AF574331

Prose Fiction and Early Modern Sexualities in England, 1570–1640

Early Modern Cultural Studies

Ivo Kamps, Series Editor

Published by Palgrave Macmillan

Idols of the Marketplace: Idolatry and Commodity Fetishism in English Literature, 1580–1680
by David Hawkes

Shakespeare among the Animals: Nature and Society in the Drama of Early Modern England
by Bruce Boehrer

Maps and Memory in Early Modern England: A Sense of Place
by Rhonda Lemke Sanford

Debating Gender in Early Modern England, 1500–1700
edited by Cristina Malcolmson and Mihoko Suzuki

Manhood and the Duel: Masculinity in Early Modern Drama and Culture
by Jennifer A. Low

Burning Women: Widows, Witches, and Early Modern European Travelers in India
by Pompa Banerjee

England's Internal Colonies: Class, Capital, and the Literature of Early Modern English Colonialism
by Mark Netzloff

Turning Turk: English Theater and the Multicultural Mediterranean
by Daniel Vitkus

Money and the Age of Shakespeare: Essays in New Economic Criticism
edited by Linda Woodbridge

Prose Fiction and Early Modern Sexualities in England, 1570–1640

Edited by

Constance C. Relihan
and
Goran V. Stanivukovic

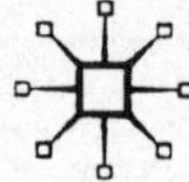

First published 2003 by
PALGRAVE MACMILLAN™
175 Fifth Avenue, New York, N.Y. 10010 and
Houndmills, Basingstoke, Hampshire, England RG21 6XS
Companies and representatives throughout the world

PALGRAVE MACMILLAN is the global academic imprint of the Palgrave Macmillan division of St. Martin's Press, LLC and of Palgrave Macmillan Ltd. Macmillan® is a registered trademark in the United States, United Kingdom and other countries. Palgrave is a registered trademark in the European Union and other countries.

ISBN 1–4039–6388–6 hardback

Library of Congress Cataloging-in-Publication Data
Prose fiction and early modern sexualities in England, 1570–1640 / edited by Constance C. Relihan and Goran V. Stanivukovic
p. cm.—(Early modern cultural studies)
Includes bibliographical references and index.
ISBN 1–4039–6388–6
1. English fiction—Early modern, 1500–1700–History and criticism. 2. Sex in literature. 3. Sex customs—England—History—16th century. 4. Sex customs—England—History—17th century. 5. Erotic stories, English—History and criticism. I. Relihan, Constance Caroline. II. Stanivukovic, Goran V. III. Series.

PR839.S49P76 2004
823′.3093538—dc22 2003058080

A catalogue record for this book is available from the British Library.

Design by Newgen Imaging Systems (P) Ltd., Chennai, India.

First edition: January, 2004
10 9 8 7 6 5 4 3 2 1

Printed in the United States of America.

To Tom, Maeve, and Meg

CONTENTS

List of Illustrations

Series Editor's Foreword

Prose Fiction and Early Modern Sexualities in England, 1570–1640, is the first title in the Early Modern Cultural Studies Series that focuses explicitly and almost exclusively on representations of sexual thoughts, feelings, and practices. It does so in a way that reveals these thoughts, feelings, and practices to be culturally specific, and crucial in the production of human subjects as individuals. The study of early modern sexuality is of course not a new phenomenon, but *Prose Fiction and Early Modern Sexualities* makes a crucial contribution to this field of inquiry because it explores a genre – prose fiction – that has hitherto been unfairly slighted in favor of the drama and poetry. As Constance C. Relihan and Goran V. Stanivukovic, the editors of *Prose Fiction and Early Modern Sexualities*, observe, "our picture of early modern sexualities will never be complete if we do not delve into the erotically rich narratives of early modern fiction." But Prose Fiction and Early Modern Sexualities does of course much more than merely study a neglected genre. Gathered here are essays dealing with constructions of "geographic otherness" in the early modern novella, "passion and reason" in Philip Sidney's *Arcadia*, the impact of Greek Romances on early modern conceptions of marriage, "sexy dressing" in Sidney's *New Arcadia*, "supernatural desires" in Mary Worth's *Urania*, "urban seductions" and homoerotic male bonding, print culture's "gelding" of Gascoigne, the undoing of sexual binaries in Lyly's *Euphues*, and, indeed, much more.

The word "sexualities" in this volume's title is deliberately used in its plural form, and the essayists assembled here – Darlene Greenhalgh, Lisa Hopkins, Steven Mentz, Sheila Cavanagh, Stephen Guy-Bray, Morgan Holmes, Alan Stewart, Elizabeth Sauer, Robert Maslen, and Lori Humphrey Newcomb – firmly underscore our suspicion that the early modern English never lived by a single, unified, dominant discourse of sexuality (with the grudging recognition that marginal individuals or small groups of individuals might gave practiced deviant behaviors). Indeed, what the examination of romances, novellas, translations of romances, and rogue literature points toward is that most of the representations of sexuality and desire in prose texts altogether defy the familiar traditional discourses of moderation and self-control. Exploring knightly romances, for instance, one contributor argues that the texts offer the early modern reader with a range of generally positive representations of same-sex erotic desire – representations that do not fit the traditional categories of "loyal friend and courting knight."

What emerges most powerfully from *Prose Fiction and Early Modern Sexualities* is that discourses of sexuality are both amazingly varied and closely intertwined with other cultural discourses. Furthermore, influenced by the best tendencies of new historicism, the authors here allow for dynamic, reciprocal interaction between different cultural spheres, always refusing to explain sexualities in prose fiction in terms of other, seemingly more authoritative, discourses such as medical, political, or theological discourses, with which they may or may not coincide. Nor are they satisfied to understand sexualities within the generic constraints and conventions of the prose genre. In fact, because of prose fiction's marginal status in early modern culture, we can reasonably argue that its authors did not feel the same duty to color within the lines as did writers of a generically more strictly defined genre such as the drama or a more highly respected genre such as poetry. Intended to be read in private, the sprawling, non-narrative character of many prose fictions is in some ways the perfect vehicle for the exploration of, and experimentations with, sexualities without imposing on them the moral judgments, plot restrictions, and social condemnations that would be required of texts performed on the public stage or that aspired to the lofty name of poetry. No matter that scholarship today has unjustly snubbed this lively and thought-provoking genre, Prose *Fiction and Early Modern Sexualities* reminds us all just why the early modern multitudes were drawn so strongly to these texts: they dealt with sexuality in all its stimulating and breathtaking variety.

Ivo Kamps
Series editor

Acknowledgments

Work on this collection was completed with the help of a joint research fellowship from the South Central Modern Language Association and The Harry Ransom Humanities Research Center at the University of Texas at Austin. We are grateful to Lori Humphrey Newcomb for her scrupulous reading of the Introduction, to Natasha Hurley for her help in the final stages of our work on this collection, and to Ivo Kamps and Farideh-Koohi Kamali for their interest in this project. At Palgrave, Roee Raz and Ian Steinberg were helpful at every stage of the book's production. Our thanks go to V. S. Mukesh as well. In Austin, Nathan Abrams's wit and enthusiasm for arguments about the history and nature of sexuality were inspiring at every stage of the work on the Introduction. We are grateful to the Bodleian Library for the permission to reproduce the illustration in Darlene C. Greenhalgh's essay, and to the Newberry Library and The Metropolitan Museum of Art for permissions to reproduce figures in Goran Stanivukovic's essay.

List of Contributors

Stephen Guy-Bray is Assistant Professor of English at the University of British Columbia. He is the author of *Homoerotic Space: The Poetics of Loss in Renaissance Literature* (Toronto, 2002) and several articles, chiefly on Renaissance poetry and drama.

Sheila T. Cavanagh is Masse-Martin/NEH Distinguished Teaching Professor of English at Emory University. She is the author of *Cherished Torment: The Emotional Geography of Lady Mary Wroth's* Urania (Duquesne, 2001) and *Wanton Eyes and Chaste Desires: Female Sexuality in* The Faerie Queene (Indiana, 1994) and numerous articles on Renaissance literature and pedagogy. She is also the Director of Emory Women Writers Resource Project, a website devoted to women's writing from the sixteenth to twentieth centuries.

Darlene C. Greenhalgh received her undergraduate degree from University of California, Berkeley, in English and Comparative Literature, and is currently completing her doctorate on Hellenistic Romance in Sidney and Shakespeare at the University of Georgia. She presently lives in Oxford where she is the program coordinator for the University of Georgia student exchange program. She has published on Shakespeare.

Morgan Holmes is the author of *Early Modern Metaphysical Literature: Custom and Strange Desires* (Palgrave, 2001). He is the Director of Rochester Communications and teaches literature and cultural studies in the Division of Continuing Education at Ryerson University in Toronto.

Lisa Hopkins is Reader in English Literature at Sheffield Hallam University and editor of *Early Modern Literary Studies.* Her most recent publications are *The Female Hero in English Renaissance Tragedy* (Palgrave, 2002) and *Writing Renaissance Queens: Texts by and about Elizabeth I and Mary, Queen of Scots* (Delaware, 2002). She is currently working on *Shakespeare on the Edge*, a study of Shakespeare's representation of the borders of early modern England, for Ashgate.

Lori Humphrey Newcomb is Associate Professor of English at the University of Illinois at Urbana-Champaign. Her study of Robert Greene's *Pandosto* and its many revisions, *Reading Popular Romance in Early Modern England*, was published by Columbia University Press in 2002. She is currently writing on print, performativity, and adaptation in plays by Greene and Shakespeare.

Robert W. Maslen is Senior Lecturer in English Literature at the University of Glasgow. He has published a book, *Elizabethan Fictions: Espionage, Counter-Espionage and the Duplicity of Fiction in Early Modern Prose Narratives* (Clarendon, 1997), and editions of Sidney's *Apology for Poetry* (2002) and Dekker and Middleton's *News from Gravesend* (forthcoming), as well as essays on sixteenth-century prose, erotic narrative poetry, and drama. He is currently writing a book about Shakespearean comedy.

Steven Mentz is Assistant Professor of English at St. John's University. He has published several articles on English Renaissance prose fiction, including studies of Thomas Nashe, Philip Sidney, and Robert Greene. He is also coeditor of a collection of essays on the early modern rogue, forthcoming in 2004 from University of Michigan Press.

Constance C. Relihan is Hargis Professor of English Literature at Auburn University. She is the author of *Fashioning Authority: The Development of Elizabethan Novelistic Discourse* (Kent State, 1994), *Cosmographical Glasses: Geographic Discourse, Gender, and Elizabethan Fiction* (Kent State, 2004), and editor of *Framing Elizabethan Fictions: Contemporary Approaches to Early Modern Narrative Prose* (Kent State, 1996).

Elizabeth Sauer is Professor of English at Brock University, where she holds a Chancellor's Chair for Research Excellence. She is the author of *Barbarous Dissonance and Images of Voice in Milton's Epics* (McGill-Queen's, 1996) and the just completed *Paper-Protestations and Textual Communities in England, 1640–1675*. She has also edited or coedited the following: *Agonistics: Arenas of Creative Contest* (with Janet Lungstrum, SUNY, 1997), *Milton and the Imperial Vision* (with Balachandra Rajan, Duquesne, 1999), winner of the Milton Society of America Irene Samuel Memorial Award; *Books and Readers in Early Modern England: Material Studies* (with Jennifer Andersen, Pennsylvania, 2002); *Reading Early Women: Texts and Manuscripts in Print, 1550–1700* (with Helen Ostovich, Routledge, 2003); *Literature and Religion in Early Modern England: Case Studies, Renaissance and Reformation* (with Jennifer Andersen, 2004). Her work in submission includes *Osiris and Urania: Milton and the Climates of Reading* and *Comparing Imperialism 1500–1900.*

Goran V. Stanivukovic is Associate Professor of English at Saint Mary's University. He has published an edited collection, *Ovid and the Renaissance Body* (Toronto, 2001); a critical edition of Emanuel Ford's *Ornatus and Artesia* (Dovehouse Editions 2003) and essays on Shakespeare and Renaissance drama, nondramatic poetry, rhetoric, early modern queerness, and the Mediterranean. He is currently completing a book on prose romances, ethnography, and sexualities in early modern England, and is editing a volume of essays on the Mediterranean and early modern English literature and culture.

Alan Stewart is Professor of Renaissance Studies at Birkbeck College, University of London, and Associate Director of the AHRB Centre for

Editing Lives and Letters. His publications include *Close Readers: Humanism and Sodomy in Early Modern England* (Princeton, 1997), *Hostage to Fortune: The Trouble Life of Francis Bacon 1561–1626* (with Lisa Jardine; Victor Gollancz, 1998), *Philip Sidney: A Double Life* (Chatto & Windus, 2000) and *The Cradle King: A Life of James VI and I* (Chatto & Windus, 2003). He is currently editing volumes 1 and 2 of Bacon's *Works* for the new Oxford Francis Bacon.

Introduction: Prose Fiction and Early Modern Sexualities in England, 1570–1640

Constance C. Relihan and Goran V. Stanivukovic

I find after all that love is nothing else but the thirst for sexual enjoyment in a desired object, and Venus nothing else but the pleasure of discharging our vessels—a pleasure which becomes vicious either by immoderation or by indiscretion.

—*Michel de Montaigne, "On some verses of Virgil,"* Essays[1]

Immoderation and indiscretion, Montaigne suggests in an essay central to early modern ideas about sexuality, characterize the viciousness and force of pleasure. They could also be said to capture the essence of the representation of sexuality—in all its various guises—in early modern English prose fiction. Although Montaigne's focus is not prose fiction explicitly, but literature more generally, his argument that "love" and its goddess, Venus, function to veil sexual desire provides a powerful foundation on which to construct an analysis of the narratival, linguistic, and symbolic implications of love in late sixteenth- and early seventeenth-century prose fiction, for beneath the narrative and rhetorical structures that seem to be grappling with notions of love and courtship, those amorous discourses, in fact, often serve as pretexts for more salacious arguments about the sexual practices and identities of men and women. Within the range of kinds of fictions produced during the period—popular, royal, and historical romances, novella, translations of Greek romances, and rogue literature—the protocols of normative and traditional discourse on love (and on courtship and marriage) contends with the persistent sexual incontinence of men and the transgressive sexual agency of women. The resulting ideological clash often manifests itself in actions and eloquent speech by male and female characters who excessively, and sometimes violently, pursue and consume desire in ways that defy traditional discourses on corporeal behavior. In this uninhibited pursuit of *erōs* and pleasure, early modern prose fiction, it might be argued, is diametrically opposed to Michel Foucault's assertion that self-mastery and moderation control and police early discourses of sexuality.[2] While the narrative structures exist to try to contain desire in early modern fiction, in other words, they are unable to effect that control.

Sixteenth-century English culture is itself suspicious of the polymorphous and transgressive implications of prose fiction's interest in eroticism and violence. Roger Ascham's *The Schoolemaster* (1570) contains a well-known attack on popular fictions, especially chivalric romances, because of what he terms their "open manslaughter and bold bawdrye." Ascham is horrified that in those texts "noblest Knightes . . . kill most men without any quarell, and commit fowlest aduoulteres by subtlest shiftes."[3] His condemnation is echoed by various humanists and Puritan preachers who were troubled by the burgeoning of popular print culture and the changes in the representation of both masculinity and femininity it prompted. Masculinity in these texts often becomes estranged from military prowess and associated with romance and courtship; femininity, although still associated with chastity, provides female characters with greater options for independent speech and action than traditional sixteenth-century English definitions of chastity allowed. The prefaces of much of the period's fiction, although containing conventional self-deprecation, may also be read as responding to such charges. Early modern fiction's pages are filled with the narratives of cross-dressed bodies, rape, pornographic voyeurism, incest, and homoerotically tinged knightly embraces. The fiction stages, in narratives usually complicated by various kinds of rhetorical and plot-driven digressions, tales of courtship, marriage, and sexual consummation often intertwined with confused identities, Moorish and Barbarian pirates attempting to rape Christian damsels, Mohametan women exciting lust in Christian knight-travelers in the Levant or in the Mediterranean Africa, Christians courting and marrying non-Christian princesses, or rogues duping connies in the chaotic alleys of London. These narrative intrigues are often marked by a sophisticated attention to geographic locations in which, to use Michel de Certeau's useful language, figurative and two-dimensional "places" become inhabited, complex "spaces" infused with multiple cultural, nationalistic, and political resonances.[4] In these tales of wandering and lust, which demonstrate the intersection of the erotic, the amorous, and the nationalistic; the forbidden, the titillating, and the corporeal, take up much more narrative space and consume more of the characters' energy than do plots of chivalric militancy. What the essays in this collection aim to demonstrate, then, is how bodies and sexualities are narrated, imagined, and fantasized about in early modern prose fiction, and how those forms of representation expand or question current arguments about early modern sexual desire and subjectivity.

But it is important to acknowledge the plurality of sexuality—the "sexualities" we insist on in this volume's title. As the plots of fiction shift, emphasizing the corporeal and romantic over the chivalric, Lorna Hutson suggests,[5] the representations of early modern sexuality acquired new dimensions. These changes, this pluralizing of sexual discourse, both expands and complicates previous understandings of the functioning and representation of sexual desire in early modern literature. The essays in this collection emerge from the now accepted ideas that sexuality is culture-specific, that it holds a crucial position at the intersection between society and the individual in the process of the construction of subjectivity and interiority, and, in a Foucauldian sense, that sexualities and desires are always produced, mediated, and denaturalized by power and hegemonic ideological structures, and that these representations reveal political subjects. The essays here attempt to explore different notions and forms of representation of a complex range of sexual subjects and their desires in early modern prose fiction. Since the early modern constructions of desire and sexuality are inseparable from the period's attitudes to the body and gender, the essays in this collection also engage in a discussion of how gender difference and behavior help mediate discourses of sexuality in prose fiction.[6] Taken as a whole, they suggest the multiplicity of ways in which ideas about sexuality were implicated in the prose fiction of early modern England. Sexualities suggests variety and multiplicity; it does not imply the ontological binary of either hetero/homosexual desire or of different sexual practices.

The multiple construction of sexualities that the essays in this collection discuss is inseparably constrained and enabled by its generic form. While certainly all texts produced during the period are intertwined with representations of sexuality, prose fiction provides a rich and unique vantage point from which to approach this field of inquiry. In talking about the "problematic . . . relations among discourses [of sexuality]," Bruce Smith warns that,

> [w]ith respect to fictional texts, the other discourses—medical, legal, ethical, whatever—chosen in a study [of sexuality] can all too readily seem to offer the key to all mythologies in the reductive way . . . There is a need to recognize that a fictional text belongs in its own right to a realm of discourse—courtly entertainment, commercial print, public theater, the manuscript culture of the nobility—and that the realm in question may or may not coincide with, say, medical discourse . . . Better still: to recognize that a fictional text is related to these other discourses in complicated, culturally specific ways that demand to be investigated.[7]

The assumption behind this argument is that literature creates its own discourse of sexual desire, one that ought to be seen as maintaining a unique position relative to other available erotic discourses in early modern culture. This position may be derived from several factors: (1) early modern prose fiction is largely plot-based, and consequently, it is characters' actions and the narrative structuring and sequencing of those actions that imply certain sexual behaviors and desires; (2) narrative conventions of early modern prose fiction are fluid; (3) the often fantastic and highly improbable situations of early prose fiction create complex opportunities for the testing of characters' agency through both actions and eloquence; (4) the frequent geographical displacement of the action of these narratives creates both conceptual and physical spaces in which pleasure may more freely be imagined and constructed; and (5) because early prose fiction is so closely tied to the marketplace, it is able to target elite and common readers, both male and female, engaging them in a seemingly private conversation about sexual desire and its representation. These four qualities of early modern prose fiction combine to make it an essential participant in any scholarly exploration of early modern sexualities. Prose fiction, then, must be recognized as providing access to an important discourse of sexuality, and one of the main goals of this collection, thus, is to explore not only some of the new avenues the interpretation of early prose fiction might take, but also to signal new conceptual and methodological directions in the study of early modern sexualities.

Current critical arguments about early modern sexualities have typically been drawn from the study of drama, poetry, religious texts, and antitheatrical tracts, travel accounts, especially of the New World, and conduct books. Prose fiction, however, has only tangentially been explored. When critics have drawn on prose fiction, they typically have focused on more canonical works, especially Sir Philip Sidney's romance *Arcadia*, and even more specifically on cross-dressing in it. The *Arcadia*, for example, enabled some of the early influential arguments about early modern sexuality: Constance Jordan's feminist arguments in reading the period's literature and her interpretation of early modern patriarchy promoted by Sidney's text, as well as Gregory Bredbeck's claims about homoeroticism and sodomy implicated by cross-dressing.[8] Early modern gender and erotic desire broadly conceived have also been studied on the model of fiction, but varied and ambiguous early modern sexualities have yet to be explored in the vast body of sixteenth- and early seventeenth-century prose fiction.[9] Yet, the burgeoning criticism of early modern sexuality, criticism that has in some cases (e.g., in feminism and queer theory) radically changed early modern studies, has hardly ever considered prose fiction. And yet the ways in which such analysis could enrich our understanding of this body of texts and sexual desire during the period is considerable. Take for example, the following passage from Barnabe Riche's "Of Nicander and Lucilla," found in his 1581 *Riche His Farewell to Militarie Profession*:

> It was in the month of July, which season in that country is extremely hot, by reason whereof Lucilla, tumbling from one side of the bed to the other, had rolled off all the clothes wherewith she had been covered so as she had left herself all naked, and in that sort he found her with corals about her neck and arms which, with the difference of their ruddy color, did set out and beautify greatly the excellent fairnes of her white body. She lay asleep upon her back, with her hands cast over her head, as for the most part young women are wont to do, so that forthwith the young prince discovered her from top to toe . . . .[10]

(This prince shortly thereafter characterizes her as "so rare a piece.")

The role of this passage in creating an erotically voyeuristic text for heterosexual male readers seems obvious; however, its function in relation to the period's construction of sexualities becomes more complex if we remember that Riche's preface establishes women as one of his specifically targeted audiences. How is this passage implicated in the construction of female desires? How are female readers to be imagined as responding to passages such as this one (of which the genre contains many)? How does this passage function to create its narrative voice as voyeuristic—the narrator is capable not only of describing this scene but also of explaining that Lucilla's posture in bed is reflective of what "for the most part young women are wont to do"? What is the effect of both raising homoerotic tensions for his female readers and distancing those readers from the passage by seeming to direct it primarily toward men (for surely female readers would not need to be told that Lucilla's posture is typical for women, if indeed it is). The effect of such a comment on female readers is likely to be to prompt either knowing identification with the narrator ("Yes, that is how we sleep," which positions female readers as voyeurs of their fellow-women's behavior—either from a female or a male-identified position), anxious questioning of their own sexual identity ("I don't sleep like that. What's wrong with me?"), suspicious concern about the narrator's sexual desires ("Why does he have so much knowledge about how women sleep?"), or derisive contempt for his assertion of privileged knowledge ("I have never known a woman who sleeps like that. What's he talking about?"). Regardless of which option—or combination of options—a female reader responds with, simple heterosexual voyeuristic pleasure is denied to female readers who do not adopt a male-identified subject position.

This is just one example of the kinds of insight the exploration of sexualities in early modern prose fiction might provide, and these insights would have broad implications for understanding early modern English culture because at the end of the sixteenth century, when the plays of Christopher Marlowe and William Shakespeare were filling the yards and galleries of the Rose and the Globe theaters, prose fiction, according to Charles Mish's analysis of the production of some of the most active printing houses in London, was more popular than drama.[11] But early prose fiction tends, generally, to be overlooked for many reasons, ranging from the tendency of many scholars to so often see it as merely derivative of continental novellas and to think of it as source material for the period's drama and not as a body of independent, literary texts, to the fact that reading dense pages of black-letter print full of interlaced plots and sequences of lengthy rhetorical speeches may seem less attractive reading material when compared to early modern drama (this is especially true when one has to read prose fiction in faraway libraries or on microfilm, usually in the back corner of a university library basement). Yet, as the essays in this collection demonstrate, our picture of early modern sexualities will never be complete if we do not delve into the erotically rich narratives of early modern fiction, whose heyday in the print market lasted from 1570–1640.

How does the study of sexualities in prose fiction, then, expand our critical methodologies, and our critical lexicon, of the ways early modern England conceptualized sexuality? Although the essays in this collection take different methodological and theoretical approaches, the critical inquiries that they employ have been enabled by what Bruce Smith has called "the syncretism of methodologies."[12] The methodological and theoretical approaches to sexualities in fiction have come out of two impulses. First, explorations of sexuality in prose fiction, explorations that have only recently, and somewhat belatedly emerged within the context of sexuality studies, have been influenced by new historicism and cultural materialism, post-structuralist and deconstructivist theories, cultural studies, theories of gender and desire, especially feminism and queer theory, and by postcolonial theory. The study of sexuality has also been expanded by what Smith has recently identified as one of the new theoretical possibilities that has propelled early modern studies of sexuality—"historical phenomenology," or what we might call "new phenomenology" to distinguish it from Roman Ingarden and Edmund Husserl's use of term in the early part of the twentieth century. Historical phenomenology is a "way of knowing" the sexual subject in its historical and conceptual specificity.[13] Some of the essays in this collection, for example, on the construction of erotic space and on the representation of same-sex erotics, make attempts in the direction of this still-developing phenomenology.[14] Second, a recent growing interest in the study of prose fiction has come out of a sense that we need to recover fiction from the archives of history, and to expand and critically scrutinize the ever-so-close intertwining of history and theory in contemporary critical practice in early modern studies. In resorting to printed and manuscript archival texts to contextualize the reading of the fiction, but also examining the strategic transmission of those archival texts in the fabric of fiction, a number of essays in the collection not only look for fiction in the archives but also for "archives in the fiction."[15]

Prose Fiction and Early Modern Sexualities is divided into three parts that together constitute a coherent overview of the new approaches to the exploration of sexuality in early modern prose fiction. In Part I, "Gender, Genre, and Sexuality," five essays unveil the fictions' intentions to express the ways sexuality and representations of gender are constructed within the idealized narratives of courtship and matrimony. This section opens with Darlene C. Greenhalgh's essay, "Love, Chastity, and Woman's Erotic Power: Greek Romance in Elizabethan and Jacobean Context," an essay on the construction of virginity, fidelity, chastity, and female sexuality, through the adventure motif in Greek romances, especially Heliodorus's *Aethiopica*, Xenophon's *Ephesiaca*, Achilles Tatius's *Leucippe and Clitophon*, Longus's *Daphnis and Chloe*, Chariton's *Chareas and Callirhoe* and their Elizabethan translations. Those translations, Greenhalgh's essay shows, were (as in other cultures and times) also cultural interpretations of the narratives of chastity and moderation, narratives that suited Protestant views of sexual ethics based on moderation and preservation of chastity. Arguing that the archetypal nature of the representation of chastity and fidelity in Greek romances does not in fact account for the culturally specific popularity of adventure romances in Elizabethan England, Greenhalgh sets out to explore Greek adventure-romances within the context of romantic love and "married chastity," pointing out that these two concepts, germane to romance and specifically related to women's "virginal and wedded chastity," enabled the plots of the Elizabethan and Jacobean adventure-romances.

If in Greenhalgh's essay the threat to woman's chastity lies in the adventure-fictions in which, because of the motif of adventure, stable erotic norms are subject to tests and threats, in Constance C. Relihan's essay, " 'Dissordinate Desire' and the Construction of Geographic Otherness in the Early Modern Novella," an analysis of the gendering of the Eastern locations in novelle collections such as William Painter's *Palace of Pleasure* (1566) and Geoffrey Fenton's *Certain Tragical Discourses* (1567), the threat to women is shown as continuing a threat to land. Employing Michel de Certeau's distinction between spaces and places, and Homi Bhabha's theory of postcolonial reading of the "othering" of the subject, Relihan shows that sexual violence converges with the fear of cultural annihilation of the Christians by the Turks. She examines the intricate convergence between the loss of male cultural identity embodied in their military prowess and sexual violence against females. Thus, Relihan shows, the West's ability to defeat the Turks is at the same time conveniently used as a pretext for the validation of sexual violence against women.

The intersection of eroticism and geography, though with a particular emphasis on the convergence of sexuality and race, is also the subject of Sheila Cavanagh's essay, "Prisoners of Love: Cross-cultural and Supernatural Desires in Lady Mary Wroth's *Urania*." Part II of Mary Wroth's romance, a fiction whose narrative brims with the possibilities for exploring a range of sexual possibilities, Cavanagh argues, "provides its audience with cautionary portraits" of Pamphilia and Amphilantus, and the unconventional erotic relationships between Pamphilia and the swarthy Tartarian Rodomandro, one that crosses both ethnic and, hence, conventional erotic boundaries. At the same time she reminds us that, in *Urania*, extramarital sexual fulfillment does not provoke loud condemnation.

Another form of a violent sexual aggression—incest, and the anxieties and taboos surrounding it—is the subject of Lisa Hopkins's essay, "Passion and Reason in Sir Philip Sidney's *Arcadia*," one of several essays on Sidney's fictional *magnum opus* discussed in this collection. Incest, announced already in the language of Sidney's dedication of *Arcadia* to his sister, has lesser importance in Sidney's romance. Yet, as Hopkins suggests, incest is explicitly inscribed in two important relationships in the romance, the one involving Philoclea's suitor and cousin, Amphialus, and it is even more pronounced in the exchanges between Pamela and her sister Philoclea. In both cases, incest complicates the idea of love and familiar loyalties upon which romance ideas of national power and stability depend. Thus in her essay, Hopkins, who also compares the incestuous implications of the *Arcadia* with those contained in John Ford's *The Broken Heart*, examines the ways in which the new *Arcadia* both codifies and redefines the notion of romantic love by showing how this codification is inextricably linked to the idea of incest.

The manipulation of gender in order to unsettle the boundaries of sexual agency in the new *Arcadia* is the subject of Steven Mentz's essay, "The Thigh and the Sword: Gender, Genre, and Sexy Dressing in Sidney's *New Arcadia*." Mentz's emphasis on the instability of erotic desire and gender construction as effects of "the semiotics of clothing," that is, cross-dressing as an emblem of the unsettling of both sexual and gender boundaries, is signified, in Sidney's fiction, both in Zelmane's "imaginative bisexuality" and Pyrocles's "bi-gendered" corporeality.

While the essays in the opening part of the collection deal with the narrative challenges of the boundaries of heteroeroticism, and gendered subjects and their sexuality, the essays in Part II, "Queer Fictions," examine the potential erotic charge created by the changing culture of male friendship, a social organization rendered both private and intense at the moment when "the new marriage model"[16] (companionate marriage) started competing with *amicitia* in society and in popular literature, especially prose. The study of masculinity, and especially of homoeroticism in the early modern English prose fiction, has not yet been the study of focused analysis, not at least since Bruce Smith's brief exploration of same-sex attraction in Robert Greene's *Menaphon*, Thomas Lodge's *Rosalynde*, and Sidney's *Arcadia*.[17] But the four essays in this section consider, with more or less emphasis, the ways in which early fictions (homo)eroticize friendship. They share a concern with what one might call a crisis of masculinity at the end of the sixteenth century, primarily with the rise of the new pragmatic masculinity that better suited the demands of urban and mercantile London and the opportunities in the courtly and legal service. Male friendship, one of the key alliances between men in early modern culture, became nostalgically revisited in these fictions and exploited, eroticized in an attempt, one might argue, to use a more traditional model of alliance as a model for male erotic alliances. Thus, in "Same Difference: Homo and Allo in Lyly's *Euphues*," Stephen Guy-Bray deconstructs and historicizes modern erotic taxonomies to explore the sexualities represented in the first section of John Lyly's *Euphues* (1578). Guy-Bray calls for a broader use of sexual binaries, one that does not involve only the *hetero* choice (meaning the other of the only two involved), but *allo* as well, including a "potentially infinite number of other people and of other differences." Arguing that sexual binaries change over time and that they are "liable to break down in practice," Guy-Bray analyzes *Euphues*'s dependence on "both difference and sameness," showing that rather than diametrically opposite, difference and sameness are, in fact, related. Their relationship, Guy-Bray shows, opens up a possibility to look at the heteroerotic, not homoerotic, relationships as sodomitical in Lyly's fiction.

While Guy-Bray's contribution explores possibilities for expanding the phenomenon of same-sex erotics in fiction, Morgan Holmes's essay, "Rogue-Sirens: Urban Seduction and the Collapse of *Amicitia*," looks at the decline of the ideal of male friendship in Gilbert Walker's 1552 chapbook of roguery, entitled *A Manifest Detection of the Most Vile and Detestable Use of Diceplay*, as an example of the fiction of "metropolitan roguery." Starting with Jean Baudrillard's distinction between *erōs* and "seduction," Holmes considers the cony's transformations from "the upstanding life" to a life of debased pleasures. Holmes's central point is that in the history of Renaissance homoeroticism, rogue fiction marks the distinction between the homoerotic *amicitia* of earlier, noble chivalry, and more "instrumental alliances" geared toward some pragmatic, fiscal gain, assuring that mercantile profit underlies erotic transactions between men. The erotics of literary roguery in Holmes's essay, then, focuses on the homoerotic relations between men, distinguishing it from that of cross-gendered desire and behavior in rogue fiction.

That production of erotic transactions within a private world of an urban life, examined by Holmes, is echoed in a similar and even more private version in Alan Stewart's "Gelding Gascoigne," an essay on the (homo)eroticization of humanist philology as it shifts from manuscript to print. In the process of this textual refashioning, textual production and sexual pleasures are juxtaposed and offered to the reader-consumers of the new humanist fiction. Stewart examines the textual relationship between George Gascoigne's 1575 *The Posies of George Gascoigne* and 1573 *A Hundreth Sundrie Flowres.* His essay examines the relationship between Gascoigne's narrative and the textual material of the *Hundreth Sundrie Flowres* anthology, which, Stewart argues, "presents itself as a voyeuristic entry into the elite amateurism of manuscript culture." The homoerotic implication, for both character relationships within the text and for the exchange of the erotic fiction between the author and his readers, occurs at the moment when F. J. exchanges Elinor's pen for a Secretary and the private act of letter writing. In that sense Gascoigne's text is "pruned," or gelded, and this "un-manning" or emasculating of the text occurs as it is shifted from manuscript to print medium. Stewart juxtaposes arguments about sexual and textual exchanges between men in Gascoigne's fiction and his (male) readers with an analysis of a similar process of "gelding" a text by the French humanist Beza, an alleged sodomite, as it moves from manuscript to print.

This part of the collection ends with Goran V. Stanivukovic's essay, "'Knights in Armes:' The Homoerotics of the English Renaissance Prose Romances," in which he examines several popular prose romances: Sidney's *Arcadia*, Robert Parry's *Moderatus, The second part of the first Booke of the Myrrour of Knighthood* (1585), and the anonymous *Palmerin of England* (1596). Stanivukovic argues that, because of their mythical timelessness and a continuing interlacing of episodes, romances provide an ideal imaginative space for the explorations of homoerotic desire. Distinguishing between nonerotic chivalric homosociality, homoerotic friendship, and sodomy as a sort of failed friendship, Stanivukovic argues that romances provided early modern readers with a variety of ways of representing same-sex erotics, most of which did not, in fact, construct that desire as either marginalized or demonized. He further argues that courtship and marriage do not offer exclusive possibilities for emotional and corporeal longing; that they, too, can coexist undisturbed by nonnormative "discrete identities"[18] that do not clearly fit into any of the two major categories of masculine representation promoted by romances: loyal friend and courting knight.

The collection closes with three essays in Part III, "Textuality and Desire," which focus on how the ideas of literary nature and the reshaping of generic expectations freed discourses of sexuality in prose fiction, especially romances. In his essay, "Sidney, Gascoigne, and the 'Bastard Poets,'" Robert Maslen argues that in the *Old Arcadia*, Sidney imitates George Gascoigne's erotic prose fiction, *The Adventures of Master F.J.* (1573). Distinguishing between the "bastard" and the "right" poet, Maslen sets out to show how Sidney creates a difference between a writer who feminizes his or her readers and one whose poetry has the capacity to impart or reveal hidden wisdom, which distinguishes the "right" poet from historians and philosophers. Poetry or literature, and illicit sex are mutually dependent in Sidney's theory of poetry, and that precept, first developed in his *Defence of Poetry*, becomes a guiding principle in the *Arcadia*. This and other romances are, Maslen argues, highly sexed texts that encourage clandestine courtship and illicit desire. Emasculation of romance, though of a romance that emerged out of the historical realities of the interregnum period in England, is also the subject of "Emasculating Romance: Historical Fiction in the Protectorate," in which Elizabeth Sauer examines the rewriting of the English romance tradition "in relation to civil war interregnum political history and strained gender relations" that were at the center of the political crisis and destabilized order in the mid-seventeenth century. Sauer looks at Richard Brathwaite's 1659 romance, *Panthalia: or the Royal Romance*, and explores its treatment of sexual politics, especially strategies of emasculation, that engender, imaginatively, political affairs in which the beheading of Charles I invoked "the king's submission to a female ruler [Henrietta Maria] as the cause of his demise."

This section ends with Lori Humphrey Newcomb's essay, "Unfolding the Shepherdess: A Revision of Pastoral," which explores the erotic implications of the gendering of pastoral labor. Newcomb focuses on the fate of the shepherdess over the period of about fifty years, from her appearance in late sixteenth-century fictions to her reemergence in Caroline print culture. The shepherdess in Newcomb's revisionist work becomes a locus of, as she puts it, "double-edged" significance. On the one hand, the shepherdess is a cultural signifier of the "social dignity [given to] women characters and poetic opportunity [entrusted to] women authors." On the other, the shepherdess is a reminder of the thwarting of women's "economic contributions" and desires.

Taken together, the essays in *Prose Fiction and Early Modern Sexualities in England* suggest a range of possibilities in which early modern fiction narrated and imagined both sexual subjects and multiple versions of sexuality. As the essays in this collection show, because of their marginal generic status in what was often loosely understood (though not named) as literature, and because of their low prestige in the print market, those fictions gave writers' erotic imagination an opportunity to exercise new aspirations in representing sexuality and sexual alliances alongside more normative forms of erotic bonding, and to direct illicit erotic energies into arenas of conventional bonds, such as marriage and male friendship. What is probably most central for the study of sexuality in fiction, and most important for the picture of sexuality that emerges in the history of early modern imaginative representations of sexuality in England, is the fact that in all the fictional modes examined in this collection, there is no sign of any, or at least, any significant, anxiety or horror attached to these various representations of sexualities, despite their often violent or nonnormative nature. This revisionism of sexual discourses should be seen as constituent of the narratives in which some crucial social institutions, for example of chivalry (and chivalric masculinity), of friendship based on traditional alliances of equal status, and of familial relations were subjected to writers' critical scrutiny. But these new discourses of sexuality in fiction also emerge at the moment when early modern English society is grappling with new ideas about privacy and subjectivity in a world filled with changing ideas about nationalism, mercantilism, accomplished and failed imperialism, and debates on royal power.

Notes

1. *The Complete Essays of Montaigne*, trans. Donald M. Frame (Stanford: Stanford University Press, 1958), p. 668.
2. Michel Foucault, *The Use of Pleasure*, Vol. 2 of *The History of Sexuality*, trans. Robert Hurley (New York: Pantheon, 1985), p. 188.
3. Roger Ascham, *The Schoolemaster* [London, 1570] (New York: AMS Press, 1967), p. 81. See also Robert W. Maslen, *Elizabethan Fictions: Espionage, Counter-Espionage, and the Duplicity of Fiction in Early Elizabethan Prose Narratives* (Oxford: Clarendon Press, 1997), pp. 40–51.
4. Michel de Certeau, *The Practice of Everyday Life*, trans. Steven Rendall (Berkeley, Los Angeles, London: University of California Press, 1988), p. 117.
5. Lorna Hutson, *The Usurer's Daughter: Male Friendship and Fictions of Women in Sixteenth-Century England* (London and New York: Routledge, 1994), p. 97.
6. For a brief recent discussion of how early modern ideas of the body and gender produce ideologies of sexual pleasure, see Valerie Traub, "Gender and Sexuality in Shakespeare," *The Cambridge Companion to Shakespeare*, ed. Margareta de Grazia and Stanley Wells (Cambridge: Cambridge University Press, 2001), pp. 129–46.
7. Smith, "Premodern Sexualities," *PMLA* 115:3 (2000): 321–22.
8. Constance Jordan, *Renaissance Feminism: Literary Texts and Political Models* (Ithaca and London: Cornell University Press, 1990). Gregory Bredbeck, *Sodomy and Interpretation: Marlowe to Milton* (Ithaca and London: Cornell University Press, 1991).
9. For the study of femininity in early modern fiction, see Constance C. Relihan, *Fashioning Authority: The Development of Elizabethan Novelistic Discourse* (Kent, Ohio and London, England: The Kent State University Press, 1994),

her edited collection, *Fashioning Authority*; Robert W. Maslen, "George Pettie, Gender, and the Generation Gap," in his *Elizabethan Fictions*; Lori Humphrey Newcomb, " 'Social Things': The Production of Popular Culture in the Reception of Robert Greene's *Pandosto*," *ELH* 61 (1994): 753–81; Maria Teresa Micaela Prendergast, *Renaissance Fantasies: The Gendering of Aesthetics in Early Modern Fiction* (Kent, Ohio and London: The Kent State University Press, 1999); and the essays dealing with gender and sexuality in *Critical Approaches to English Prose Fiction 1520–1640*, ed. Donald Beecher (Ottawa: Dovehouse Editions, 1998).

10. Barnabe Riche, *His Farewell to Military Profession*, ed. Donald Beecher (Ottawa: Dovehouse Editions, 1992), p. 210.
11. Charles C. Mish, "Best Sellers in Seventeenth-Century Fiction," *Papers of the Bibliographic Society of America* 47 (1953): 356–73; "Black Letter as Social Discriminant in the Seventeenth Century," *PMLA* 98 (1953): 627–30; "English Short Fiction in the Seventeenth Century," *Studies in Short Fiction* 6 (1969): 233–330.
12. Smith, "Premodern Sexualities," p. 327.
13. Smith, "Premodern Sexualities," p. 325.
14. We might invoke here, e.g., Wolfgang Iser's assertion that "[t]he phenomenological theory of art lays full stress on the idea that, in considering a literary work, one must take into account not only the actual text but also, and in equal measure, the actions involved in responding to that text." See Wolfgang Iser, *The Implied Reader: Patterns of Communication in Prose from Bunyan to Beckett* (Baltimore and London: The Johns Hopkins University Press, 1974), p. 274.
15. We borrow this phrase from Carla Freccero, "Archives in the Fiction: Marguerite de Navarre's *Heptaméron*," in Kahn and Hutson, *Rhetoric and Law in Early Modern Europe*, pp. 73, 73–94.
16. We borrow this phrase from Lisa Jardine. See Lisa Jardine, "Companionate Marriage Versus Male Friendship: Anxiety for the Lineal Family in Jacobean Drama," in *Political Culture and Cultural Politics in Early Modern England: Essays Presented to David Underdowne*, ed. Susan D. Amussen and Mark A. Kishlansky (Manchester and New York: Manchester University Press, 1995), pp. 235, 234–54.
17. Bruce R. Smith, *Homosexual Desire in Shakespeare's England: A Cultural Poetics* (Chicago and London: The University of Chicago Press, 1991), pp. 137–47. For an examination of homoeroticism signified through cross-dressing in the new *Arcadia*, see also Bredbeck, *Sodomy and Interpretation*, pp. 105–06; Winfried Schleiner, "Male Cross-Dressing and Transvestism in Renaissance Romances," *Sixteenth Century Journal* 19 (1988): 605–19.
18. Jonathan Goldberg, *Sodometries: Renaissance Texts, Modern Sexualities* (Stanford: Stanford University Press, 1992), p. 10.

Part I

Gender, Genre, and Sexuality

CHAPTER 1

LOVE, CHASTITY, AND WOMAN'S EROTIC POWER: GREEK ROMANCE IN ELIZABETHAN AND JACOBEAN CONTEXTS

Darlene C. Greenhalgh

That the Greek romance exerted a strong influence on Elizabethan and Jacobean prose fiction and drama, including Shakespeare, has been well documented.[1] Notwithstanding individual variations, the plots of the Hellenistic romance authors who were most influential in the Renaissance—Heliodorus, Longus, and Achilles Tatius—share an underlying structural pattern: a pair of youthful lovers meet, fall in love, separate, suffer trial and tribulation, and eventually reunite in lawful marriage. According to the classicist John J. Winkler, the Greek romances of North Africa and Asia Minor introduced "a quite specialized form of erotic story: these are love-leading-to-marriage stories, in which the necessary goal of passion itself is lawful matrimony."[2] The erotic stories that constitute the ancient prose romance genre include Heliodorus of Emesa's *Aethiopica* or *Theagenes and Chariclea* (fourth century A.D.); Longus's *Lesbiaca* or *Daphnis and Chloe* (third century A.D.); Achilles Tatius of Alexandria's *Leucippe and Clitophon* (second century A.D.). Two additional romances with less direct bearing on early modern drama and fiction are Xenophon of Ephesus's *Ephesiaca* or *Habrocomes and Anthia* (second century A.D.) and Chariton of Aphrodisia's *Chaereas and Callirhoe* (second century A.D.).[3] Typically, the hero and heroine of Greek romance persevere in a series of conventional ordeals (storms, shipwrecks, pirates, bandits). The protagonists' victory over their ill-fated mishaps ensure that their sexual attraction, which strikes instantly and with reciprocal force, is formidable enough to endure into the bond of matrimony. As David Konstan explains, "the reciprocal love between the primary couple is constituted in the Greek novels as the basis for an enduring relationship of marriage."[4] The formulaic motif of equal love in marriage guarantees the lovers' success in adversity and the story's triumphant ending.

The longstanding appeal of Hellenistic romance stretched well into Renaissance England. In *Shakespeare and the Greek Romance*, Carol Gesner has proposed an archetypal interpretation of the genre's popular storyline. Gesner draws on Northrop Frye's notion of the heroic romance quest by applying the tripartite pattern of the adventure "quest" to Greek romance: the "perilous journey," "crucial struggle," and "final discovery and recognition."[5] This symbolic interpretation of the plot pattern runs counter to what Bruce R. Smith sees as the specific cultural significance in Renaissance England of "romances like *Clitophon and Leucippe*." Such Greek romances are sites of carnival "sexual license" where misrule and lawlessness reign within the constraints of the Elizabethan "power structure": because these romance narratives represent a temporary release from societal mores, they are, in Smith's words, "not real life," "a place apart," and "time out."[6] Although Greek romance may have functioned as a "place apart," or even a wish-fulfillment "quest," there are aspects of its love-in-marriage story that engaged directly in the moral codes of the period. More specifically, the generic plot scheme reflected a critical commonplace in sixteenth- and seventeenth-century Protestant sexual ethics: the valorization of legal matrimony and wedded chastity over celibacy and single life. The ancient romance plot—as it arises in the *Aethiopica*, *Leucippe and Clitophon*, and *Daphnis and Chloe*—presented a version of erotic love that conformed to the new ideas of married chastity and the sanctity of holy matrimony. It also promoted fidelity as a dominant characteristic in the cultivation of romantic and married love; in addition, Greek romance endorsed the state of virginity as a prerequisite for honorable female (as well as male in Heliodorus) conduct in courtship.

Mikhail Bakhtin's discussion of Greek romance provides a theoretical lens through which to analyze the ancient genre in relation to Protestant views on romantic love. According to Bakhtin, Greek romance falls under the rubric of the "adventure novel of ordeal" since its literary *chronotope* or "time space" corresponds to the pattern of novelistic "adventure-time."[7] Bakhtin locates the nature of adventure-time within the plot framework: "The first meeting of hero and heroine and the sudden flareup of their passion for each other is the starting point for plot movement; the end point of plot movement is their successful union in marriage" (p. 89). In essence, all the action of the novel transpires between these two poles, meeting and matrimony. For Bakhtin, the concept of adventure-time entails that the hero and heroine undergo a series of ordeals that test virtuous behavior. Between the two poles of plot movement, the awakening of passion and its fulfillment in lawful matrimony, the young lovers experience a variety of situations and adventures. The hero and heroine meet not only with perils throughout the course of the story but also with a variety of temptations and enticements; as such, they often find themselves in compromising situations and yet somehow manage to keep their integrity whole. While the young lovers exemplify a variety of physical virtues—fortitude, strength, and intrepidity—the moral qualities most often tested are fidelity and chastity. The loyalty and constancy of the hero and heroine contribute to a principal characteristic of Greek romance and demonstrate the lovers' mutual rectitude and probity. Thus, the symmetrical love of the hero and heroine remains unaltered throughout the novel, so that "[t]heir chastity is also preserved, and their marriage at the end of the novel is *directly conjoined* with their love—that same love that had been ignited at their first meeting at the outset of the novel" (p. 89).

The narrative scheme of love-in-marriage would have found favor with a Renaissance reformation audience who theoretically regarded matrimony as a state equal to (if not surpassing) celibacy, and considered mutuality in love as an integral condition within the bonds of marriage itself.[8] For religious reformists such as Luther and Calvin, the state of marriage was not conceived as a remedy for the ills of copulation, according to the standard interpretation of Gratian's *Decretum* (ca. 1140), but rather a beneficial condition and blessing in itself.[9] No longer a sacrament, matrimony became the natural endpoint of erotic impulses. Thus, sixteenth- and seventeenth-century religious reformers embraced a more optimistic view of sex and marriage than was conventional in medieval canonical thought, although they realized that sexual passion had the power to vex human relationships, generate brutal behavior, and divert attention away from spiritual concerns.[10] As such, reformed theologians asserted the necessity of piety and reverence in sexual conduct; yet, they also considered sex in marriage a positive aspect of nuptial relations, so that lawful sexual union between a man and woman was not a defect in human nature caused by original sin, but a gift in its own right.[11]

The reformists' idea of chaste marriage, a doctrine that "claimed for marriage the spiritual prestige which had previously been reserved for celibacy,"[12] is consistent with the two most important elements of the Greek romance plot: the moment of love (or love-at-first-sight) and the moment of mutual union in marriage. The ancient romance plot, as it progressed from erotic passion to solemnized marriage, subscribed to the idea of conjugal love and chaste marital relations as crucial factors in matrimony. Likewise, the Protestant view of marriage as a validation of sexual relations between husband and wife not only championed the notion of romantic love as a positive force in marriage, but it also laid open to criticism the belief that sexual desire is *ipso facto* a destructive power in human relationships, reducing lovers to irrational or lustful conduct. Sex, a natural and powerful drive, gains legitimacy within the institution of holy matrimony.[13] The concept of married love occupied a fundamental position in courtship and marriage in the Tudor and Stuart period. In view of the elevated status of love in marriage, early modern historian David Cressy contends that love, in this era, appears to have been "a common and expected ingredient in the majority of matches."[14]

I

The newly translated Greek romances enjoyed a tremendous readership in early modern England and in Continental Europe. English translations of

Greek romance first appeared in Elizabeth I's reign. Angell Daye's edition of Longus's romance *Daphnis and Chloe* was issued in 1587; this translation was based largely upon Jacques Amyot's 1559 popular and influential French rendering, *Les Amours pastourales de Daphnis et Chloé*. William Burton's *The most Delectable and pleasant Historye of Clitiphon and Leucippe* appeared a decade later, and it was followed by Anthony Hodges's English version of Achilles Tatius's romance in 1638. Prior to Burton's translation of *Leucippe and Clitophon*, the romance had been widely available: it had been translated into Latin in 1554, Italian in 1546, and French in 1568. By far the most popular and esteemed of the Greek romances in the early modern period was Heliodorus's *Aethiopica*. The first translator of the complete *Aethiopica* into English, Thomas Underdowne, closely followed the 1552 Latin translation of the romance undertaken by the Polish knight Stanislaus Warschewiczki.[15] Underdowne's 1569 version, *An Aethiopian historie*, was reprinted numerous times: in 1577, 1587, 1605, 1622, and 1627.[16] The decision to translate Heliodorus in the vernacular was, in all likelihood, inspired by such successful translations as Jacques Amyot's *L'Historie Aethiopique de Heliodorus, contenant dix livres, traitant des loyales et pudiques amours de Théagènes Thessalien, et Chariclea Aethiop ene*, a version that saw print no fewer than twenty-five times between 1547 and 1626, or Leon Ghini's popular Italian rendering, *Historia di Heliodoro delle cose Ethiopiche*.[17]

The *Aethiopica* was an exemplary piece of romantic fiction in the Elizabethan period largely due to the sexual purity of its hero and heroine. What is particularly noteworthy about Underdowne's English translation is that it helped fashion the moral tenor of the *Aethiopica* by defending its amatory content. As the full title of Amyot's *L'Historie Aethiopique* indicates, Underdowne was not the first early modern translator to interpret the story of Theagenes and Chariclea as a commentary on loyal and modest love ("loyales et pudiques amours"). Nonetheless, in the 1577 and later reprints of *An Aethiopian historie*, he praises the book anew for its chaste love story, while noting its secular subject matter:

> I am not ignorant that the stationers shops are to full fraughted with books of smal price, wither you consider the quantitie or contents of them, and that the loosenesse of these dayes rather requireth grave exhortations to vertue, then wanton allurements to leudness, that it were meeter to publish notable examples of godly christian life, then the most honest (as I take this to be) historie of love.[18]

Unlike other books that encourage "wanton allurements to leudness," the *Aethiopica* chronicles, as Underdowne has it, the most honest history of love. According to the *OED*, the word honest in the sixteenth century included the meaning of "chaste" and "virtuous," especially in reference to a woman's sexual conduct. Since the *Aethiopica*, however, is a story about the reciprocal love of Theagenes and Chariclea, "honest" presumably refers to the virtue and chastity of both the hero and heroine. The idea of mutual chastity reinforces Underdowne's moralistic proclivity, and he goes on to contrast the teaching of the *Aethiopica* with other stories of "smal price": "If I shall compare it with other of like argumente, I thinke none commeth neere it. *Morte Darthure, Arthur* of little *Britaine*, yea, and *Amadis* of *Gaule*, [etc] accompt violent murder, or murder for no cause, manhoode: and fornication and all unlawfull luste, friendly love" (sig. iii). These chivalric romances fail to provide sound ethical instruction to the reader since they equate violence with manhood and unlawful passion with love. "These bokes," writes Lodovicus [Juan Luis] Vives about such fiction, "do hurt both man & woman, for they make them wylye & craftye, they kyndle and styr up covetousnes, inflame angre, & all beastly and filthy desyre."[19] The chivalric tradition, in general, tended to privilege the escapades of a knight in love with a lady already married over the story of chaste lovers, shared adventures, and their union in lawful matrimony.[20] Accordingly, their gratuitous violence and illicit sex differentiate them from Heliodorus, whose "booke punisheth the faultes of evill doers, and rewardeth the well livers" (sig. iii).

As Underdowne's appraisal of the *Aethiopica* indicates, early modern readers of Heliodorus frequently interpreted the story's theme of honest love as a paradigm of romantic relations. This interpretation, one repeatedly applied to Heliodorus, extended well into the seventeenth century. For example, in his 1638 verse translation, *The famous historie of Heliodorus* (originally titled *The Faire Ethiopian* in the edition of 1631), William Lisle appends the document "Testimonies of Learned Men concerning Heliodorus." These testimonies substantiate the value of the *Aethiopica* by enumerating its wide range of virtues, including, of course, its chaste love story. A testimonial from the scholar Thomas Dempster states cogently: "Heliodorus the Phoenix of Phoenicia: an Elegant writer of chast Love, and in the contexture of this History, a most elaborate Author."[21] Later in the century, Nahum Tate and a "Person of Quality" affix similar testimonials to their 1686 translation of the romance, *The Aethiopian History of Heliodorus.* This title undergoes a transformation in the 1687 second edition to read in full: "The Triumphs / Of Love / And / Constancy: / A / Romance. / Containing the Heroick Amours of Theagenes & Chariclea / In Ten Books." Along with the "Heroick Amours" of the hero and heroine, the title proclaims love and constancy as its main premise, and the testimonials of "Eminent Persons, Ancient and Modern" corroborate this claim. One such person, "Vicentius Obsopoeus," the first editor of the *Aethiopica* in print (1534), is quoted as saying:

> I Recommend The Aethiopian History of Heliodorus, as the most absolute Image of all humane Affections; a perfect Example of Conjugal Love, Truth and Constancy being Wonderfully drawn in the Characters of Theagenes and Chariclea.[22]

This Protestant critic defines the story as an ideal model of romantic love: the devotion of the hero and heroine is "the most absolute" of human affections and a "perfect Example" of marital love, truth, and constancy.[23] Concomitantly, another testimonial from a Dr. Peter Heylin indicates that the lovers' "honest and chaste affection" is suitable for even the "chastest Ear":

> A piece indeed of rare contexture and neat contrivance, without any touch of loose or lascivious Language, honest and chast affection being the subject of it, not such as Old or Modern Poets show us in the Comedies or other Poems: for here we have no Incestious mixtures of Fathers and Daughters: no Pandorism of Old Nurses: no unseemly action specified, where heat of Blood and opportunity do meet: nor indeed any one passage unworthy of the chastest Ear. (sig. a5)

Although there is no direct reference to a specific comedy or poem in this comparison, it appears that Heliodorus's romance would afford the stage worthy material, for the story supercedes less virtuous tales of passion, including presumably those of New Comedy in which the subject of love is often sexualized or illicit.

Other English translations of Greek romance share a similar emphasis on the merit of honest love. In Daye's *Daphnis and Chloe* the title page makes good on the virtue of honorable courtship, among other themes: "Daphnis and Chloe / Excellently / describing the weight / of affection, the simplicities of love, the purport / of honest meaning, the resolution of men, and disposition of Fate."[24] Likewise, the title page of Hodges's seventeenth-century translation of Achilles Tatius's *Leucippe and Clitophon* accentuates the romantic love between the hero and heroine: "The Loves / of Clitophon / And Leucippe. / A most elegant History, written in / Greeke by Achilles Tatius."[25] In the same translation, a sonnet accompanies an illustration on the frontispiece (see figure 1.1). It depicts the hero and heroine in the throes of a storm at sea: "See for the sceane a troubled Sea, whereon / Float faire Lecuippe and her Clitophon." Clutching one another, the lovers receive little succor from the element: "But churlish Neptune (who for Venus sake / Me thinkes on Lovers should some pitie take) / Quels not the raging Ocean, while each wave / Presents the ship, and passengers, a grave." The sonnet concludes with Venus's dispatch of Cupid to the lovers' rescue: "... Loves Queene... Sets Cupid at the sterne; who well may free / These paire of Turtles from the tyranny / Of angry Neptune... " (sig. A1^{v}). The shipwreck off the coast of Alexandria refers to Leucippe and Clitophon's first adventure and separation, and it initiates the series of trials that lead up to the couple's marriage. The powerful drive of erotic love—which is often associated with the frenzy, sickness, and derangement induced by Cupid's arrow in the Petrarchan or Ovidian tradition—is now depicted as a benevolent and benign force that saves lovers from the threat of destructive elements. As the placement of the sonnet and illustration indicates, these Renaissance printers and translators of Greek romance stressed the amorous virtues represented in these stories, including the triumph of mutual love tested by adversity.

Even though Achilles Tatius, Longus, and especially Heliodorus received praise for the didactic nature of their stories, such writers also incurred the condemnation of early modern critics. An infamous critique can be found in

On the Frontiſpiece.

SEE for the ſceane a troubled Sea, whereon
Float faire Leucippe and her Clitophon:
But churliſh Neptune (who for Venus ſake
Me-thinkes on Lovers ſhould ſome pitie take)
Quels not the raging Ocean, while each wave
Preſents the ſhip, and paſſengers, a grave.
No Caſtor here, or Pollux to be ſeene,
But the celeſtiall influence of Loves Queene,
Which ſeeing her Darlings to ſuch ſtraits were come,
As to take boat to goe t'Elyſium,
Sets Cupid at the ſterne; who well may free
Theſe paire of Turtles from the tyranny
Of angry Neptune, ſince from his firſt birth
Ha's beene the Lawgiver to Sea and Earth.

Figure 1.1 Engraved frontispiece and sonnet from *The Loves of Clitophon and Leucippe* by Achilles Tatius and translated by Anthony Hodges, 1638. By permission of the Bodleian Library, University of Oxford, Douce T 206 (sig. Al[v], A2).

Stephen Gosson's *Playes Confuted in Five Actions* (ca. 1582). Gosson singles out the "*Aethiopian historie*" as one in a group of indecent, low-brow stories and dramatic works that had been "throughly ransackt" to supply material for the London playhouses:

> The *Palace of pleasure*, the *Golden Asse*, the *Aethiopian historie*, *Amadis of Fraunce*, the *Rounde table*, baudie Comedies in Latine, French, Italian and Spanish, have been throughly ransackt, to furnish the Playe houses in London. How is it possible that our Playemakers headdes, running through Genus and Species & every difference of lyes, cosenages, baudries, whooredomes, should present us with any schoolemistres of life, looking glasse of manners, or Image of trueth?[26]

In part, Gosson's complaint is that such common fiction not only contains vile subject matter, "lyes, cosenages, baudries, whooredomes," but presents an illusory and thus false image of reality because it distorts the "looking glasse of manners, or Image of trueth." About this much-quoted passage, Hallet Smith states, "[t]he Greek romances would have been scorned by the enemies of the stage, like Gosson," who regarded them as extravagant and foolish.[27] Although Gosson denounces the *Aethiopica*, his criticism suggests that at least one Greek romance provided playwrights with a repertoire of incidents and characterizations. Indeed, in *The Lost Plays and Masques, 1500–1642*, Gertrude Marian Sibley lists a play called *Theagines and Cariclea*, performed at court in 1572 for the Christmas festivities, and also one titled *The Queen of Ethiopia* (identified with *Theagines and Cariclea*), acted by Lord Howard's men for the major of Bristol in 1578.[28] It was theoretically conceivable that Gosson's "Playemakers" were reading and scripting Underdowne's English translation of Heliodorus, which would have been available to them in 1569 and again in 1577. Underdowne's 1577 epistle to the reader in support of the *Aethiopica* also appears in approximately the same period that Gosson launches his attack on playwrights. Whether or not Underdowne was ambivalent about the transference of his work to the stage, or whether his translation did in fact encourage dramatic adaptations of the prose romance, he upholds the *Aethiopica* as a celebrated testimony to "honest love."

Heliodorus's *Aethiopica* seemed to set the standard for the Greek romance genre. Apparently, Heliodorus created its paragon, "the most honest... historie of love" (Underdowne, sig. iii), as well as "a perfect Example of Conjugal Love" (Tate, sig. A5^v). Indeed, one compliment paid to Hodges on his translation of Achilles Tatius was the author's comparison to Heliodorus: "Friend, I thy boke compare with swilk of yore, / With mighty deeds of worthy Heliodore" (sig. A6^v). Moreover, in Burton's 1597 translation of *Leucippe and Clitophon*, the translator compares the merit of Achilles Tatius's work to Heliodorus's: "(as Crucius saith uppon Heliodorus) there is none who is learned, and desirous of good instructions, which once having begun to read him, can lay him aside, untill he have perused him over."[29] This reverence for Heliodorus venerates the *Aethiopica*, even though chronologically it was written after both the works of Achilles Tatius and Longus.[30]

Given similarities in plot and theme, why did Heliodorus's *Aethiopica* stand apart from its romance counterparts in the early modern period? An explanation of the *Aethiopica*'s singularity may lie in the story's emphasis on the virginal purity of both the hero and heroine. At this point, a further distinction needs to be made within the genre of Greek romance. In his study of the Greek novel, David Konstan argues that the primary virtue of the Hellenistic romance hero and heroine resides in the preservation of their mutual fidelity, not necessarily in the strict enforcement of their physical chastity. He states:

> In the Greek novels, the body is not the primary site on which the problem of love and fidelity is transacted. In the absence of a strong opposition between love and lust, where sex is constructed as the specific object of lust and is resisted in the name of true love, the Greek novel does not focus on sex per se as the hallmark of virtue. In certain situations, the protagonist, male or female, accepts a sexual association with another partner, but this is not registered in the text as a failure of fidelity.[31]

In support of this observation, one could cite Clitophon's seduction by an Ephesian wife or Daphnis's copulation with a married woman. Rather than an absolute adherence to chastity, the integrity of the Greek romance hero and heroine consists in maintaining a commitment to their pledge of fidelity. In essence, a sexual peccadillo, usually committed in extremity, does not damage the lovers' unshakable resolution to remain together. However, Konstan perceives that in Heliodorus a different type of relationship between the hero and heroine develops, one in which virginal purity begins to take the place of mere fidelity as the story's principal virtue. What makes this shift in emphasis especially significant in Heliodorus is that the ideal of premarital virginity applies equally to the male as well as to the female protagonist. As will be shown, the importance given to both female and male chastity in the *Aethiopica* distinguishes the story from its Greek romance counterparts in *Leucippe and Clitophon* and *Daphnis and Chloe.*

In the *Aethiopica*, the love-leading-to-marriage plot fosters the motif of reciprocal chastity, and the emphasis on the virginal pureness of the hero and heroine occurs almost as soon as the protagonists meet. Theagenes, a Thessalian and descendant of Achilles, has come to Athens to perform ceremonial rites in honor of his ancestors. Chariclea, an Athenian priestess of Diana, oversees the ritual. In actuality, the heroine is an Ethiopian princess born with white skin because her mother, Persina, gazes on a picture of Andromeda during her daughter's conception. Chariclea's light skin color forces Persina, who fears accusations of adultery, to convey her daughter secretly from their native land, an action that places Chariclea under the guardianship of an Athenian, Charicles. During the festivities of the Pythian Games, Theagenes and Chariclea fall in love at first sight (Book Three). The narrator describes Cupid as the "moderatour" and "Arbiter" of the festivities in order to show that the couple's romantic and eventual sexual union are ultimately controlled by a higher, goodly power. By having a judicious Cupid oversee the love match, Heliodorus sets the scene for the couple's chaste and discreet pairing: "The nexte daie Apolloes games did ende, but youthfull disportes begane, Cupide (in mine opinion) moderatour, and Arbiter thereof, beeing in full determination, to declare his force, in most ample wise, by these two champions, which he had sette together" (sig. F8[v]). Consequently, in Book Four the modest Chariclea resists her ardent passion for Theagenes, fearing that her lovesickness will denigrate her virginal state. She says to the Egyptian sage Calasiris: "Although mine increasing disease doth muche greeve me, yet that greeveth mee more, that at the firste I overcame it not, but am yeelded unto love, which by hearing onely doth defile the honorable name of virginitie" (sig. G6[v]). Calasiris convinces Chariclea of the naturalness of her desire, and that her strong affection for Theagenes can only find legitimization in holy matrimony. Therefore, he pacifies the heroine:

> But now we consider howe presently you may best order your businesse, in as much as at the firste, not to be in love, is a kind of happinesse, but wh you are taken, to use it moderately, it is a point of excellente wisedome, which thing

> you may well doo, if you will beleeve mee, by putting away the filthy name of luste, and imbracing the lawfull bande of wedding, and turning your disease into matrimony. (sig. G6^{v}–G7)

Calasiris does not prize virginity over wifehood, but he does indicate that sexual desire should be properly channeled via the rite of marital union.

In a larger context, Calasiris's differentiation between virginal and wedded chastity would have been acknowledged by Elizabethan and Jacobean readers as a legitimate distinction, especially, though not exclusively, for women. In Marie Loughlin's definition, virginal chastity in the early modern period involved "sexual abstinence usually undertaken by religious women and men," while wedded chastity referred to "virginity aimed . . . at the dissolution of its integrity in the lawful sexual initiation of marriage."[32] The logical conclusion is that wedded chastity was, writes Loughlin, "a state that Protestants valued more highly than the older ideal of lifelong abstinence."[33] We find, for example, a pertinent explanation of the place of chastity in wedlock in a sixteenth-century treatise on marriage. In *Gods Arithmeticke* (1597), Francis Meres explains that the Devil and his workers (the Catholic Church) "bannished out of the bondes of Christianitie, that most famous and glorious Empresse Ladie Matrimonie and exalted in her Throne fained Dame Chastitie, which beeing pure is not to be preferred before holy Wedlocke."[34] According to Meres, because God ordained Adam and Eve to increase and multiply, the Catholic dogma that elevates virginity over sexual relations in marriage contradicts the Creator's commandment. Hence, "Virginitie is the daughter of Marriage, and through marriage is made a Cittizen and Indweller of Paradice."[35] Interestingly, an Elizabethan translation of Heliodorus emphasizes the very idea of wedded chastity. In *The Amorous and Tragicall Tales of Plutarch* (1567), James Sanford appends Book Four of the *Aethiopica* to a series of Plutarch's tales. Significantly, Sanford's rendering of Heliodorus's romance places greater weight on the sanctity of wedded chastity than does Underdowne's translation, which follows Warschewiczki's Latin version more closely. Unlike Plutarch's more sordid tales of lust and murderous passion, the section of the *Aethiopica* that Sanford chooses to translate describes the spotless inception of Theagenes's and Chariclea's symmetrical love: their pledge of fidelity and wedded chastity.

The scene in question occurs just before the lovers' elopement. When Chariclea's father arranges for her to marry his nephew, Theagenes and Chariclea decide to elope in order to remain together. Sanford's Chariclea insists that Theagenes not violate her until their nuptials have concluded: she demands that "Theagenes establishe with an othe [her] securitie and suretie, that he shall not bed with [her], untill the espousalls bee ended." Disappointed that Chariclea should suspect him so weak as to need an oath of chastity, Theagenes did "sware, that he had injurie shewed him, saying":

> That faith might be broken by preventing the oath, and onely to be performed willingly with promise of mind, neither that hee could commende that minde, which for feare of one more stronger seemeth to be compelled.

The narrator continues:

> yet he sware by Apollo of Delphos, and by Diana, & Venus hir selfe, that he would doe all things as Chariclea desired. And he and she calling the Gods to witnesse, made the agreement betwene themselves.[36]

In Heliodorus's story, Theagenes and Chariclea have not been publically married during the course of their adventures, though at this point in the narrative they exchange private vows of fidelity and sexual continence. It is possible that an early modern reader of this passage might interpret this literary presentation of the couple's private oath as a clandestine marriage, one based on the late medieval and Renaissance theological precept of *verba de presenti* (present consent) and *verba de futuro* (future consent): a theory of legal marriage based on the sole mutual consent of a couple.[37] The historian Cressy writes that a lawful and binding marriage contract in the medieval and early modern period "could be expressed in *verba de presenti*, making an immediate and indissoluble commitment expressed by the words 'I do'; [or] *verba de futuro*, a promise of future action expressed by the words 'I will.' "[38] Diana O'Hara states further that "Words of future consent (*verba de futuro*) and *conditional* contracts did not instantly create valid unions, but became absolute once sexual intercourse occurred and any specified conditions were fulfilled."[39] She adds, "Local customs such as the use of gifts and rings, and other formalities which involved familial agreement and betrothal before witnesses, were called for but were not in fact essential for legal validity."[40] Alone, Sanford's Theagenes and Chariclea exchange vows that countenance mutual sexual abstinence until "the espousalls bee ended," so that the clandestine ceremonial pact between the lovers (in the language of *verba de futuro*) reinforces the principle of mutual chastity before lawful marriage. However, the same passage in Underdowne's *An Aethiopian historie* gives a notably different reading. Here, Chariclea has Theagenes swear to his chastity in these terms: "that he shall not fleashly have to doo with me, untill I have recovered my countrie, and parentes, or if the Godds be not content herewith, at least untill I by mine owne free will be content he shal marrie me. Other wise never" (sig. H3). Not only does Chariclea wish to choose the time of her marriage, but she concedes, it seems, to the possibility of sex before the event of a solemnized marital union, one formally witnessed by her parents. In Underdowne, Chariclea possesses more sovereignty than in Sanford's characterization of her. Although *Amorous and Tragicall Tales* was published two years before the first printing of Underdowne's *An Aethiopian historie*, the variations in the two passages reveal Sanford's concern with fashioning a more orthodox picture of the hero's and heroine's equal commitment to marriage and sexual temperance.

In another Elizabethan translation of Heliodorus, the subject of wedded chastity arises once again as a significant theme. Abraham Fraunce in *The Countesse of Pembroke's Yuychurch* (1591) appends a small excerpt from Book One of the *Aethiopica* to his *Amyntas Pastorall*, a dramatic poem based on

Torquato Tasso's *Aminta*. While this small excerpt from the love story of Theagenes and Chariclea may have been merely a literary exercise in Greek translation, its inclusion in Fraunce's publication is more than fortuitous. Similar to the love-leading-to-marriage pattern in Heliodorus's romance, what is exalted in *Amyntas Pastorall* is not virginal chastity, but virginity that culminates in holy wedlock. This theme is not totally incongruent with the Catholic ideal of chaste conduct before and during matrimony, an ideal that one might find in a writer such as Tasso. About this issue, Ruth Kelso argues, "chastity, synonymous with virginity in the maid, was obviously not conceived by Catholics as ending with virginity in marriage, but . . . was counted the greatest virtue of the wife in her fidelity to her husband."[41] Initially, the virginal Phillis cruelly rejects the affection of Amyntas; yet, when she discovers that Amyntas's supposed death is brought on by her own proud disdain, Phyllis repents her scorn: "my scornefull pryde, that I then my Chastyty called, / And it Chastyty was, but Chastyty noe-pyty-taking, / Now I repent it alas, but now too late I repent yt."[42] After Phyllis realizes her folly, her lack of compassion in love, she gives herself to the revived Amyntas in marriage. Phyllis's self-realization corresponds to Chariclea's maturation from a reclusive virgin to a chaste bride. Before Chariclea's enamorment of Theagenes in the *Aethiopica*, her father laments, "Shee hath bidden mariage farewell, and determineth to live a maiden stil, and so becomming Dianas servant, for the most parte, applieth her selfe to hunting, and doth practice shooting." He goes on to describe the heroine's resolve to remain celibate: Chariclea "commending virginitie with immortall praise, and placing it in Heaven by the Gods, calleth it immaculate, unspotted, and uncorrupted: as for love, Venus disporte, and every Ceremonie, that apperteineth to marriage, shee utterly dispraiseth" (sig. E4^{v}–E5). As does Chariclea, Phyllis eventually abrogates the state of maidenhood for the sanctioned contract of marriage.

In "The second part of the Countesse of Pembrokes Yuychurch," based on a translation from Thomas Watson, the poem describes Amyntas's inconsolable grief over the death of Phyllis on their wedding day. This poem, when read together with Fraunce's translation of Helidorus's Book One, has further thematic links with the notion of wedded chastity. Unwilling to live without his beloved, Amyntas mortally wounds himself, and, as a tribute to his undying faith, the gods transform the dying Amyntas into the Amaranthus flower; not remarkably, Cupid appropriates the flower. Even though this love story does not conform strictly to the Greek romance scheme of happily-ever-after, it appears that Fraunce draws from the story of Theagenes and Chariclea to suggest the idea of mutual chastity even in death; for, the Heliodoran lovers uphold their pledge of fidelity to such a degree that they would rather chose death than lose their virginity to any other person. For example, in Fraunce's "The Beginning of Heliodorus his Aethiopical History," the reader meets Chariclea and Theagenes, learns of their devotion, and views their courage in the face of shipwreck and Egyptian thieves. One of the high points of this section occurs when Chariclea, threatening suicide, staves off capture by a large group of bandits, whose leader is Thyamis. Defending the wounded Theagenes and guarding her own person, the heroine, in Fraunce's words,

> cleaved fast to the yongman,
> And held yongman fast, and every way shee declared;
> Unles yongman went, she never meant to be going,
> Unles yongman went, herself shee meant to be murdring,
> And with a knife in her hand to her hart shee begins to be poynting. (sig. M3)

Similar to Amyntas, who stabs himself in the breast, Chariclea chooses death over the possibility of life without her betrothed, though she is saved here from actual suicide. Chariclea's defense of Theagenes also implies a defense of her own virginity. Surrounded by a group of bandits who profess utter astonishment over Chariclea's rare beauty, the heroine perhaps senses a palpable threat to her person and chastity. A little later, when Thyamis captures the hero and heroine, Chariclea declares her determination to remain true to Theagenes or else die: "but rather then any man should filthely know me, which Theagenes never did, truely with haulter I woulde ende my life, reserving my selfe pure and chaste (as hitherto I have done) even unto deathe, and thereby gaine a beautifull Epitath for my singular virginitie" (Underdowne, sig. A5). Importantly, Theagenes had been injured in an earlier skirmish when he was attempting to protect the heroine's maidenhead. At that earlier point, he and Chariclea took up arms "Syth force and violence were offered unto [her] person" (Fraunce, sig. M2^{v}).[43] Theagenes's and Chariclea's single-minded tenacity to consummate their passion in marriage remains a thematic feature of the first book.

If readers were to continue where Fraunce's translation leaves off, they might observe that the preservation of the hero's and heroine's virginity often depends upon the lovers' ability to pass as brother and sister. The use of this plot device indicates the physical and psychological mirroring of the primary couple: beautiful, chaste, and valiant, Theagenes and Chariclea resemble each other to such a degree that they often succeed at simulating a brother-and-sister relationship. Although romantic love happens as the product of spontaneous attraction in Greek romance, it occurs within the confines of a predetermined social and economic boundary: not only do the hero and heroine physically resemble each other, but they belong to the same social and economic class.[44] For example, in the *Aethiopica* the couple Theagenes and Chariclea both claim noble ancestry; the hero is a direct descendant of Achilles, and the heroine learns that she is the daughter of an Ethiopian king and queen. In Longus's pastoral *Daphnis and Chloe*, the hero and heroine, as shepherds, both discover at the story's conclusion that each possesses an affluent father in Mytilene. In Achilles Tatius's *Leucippe and Clitophon*, the lovers are even half cousins. To further this sense of homogeneity, the romance hero and heroine often mirror each other by being the most attractive, pure, or virtuous of their sex. In the narrative context of Greek romance, the hero and heroine freely choose love; however, the objective of this love, lawful marriage, takes place within the bounds of the couple's established social order.

The lovers' similitude in the *Aethiopica* allows the hero and heroine to put on the guise of brother and sister in order to ward off potential threats to their chastity. Both Theagenes and Chariclea use this tactic. For example, when the robber Thyamis (who is really a high priest of Memphis) desires Chariclea as his lawful wife, the heroine invents a story that keeps Theagenes from harm and her virginity intact. About her "brother" Theagenes, she says to Thyamis: "When we came to the age of fourtene yeeres, by the lawe (whiche calleth such to the office of priesthood) I was made priest, to Diana, and this my brother of Apollo" (sig. B6). When Chariclea deceptively requests that Thyamis allow her to surrender her priesthood at an appropriate shrine of Apollo before she marries him, Chariclea gains valuable time to forestall a marriage with Thyamis, while simultaneously quelling Thyamis's jealousy of Theagenes. But Theagenes does not understand this dissimulation. Bewildered by Chariclea's apparent plan to wed another, Theagenes accuses the heroine of forsaking her pledge to him. Chariclea counters this accusation by restating her immutable loyalty to Theagenes. She states:

> In one thing onely I knowe, I have not ruled my selfe, that is, in the love that I have borne to you, from the beginninge, but notwithstanding it is both lawfull, and honeste: for I not like your lover, but at the first concluding marriage with you, have committed my selfe to you, and have lived chastely without copulation hitherto, not without refusing you oftentimes, profering me such things, and have waited for occasion to be married, if any where it might lawfully be done, whiche thing, at the first, was decreed betweene us, and above all things, by othe established. (sig. B7^{v})

Implicitly, Chariclea reminds Theagenes that her scheme—to wed Thyamis—is merely a ploy to keep her troth plight. Just as Chariclea safeguards her virginity by blocking an unwanted suitor (and evidently also refusing Theagenes), Theagenes also blocks the sexual advances of the character Arsace, sister to the king of Memphis. Theagenes subdues the envy of Arsace by feigning that Chariclea is his sibling.

Books Seven and Eight of the *Aethiopica* focus largely on the preservation of Theagenes's virginity and his sexual commitment to the heroine. When the hero and Chariclea arrive in Memphis, the seductress Arsace becomes "inflamed when shee had seene Theagenes excellent beautie, which farre passed all that ever shee had seene before" (sig. M5^{v}). Secretly plotting to entrap Theagenes, Arsace invites the couple to stay with her after their guardian Calasiris dies. As Theagenes considers "howe wantonly with steady eyes, continually shee beheld him, so that her becks declared scante a chaste minde" (sig. M8), he apprehends Arsace's capacity for lust and her jealousy of Chariclea. Prompted by the heroine, Theagenes tells Arsace's bawd that they "be brother and sister" (sig. M8^{v}). The bawd "was very gladde to heare the names of brother and sister, thinking then surely that Cariclia should be no impediment to Arsaces disports" (sig. M8v). When by necessity Theagenes reveals to Arsace that Chariclea is really his plighted wife, the hero suffers torture but does not succumb to Arsace's repeated attempts upon his virginity: "by reason of his chastity," Theagenes delights in his torture: "he now had occasion to declare what good will he bare to Cariclia" (sig. O6–O6v). This physical trial only serves to strengthen Theagenes's dedication to Chariclea and reinforces his pledge of chastity: "he tooke a lofty stomach to him, and rejoyced, and gloried in that fortune" (sig. O6–O6v). In order to draw attention to the reciprocal nature of the couple's commitment, Heliodorus has Chariclea incarcerated with the hero on a trumped up charge of murder. Fettered togther, the couple interprets their perseverance in adversity as a testament to a shared allegiance to constancy and virginal integrity:

> But they compted this a comfort, and to be pained alike they thoughte it a vauntage, and if either had lesse torments then the other, eche supposed hym selfe vanquished, and as it were more faint, and weake in love. For nowe was it lawfull for them to be together, and encourage eche other to take in goodly wise what fortune so ever came, and refuse no perill which shoulde insue of their unfained chastitie, and stedfaste faith. (sig. P2)

The passage underlines the common trials of the hero and heroine. Each experiences pain and hardship on account of the other, and each wishes the other to suffer less. The lovers' anguish only fortifies their impervious bond, their "unfained chastitie," and "stedfaste faith."

The final test of the couple's chastity takes place in the last book. This episode supports the ethic of male and female celibacy before marriage. In a series of events too complicated to summarize here, Theagenes and Chariclea arrive as prisoners in the heroine's native Ethiopia. Once again, they act as brother and sister. Chariclea's father, Hydaspes, has just won victory over the Persians and intends to sacrifice both a male and a female virgin to his country's gods. Unaware that Chariclea is his own daughter and Theagenes his future son-in-law, Hydaspes hopes to offer the heroine to the Moon, the hero to the Sun. But before Hydaspes initiates the sacrifices, he tests the pair for their sexual purity: "the lawe willeth that shee be as well cleane also, that is offered to the Moone, as he that is sacrificed to the Sunne" (sig. R7v). To test their innocence, the hero and heroine must walk through fire because "it would burne every unchast person" (sig. R7v). Not surprisingly, the couple proves chaste. What amazes the spectators, though, is not the virginity of the heroine, but the hero's maidenhood: "After Theagenes also put his foote to the fire, and was founde a maide, there was great wondering, both for that he being so tall and beautifull, as also because he was young and lusty, and had never to do with any woman" (sig. R8). The logic is that the young, attractive hero should have by now submitted to his carnal passions. The public trial of virginity not only affirms the spotless attachment of the hero and heroine, but it paves the way for their lawful wedding at the story's conclusion.

The concepts found in Bakhtin's treatment of Greek romance seem to relate particularly to Heliodorus's story of reciprocal love and sexual continence; in his words, the main protagonists "are placed in the most ticklish situations, but they always emerge with their honor intact" (p. 106). Yet, this model does not wholly correspond to the presentation of love and chastity in the storylines of Longus and Achilles Tatius. This is not to say that the concept of mutual sexual temperance does not figure largely into the design of their narratives. It does. In these romances, however, the hero's desire for sexual intimacy with the heroine or his physical indiscretion with another woman, which usually occurs at a moment of crisis in the course of his ordeals, is excused or tolerated as a common aberration in male conduct.

In *Leucippe and Clitophon*, the lovers learn to cultivate the virtue of chastity during the course of their adventures. If Theagenes and Chariclea possess an innate understanding of the necessity of wedded chastity, Achilles Tatius's plot teaches the primary couple to abstain from sexual relations before marriage. In Book One, Clitophon falls head-over-heels in love with Leucippe during their first encounter, and he is coached into seducing her by his sexually sophisticated cousin, Kleinias. In his attempt to bed the heroine, Clitophon convinces Leucippe that, if the couple exchange private vows of love, they can licitly consummate their passion. No longer satisfied with mere kissing, he urges her to "do the rest which lovers most of all desire: therfore first let us contract our selves togither, for if we will sacrifice to Venus, we shall not find any god more favourable unto us then this" (sig. F1). The hero mitigates Leucippe's anxiety of premarital sex by assuring her of the legality of their secret troth plight. Soon after Leucippe agrees, their attempt at love-making is stymied by Leucippe's mother, Panthia. Due to the circumspection of Panthia and because Clitophon's father wants him to marry his half sister, the pair decide to elope. It is during the first separation of the lovers that a new alliance is forged between the couple, one based on the prospect of wedded chastity or mutual sexual abstinence before lawful matrimony. Unlike Theagenes's and Chariclea's vow of chastity before their elopement, the hero and heroine in Achilles Tatius's novel come to their agreement of abstinence only after their elopement and only after the onset of their initial trials, which include a shipwreck, capture by Egyptian outlaws, and the heroine's faked immolation. When the pair eventually reunite after their first set of adventures, Leucippe forestalls Clitophon's request for sex, his "frutes of Venus" (sig. K1^{v}), by relating to him the contents of a dream. In this dream, the goddess of chastity, Diana, reveals herself as Leucippe's guardian: "in my dreame Diana seemed to appeare unto me, saying; doo not weepe, for thou shalt not die, I my selfe will helpe thee, keepe thou as yet thy virginitie, until I shall otherwise appoint thee, for thou shalt marry none but Clitiphon" (sig. K1^{v}). Although privately betrothed to the hero, Leucippe at once resolves to remain a virgin until lawful matrimony. Coincidentally, Clitophon has had a similar dream. He recounts that, while standing in a temple of Venus, a woman appears before him, saying, "as yet it was not lawfull for me to enter into the temple; but if that I would stay a little space, it should come to pass, that the doores would open of theyr owne accord, and also that I should be created a Priest unto the goddesse" (sig. K2). The apparition in the dream forewarns Clitophon of the illegality of intercourse before marriage. On account of Leucippe's vision of Diana and Clitophon's dream in the temple of Venus, the hero now determines to exercise sexual temperance with the heroine: "neyther did I strive to offer her [Leucippe] violence any more" (sig. K2). Leucippe retains her virginity throughout her ordeals, but not without much suffering and tribulation.

As we begin to see, the heroine's ability to defend her virginity is a key ingredient of this love-in-marriage plot. The trials over which Leucippe prevails largely measure the heroine's ability to defend her virginity; for, after the revelation of the dreams, a series of assaults is made upon the heroine's maidenhead. At this crucial point in the narrative, the issue of wedded chastity gives way to the problem of the preservation of the heroine's virginity from outside forces. Leucippe manages to protect her virginity from malefactors through a sequence of bizarre and chance events. Just before her arrival in Ephesus, an Egyptian general, Charmides, who has just saved Clitophon from a band of marauders, seeks the heroine for his own pleasures, but before he is able to violate her, Leucippe must overcome yet another attempt upon her maidenhead. This time, an Egyptian soldier falls in love with Leucippe; in order to seduce her, he concocts an "amorous Potion" (sig. L3). Unfortunately, the heroine receives too much of the love tonic and is consequently inflicted with madness. From this event, a third assay on Leucippe's virginity comes to pass when an Egyptian doctor treats the heroine's disease only because he has fallen in love with her as well: "[he] gave her the medicine hoping to have occasion therby to come into acquaintance with her, and that he might preserve her for himself" (sig. M2). Since the Egyptian doctor understands that Leucippe's virtue remains unassailable, he devises a scheme to kidnap her by transporting the heroine onboard a ship. Prior to her attempted ravishment, a group of pirates on the sailing vessel intervene (as can now be expected) and sell her to a steward in Ephesus.

The most powerful defense of Leucippe's virginity unfolds during her stay in Ephesus. Once she reaches Ephesus, the city whose patron goddess is, of course, Diana, a slight change takes place. The heroine can no longer rely merely on chance to save her. Now she must actively begin to oppose assaults upon her virginity. Leucippe is enslaved at a great house of Ephesus because she refuses to submit to its steward's "filthie desire" (sig. N3^{v}). The steward, Sosthenes, purchased the heroine from the band of pirates for two thousand gold pieces. Not only has Sosthenes developed a licentious appetite for Leucippe, but the master of the same estate, Thersandros, has as well. Lovesick and fearing that Leucippe is truly married to Clitophon, Thersandros is consumed with such lustful desire that he forces himself on the heroine. To repulse the concupiscence of Thersandros, the heroine uses a progression of stratagems. She first reminds him of the profanity of his desires: "But heare you sir, doo you reverence Diana heere; and go about to ravish a virgin in a virgins Cittie?" (sig. Q4^{v}). Leucippe furthers his sense of guilt by comparing her stalwart virtue with his brute savagery: "this is the most famous commendation and to be preferred before all, that Leucippe keepe her maydenhead against the force of Thersander, more savadge then all the pyrates" (sig. Q4^{v}). Finally, the heroine brandishes her most important weapon against her despoilers, her volition and personal liberty: "I am both naked, alone, and a woman: and have no defence, except my liberty, which can neither be whipped with rods, nor cut with iron, nor burnt with fire: that will I never leese, and if you cast me into the middle of the flame: there will not bee force inough therein to take it from me" (sig. Q4^{v}). Leucippe's obstinacy and declaration of liberty deter Thersandros from further physical assault, even though he later tries to abduct the heroine while attempting to have Clitophon executed for murder.

In the *Aethiopica*, both Theagenes and Chariclea successfully guard their virginity from various assailants. In Achilles Tatius's adventure romance, however, the hero struggles to remain chaste to his betrothed, but his dedication to chastity does not equally match the heroine's physical constancy when it is put to the test. When Clitophon wrongly discovers that pirates have decapitated Leucippe, he mourns her death (and attempts suicide), yet he is ultimately persuaded into another marriage with a wealthy and beautiful woman who also believes her spouse has died: she is Melite, wife of Thersandros. Melite has fallen desperately in love with Clitophon. Although Clitophon successfully keeps Melite at bay for awhile, he ultimately falls prey to Melite's desire to wed and to his own youthful impulses. Clitophon's only stipulation to this new marriage concerns the solemnization of his marriage vow: "I sware when I lost Leucippe, that heere never any shoulde have my Virginitie" (sig. N1^{v}).[45] In other words, Clitophon will not consummate the union with Melite in the same country where Leucippe has supposedly died. Despite his dedication to Leucippe's memory and loyalty to her love, Clitophon not only agrees to marry Melite in the temple of Isis, but it appears that he pledges to her his complete affection:

> I also tooke my oath that I loved her as sincerely as ever I did Leucippe before: shee likewise did sweare that I should bee her husband, and shee would make me Lorde of all her substance: all which was confirmed there betweene us, but the nuptials should not bee solemnized before wee came to Ephesus, and that there as I had sworne before, Melite should succeede in Leucippes place. (sig. N2)

Clitophon's marital oath resembles a contract made *verba de futuro* with the stipulation that the marriage would not be solemnized until consummation in Ephesus. While Burton's above translation emphasizes Clitophon's change of heart,[46] the hero does stay true to his temporary pledge of chastity—not to have sex with Melite in the same place where Leucippe has died. Just after his arrival in Ephesus, the city where Clitophon is to consummate his union with Melite, the hero discovers, to his chagrin, that Leucippe is actually alive. To express his utmost devotion and fidelity to Leucippe and to indicate that his "marriage" to Melite is not lawful since it was not consummated, Clitophon explains away his apparent betrayal of the heroine. In a letter to Leucippe, the hero writes that he has refrained from sexual intercourse with his new bride: "you shal find that my virginitie (if there be any virginitie of men) hath followed your example" (sig. O1^{v}). At this moment, Clitophon's statement is true. He has not engaged in a sexual liaison with Melite. Despite Clitophon's physical continence up until this point (and as if to foreshadow the lacuna of "any virginitie of men"), the hero eventually capitulates to Melite's demand for sex. He rationalizes coitus with Melite by pointing out that he and Melite are no longer contractually bound together since Leucippe is still alive. Therefore, copulation with Melite would not indicate a legally binding act of marriage.

The disparity between the hero and heroine at this juncture intensifies when Leucippe is made to take a public virginity test at the story's conclusion. The hero is not. The heroine triumphs in her test of chastity when music issues forth from a cave of Diana, a sign that evidences a woman's bodily pureness. By contrast, Clitophon is never compelled to perform a chastity test, nor does he fail to omit his copulation with Melite when he recounts his adventures to a group of banquet guests, which include Leucippe's newly arrived father, Sostratos. Clitophon says falsely: "I doo keepe my virginitie (if men have any as yet untouched, as Leucippe doth hers) since that I hadde learned long before to consecrate it to the honour of Diana" (sig. T1^{v}). With so much emphasis given to the preservation of the heroine's virginity, it is paramount that the heroine stay virginal until a marriage has been conducted with at least one parental witness. As Clitophon says to Sostratos, ironically or not: "wee would not celebrate our marriages our father being away, hee is now heere present" (sig. T1^{v}). The lovers return to celebrate their nuptials first in the hero's homeland of Tyre.

In *Daphnis and Chloe*, a similar preoccupation with the issue of the heroine's virginity emerges. Unlike the main protagonists' experience of love-at-first-sight in the plots of Heliodorus and Achilles Tatius, the love of the hero and heroine in Longus's story develops more slowly, although there is a precise moment in the narrative when each is suddenly and irrevocably taken by the beauty of the other (specifically during Daphnis's bath at the shrine of the Nymphs and the prize of Chloe's kiss during the beauty contest between the hero and Dorcon in the first book).[47] When Daphnis and Chloe communicate to each other their shared love, they also exchange vows of mutual commitment: "they iointly agreed to give eche to other an interchangeable oth" (sig. M4v). But because Daphnis has sworn his faith by the "wanton" and "verie subtil and amorous" god Pan, Chloe has Daphnis undertake a separate oath of constancy, so that he "swore unto Chloe the othe and assurance she required" (sig. N1).

The conventions of the Greek romance genre require that the hero and heroine withstand trials of their love, and the love trials in this pastoral romance are less spectacular than the ones in the *Aethiopica* or *Leucippe and Clitophon*;[48] even so, Chloe's relatively minor adventures leave her a virgin at the story's end, while Daphnis's ordeals do not. Chloe's tribulations include the cowherd Dorcon's bungled attempt to violate her, capture by warring Methymneans, and abduction by the cowherd Lampis. In these instances, fate miraculously intervenes to deliver the heroine from harm. On the hero's part, Daphnis survives injury from the Methymnean band of youths and even repulses the wooing of Gnatho, his brother's male servant.[49] Aside from these obstacles, Daphnis yields to the erotic longings of his married neighbor Lycaenion (she is appropriately named the "she-wolf"), who seduces the hero into intercourse. In his 1587 version of the romance, Daye omits this vital seduction scene from his version only to replace it with "The Shepheards Holidaie," a group of songs and eclogues in praise of Elizabeth I.

One of the effects of this scene's exclusion from the Elizabethan edition concerns the forfeiture of viewing the hero's sexual initiation. If we look to a modern translation of the scene, it reads: "Daphnis did not resist [Lycaenion] but was delighted. Being a rustic, a goatherd, in love and young, he threw himself at the feet of Lycaenion and begged her to teach him, as soon as possible, the skill that would make him able to do what he wanted to Chloe."[50] The loss of the hero's virginity, like Clitophon's sexual involvement with Melite, is in some sense construed as the result of a young man's natural ardor; perhaps more important, it indicates a necessary and formidable step in Daphnis's sexual development, even a kind of sacrifice for his future wife. Although the adulterous act is omitted from its Elizabethan version, there is no apparent stigma in the Greek romance against a young man who is initiated into the art of lovemaking. Despite his lessons in love, Daphnis refrains from intercourse with Chloe due to Lycaenion's warning of Chloe's hymenal bleeding: "Chloe would easily have become a woman if the thought of blood had not disturbed Daphnis" (p. 327). It appears that providence conspires to keep the pair of young lovers chaste until wedlock. As a result, Chloe's worth as a young woman, like Leucippe's, is based on the preservation of her maidenhood until the rites of lawful matrimony have been performed. The following episode concurs with this assumption. When Daphnis's father, Dionysophanes, considers Chloe's worthiness as his son's future bride, he asks a crucial question—if she be a virgin: "Daphnis swore that nothing more had taken place between them than kissing and vows; so Dionysophanes was pleased" (p. 345). It seems reasonable to conclude that the heroine's virginity, not necessarily the hero's, makes possible the legitimate and hallowed marital union that constitutes a fundamental aspect of the Greek romance plot in Longus and Achilles Tatius.

Over and beyond the charm of its chaste love plot and its emphasis on the mutual affection of the hero and heroine, the Greek adventure-romance engaged its audience with a somewhat patriarchal view of women and marriage that would not have been totally foreign to English readers in the sixteenth and seventeenth centuries. According to Brigitte Egger, the Greek romance of Hellenism generated a complex attitude toward marriage that blended together the patristic laws of classical Greece with the more liberal marital laws of Hellenism. In classical Greek or Attic law, the legal contract of marriage regarded the woman solely as an object of barter: it was a transaction between her legal guardian (most often her father) and the groom: "The dowry was entirely at her husband's disposal as long as the marriage lasted, and afterward had to be returned to her male relatives. She certainly had no right of choice; her consent either to marriage or to divorce was unnecessary."[51] However, the transition from classicism to Hellenism brought about significant changes for women and marriage. Along with increased control over the dowry and the ability to own property, Greco-Egyptian women now participated in the marriage negotiations; the matrimonial contract became a consensual agreement between the male and female rather than an economic arrangement between the heads of families. A further indication of woman's new legal status was, in Egger's words, the idea of "the *autoekdosis* ('self-handing-out'): their capacity to give themselves in marriage, with a family member as a witness, but by their own authority."[52] We have seen earlier that Heliodorus's Chariclea invokes the premise of *autoekdosis* in her dealings with Theagenes when she declares her choice of a partner and the time and place of marriage. She states: "[Theagenes] shall not fleashly have to doo with me, untill I have recovered my countrie, and parentes, or if the Gods be not content herewith, at least untill I by mine owne free will be content he shal marrie me" (Underdowne, sig. H3). In spite of the significant allowances authors of Greek romance made to accommodate an audience that enjoyed the entitlements of the new marital laws, the writers did not completely integrate the recent thinking on marriage into the construct of their fictional worlds. Egger finds that the stories often place restrictions and constraints on their female characters that did not altogether comport with the nuptial liberties of their contemporary readers. Egger's theory is dependent on the idea that romance plots do, indeed, reflect the marriage laws and attitudes of a culture.

One of the consequences of male bias in Greek romance was that it tended to prescribe a male-centered view of female virtue in love and marriage. This type of bias, one that restricts a woman's role in courtship and matrimony, shares affinities with some representations of women and marriage in Elizabethan and Jacobean reformist marriage literature: social subordination in wedlock acts as a metaphor for the type of patriarchal constraint that can be detected in Greek romance. A brief analysis will serve to illustrate this point. While many religious reformists and sixteenth- and seventeenth-century domestic writers, such as William Googe, Edmonde Tilney, and William Whately, advocated the idea of the companionate marriage, conjugal affection, and the shared obligations of the spouses, they did not totally consider the wife as an equal to man: "They all agreed in regarding the wife as subordinate to the husband," a "second helper," or "servant."[53] In Tilney's popular *A brief and pleasant discourse of duties in Marriage* (1568), the author provides a clear example of the importance at this time placed on the ideal of married love: "[f]or perfite love knitteth lovinge heartes, in an insoluble knot of amittie. Love indifferent serveth not, love fayned prospereth not. Wherfore it must be true, and perfite love, that maketh the *Flower of Friendship* betweene man and wyfe freshly to spring."[54]

Despite this principle of conjugal affection and friendship, Tilney prescribes the subservience of the wife in marriage. He commands the wife to obey her husband in all affairs, for the husband is far superior to his spouse in most everything: "[he] is, most apt for the soveraigntie being in government, not onely skill, and experience to be required, but also capacite to comprehend, wisedome to understand, strength to execute, solicitude to prosecute, pacience to suffer, meanes to sustaine, and above all, a great courage to accomplish, all which are commonly in a man, but in a woman very rare" (sig. Ei). Whereas Tilney advises the husband to acquire such traits as eloquence, courtesy, and wisdom, one of the greatest attributes that a woman brings to her marriage remains matronly chastity: "For the happinesse of matrimonie, doth consist in a chaste matrone, so that if suche a woman bee conjoyned in true, and unfayned love, to hir beloved spouse, no doubt their lives shall be stable, easie, sweete, joyfull, and happie" (Diiii). While Tilney supports the idea of mutual love in marriage, a woman must remain true, chaste, and inferior in wedlock.

A similar view on love in marriage can be found in William Whately's *A Bride-Bush or a Wedding Sermon* (1617). Although Whately opines that love "is the life, the soule of marriage,"[55] he also recommends woman's subordination in wedlock: the wife is "to acknowledge her inferiority: the next, to carry her selfe as inferiour. First then the wives judgement must be convinced, that shee is not her husbands equall, yea that her husband is her better by farre; else there can bee no contentment, either in her heart, or in her house" (sig. E4^{v}). Whately expands on the requirement of the wife's inferiority: she is "a dutifull wife, when shee submits her-selfe with quietnesse cheerefully, even as a wel-broken horse turnes at the least turning, stands at the least check of the riders bridle, readily going and standing as he wishes that fits upon his backe" (sig. F4). Whately's statements suggest that mutual love in marriage does not correspond to equality in marriage. For example, Whately advocates the sharing of responsibilities in marital duties, but he privileges the husband's ability over the wife's: "the husband should bee most abundant, knowing that more of every grace is looked for in him, than from the weaker vessall." He continues to define the concept of mutuality in marriage duties: "Wee call them not therefore common or mutuall, because both should have a like quantity of them; but because both must have some of all, and the husband most of all" (sig. BI^{v}). As these examples show, the idea of the companionate marriage, in which husband and wife participate lovingly in domestic obligations, did not indicate equality between man and woman. Likewise, male bias in Hellenistic romance, which both exploits and contains woman's erotic power, can be read as an analogy of patriarchal bias in these marriage pamphlets.

For its early modern audience, the love-leading-to-marriage plot of Greek romance invoked a version of romantic love that conformed to the Protestant ideal of wedded chastity and mutual affection in marriage. The problem of premarital sex represented, on the one hand, a temporary suspension in the hero's virtuous behavior to which he was quickly restored.

On the other, the lapses in male chastity also added to the attraction of the story. Northrop Frye's theory that the fantasies of a culture can be revealed in the structure of romance applies to the trials of chastity of the romance plot.[56] The heroine, who is the apex of feminine beauty and intelligence, repeatedly defends her virginity from various scoundrels in erotically charged scenes of seduction and attempted rape. The hero, however, is allowed sexual intercourse in similar situations (Longus and Achilles Tatius). In as much as the ultimate male fantasy is that a woman remain indisputably chaste while sacrificing her security and well-being for a potentially lawful marriage, the Greek romance love plot becomes increasingly patriarchal in its shape and scope. True, the virtuous and devoted romance hero, with his passion for love and romantic sentiments, was, in the most conventional sense, an engaging character. In fact, in sixteenth- and seventeenth-century England such popular fiction as Greek romance catered to a growing, and by no means exclusively, female readership whose members inclined toward the courtly.[57] We have seen that the romance heroine possessed a good deal of wit and moral excellence. But it is not perplexing that this audience valued the romantic plot and thematic features of the genre, especially given the potential for arranged marriages among the aristocracy.[58] Unlike some of their readers, the hero and heroine freely choose their martial partners, triumphing in trials of honor and virtue. Furthermore, because the primary couple resemble each other, their union in marriage affirms their social and economic homogeneity. Despite the couple's uniformity in love, the erotic suffering of the Greek romance hero differs in content and degree from the heroine's; it often lacks the sexual titillation and provocative suggestion that find repeated expression in the heroine's trials of chastity. This expression of female objectification demonstrates the story's interest in woman's eroticism. Thus, Egger's thesis applies especially here: "The price paid for women's erotic centrality [in the Greek romance] is their social containment in the realms of law and marriage, among others."[59] The fantasy of woman's erotic power, combined with the cultural and legal constraints imposed on her, may have contributed to the attraction of the Greek romance as edifying and recreational literature for its Renaissance readership. The importance of readers envisioning that men and woman share equally in trials of fidelity and chastity (the *Aethiopica*), of female virginity and honor in love (*Leucippe and Clitophon*), and of imagining a pastoral world of sexual innocence and purity (*Daphnis and Chloe*) is finally counterbalanced by a male-centered fantasy of women's erotic power and its obsessive interest in female chastity.

NOTES

1. I would like to thank Christy Desmet for her helpful suggestions in the revision of this essay. For a discussion of the plot affinities between the Greek novel and Elizabethan prose fiction and drama, see Samuel Lee Wolff, *The Greek Romances in Elizabethan Prose Fiction* (New York: Columbia University

Press, 1912); see also Carol Gesner, *Shakespeare and the Greek Romance: A Study of Origins* (Lexington: University of Kentucky Press, 1970).

2. John J. Winkler, "The Invention of Romance," in *The Search for the Ancient Novel*, ed. James Tatum (Baltimore: Johns Hopkins University Press, 1994), p. 24. In Chariton and Xenophon, the primary lovers are already married before they separate.
3. The romances of Xenophon and Chariton were not translated into English until the eighteenth century. For the approximate dates of the composition of the Greek romances, see E. L. Bowie "The Greek Novel," in *Oxford Readings in the Greek Novel*, ed. Simon Swain (Oxford: Oxford University Press, 1999), pp. 39–59; and Niklas Holzberg, *The Ancient Novel: An Introduction*, trans. Christine Jackson-Holzberg (London: Routledge, 1995), pp. 103–05.
4. David Konstan, *Sexual Symmetry* (Princeton: Princeton University Press, 1994), p. 36. Konstan's central argument is that the Greek romances as a genre "portray *eros* as a fully reciprocal passion between equals" (p. 33).
5. Gesner writes, "In Greek romance the 'quest' usually is begun when a pair of youthful lovers—frequently married—are separated. Their desire for reunion usually motivates the journey." Genser continues to explain the plot and its outcome: "Eventually the [heroine] is restored to the hero, most often at the conclusion of the romance in a triallike recognition scene in which all mysteries are explained and all loose threads are knitted up again" (*Shakespeare and The Greek Romance*, p. 4). For Northrop Frye's theory, see *Anatomy of Criticism: Four Essays* (Princeton: Princeton University Press, 1957), pp. 186–206.
6. Bruce R. Smith, *Homosexual Desire in Shakespeare's England* (Chicago: The University of Chicago Press, 1991), pp. 126, 128, 122–23. Smith compares Achilles Tatius's romance to native English folk festival. In both contexts, male homosexual desire finds playful expression, enjoying a momentary refuge from the dominant heterosexual ideology. In Achilles Tatius, Clitophon's cousin Kleinias is involved in a homosexual relationship with a young man, who tragically dies in a horse riding accident early on in the story. David Konstan argues persuasively that homosexual relationships in Greek romance, especially pederastic ones, often serve as a asymmetrical contrast to the symmetry of the heterosexual hero and heroine, *Sexual Symmetry*, p. 28.
7. Mikhail Bakhtin, "Forms of Time and Chronotpe in the Novel," in *The Dialogic Imagination*, ed. Michael Holquist, trans. Caryl Emerson and Mikhail Holquist (Austin: University of Texas Press, 1981), pp. 84–258. Citations of Bakhtin's essay refer to this edition, and they will be cited parenthetically. For further information on Bakhtin's novelistic theory, see Katerina Clark and Michael Holquist, *Mikhail Bakhtin* (Cambridge, Mass.: Harvard University Press, 1984), pp. 275–94.
8. About the idea of the companionate marriage in Protestant doctrine, see Lawrence Stone, *The Family, Sex, and Marriage in England, 1500–1800* (London: Weidenfeld and Nicolson, 1977), p. 136.
9. James A. Brundage, *Sex, Law and Marriage in the Middle Ages* (Aldershot, Hampshire: Variorum; Brookfield, Vt.: Ashgate Publishing, 1993), p. 364.
10. James A. Brundage, *Law, Sex, and Christian Society in Medieval Europe* (Chicago: University of Chicago Press, 1987), p. 552.
11. Eric Fuchs, *Sexual Desire and Love* (Cambridge: James Clarke; New York: Seabury Press, 1983), pp. 157–63.

12. Juliet Dusinberre, *Shakespeare and the Nature of Women*, 2nd edition (Houndsmills: Macmillan Press; New York: St. Martin's Press, 1996), p. 24.
13. Merry E. Wiesner-Hanks, *Christianity and Sexuality in the Early Modern World* (London and New York: Routledge, 2000), p. 63.
14. David Cressy, *Birth, Marriage & Death* (Oxford: Oxford University Press, 1997), p. 261. Cressy argues against Lawrence Stone's findings that marriage at this time lacked romantic intimacy. Cressy also points out that Puritans often advocated the idea of the "companionate marriage": the equal affection between a married couple "based on 'mutual society, help, and comfort' " (p. 297).
15. Consequently, Underdowne repeats several of his predecessor's mistakes. See Tomas Hägg, "The Renaissance of the Greek Novel," in *The Novel in Antiquity* (Berkeley and Los Angeles: University of California Press, 1983), pp. 192–213. See also F. A. Wright's introduction to Underdowne's translation, *Heliodorus: An Aethiopian Romance* (London: Routledge, n.d.), pp. 1–5.
16. Sterg O'Dell, *A Chronological List of Prose Fiction in English Printed in England and Other Countries, 1475–1640* (Cambridge, Mass.: Technology Press of MIT, 1954), pp. 39–98 passim.
17. Carol Gesner gives a comprehensive listing of the publication dates and reprints of Greek romance in England and on the Continent, *Shakespeare and the Greek Romance*, pp. 159–60.
18. Thomas Underdowne, *An Aethiopian Historie* (London, 1577), sig. iii. Citations of *An Aethiopian Historie* refer to the 1577 edition unless indicated otherwise, and they will be cited parenthetically.
19. Lodovicus Vives, *The Office and Duetie of an Husband* (London, 1554), sig. O7^{v}.
20. For further discussion of the chivalric tradition, see C. S. Lewis, *The Allegory of Love* (Oxford: University of Oxford Press, 1936), pp. 22–43.
21. William Lisle, *The Famous Historie of Heliodorus* (London, 1638), sig. A2^{v}.
22. N.[ahum] Tate, *The Aethiopian History of Heliodorus* (London, 1686), sig. a5^{v}. Further citations refer to this edition, and they will be cited parenthetically.
23. Margaret Anne Doody states that the first printing of Heliodorus's romance was linked with the Protestant movement: "The first edition of the *Aithiopika* was published in 1534, in Basel, edited by Vincentus Obsopaeus, a humanist who translated some of Luther's works from German into Latin. Obsopaues' association with the new Lutheran movement may have made the novel the more appealing to new Protestants in northern countries," *The True Story of the Novel* (London: Fontana Press, 1998), pp. 233–34.
24. *Daphnis and Chloe: The Elizabethan Version: From Amyot's Translation By Angel Day: Reprinted from the Unique Original*, ed. Joseph Jacobs (London: David Nutt, 1890), p. 1. Citations from *Daphnis and Chloe* refer to this reprint of the 1587 edition, and they will be cited parenthetically unless indicated otherwise.
25. A. [nthony] H. [odges], *The Loves of Clitophon and Leucippe* (Oxford, 1638), title page. Further citations from Hodges's translation refer to this edition, and they will be cited parenthetically.
26. Gosson, *Playes Confuted in Five Actions*, in *The English Stage: Attack and Defenses, 1577–1730*, ed. Arthur Freeman (New York: Garland, 1972), sig. D5^{v}.

27. Hallet Smith, *Shakespeare's Romances* (San Marino, Calif.: The Huntington Library, 1972), p. 9.
28. Gertrude Marian Sibley, *The Lost Plays and Masques, 1500–1642* (Ithaca: Cornell University Press, 1933), pp. 157–58.
29. *The Loves of Clitophon and Leucippe. Translated from the Greek of Achilles Tatius by William Burton. Reprinted for the first time from a copy now unique by Thomas Creede in 1597*, ed. Stephen Gaselee and H. F. B. Brett-Smith (Oxford: B. Blackwell, 1923), sig. A4. Further citations of the romance refer to this reprint of the 1597 edition unless indicated otherwise, and they will be cited parenthetically.
30. See note 3.
31. David Konstan, *Sexual Symmetry*, p. 48.
32. Marie H. Loughlin, *Hymeneutics: Interpreting Virginity on the Early Modern Stage* (Lewisburg: Bucknell University Press, 1997), p. 54.
33. Loughlin, *Hymeneutics*, p. 54.
34. Francis Meres, *Gods Arithmeticke* (London, 1597), sig. A2^{v}.
35. Meres, *Gods Arithmeticke*, sig. A2^{v}.
36. J.[ames] Sanford, *The Amorous and Tragicall Tales of Plutarch* (Ann Arbor, Mich.: University Microfilms, 1964), sig. D5, D5–D5^{v}.
37. R. B. Outhwaite, *Clandestine Marriage in England, 1500–1850* (London: The Hambledon Press, 1995), pp. 1–17.
38. Cressy, *Birth, Marriage & Death*, p. 267.
39. Diana O'Hara, *Courtship and Constraint* (Manchester: Manchester University Press, 2000), pp. 10–11. Jack Goody also explains the difference between present and future consent: "Consent alone, and not coitus, made a marriage valid, at least in terms of its 'present' form. With future consent, an indissoluble bond was created only by means of sexual relations," *The Development of the Family and Marriage in Europe* (Cambridge: Cambridge University Press), p. 149.
40. O'Hara, *Courtship and Constraint*, p. 149.
41. Ruth Kelso, *Doctrine for the Lady of the Renaissance* (Urbana: University of Illinois Press, 1956), p. 273.
42. Abraham Fraunce, *The Countesse of Pembrokes Yuychurch* (London, 1591), sig. E3^{v}. Further citations refer to the 1591 edition, and they will be cited parenthetically.
43. In Underdowne's translation, Chariclea states that she and Theagenes fought "to repell the violence which was proffered to [her] virginitie" (*An Aethiopian historie*, sig. A3).
44. Konstan writes: "The primary couple, invariably heterosexual, are either fellow citizens or members of the same social class and are of more or less the same age—very young" (*Sexual Symmetry*, p. 33).
45. Whether Clitophon is actually a virgin or not appears to be unclear in the story; e.g., John J. Winkler's modern translation does not mention the issue of the hero's virginity. Clitophon merely says: "I have already taken a vow never to copulate in this part of the world, where I lost Leukippe," *Leucippe and Clitophon*, in *Collected Ancient Greek Novels*, ed. B. P. Reardon (Berkeley and Los Angeles: University of California Press, 1989), p. 239.
46. Compare Winkler's modern translation to Burton's. His provides a different interpretation of the passage, one that suggests that Clitophon is less than eager to marry Melite: "On the next day we had agreed to meet at Isis's

temple to speak further and to exchange vows with the goddess as our witness. Menelaos and Kleinias accompanied us. I pledged to cherish her without guile; she pledged to name me her husband and declare me master of all her properties" (*Leucippe and Clitophon*, p. 240).

47. The scene in which Chloe watches Daphnis bathe does not occur in Daye's translation. For the controversy surrounding this lost passage, see Joseph Jacob's discussion in *Daphnis and Chloe: The Elizabethan Version from Amyot's Translation*, pp. xviii–xxv.
48. It is important to note that in *Daphnis and Chloe* the hero and heroine never leave their country for any substantial time; adventure comes to the lovers rather than vice-versa. For a discussion of the generic differences in *Daphnis and Chloe*, see Bakhtin, *The Dialogic Imagination*, p. 103.
49. In the Elizabethan translation, Burton calls Gnatho an "unnaturall beast" who acts "against nature" (*Daphnis and Chloe*, sig. T2^{v}). Such vituperation does not occur in Longus.
50. I cite from Christopher Gill's translation of *Daphnis and Chloe*, in *Collected Ancient Greek Novels*, ed. B. P. Reardon, p. 325. Further citations of this modern translation refer to this edition, and they will be cited parenthetically.
51. Brigitte Egger, "Women and Marriage in the Greek Novels," in *The Search for the Ancient Novel*, ed. James Tatum (Baltimore: The Johns Hopkins University Press, 1994), p. 266.
52. Egger, "Women and Marriage," p. 267.
53. Stone, *The Family, Sex and Marriage*, p. 136. Stone argues that the tenets of Protestantism, which gave fathers and husbands, not the Church, power over the family unit, reinforced the authority of the patriarchy (esp. pp. 151–218). For further discussion of the concept and problems of equity in marriage in the early modern period, see Constance Jordan, *Renaissance Feminism* (Ithaca: Cornell University Press, 1990), esp. pp. 21–64 and Ralph A. Houlbrook, *The English Family, 1450–1700* (London: Longman, 1984), pp. 96–105. For a theory of marital relationships in the early modern period that challenges the notion of the absolute supremacy of the husband, see Keith Wrightson, *English Society, 1580–1680* (London: Routledge, 1982), pp. 89–104.
54. Edmonde Tilney, *A brief and Pleasant discourse of duties in Marriage* (London, 1568), sig. Biiii. Citations refer to the 1568 edition, and they will be cited parenthetically.
55. William Whately, *A Bride-Bush* (London, 1617), sig. B2. Additional citations will refer to the 1617 edition, and they will be cited parenthetically.
56. Frye writes: "The romance is the nearest of all literary forms to the wish-fulfilment dream, and for that reason it has socially a curiously paradoxical role. In every age the ruling social or intellectual class tends to project its ideals in some form of romance, where the virtuous heroes and beautiful heroines represent the ideals and the villains the threats to their ascendancy" (*Anatomy of Criticism*, p. 186).
57. For an account of the rise of a female readership in recreational literature, see Suzanne Hull, *Chaste Silent and Obedient* (San Marino, Calif.: The Huntington Library, 1982), pp. 71–90. See also Caroline Lucas, *Writing for Women* (Milton Keynes: Open University Press, 1989), p. 48. Lucas argues that the Greek romance and its Elizabethan offshoots were directed toward both a female and a courtly audience.

58. On the complex subject of the arranged marriage among the sixteenth- and seventeenth-century upper class, Keith Wrightson writes: "It is clear that even in the higher social ranks where families had most to lose by an imprudent match, the situation was far from monolithic when it came to the selection of future spouses. The 'arranged' match, initiated by parents, which left the child with nothing more than a right of veto was undoubtedly a reality throughout our period. But even among the social élite it presents a picture which is too stark unless accompanied by considerable qualification" (*English Society, 1580–1680*, p. 74). Recently, Diana O'Hara has explored the critical assertion that the poor and middle levels of society experienced greater freedom in choice of marriage partners and in courtship (*Courtship and Constraint*, pp. 30–56).
59. Egger, "Women and Marriage," p. 273. Egger contends that the patriarchal fantasy of woman's eroticism appeals to readers today in such books as the Harlequin romance.

Chapter 2

"Dissordinate Desire" and the Construction of Geographic Otherness in the Early Modern Novella

Constance C. Relihan

In the dedication of his 1566 *Palace of Pleasure* to the earl of Warwick, William Painter writes that the tales he has collected display:

> the uglye shapes of insolence and pride, the deforme figures of incontinencie and rape, the cruell aspectes of spoyle, breach of order, treason, ill lucke and overthrow of states and other persons . . . some of these may seeme to intreat of unlawfull love and the foule practises of the same, yet being throughly read and well considered, both old and yonge may learne how to avoyde the ruine, overthrow, inconvenience and displeasure, that lascivious desire and wanton wil doth bring to their suters and pursuers. All which maye render good examples, the best to be followed, and the worst to be avoyded: for which intent and purpose be all things good and bad recited in histories, chronicles and monumentes, by the first authors and elucubrators of the same.[1]

Certainly, there is a conventional component to this claim that the stories he is about to present will serve a didactic purpose, but the passage also reveals what is a very substantial concern for the English collectors and translators of novelle in English. Geoffrey Fenton's dedication to Mary Sidney beginning his *Certaine Tragical Discourses* (1567) also asserts a didactic goal.[2] Fenton wants to help correct the ill behavior of his age; he also asserts in this letter that all classes of English society need knowledge of

> worldly thinges . . . [which] can not be gotten but by the assistance of histories, who are the onelye and true tables whereon are drawne in perfecte coollers the

> vertues and vices of everye condicion of man ... that excellent treasore and full librarye of all knowledge yeldes us frelye presidentes for all cases that may happen; both for imytacion of the good, detestynge the wycked, avodynge a present mischiefe, and preventynge any evil afore yt fall.[3]

Histories, in other words, are by their very nature instructive. And, as Lorna Hutson demonstrates in *The Usurer's Daughter: Male Friendship and Fictions of Women in Sixteenth-Century England*, Fenton's concern here is with factual military histories as much as it is with the fictional romantic histories he is about to present. She succinctly observes that "it was classical military history which offered the primary conceptual model for fictions of civil courtship."[4] Histories and fiction both provide exempla; both are instructive, although certainly the degree to which we should take their ability to function in this role is open to question.

The nature of the didactic dimension of these early modern novella collections varies in emphasis once the writers leave their dedications behind and turn to the tales themselves, but that didacticism becomes significantly gendered, as the subject matter and frequent direct addresses to readers show.[5] This gendering is not merely the result of a desire to appeal to female readers, but it also reflects a desire to construct and channel male constructions of identity. As Hutson observes:

> The centrality of women to [novella collections] is not, then, necessarily a concession to the tastes of women readers, nor even a concessionary move from the "public" to the "private" sphere. Rather it is that fictions of women, focusing men's narratives of persuasive efficiency, become coextensive with the enterprise of authorship itself as the medium of masculine social advancement. For, as humanism relocated the space of trial for masculine *virtus* from battlefield to text, so anthologies (rhetorical "gatherings" of poetry and fictional history), appearing in print before men's eyes, became the new place in which men displayed the cerebral equivalent of chivalric prowess, in virtuoso deployments of their skill in probable argument.

These collections demonstrate their authors' cerebral prowess generally within the framework of fictional romantic histories that interrogate the nature of relationships between men and women, and the more narrow analysis of the functioning of reason and passion; and definitions of orthodox and transgressive desire. They afford male authors the opportunity to explore strategies for defining, describing, and satisfying heterosexual male desire in ways acceptable to a culture that was seen as increasingly turning from the battlefield to the bedchamber as its site of military confrontation—as can be seen in Barnabe Riche's prefaces to his *Farewell to Militarie Profession* (1581) or even the opening soliloquy of Shakespeare's *Richard III*.

Moreover, this movement from battlefield to bedroom is coexistent with an additional geographic movement.[6] Perhaps simply because stories must be set somewhere—as Michel de Certeau puts it: "every story is a travel story,"[7] the novelle presented by Painter, Fenton, Pettie and others provide their readers with specific links between the construction and containment of desire and the colonizing discourse that so often masks itself as geographic didacticism and ethnography.

While most of these geographic references are to Italian cities and provinces, as should be expected since Italian authors provide the majority of the source material, the novelle collections also provide information about non-European, non-Christian cultures. Fenton's *Discourses* provides many instances of this kind of characterization of the East, for example: "a company of effemynate Persians" (II.59), "th'incursions of the blasphemous infidells and ennemies of our religyon" (II.104), "the desperat Persyans" (II.111), "the barbarous disposicion of the Turke, or Moare, or other infidell withoute religion or faith" (II.209–10), "the most furious and savage beastes that ever bredd in the desertes of Lybya" (II.268). These nuggets of information and innuendo act to stigmatize and place the East under European discursive control. And the importance of this cultural or geographic didactic element, which might be aligned with the "nationalist pedagogy" Homi Bhabha finds present in the textual production of a culture.[8] Matteo Bandello, writing in a dedicatory epistle contained in his collection of *Novelle* (1554), one of the most influential Italian collections, explores more fully the need for education about geographical difference in general, and the threat posed by the East more specifically:

> Again, in worldly matters this age of ours has seen the Turks take all of Syria, and the Sultan defeated with his mercenary crew, Belgrade conquered, Rhodes at war, most of Hungary subjugated, and Vienna in Austria besieged, and great damages done in those countries, with the expectation of worse, to the unspeakable shame of all Christendom, which has by now been reduced to a corner of Europe thanks to the discords which now grow greater every day among Christian princes. Those who ought to stand up against the Turkish might and cruelty have spilled so much Christian blood that it would have been sufficient to recapture the Empire of Constantinople and the Kingdom of Jerusalem . . . We have seen the Great Shepherd of Rome, a prisoner of the Germans and Spanish, buy his freedom from the Emperor Charles, and Rome cruelly sacked, the churches pillaged, the nuns raped, and all cruelties one can imagine perpetrated, so that the Goths of former times were more merciful . . . The Emperor and the King of France are now at war and now at truce, and yet one sees no peace agreement. The Venetians have been forced to buy peace from the Turks and to give them part of their land . . . And certainly we can say that very few ages have seen as sudden changes as we see daily, nor do I know where all these things will end, because it seems to me that we are going from bad to worse and that among the Christians there is more discord than ever.[9]

Bandello's lament focuses on early modern European anxiety about the dissolution or erasure of national and cultural identities, an anxiety that often manifests itself in the kind of brief geographical allusion described earlier and in tales that use the East as an important location. The fear that Bandello enunciates of "going from bad to worse" often translates to the page in terms of the interplay among different places and different cultures, and sexual violence is intimately folded into this set of cultural fears. The raping of nuns merits Bandello's emphasis as a new and particularly heinous form of violence created by the Christian inability to eliminate the threat the Ottoman Empire poses to the West, and this violence crosses both sexual and cultural boundaries—its victims are both women and representatives of Bandello's culture: their rape is an aggressive military act of cultural annihilation as much as it is a private act of personal, sexual assault. It straddles the boundaries between the arenas of *virtus* Hutson describes.[10]

When eastern locations are not used in brief allusions within these tales but as locations that figure in the narratives' plots, they are often likely to be linked to qualities the European male reader fears and that become narratively linked to violence against women: the domination of passion, the erasure of reason, and fear of male subordination to women. One tale in which this link is clearly established is in William Painter's tale "Of Amadour and Florinda" (I.53), which he derives from Marguerite de Navarre. Painter summarizes the tale as presenting "The loue of Amadour and Florinda: wherein be conteined mani sleightes and dissimulations, together with the renowmed chastitie of the said Florinda" (2.129). Florinda's chastity doesn't just resist "mani sleightes and dissimulations," it resists two rape attempts, the second of which is fairly graphically described. The tale charts the progress over several years of the love of Amadour, a valiant Spanish gentleman, for the young, aristocratic Florinda. During the course of the tale Amadour marries in order to provide a cover for his virtuous passion for Florinda, and he pursues a mistress in order to provide further distraction for those suspicious individuals who think he may love her; she falls in love with one nobleman who loves someone else and then enters into a loveless marriage out of political necessity. Eventually, Amadour, who "through the force of love had lost al reason" (2.142), attempts to rape her. During the first of the attempted rape scenes, we are simply told that "he attempted that which the honor of womanhode doth defend" (2.142) and that he "pursued his purpose so earnestly as he could" (2.142). She, believing he is sick and not ill-intentioned, fends him off by calling in the aid of a gentleman in the next room. Subsequently, Florinda remains suspicious of Amadour and in preparation for the second scene of attempted rape, she "tooke up a stone which was within the chapell, and gave her selfe so great a blowe on the face that her mouthe, eyes and nose, were altogether deformed"; she then intentionally "fell downe uppon a great stone" (2.146). This second scene builds on that description of self-violence:

> Florinda sawe his face and eyes so altered, and that the fairest die and colour of the world, was become so red as fier, with his most pleasaunt and amiable loke transformed into horrible hew and furious, and therewithall discried the very hote burning fier to sparkle within his harte and face: and how in that fury with one of his strong fistes he griped her delicate and tender hands: and on the other side shee seeing all her defences to fayle her, and that her feete and

> handes wer caught in such captivitie as she could neither run away nor yet defend her selfe. (2.146)[11]

She tries to reason with him, but his response is to say, "since I can get nothing of you but the bare bones and carcase, I will holde them so fast as I can" (2.147). She finally thwarts his attack by crying out for her mother, who had arranged this meeting between the two characters in the first place.

In the tale of Amadour and Florinda cultural difference and military prowess frame these scenes of sexual violence in which the violence is self-evident and its thematic significance is fairly clear: the text makes literal the frequently used Petrarchan metaphor of war as emblematic of the conflict love creates between reason and passion. One of the goals of this novella is to provide a means by which the struggle between reason and passion may be played out and explored; however, as Marcel Tetel has observed, in Marguerite's version of the tale the military image is used "at a very earthy level." It is reduced to "the conquest of a woman by a man and the incessant confrontations between the two in order to effectuate this conquest."[12] Painter's version operates similarly, although his imagery is not as consistent as hers. Before the first scene of attack, Amadour's profession of love to Florinda and his subsequent behavior had spurred her to jealousy. Upset with her reaction, he decides "to dissemble mine anger" (2.136)[13] and to return to a military life. We are told that he fights with the King of Spain at Perpignan, and is ultimately confronted by the troops of the King of Tunis. Their superior strength convinces him that it would be "better to render himself, than to be cause of the losse of so many good souldiours as were under his governmente" (2.139), and so he surrenders and is taken as a prisoner to Tunis. He remains a prisoner of the Turks for two years until he is finally permitted to go seek his ransom: this reprieve comes just when we are told by the text that "the king [of Tunis] was minded to offer him the gibbet, or els make him renounce his fayth, for the desire hee had to retaine him still, and to make him a good Turke" (2.140). The second scene of attempted rape is also followed by reference to the non-Christian world, a reference that makes explicit the parallels between sexual imperilment and cultural dissolution. Amadour is appointed to do battle against the Moors led by the King of Granada. In this battle Florinda's husband is killed and her brother is wounded. Amadour finds himself surrounded by the enemy. He decides, we are told by the narrator, that

> because he would bee no more taken, as well to verifie his faith towardes God as also his vowe made to his lady, and also considering that if he were prysoner to the kyng of Granado, either hee should cruelly be put to death, or els forced to renounce his faith, he determined not to make his death or taking glorious to his enemies (2.150)

He makes this decision so that he will not be forced to renounce Christianity: he kisses the "crosse of his sworde" and impales himself on it. Florinda ends the tale by entering a convent and focusing her attentions on "the perfit love of God" (2.150). Interestingly, Painter tried to recoup Amadour's reputation here, just as he had tried to soften Marguerite's tone toward him throughout the tale. In Marguerite's version, the corresponding passage explicitly refers twice to his abuse of Floride: "as he had failed to take his lady," his enemies will fail to take him; and, "his faith to her he had broken," but his vow to God he would not break (p. 152).

Amadour's initial attempt to suppress his anger at Florinda's jealousy places him in the world of the Turks where he attempts, in Tetel's phrase, to "reassert himself after sentimental defeats" (Tetel, p. 30). There he does not become a victorious warrior; rather, he is captured, resulting in an "immeasurable loss" (as Patricia Frances Cholakian, referring to Marguerite de Navarre's tale, has called it) to his country.[14] He is an exemplary hostage whom the King of Tunis would like to make "a good Turk." When he returns to Europe, he does not do so in absolute terms: he returns to drum up his ransom, still linked to the non-European world—he drags that realm with him.[15] His transgression of the bounds of a *serviteur* removes him from full participation within the Christian, European world. The violence of the rape scenes is then infused with traces of the non-European Turk and that world may be said to be implicated in the failure of reason to restrain Amadour's passion. The gross violence to which Amadour succumbs may be read, then, as a sign of his inability to channel his desire in humanistically acceptable ways and of his affiliation with the non-European Other. And his decision to kill himself rather than be captured a second time and forced to renounce his faith makes literal his desperate fear of losing his Christian, "reasonable" identity. This fear had been triggered by Florinda's jealousy, enhanced by his captivity by the Turks, and brought to a crisis by the violence of his attempted rape of her and the later military supremacy of the Turks. That the violence prompted by unrestrained sexual desire results in fear of cultural annihilation is evident in Amadour's language in Marguerite's version even more clearly than Painter's: just before his suicide rather than being subject to the gibbet, in her text he chooses self-impalement rather than the impalement that the King of Tunis had planned for him; he chooses to phrase his decision in relation to his earlier actions with Floride "[e]ven as he had failed to take his lady, so now his enemies would be frustrated in taking him" (p. 152): loss of cultural identity in the male is equated with sexual violence against the female. In other words, fear of cultural loss becomes played out on the female body: it becomes symbolically enacted not only as his failed attempt to take her by force, but also as her violence against herself. She becomes the agent of her own objectification and disfiguring.

This objectification meets with specific approval in the period itself from George Pettie, who valorizes her behavior as part of his commentary on the tale of Pygmalion, contained in his 1576 *A Petite Palace of Pettie His Pleasure*:

> ...so may *Florinda* bee a fruitfull example to the feminine sorte, to doe the like, who bearyng sutch fervent affection to fer freinde *Amadour*, that shee

> helde him more dere then her owne life, that she received more contentacion in the companie of him, then of husband, father, mother, [childe, *B-F*] freinde or whosoever: yet shee was so far of from filthy affection towards him, that shee avoyded, so neare as shee could, all occasions which might draw him into any disordinate desire towardes her. In so mutch, that havyng occasion of privie conference with him in a private place, beefore she came, shee fouly defaced her face, and bruised it with a stoane, that hee might not bee inflamed with the feature thereof, and divers other wayes at divers other times, valiantly withstoode all alarms of lust. Therfore they are no doubt deceived, which thinke that love cannot bee without lust, neither fervent affection without fleshly fancie.[16]

She tries, Pettie asserts, to prevent the creation of "disordinate" desire: she acts to "order" Amadour's desire by becoming violent against herself in order to try to enable Amadour to create a socially acceptable version of his desire. The extremity and severity of the wounds she inflicts upon herself suggest the strength of Amadour's desire and the insufficiency of conventional erotic outlets for it—it is only the military world of aggression against the Turk that provides a culturally sanctioned means for the assertion of his *virtus.*

Geoffrey Fenton's *Certaine Tragicall Discourses* provides a good text from which to draw further examples of the ways in which setting a narrative within a location of geographic and cultural Otherness, particularly that of the non-Christian East, becomes linked to scenes of violence against women because it is among the earliest collections to import the Italian tales into England. (William Painter's *The Palace of Pleasure*, vol. 1 was published in 1566. Fenton's collection appeared before the second volume of Painter's collection was published in 1567.) The text contains thirteen tales based on Bandello's novellas as they were translated into French by Belleforest. In general, as René Pruvost observed in 1937, Fenton tends to amplify his models greatly, adding more passages of rhetorical grandiloquence, much more moralizing, and more consistent attempts at analysis of his characters than Painter or his sources do.[17] This moralizing tone emerges from his desire to authorize his text as didactically significant, as well as from Fenton's patriotic, anti-Italian, and anti-Catholic biases (Pruvost, p. 190).

Fenton's Discourse 12, "Perillo suffreth muche for the love of Carmosyna, and marienge her in the ende, were both two striken to deathe with a thonderbolte, the firste night of their unfortunat mariage" (II.213), like the tale of Amadour and Forinda, also involves an episode of imprisonment by Turks. Unlike that tale, however, in which contact with the East prompts a loss of reason in the male that then results in violence against the female and her own violence against herself, here contact with the East empowers the female. In an attempt to earn the approval of Carmosyna's father for their marriage Perillo joins a merchant voyage to Alexandria that is blown to the Barbary Coast where it is set upon by Moorish pirates (II.225), and he is imprisoned in Tunis "to lyve in extreme miserye under the servile yoke of the barbarous nations" (II.226). Perillo is eventually released, undertakes a second merchant venture (funded by Carmosyna), which earns him enough money to be granted her father's permission to marry her. As in the tale of Amadour and Florinda, it is the intervention of the East that facilitates Carmosyna's willingness to aid her beloved: before his capture she tells him she must rely on her parents' will in determining their future. After his imprisonment she is willing to supply him with funds and to plan to find a means to effect his release (although he is released before she is able to implement her plan). There seems to be some element that the "barbarous nations" represent, that empowers Carmosyna to control money (Carmosyna does not fund his initial voyage) and to take an active role in ensuring her union with the man she selects: the East seems to free her to act both economically and sexually. Also as in the Amadour and Florinda narrative, contact with the East seems to provoke an ability to abandon certain European, Christian conventions: in Marguerite and Painter's tales, it authorized the destructive releasing of Amadour's passions and subjected Florinda to the dehumanizing violence of them. In Fenton's text, the result of Turkish imprisonment may be even more threatening to an English audience: it displaces the influence onto the female character in the narrative (as was ultimately the case in the Amadour/Florinda tale), not to victimize her, but to authorize her economic independence. Fenton's "Perillo and Carmosyna" differs from the Amadour and Florinda tale in interesting ways: whereas contact with and imprisonment by the Turks prompts Amadour to violence and unrestrained passion, in Fenton's discourse it stimulates the female character to economic and sexual action. It eliminates her passivity and objectification whereas it prompts Amadour to view Florinda in just such objectifying terms.[18] Regardless of these differences, however, there is an intriguing similarity between the two tales: Carmosyna, like Florinda, is prone to self-violence. After learning of Perillo's capture, she falls "into suche presente rage that she was redy to use force against herselfe" (2.227) and must be physically restrained from taking action against herself. Regardless of the varying effects of contact with the East on male desire, its ultimate effect on female characters bears this troubling similarity.

Fenton's *Discourses* provides further ways in which locating a novella in an Eastern location becomes a kind of touchstone, unleashing threatening behavior in Christian Europeans as well as examples of ways in which Eastern allusions present more explicit threats of physical violence against women. Fenton's fourth tale, "An Albanoyse Capteine, being at the poynte to dye, kylled his wyfe, because no man should enjoye her beawtie after his deathe,"[19] begins with the following sentence:

> Duringe the sege and miserable sacke of Modona (a cytye of the Mores, confyning upon the sea Peloponese, not farr from the straite of Ysthmyon, by the whiche the Venetians conveighe theire great traffique and trade of marchandise) Baiazeth, th'emperour of the Turkes, and great grandfather to Sultan Solyman who this daye governeth the state of th'oriente, used so many sortes of inordinat cruelties in the persecution of those wretches whom fate, with

> extreme force of his warr, had not onlye habandoned from the soyle of their ancient and naturall bode, but also (as people ful of desolation and voide of succour euery ways) forced them to craue harbor of the lymytrophall townes, adjoyning their countrey, to shroude ther weary bodyes, bledinge still with the woundes of their late warre, and overcome besides wth the violence of hungar and cold—ii comon enemies that neuer faile to followe the campe of miserie. (I.165)

From these "lymytrophall townes" the captain flees to Mantua with his wife. The Turkish wars do not figure again in Fenton's tale, but they have established the captain and his wife as exiles, as characters thrust into the events of the narrative by the horrors of war against the Turks. (It is perhaps significant too, in our attempt to explore the ways in which cultural difference and racism function in the text to notice that Modona is called a city of the "Mores"; that is, it is part of the province of Greece formerly known as Morea, but a term that also cannot help but echo with associations to North African Moors. This strategy is also used in another collection that we will later consider, William Averell's *A Dyall for Dainty Darlings* (1584).) This opening also serves to remind readers of current political affairs in the region: Baiazeth is the great grandfather of Soliman, the current ruler of "the state of th'oriente," the ruler that Painter—also writing in 1567—had warned his readers about. Had not the Turks disrupted the lives of the tale's central characters, the Captain would not have been driven to his murderous actions, for he is driven to suicidal despair by the death of his protector (I.182). In this case, contact with the non-European prompts loss of reason in the male and violent victimization of the female, although not the additional self-violence to which Florinda had been subjected.

Within the framework of a collection of "histories" that has as part of its stated intention the "avodynge a present mischiefe, and preventynge any evil afore yt fall," the use of the Turkish contact provides a subtle attempt to link violence against women to the need to colonize and destroy the Ottoman Empire. Further didactic moments in the tale are more explicit. The Captain's unfortunate wife, for example, hoping to save her own life and comfort her husband, explains to him that

> the scripture . . . forbides us to yelde any debte or dutie at all to suche as be alredie passed out of the worlde, and muche lesse to sacrifyze ourselves for their sakes upon their tombes (accordynge to the supersticious order of the barbarians in olde time, remeinyng at this daye in no lesse use amonge the people of the weste worlde) . . . . (I.185)

A marginal gloss at this point informs the readers that we are here learning about: "A ceremonie amongst the barbarians to sacrafise themselves uppon the tombes of their deade frendes" (I.185). Slightly later in the text, as the jealous captain is about to stab his blameless wife to death, the narrator informs us that his rage was "far excedinge the savage and brutishe maner of the tiger, lyon, or libarde, bredd in the desertes of Affrike, the common norsse of monsters and creatures cruell without reason" (I.188–89). These two moments in the story differ in degree more than kind. The first is an attempt to teach readers about ancient customs practiced by non-Christians; the second example allows its prejudices to speak more openly. Its goal is not to teach the reader about a custom or part of natural history; its goal is to characterize the savagery of the captain, to dehumanize him and Africa under the guise of didacticism. And these moments occur within a larger framework of Eastern savagery and aggression against which heterosexual male desire becomes figured as requiring violence against women.

An additional Fenton tale also includes the East, although in the form of Turkish pirates, not soldiers. In "Luchyn is Longe in Love wyth a Simple Mayde, whom he woeth and cannot wyn by any passion hee endureth...." (II.129),[20] the "simple mayde," Janiquetta is not threatened by physical violence (either at her own hand or that of another), but she is forced to propose prostituting herself as a result of the poverty into which she falls after her husband is captured by Turkish pirates. Explicit references to the East in this tale are few—in addition to learning that her husband is imprisoned in "a towne subject to the Turkishe governmente" (II.159), there is mention of Cleopatra (II.137) and "Orient coullers" (II.153). Nonetheless, the East is a necessary precondition for the events of the tale: it prompts her to prostitution as well as Luchyn's sublimation of his desire for her (for he helps her without demanding that she submit herself to him). She is kept from the sexual violence of forced prostitution and Luchyn is praised for his "heroicall vertue" (II.163) at the end of the tale. Moreover, the tale concludes with Janiquetta's husband still imprisoned by the Turks, suggesting that Janiquetta is saved from violence only by isolating her from male desire that has been tainted by the East. She ends the tale chastely and safely, but only by sacrificing a Christian male to the barbarous Eastern Other.

The link between the East and the violent effects of male desire on female characters continues through later collections of *novelle* as well. George Whetstone's *An Heptameron of Ciuill Discourses* (1582), a text combining elements of the Boccaccian collection with courtesy literature,[21] emphasizes even more than Marguerite de Navarre had, the philosophical discussions about marriage and gender relations that surround the narratives.[22] The best-known story in the collection is the tale of Promos and Cassandra, told on the fourth day by the only female narrator within the text; she tells her tale to demonstrate that men are much more capable of "treacherie" (p. 125) than women. Like many of the tales already considered, it is set in Europe, but is framed against the East. It begins:

> At what time *Corvinus* the scourge of the *Turkes*, rayned as Kinge of *Bohemia*: for to well governe the free Cities of his Realme, hee sent divers worthy Majestrates. Among the rest, he gave the Lorde *Promos* the Lieutennauntship of *Julio*: who in the beginning of his government, purged the Cittie of many ancient vices, and severely punished new offenders. (p. 125)

Diane Sklanka, citing C. T. Prouty, identifies "Julio" as Jula or Gyula in Eastern Hungary.[23] While Corvinus is not a Turk, and "Julio" is not an

Eastern location in itself, both have Eastern connections: the first because his reputation during the sixteenth century was established not only as a just administrator but as a defender of the West against the Turks—Painter had called him "the first ['of any Prynce that governed that kingdome'] that was Famous, or feared of the Turks";[24] the second because it would be on the edge of the territory the Ottomans attempted to conquer.

The plot of the tale is very similar to that of Shakespeare's *Measure for Measure*, except that in Whetstone's prose version the heroine must submit to the rape prompted by Promos' sexual blackmail.[25] After Corvinus has revealed Promos' crime, the lieutenant is married to Cassandra and sentenced to be executed, a punishment that is remitted through Cassandra's pleas and Promos' repentance. The narrator concludes the tale by telling her audience that "from betweene the teethe of daunger, every partie was preserved, and in the ende establyshed in their hartes desire" (p. 137). Again the Eastern frame contextualizes the violent exercising of male desire and power: Corvinus is the "scourge of the Turks." Moreover, the tale is set in Hungary, which was positioned on the edge of mid-sixteenth-century Turkish incursions into Christian Europe. As such, the narrative situates itself as part of the cultural apparatus concerned with staving off threats to its autonomy, its structures, its values. In other words, the frame of this tale signals that it is treatment such as that given to Cassandra that has been protected by Corvinus's repulsion of the Turks: it emphasizes the abuse of Cassandra as part of the strengths of European culture. Whereas the East provided the spur to the violent exercising of desire, in this case the violence has been internalized. The ability of the West to defeat the Turks becomes simultaneously figured as the ability of the West to authorize and validate sexual violence against women: Promos' rape of Cassandra is legitimated by marriage and all the characters ultimately achieve "their hartes desire" (p. 137).

Significant, too, is what this tale does to the text as a whole—after it is told, no other extended narratives are included within the text until the last day when the host, Signor Philoxenus, whose name means "friendly to strangers,"[26] inserts a tale about two Ionian lovers whose marriage brings peace to their parents' warring cities, a narrative move that may suggest a radically different view of the functioning of desire than the tale of Promos and Cassandra suggests. While Philoxenus may be friendly to strangers, both by permitting the disputants of Whetstone's text to stay at his villa and permitting the Eastern characters of his Ionian tale to achieve a happy ending (these lovers are ultimately transformed into a pair of turtledoves [p. 226]), the text as a whole is more reflective of the sexual violence the tale of Promos and Cassandra suborns.

William Averell's *A Dyall for Dainty Darlings rockt in the cradle of Securitie: A Glasse for all disobedient Sonnes to looke in. A Myrrour for vertuous Maydes. A Booke right excellent, garnished with many woorthy examples, and learned aucthorities, most needefull for this tyme present* (1584) also uses the unleashing of violence against the female as a means of characterizing the abject Otherness of the East to edify its readers, both male and female.

In a heavily moralized text (even more prone to moralizing digressions than Pettie's *Petite Palace*), his narrator tells us about

> the example of a Captained wife of Constantinople, whose detestable pride, was so lothsome in the eyes of the Lord, that it procured his iustice to worke reuenge vpon her stincking carcase. The report whereof as I haue breefely read, so the discourse thereof, I will shortly write, trusting that all these in whome the sparkes of vertue are kindled, will by her example growe into a greater increase of vertue, and they whome the water of follie hath quenched thyr good desyres, will warme themselues at the flames of wisedome, to drie vp the moisture of theyr vicious mindes.[27]

In other words, not only is the narrative true, but it will satisfy a didactic goal by teaching us the evils of pride, made more loathsome by being illustrated by a woman, the wife of a Venetian captain, living in the lymytrophall location of Constantinople. This woman is so proud she refuses to bathe herself in common water or to feed herself. Eventually God punishes her, causing her body to rot in "euery parte of this her pampered body, so that no member, no joint, nor part therof was free from the mouldred plague of putrifaction" (p.12). The stench from her rotting body creates "an intollerable stincke" (p. 13) that drives away all her friends and all but one of her servants. The bodily destruction and isolation she suffers here—which provides Averell with the opportunity to discuss the evils of pride and to exhort women "to auoide curiositie" (p. 13)—is reminiscent of what Florinda hoped she would achieve by the violence she inflicted upon herself, but in this case it is a Christian God who unleashes violence against the woman, who is placed in the Eastern context of Constantinople and whose own hedonistic desires are responsible for her suffering.

Another pair of collections, *The Cobbler of Canterbury* (1590), revised as *The Tinker of Turvey* (1630), also include a tale that occurs largely within the framework of the East, again showing the kind of cultural disruption that Eastern contact, even benevolent contact, can cause. This tale, the Scholar's tale about two young lovers who flee their warring families in Sicily and are captured by Tunisian pirates, begins thus:

> When the King of Tunis was beaten out of his kingdom and sought to enter again by force, Jacomine Pierro and Alexander Bartolo, two noblemen of Sicilia, and both of Palermo, for the good will they bore the king, prepared certain tall barks, and with their aid, maugre his enemies, placed the king safe again in his kingdom. (p. 175)[28]

After this initial reference to the East, the text focuses on the emerging love of the children of the two nobles, the family feud that erupts and keeps them apart, and the young lovers' decision to try to sail to Spain in order to be together. At sea they are captured by Tunisian pirates, the woman is transported to the seraglio of the King of Tunis and her beloved roams dejectedly about the city looking for her until he spies her just before he is about to abandon hope and leave. He sneaks into her room and they consummate their marriage just before the King decides that it is time for him to come to her for the first time. The threat of the woman's rape by the Tunisian king is replaced by the threat of death for both lovers after the Tunisian king, who discovers the two Sicilians together in her bed, decrees that they shall be burned at the stake. This tortuous death is only forestalled by the recognition by the King's High Admiral that they are the offspring of the Italian defenders of the Tunisian monarch. At this point, the King pardons them and they thank him for his mercy. The young man is then knighted by the king, who provides them with a ship laden with treasure in which to sail home (pp. 182–83).

This Tunisian knighthood links the tale with that of Amadour and Florinda: like Painter's Amadour, his return to the Christian West carries elements of the East with it. As in the other examples we have examined, in other words, contact with the Turk—here in the form of the earlier generous military support of the lovers' fathers—precedes the unleashing of unrestrained desire (we are given no explanation for the feud that erupts between the families). And this benevolent action has as its ultimate result, the importation of a Tunisian noble (the knighted Italian) into Sicilian culture: cultural annihilation is never discussed in the text, but the threat posed by this event echoes with Philip Sidney's fear that all of Europe will "turn Turk."[29]

More examples could be cited of early modern *novelle* in which the East figures similarly. It decenters European, Christian values as they are present in the male and it demonstrates the effects of that decentering as the unleashing of violent, unrestrained desire that threatens the female character—either at her own hand or that of a male figure tainted by the East. The female's action then becomes emblematic of the dangers of cultural annihilation that the East represents: Florinda and Carmosyna become violent against themselves, Carmosyna becomes economically active, the Captain's wife endures an entirely pointless death. Within the didactic framework of collections of "histories" that, as Fenton puts it, are at least partly designed to encourage the "avodynge a present mischiefe, and preventynge any evil afore yt fall," the use of contact with the Turks provides a subtle attempt to educate early modern readers to the need to textually if not politically colonize the Ottoman Empire by reducing it to a threatening Other that would dehumanize all those who encountered it. Because of a variety of European cultural fears, provoked by the Reformation as well as by the Turks' military strength,[30] the Ottoman Empire became for writers and translators of novelle an essential imaginative location. It became, as Foucault writes in *The Order of Things*:

> the Other that is not only a brother but a twin, born, not of man, nor in man, but beside him and at the same time, in an identical newness, in an unavoidable duality. . . . it is both exterior to him and indispensible to him . . . .[31]

NOTES

1. William Painter, *The Palace of Pleasure*, 4 vols. (London: Cresset Press, 1929), with an introduction by Hamish Miles and illustrations by Percy Bliss. All references to Painter's text will be to this edition by volume and page.
2. Walter Davis asserts that the early novella usually "maintained an air of factuality whose main attributes were realistic detail and a remorseless detachment from ideals," and he further observes that the novella "usually presents love from the fabliau's point of view, and it presents tragedy in a world unrelieved by divine grace" (*Idea and Act in Elizabethan Fiction* [Princeton: Princeton University Press, 1969], p. 155).
3. Geoffrey Fenton, *Certain Tragical Discourses of Bandello*, 2 vols., 1898 (Rprt. New York: AMS, 1967), with an introduction by Robert Langton Douglas.
4. Lorna Hutson, *The Usurer's Daughter: Male Friendship and Fictions of Women in Sixteenth-Century England* (New York: Routledge, 1994), p. 107.
5. See Jane Collins's forthcoming "Publishing Private Pleasures: The Gentlewoman Reader of Barnaby Riche and George Pettie," and Juliet Fleming's "The Ladies' Man and the Age of Elizabeth," as well as Caroline Lucas and Lorna Hutson more generally on the nature of these addresses. The Hutson quotation that follows comes from p. 97. On the didactic dimension of Painter's text and the link between its didacticism and Painter's female readers, especially of the 1567 volume, see Helen Hackett, *Women and Romance Fiction in the English Renaissance* (Cambridge: Cambridge University Press, 2000), pp. 35–38. Hackett also discusses the appeals to female readers of Fenton's and Pettie's *novelle* collections.
6. There is not room here to raise the significant discursive links between geography and same-sex as well as heterosexual desire; however, Winfried Schleiner, raising briefly one dimension of the complexities of homosexual desire in the period, notes, "Renaissance accounts of 'unnatural acts' ascribe same-sex love to the religious and cultural other, the Turk" (p. 98).
7. Michel de Certeau, *The Practice of Everyday Life*, trans. Steven F. Rendall (Berkeley: University of California Press, 1984), p. 115.
8. Homi K. Bhabha, *The Location of Culture* (New York: Routledge, 1994), p. 145.
9. III.62: "From Bandello to The Very Kind Gentleman Domenico Cavazza," in Janet Levarie Smarr, trans. *Italian Renaissance Tales* (Rochester, MI: Solaris Press, 1983), pp. 229–30.
10. This impulse might also be linked to the utopian discursive impulse that Amy Boesky, in *Founding Fictions: Utopias in Early Modern England* (Athens: University of Georgia Press, 1997), ably describes in early modern culture. The idealized representation of culture, as she explains, "depended on inaccessibility" (p. 177). The geographic anxiety of *novelle* manifests itself by constructing inaccessible locations while simultaneously gesturing toward their accessibility through geographic discourse.
11. Note the faithfulness with which Painter translates Marguerite's version of the passage:

> [Amador's] face was contorted with a terrifying violence, as if there was some raging inferno belching fire in his heart and behind his eyes. One powerful fist

roughly seized hold of her two weak and delicate hands. Her feet were held in a vice-like grip. There was nothing she could do to save herself. She could neither fight back, nor could she fight free.... (p. 147)

P. A. Chilton, trans. and ed. Marguerite de Navarre, The Heptameron (New York: Viking Penguin, 1984). All further references to de Navarre's text will be to this edition by page number.

12. Marcel Tetel, *Marguerite de Navarre's Heptameron: Themes, Language, and Structure* (Durham, NC: Duke University Press, 1973), p. 28. Tetel also calls attention to the use of the verb *guerroyer* in tale 10 to describe the verbal exchanges between Amador and Florida, further emphasizing the importance of military imagery within the text (p. 29).
13. Here Painter seems to mistranslate Marguerite. In the *Heptameron*: "... to hide my anger just as...I've hidden my joy" (p. 134). In Painter: "to dissemble my anger and contentation." In the *Heptameron* he is not doing both simultaneously. The shift seems part of a plan to ennoble Amadour.
14. Patricia Francis Cholakian, *Rape and Writing in the Heptameron of Marguerite de Navarre* (Carbondale: Southern Illinois University Press, 1991), p. 91.
15. Langer also briefly alludes to the role of place in de Navarre's *novelle* and early modern *novelle* as a whole, suggesting that references to rulers and the places they govern, which typically occur at the beginning of a narrative, function to establish a framework in which justice will be enacted, thereby permitting satisfying narrative closure (p. 327). For more on the ransoming of European captives in the East and the nature of Mediterranean pirates, see Richard Wilson, "Voyage to Tunis: New History and the Old World of *The Tempest*," *ELH* 64: 2 (Summer 1997): 333–57.
16. George Pettie, *A Petite Palace of Pettie His Pleasure*, ed. Herbert Hartman (London: Oxford University Press, 1938), pp. 235–36.
17. René Pruvost, *Matteo Bandello and Elizabethan Fiction* (Paris: Librairie Ancienne Honoré Champion, 1937), p. 180. Margaret Schlauch finds Fenton guilty, in his eleventh tale, of "Elizabethan stylistic padding at its worst" (p. 423).
18. An additional geographical point may merit emphasis at this point: the novella form flourished in Europe during the sixteenth century as a form that easily combined opportunities for originality with the drive to imitate (see Tetel, *Marguerite de Navarre's Heptameron*, p. 191).
19. Douglas, Robert Langton, ed. and introduction, *Certain Tragical Discourses of Bandello Translated into English by Gefraie Fenton, anno 1567*, 2 vols. (London: David Nutt, 1898; Rprt. New York: AMS Press, 1967), I.163.
20. Pruvost writes of this tale that in Bandello's version it is 4 pp. long; in Fenton's it is 45 pp. Fenton "as usual plays sundry rhetorical variations round the text of Belleforest without altering its substance. Everywhere the situations indicated in a few lines by Bandello are developed at great length; everywhere the heroes launch into long speeches; everywhere an attempt is made at analysing their feelings. Particularly noticeable in this respect is the expression of Luchyn's despair when he finds that Janiquetta will not grant him his suit. Here again Belleforest makes him pour his sorrow out in verse. Fenton omits his poetry, but for the rest he consistently follows the lead of his model" (Pruvost, *Matteo Bandello*, p. 158).

Caroline Lucas observes, "Fenton's prose was more rhetorically elaborate than Painter's" and that George Pettie's style is more elaborate than Painter's, Caroline Lucas, *Writing for Women: The Example of Woman as Reader of Elizabethan Romance* (New York: Open University Press, 1989), p. 42. This seems a conventional and fair thing to say. Pettie's elaborations become more euphuistic. On the implications of euphuism, see Joan Pong Linton, "Lyly's Euphuistic Romances..." in *Framing*. Euphuism itself serves a didactic aim.

21. Thomas F. Crane, in 1920, called it "the most elaborate original production of [its] kind in English literature," *Italian Social Customs of the Sixteenth Century and Their Influence on the Literature of Europe* (New Haven: Yale University Press, 1920), p. 520.
22. On the intricacies of the structure of Marguerite de Navarre's *Heptameron*, see Josephine Donovan's recent *Women and the Rise of the Novel, 1405–1726* (New York: St. Martin's, 1999), in which she links the early modern framed novella collections, including de Navarre's, with the dialogic structure of the novel.
23. Diane Shklanka, ed., *A Critical Edition of George Whetstone's 1582: An Heptameron of Civill Discourses* (New York: Garland, 1987), p. 331. Langer, in his treatment of de Navarre's *Heptameron*, discusses novella openings such as this one in the context of their emphasis on the identification of the prevailing ruler who will ultimately "encourag[e] a just resolution of a conflict" (p. 327). He does not specifically discuss Whetstone's text and the role of geography in these tales remains unexplored in his analysis.
24. Shklanka, *A Critical Edition of George Whetstone's An Heptameron*, p. 331, citing Painter's "A Lady of Bohemia" (II.28). She's quoting from the Jacobs' edition.
25. Hutson discusses this point briefly in reference to Whetstone's dramatic version of the tale. See *The Usurer's Daughter*, p. 190.
26. Shklanka, *A Critical Edition of George Whetstone's An Heptameron*, p. 245.
27. From the Chadwick-Healey database, p. 9.
28. References are by page number to the text in Charles C. Mish, ed., *Short Fiction of the Seventeenth Century* (New York: Norton, 1963). Margaret Schlauch calls this tale the "least interesting" of the narratives presented in the first version of the collection, the *Cobbler of Canterbury*. She points out that the tale is loosely based on Boccaccio 5.6, but observes that in Boccaccio's version the magnanimous king is not from Tunis, but Sicily. The French source for the tale, *Flores and Blancheflour*, contains a Saracen king (Margaret Schlauch, "English Short Fiction in the Sixteenth and Seventeeth Centuries," *Studies in Short Fiction* 3 (1966): 431). Boccaccio's version does not involve Tunis and is structured considerably differently. The tale does bear some relation to the fourth narrative of Barnabe Riche's *Farewell to Militarie Profession* (1581). See my discussion of it in *Fashioning Authority*.
29. See Sidney's letter VIII to Languet, dated December 19, 1573: "Nonne rides nos Saxones etiam jam Turkanifare?" (Feuillerat, pp. 80–81). On the historical realities of this phenomenon, see N. I. Matar, "'Turning Turk': Conversion to Islam in English Renaissance Thought," *Durham University Journal* (January 1994): 33–41. See also Barbara Fuchs, *Mimesis and Empire: The New World, Islam, and European Identities* (Cambridge: Cambridge University Press, 2001), pp. 118–38, for more detailed discussion of the Christian "renegado" who converts to Islam.

30. See Jeffrey Knapp, "Rogue Nationalism," *Centuries' Ends: Narrative Means* (Stanford: Stanford University Press, 1996), p. 140. Knapp discusses—in the context of an analysis of vagrancy and rogue literature—English fears that the Reformation would tear England apart by promoting factionalism.
31. Michel Foucault, *The Order of Things* (New York: Vintage, 1973), p. 326.

Chapter 3

Passion and Reason in Sir Philip Sidney's *Arcadia*

Lisa Hopkins

Although the old and new *Arcadias* are different in many significant respects, at the heart of both lies the prophecy received by Basilius from the Delphic oracle, and the consequences of his futile attempts to avoid its fulfillment. This motif of a king's attempt to thwart an oracle is not, of course, confined to the *Arcadia*. Variations on it recur in both *The Winter's Tale* and Ford's *The Broken Heart*, which is clearly indebted both to the *Arcadia*, like so much of Ford's other work, and also, it has been argued, to the life of Sidney himself and his ill-fated love affair with Penelope Devereux, to whom Ford, many years earlier, had dedicated his first published work. A rather different inflection of the motif is found in another Renaissance play, Webster's *The Duchess of Malfi*, where the astrological predictions concerning the Duchess's first son by Antonio may or may not be fulfilled. Most obviously, it is also the driving force of the events of Sophocles's *Oedipus Tyrannus*. And in all these plots, it is inextricably bound up with fears and taboos about incest. In this essay, I want to show how the new *Arcadia* codifies a definition of romantic love in which negotiation with the idea of incest becomes an inevitable corollary of the young aristocrat's development of a personal and romantic identity. Sidney is sensitive both to the threat of endogamy and the dangers of exogamy, and to the ways in which love both disrupts families and is a prerequisite for the formation of new ones. In the new *Arcadia*, therefore, he alerts his audience to these hazards and, by showing how passion must and can be tempered by reason, offers them the knowledge that may enable them to plot a path safely between the Scylla of the family and the Charybdis of the heart.

In the new *Arcadia*, the protocols of love and desire are clearly and rigidly structured, far more so than in the older version: Margaret M. Sullivan, for instance, points out, "[b]oth texts dramatize the analogical relation between monarchy and patriarchy, but only the revised text subjects its male Amazon to the same gender code that paralyzes Basilius's daughters,"[1] and Victor Skretkowicz observes of Pyrocles that "[h]is rewritten role demands . . . that his behaviour falls within the moral constraints of long established chivalric codes. We are less likely in a heroic novel to accept the early description of the torrid embrace between Pyrocles and Philoclea than the revision with its clear position on respect for a virgin's wishes."[2] Equally, Clare Kinney points out how "even as the author recasts his earlier work, his redeployment of Ovidian allusion and his variations on Ovidian themes illuminate the new emphases of the exfoliating romance" to produce a "complex reexamination of the *Old Arcadia*'s narratives of *eros.*"[3] In the new *Arcadia*, then, what we are offered is in effect a comprehensive definition and anatomy of love and desire, together with a rather less well developed and codified set of initial formulations for a code of practice for its proper operation in society.

A wide variety of aspects of love is examined during the course of the romance. There are, for instance, clear protocols structuring the ways in which it must be experienced and expressed. True love is so powerful and overwhelming a force that in the truly sensitive it can be activated by proxy means such as paintings, though, as Lamon's song of Claius and Strephon at the end of Book One informs us when he describes the techniques of Cupid, the lower classes are not similarly susceptible:

So now for prey these shepherds two he took,
    Whose metal stiff he knew he could not bend
With hear-say pictures, or a window-look;
    With one good dance, or letter finely penn'd
That were in court a well-proportion'd hook,
    Where piercing wits do quickly apprehend:
        Their senses rude plain objects only move,
        And so must see great cause before they love.[4] (p. 201)

Once activated, however, love operates just as durably and effectively amongst shepherds as amongst their betters, as the continued devotion of Strephon and Claius to Urania makes clear. This is a point to which Sidney will recur. Though much is made of status distinctions in the romance, and Pyrocles, Musidorus, Philanax, Kalander, and Pamela are all happy to make plain their disdain for Dametas, Miso, and Mopsa, Sidney nevertheless slyly insists on small but telling similarities between the emotions and motivations of these two groupings, which suggest that it is in externals rather than essentials that they primarily differ.

Also, it is only unrequited love that finds outward expression. Thyrsis will not sing with Philisides because "he should within few days be married to the fair Kala; and since he had gotten his desire, he would sing no more" (p. 426). And when Musidorus (in disguise as Dorus) has offended Pamela by his attempt to kiss her and taken refuge in the woods, the idea that she might pity and understand him when he is dead

> found such friendship in his thoughts that at last he yielded, since he was banished her presence, to seek some means by writing to show his sorrow and testify his repentance. Therefore getting him the necessary instruments of writing, he thought best to counterfeit his hand (fearing that as already she knew his, she would cast it away as soon as she saw it) and to put it in verse, hoping that would draw her on to read the more, choosing the elegiac as fittest for mourning. (p. 437)

What this means is that any love affair that is discussed in the *Arcadia* is likely to be an unfulfilled or an unconsummated one. Few relationships have progressed to marriage. Exceptions include Erona and Antiphilus, though theirs, as Antiphilus's name with its meaning of "anti-love" clearly suggests, consists of an entirely one-sided devotion, and Basilius and Gynecia, who, like Dametas and Miso, show each other no affection and are only too glad to escape from each other's company. The one instance of a married couple who are genuinely in love is Argalus and Parthenia, and the one *vignette* of their married life finds them rather curiously engaged:

> The messenger made speed, and found Argalus at a castle of his own, sitting in a parlour with the fair Parthenia, he reading in a book the stories of Hercules, she by him, as to hear him read; but while his eyes looked on the book, she looked on his eyes, and sometimes staying him with some pretty question, not so much to be resolved of the doubt as to give him occasion to look upon her. A happy couple: he joying in her, she joying in herself, but in herself, because she enjoyed him: both increasing their riches by giving to each other; each making one life double, because they made a double life one; whereas desire never wanted satisfaction, nor satisfaction ever bred satiety: he ruling, because she would obey, or rather because she would obey, she therein ruling. (p. 501)

A number of phrases here will echo resonantly down the ages: that oddly modern and banal description of them as "a happy couple" jostles shoulders with a prolepsis of the spirit if not the letter of "He for God only, she for God in him." What is particularly notable for my purposes, though, is that although Argalus and Parthenia are seated in a "parlour," a room whose very name designates a space envisaged as being for talking in, they are not conversing; he is reading, albeit aloud, and she is listening to him. The shared fact of reading might initially appear to allow for an identification between Argalus and the reader, but the subject matter disables that: we are reading a scene of love, but he is reading a book of war. The sense of our own exclusion from the intimacy apparently offered by the scene is deepened by the fact that at the heart of the experience described by Sidney lies Argalus's reading voice, which we cannot hear.

Argalus is the only character in the new *Arcadia* whom we ever see reading for pleasure. Even when they are in captivity, Pamela sews and prays,

Philoclea exercises her humility, and Zelmane paces up and down her cell. Moreover, unlike so many other characters of subsequent romances, none of those of the new *Arcadia* are presented as having been formed by their reading (the obvious contrast here is with *Don Quixote*, but the idea will become a staple of romance). Nor have any of them derived their ideas of chivalry or of any other aspect of their own world from books; to all intents and purposes, all the characters except Argalus live in an entirely oral culture (and even he is here participating in it), *hearing* of each other's doings and passing on the recital of them with varying degrees of formality and of self-conscious narration. At various stages of the romance, Philoclea, Basilius, Musidorus, Pyrocles, Philisides, the other shepherds, and even Miso all tell, sing, or recite stories.

To some extent this is a product of the myth of Arcadia, the *ur*-location of the pastoral that is experienced directly and personally rather than vicariously through literature; the absence of books is thus an aspect of the plenitude of the experience, as in Shakespeare's *As You Like It* where the only books are those to be found in the sound of the brook. Pyrocles and Musidorus are no Elizabethan gentlemen merely playing at pastoral by taking their books outdoors to be painted by Hilliard or Oliver, but the thing itself, and they have no patterns other than their own deeds, of which they hear a number of orally recounted versions during their travels. The booklessness of the culture also has another effect, however. If it is only unrequited lovers who sing, write, or speak their passion, and only requited ones (and male ones at that) who read, then we by the very fact of being readers ourselves are implicitly forced into alignment with the requited lovers, and distanced emotionally and in terms of shared experience from the unrequited ones, whom we are thus invited to survey with an eye less of identification than of judgment.

This idea of separability and the forcing apart of points of view and positions of identification recurs in the *Arcadia*'s extensively developed interest in the *sine qua non* of heterosexual romance, gender distinction.[5] The question of proper gender roles is thoroughly discussed by Musidorus when he first sees Pyrocles in his disguise as the Amazon Zelmane (an episode entirely original to the revision, since in the *Old Arcadia* Musidorus himself had collaborated in the transformation of his cousin):

> And is it possible that this is Pyrocles, the only young prince in the world formed by nature and framed by education to the true exercise of virtue? Or is it indeed some Amazon that hath counterfeited the face of my friend in this sort to vex me? For likelier sure I would have thought it that any outward face might have been disguised than that the face of so excellent a mind could have been thus blemished. O sweet Pyrocles, separate yourself a little, if it be possible, from yourself, and let your own mind look upon your own proceedings; so shall my words be needless and you best instructed. See with yourself how fit it will be for you in this your tender youth, born so great a prince, and of so rare not only expectation but proof, desired of your old father, and wanted of your native country, now so near your home to divert your thoughts from the way of goodness to lose, nay, to abuse your time. Lastly to overthrow all the excellent things

> you have done, which have filled the world with your fame; as if you should drown your ship in the long desired haven, or, like an ill player, should mar the last act of his tragedy. Remember (for I know you know it) that if we will be men, the reasonable part of our soul is to have absolute commandment, against which, if any sensual weakness arise, we are to yield all our sound forces to the overthrowing of so unnatural a rebellion; wherein how can we want courage, since we are to deal against so weak an adversary that in itself is nothing but weakness? Nay, we are to resolve that if reason direct it, we must do it; for, to say "I cannot," is childish, and "I will not," womanish. (pp. 132–33)

For Pyrocles to adopt female disguise "vexes" Musidorus because he sees it as "blemishing" Pyrocles's mind. However, his proposed remedy for the situation suggests a curiously splitting effect when he advises Pyrocles to "separate yourself a little, if it be possible, from yourself, and let your own mind look upon your own proceedings," implying that masculinity depends on self-division and rigorous enforcement of a performed rather than an innate identity. There is a curious tension between the vagueness of action that Musidorus counsels—"separate"—and the increasing specificity and concreteness of the ones that he sees Pyrocles as already actually performing by virtue of his female disguise: "divert," "abuse," "overthrow," "drown," and "mar." All these are energetic, performative actions that in other contexts might well be thought suitable only to the masculine rather than the feminine sphere, and yet it is Pyrocles's assumed femininity that is figured as underpinning them.

Things become even more provisional when Musidorus begins his exhortation to Pyrocles, "[r]emember . . . that if we will be men." The "if" signals that there is an alternative to this possibility, and thus confirms that manhood is *not* the inevitable state of those biologically gendered male. Moreover, manhood proves, paradoxically, to depend not on self-assertiveness, as Musidorus's earlier advice to Pyrocles to supervise himself had seemed to imply, but on a form of submission: "if we will be men, the reasonable part of our soul is to have absolute commandment, against which, if any sensual weakness arise, we are to yield all our sound forces to the overthrowing of so unnatural a rebellion." Though men may overthrow, they must also "yield" and cede "commandment," and their victory is assured only by the weakness of their adversary.

Musidorus's argument is, of course, underpinned by a belief in the inferiority of woman to man. He images womanishness as equivalent to childishness in that the two together represent the pitfalls a man must avoid to be manly. He thus opens up the whole question of the *querelle des femmes*, so often a topic of medieval romance, as Pyrocles in his reply is quick to point out by his spirited defense of womanhood:

> this must I confess, that I am not yet come to that degree of wisdom to think light of the sex of whom I have my life, since if I be anything (which your friendship rather finds than I acknowledge) I was, to come to it, born of a woman and nursed of a woman. And certainly (for this point of your speech

> doth nearest touch me) it is strange to see the unmanlike cruelty of mankind, who, not content with their tyrannous ambition to have brought the other's virtuous patience under them, like childish masters think their masterhood nothing without doing injury to them who (if we will argue by reason) are framed of nature with the same parts of the mind for the exercise of virtue as we are. And for example, even this estate of Amazons (which I now for my greatest honour do seek to counterfeit) doth well witness that if generally the sweetness of their disposition did not make them see the vainness of these things which we account glorious, they neither want valour of mind, nor yet doth their fairness take away their force. (pp. 134–35)

Pyrocles deploys the "third term" of childishness in direct opposition to the purposes for which his cousin had earlier attempted to commandeer it, aligning it with masculinity rather than femininity and proposing an apparently entirely new set of criteria for proper manhood, which is based on admiration for womanhood and its values rather than an attempt to separate itself from them, while women say not, as in Musidorus's formulation, "I will not," but "I could, but it's not a good idea." However, there prove to be some significant points of convergence between Pyrocles's view of manhood and that of Musidorus to which he presents it as antithetical. Both depend on an association of manhood with subservience or submissiveness to something other than itself per se, and both posit an innate separability between manhood and men themselves. For Pyrocles, as for Musidorus, "mankind" can be "unmanlike," and even if their definition of childishness differs, both agree that men can become like children.

The separability and propensity to fragmentation that characterize both men's view of manhood confirms that there is more at stake here than the old debates of the *querelle des femmes*; there is also the far more alarming question of the degree of correlation between assigned gender and biological sex. This becomes even clearer in the second part of Musidorus's admonition to Pyrocles:

> And see how extremely every way you can endanger your mind: for to take this womanish habit, without you frame your behaviour accordingly, is wholly vain; your behaviour can never come kindly from you but as the mind is proportioned unto it: so that you must resolve it, if you will play your part to any purpose, whatsoever peevish imperfections are in that sex, to soften your heart to receive them – the very first down-step to all wickedness. For do not deceive yourself, my dear cousin, there is no man suddenly either excellently good or extremely evil, but grows either as he holds himself up in virtue or lets himself slide to viciousness. (p. 133)

Here Musidorus goes even further in warning against the possibility of the separability of sex and gender and the danger that a man might actually degenerate into a woman,[6] because it is, it seems, not the body that determines behavior and thus conformity to the appropriate gender, but the mind. A man, in order to remain a man and a practitioner of "virtue" (of whose root in the Latin *virtus*, manliness, Sidney would have been very well aware), must continually "hold himself" in it; it is a position that needs to be consciously occupied rather than one innate and inevitable.

What has caused all the trouble is love. Of this, too, Musidorus has a definition to offer:

> And let us see what power is the author of all these troubles: forsooth love, love, a passion, and the basest and fruitlessest of all passions. Fear breedeth wit; anger is the cradle of courage; joy openeth and enableth the heart; sorrow, as it closeth, so it draweth it inward to look to the correcting of itself; and so all of them generally have power towards some good by the direction of reason. But this bastard Love (for indeed the name of love is most unworthily applied to so hateful humour) as it is engendered betwixt love and idleness; as the matter it works upon is nothing but a certain base weakness which some gentle fools call a gentle heart; as his adjoined companions be unquietness, longings, fond comforts, faint discomforts, hopes, jealousies, ungrounded rages, causeless yieldings; so is the highest end it aspires unto a little pleasure with much pain before and great repentance after. (p. 130)

Love, according to Musidorus, is a passion, and the worst of the passions at that. Love is opposed to reason, the fundamental guarantor of humanity.

The narrative as a whole provides abundant reinforcement for the absolute identification of love as a passion. Philoclea interrupts her tale of Plangus to observe "if that may be called love, which he rather did take into himself willingly than by which he was taken forcibly" (pp. 312–22), implying that love is not love if it fails to disable the operation of the will and judgment. The second Eclogues openly oppose Passion to Reason (p. 407). And Basilius describes the non-love of Artesia and Phalantus thus:

> But in that court he saw and was acquainted with this Artesia whose beauty he now defends; became her servant; said himself (and perchance thought himself) her lover. "But certainly," said Basilius, "many times it falls out that these young companions make themselves believe they love at the first liking of a likely beauty; loving, because they will love for want of other business, not because they feel indeed that divine power which makes the heart find a reason in passion, and so, God knows, as inconstantly leave upon the next chance that beauty casts before them." So therefore taking love upon him like a fashion, he courted this lady Artesia, who was as fit to pay him in his own money as might be: for she, thinking she did wrong to her beauty if she were not proud of it, called her disdain of him chastity, and placed her honour in little setting by his honouring her; determining never to marry but him whom she thought worthy of her, and that was one in whom all worthinesses were harboured. And to this conceit not only nature had bent her, but the bringing-up she received at my sister-in-law Cecropia had confirmed her; who, having in her widowhood had taken this young Artesia into her charge because her father had been a dear friend of her dear husband's, had taught her to think that there is no wisdom but in including both heaven and earth in oneself; and that love, courtesy, gratefulness, friendship, and all other virtues are rather to be taken on than taken in oneself. And so good a disciple she found of her that, liking the fruits of her own planting, she was content (if so her son could have liked of it) to have wished her in marriage to my nephew Amphialus. (p. 154)

Basilius concurs with Musidorus in believing love to be an insistent, elemental force, rather than an operation of reason or willed choice that can be adopted "like a fashion," that is, as if it were something external, as Phalantus and Artesia both believe it to be—the latter, significantly, having been encouraged in this belief by the atheist Cecropia, who believes in no external power, and is so well pleased with the results of her teaching of Artesia that she is described, in a passage that smacks almost of incest, as wishing to offer her as virtually a surrogate self in marriage to her son Amphialus, who is repeatedly described as the only love-object of Cecropia herself.

When Musidorus himself falls in love with Pamela, he might well be expected to change his tune on the subject of love in general. In fact, however, though Musidorus readily confesses himself entirely enslaved, his definition of love remains remarkably constant. Disguised as Dorus, and unable to devise a way to make either his love or his identity known to Pamela, he recounts to Pyrocles how

> Many times have I, leaning to yonder palm, admired the blessedness of it that it could bear love without sense of pain. Many times, when my master's cattle came hither to chew their cud in this fresh place, I might see the young bull testify his love, but how? With proud looks and joyfulness. (p. 222)

Complaining not that love debases man by reducing him to the level of a beast but merely about the fact that the privileges of beastliness or of the vegetable state are withheld, Musidorus makes no distinction between his own love and that manifested by the bull (with, presumably, a play of words on "testify.")

Ironically, for all Musidorus's contempt of Dametas and his family, there is in fact virtually no difference between his perception of love and that which will later be offered in the context of the story told by Miso, as she recounts a conversation she had with an old woman in her youth:

> "Minion," said she (indeed I was a pretty one in those days, though I say it) "I see a number of lads that love you. Well," said she, "I say no more; do you know what love is?" With that she brought me into a corner, where there was painted a foul fiend I trow, for he had a pair of horns like a bull, his feet cloven, as many eyes upon his body as my grey mare hath dapples, and for all the world so placed. This monster sat like a hangman upon a pair of gallows. In his right hand he was painted holding a crown of laurel, in his left hand a purse of money; and out of his mouth hung a lace of two fair pictures of a man and a woman, and such a countenance he showed as if he would persuade folks by those allurements to come hither and be hanged. I, like a tender-hearted wench, shrieked out for fear of the devil. "Well," said she, "this same is even love: therefore do what thou list with all those fellows one after another, and it recks not much what they do to thee, so it be in secret; but upon my charge, never love none of them." "Why mother," said I, "could such a thing come from the belly of fair Venus?"—for a few days before, our priest (between him and me) had told me the whole story of Venus. "Tush," said she, "they are all deceived"; and therewith gave me this book which she said a great maker of

> ballads had given to an old painter, who, for a little pleasure, had bestowed both book and picture of her. "Read there," said she, "and thou shalt see that his mother was a cow, and false Argus was his father." And so she gave me this book, and there now you may read it. (p. 308)

Miso, whose name means "I hate" and who seems to have followed the old woman's advice never to love, thinks of love in terms of a bull just as the virtuous, high-minded, and romantically devoted Musidorus does.[7]

Love, therefore, must be overwhelming and in direct opposition to reason before it can be counted as love in the world of the *Arcadia*. One aspect of this incompatibility between love and reason is that throughout the *Arcadia*, Sidney imagines and constructs love and desire as drives acting almost entirely in opposition to earlier allegiances in the shape of familial and also to national loyalties. Although the idea of love as often conflicting with family demands is common enough in Renaissance literature, in the new *Arcadia* desire comes to be defined almost exclusively as an impulse not merely directed outside the family but acting in direct opposition to it.

This first becomes apparent when we are introduced to the story of Argalus and Parthenia. Parthenia's mother violently opposes her marriage to Argalus, whom she is even prepared to murder, because the mother wishes her instead to marry her neighbor Demagoras, with whom the mother bonds very closely in their mutual hatred of Argalus. But even the marriage with Demagoras would not have secured family harmony, since Parthenia's uncle Kalander was opposed to it (p. 88). It is, it seems, impossible to imagine a marriage that does not cut across familial bonds.

This becomes even clearer as the narrative progresses. Love takes Pyrocles from his cousin (p. 116), and love causes disruptions and tensions in the family of Basilius for which no possible solution seems imaginable, since it is out of the question for Basilius, Gynecia, Philoclea, and Pamela all to be made happy, not least because three of them all desire the same love-object. Love drives Amphialus to rebel against his uncle and, eventually, to bring about the death of his mother, just as love also leads Andromana to cause the death of her son. (A notable feature of the *Arcadia* is the astonishing weakness of the majority of parent–child bonds, most spectacularly in the case of Gynecia, which points up the strength of other bonds.)

Indeed throughout the new *Arcadia*, love is consistently counterpointed with violence. It was also so in the *Old Arcadia*, of course, where there were deaths aplenty and where Musidorus acutally attempted to rape Pamela. Some of this is actually toned down in the new *Arcadia*, where the mere attempt at a kiss produces such anger on Pamela's part that Musidorus, beside himself with shame, has to spend two days in the woods. Nevertheless, scenes of love still find themselves insistently echoed, followed, or paralleled by scenes of violence, and ideas of love and violence are repeatedly interwoven or paired, sometimes in conjunction with the idea that since unfulfilled love must find expression, violence may actually be the only alternative form to poetry as a means of that expression: Anne Sussman suggests that in the *Old Arcadia*, "poetic production . . . is the aftermath of a merger between love and violence . . . The continuous interplay between love and violence is so intrinsic to the conjoined production of verse and narrative that it effectively functions as a poetic of sexual violence," while "[b]y the time he came to revise the *Arcadia*, some three years later, his perspective will have changed, and his poetic of sexual violence will prove a hindrance, rather than an inspiration, to poetic production."[8] Love is the enemy inside Amphialus's defenses, undermining his otherwise impregnable castle from within, and Zelmane, like Astrophil, draws on metaphors of war to express her love:

> Her loose hairs be the shot; the breasts the pikes be;
> Scouts each motion is; the hands be horsemen;
> Her lips are the riches the wars to maintain (p. 432)

It is also notable how many of those who die in the new *Arcadia* have been defined primarily or entirely in terms of whom they love or simply by the fact of their being in love. These include Andromana, Antiphilus, the nameless young rebel farmer who loved Zelmane, Dido, Palladius, the original Zelmane, Amphialus, Argalus, Parthenia, and Agenor, a character who indeed seems introduced expressly in order to be described as a lover and then to die (pp. 467–68). Strikingly, too, the passage telling of Agenor's death is followed by a section of the narrative that is clearly influenced by that *ur*-tale of love-caused war, the *Iliad*, with descriptions of conflict highly reminiscent of the Homeric style and the presence of a number of *Iliad*-derived names such as Memnon and Sarpedon.

The conflicted relationship that Sidney proposes between love and the maintenance of familial or even personal identity means that love in the *Arcadia* is envisioned not so much as a potential force for social cohesion and alliance-forming but as a threat to society. One marked manifestation of this is the stress throughout the romance on the extent to which love is at least as likely to be endogamous as exogamous. The Greece that Sidney presents is one whose political structure is entirely underpinned by a complex network of intermarriages that have produced alliances and bonds, and in this it comes very close to the structures of both the English aristocracy of which he formed at least an honorary part and also of the Renaissance Europe in whose diplomatic alliances he was so closely involved. However, Sidney's own marriage was made for social rather than amatory reasons; he saw the woman he loved unhappily tied to a loathed husband, and he was well aware that his whole family's position was dependent on the entirely irregular relationship (whatever its precise nature may have been) between the Queen and Sidney's uncle the Earl of Leicester, which the latter, despite his best attempts, had never succeeded in cementing by marriage. Few people were better placed to grasp the ways in which both marriage was both politically and socially essential for the maintenance of the aristocratic order by which chivalric values were supported, but also unlikely to coincide with the personal emotional and romantic needs to which chivalry encouraged attention to be paid.

Indeed Brenda Cantar suggests, "[t]hat Sidney wrote his romance originally for his beloved sister, the Countess of Pembroke, who, like Gynecia, was married to a man many years her senior might... account for the narrative ambivalence and oscillation between the detailing of Gynecia's sinful and unnatural conduct, and the profuse explanations that seem designed to solicit the reader's empathy and sympathy."[9]

Such tensions abound in the *Arcadia*. Although Greece as the characters know it may have been shaped by marriage alliances, there is for much of the narrative no prospect of the contraction of any more such by which the future may be secured. Romantic attraction is, indeed, at least as likely to be endogamous as exogamous: Amphialus wishes to marry his cousin Philoclea, Palladius loves his cousin Zelmane, the King of Iberia marries his son's former mistress, and Erona chooses the son of her nurse rather than a prince (and loses her throne for her pains). In one sense, the marriages of Pyrocles to Philoclea and of Musidorus to Pamela will be exogamous, uniting Arcadia to Thessaly and Macedon, but they will in another be equally endogamous, since the marriage of the two cousins to two sisters will further cement the bonds between them (which are already unusually strong because they are cousins not just on the side of one parent but of both). Even where proposed marital alliances are in fact exogamous, they are more likely to be received as threats than as forms of social bonding. Parthenia's mother wishes her daughter to marry her neighbor rather than the new acquaintance Argalus, and Basilius does not wish his daughters to marry at all but to confine them with his own family circle and that of his trusted Dametas.

It is of course a commonplace in romance that the older generation will seek to thwart the wishes of the younger, but it is less frequent to find the younger people themselves thus voluntarily limiting their choices within the circle of the known. That this is so in the *Arcadia* suggests that there are other fears and desires at work, and, as I outlined at the beginning, I want to argue that one way of illuminating the nature of those fears and desires is to compare the *Arcadia* with a small group of later works that are all obviously indebted to it and which all also share a common interest in the idea of incest.

The writer most obviously associated with explorations of incest in Renaissance England is of course John Ford. There are strong parallels between the *Arcadia*, Ford's work in general, and *The Broken Heart* in particular. In *The Old Arcadia*, Pyrocles's name when in disguise is Cleophila, in honor of Philoclea, and this is the name of the heroine's sister in *The Lover's Melancholy*; Pamphilus in the new version womanizes in the same way as Ferentes in *Love's Sacrifice*, and suffers the same fate of death at the hands of those he has deceived.

Most obviously, the Prologue to *The Broken Heart* asserts that

> What may be here thought a fiction, when time's youth
> Wanted some riper years, was known a truth.[10]

This has often been taken to refer to the real-life relationship between Sidney and Penelope Rich, sister of the Earl of Essex and the "Stella" of *Astrophil and Stella*,[11] and, as her blonde hair and black eyes (p. 146) and Pyrocles's reference to her as "my only star" (p. 741) make plain, the model for Philoclea. The story of Orgilus and Penthea certainly does have elements in common with that of Sidney and his Stella, while the names of Ford's characters may well seem to echo those of Argalus and Parthenia, who feature in one of the numerous sub-plots of the new *Arcadia*, and "the general indebtedness of Ford's play to Sidney's *Arcadia* has been noticed."[12]

Incest, the major theme of Ford's *'Tis Pity She's a Whore*, haunts *The Broken Heart* too. When the pathologically jealous Bassanes finds his wife Penthea alone with her twin brother Ithocles, incest is the conclusion to which he immediately leaps. Incest is also a recurring nightmare in the other plays linked to the *Arcadia* by a shared reliance on the oracle motif. In *The Winter's Tale*, Paulina directly cautions Leontes against harboring incestuous feelings for his daughter Perdita, while in the source narrative on which Shakespeare based his play the equivalent relationship is actually consummated. In *The Duchess of Malfi*, which has many borrowings from the *Arcadia* and reuses its echo motif, it is difficult not to see an incestuous element in Ferdinand's excessive interest in his sister's body, and in *Oedipus Tyrannus*, to which the *Arcadia* is so obviously indebted, incest is at the heart of both plot and prophecy.

Incest may well seem to be of far less importance in the *Arcadia*. Though the prophecy warns that Philoclea will embrace an unnatural love, and Philanax worries about "banishing [the princesses] from company, lest I know not what strange loves should follow" (p. 81), the plot soon makes it apparent that this refers merely to the Amazon disguise of the actually male, and unrelated, Pyrocles, and since Philoclea has no close male relative but her father, whose mind is abundantly occupied with thoughts of the supposed Zelmane, the plot seems to afford no scope for incest or the threat of it.

Nevertheless, it does surface. Not only is Philoclea's suitor Amphialus also her cousin, but the lover of Plangus, Prince of Iberia, becomes his stepmother and still seeks to continue the liaison.[13] (Indeed, as I have suggested earlier, so complex is the web of interrelationships between the various rulers mentioned in the romance that incest is almost inherent in any royal marital alliance.) The King of Paphlagonia is blinded, the traditional punishment for the incestuous, a fate with which Miso is also threatened by Basilius (p. 326) and Ferentes by one of his discarded mistresses (p. 335). Incest is even more surprisingly and directly flirted with in the description of a conversation between Philoclea and her sister Pamela. Philoclea begs Pamela to share the cause of her sorrow with "your sister, yea and servant Philoclea":

> These words won no further of Pamela but that telling her they might talk better as they lay together, they impoverished their clothes to enrich their bed which for that night might well scorn the shrine of Venus: and there, cherishing one another with dear though chaste embracements, with sweet though cold kisses, it might seem that love was come to play him there without dart, or that, weary of his own fires, he was there to refresh himself between their sweet breathing lips. (p. 254)

There are several things of interest here. Though we are expressly told that the proceedings are all "chaste," we may well wonder why we should ever have been expected to require such a reassurance in a scene focused on siblings. (Though Aubrey was later to recite gossip that Sidney himself had been the lover of his own sister Mary, Countess of Pembroke, and the father of her son Philip, I know of no evidence for the existence of any such rumors during Sidney's lifetime.) Philoclea describes herself as Pamela's "servant," the term often used of a Petrarchan lover, while "lay together" was regularly used to mean "had sexual intercourse." Moreover, one cannot help but note that although Pamela does eventually speak of what is troubling her, the immediate effect of retiring to bed is to hinder her as much as it helps her, since she is taken up with kissing instead of talking.

Why might the possibility of incest be raised here, however briefly and indirectly? To some extent, incest is always the other side of the coin of the identity theme so prominent in the *Arcadia*, in which so many of the characters are not only disguised themselves but also find themselves fighting unknown opponents or employing disguised page boys. Although the *Arcadia*'s affiliations with Richardson—who named his first heroine after Pamela—have more often been remarked, it also has much in common with *Tom Jones*, whose wandering hero has to learn who he and other people are, and thus stands squarely in a tradition of Oedipus-influenced English fiction from *Moll Flanders* to *Evelina* in which origins are discovered and unwitting incest or marriage with close kin narrowly (or not) avoided. Indeed Sidney himself describes his own work in terms both precisely reminiscent of the fate of Oedipus and also unmistakably suggestive of a joint parenting enterprise between himself and his sister when he writes in his dedication of it to her, "For my part, in very truth (as the cruel fathers among the Greeks were wont to do to the babes they would not foster) I could well find in my heart to cast out in some desert of forgetfulness this child which I am loth to father" (p. 57).

And perhaps this striking occurrence of the language of incest in Sidney's dedication to his sister, like the apparently unnecessary insistence on the chastity of Pamela's and Philoclea's embraces, brings us to the heart of the matter. There is clearly a relationship between Sidney's own family and several of the events of the *Arcadia*. Quite apart from his dedication of the work to his sister, whose continuing Sidney identity he insists on, the sudden and unexpected deformity of Parthenia (p. 90) may be compared with the horrific scarring that smallpox caused on the face of his mother, while Amphialus's displacement from the succession following the birth of children to Basilius echoes Sidney's similar demotion as heir to his uncle the Earl of Leicester after the birth of the latter's son. One might even see a parallel between Parthenia's vicarious enjoyment of Argalus's reading and the processes of composition that Sidney describes in his dedication of the work "To my dear lady and sister, the Countess of Pembroke": "Your dear self can best witness the manner, being done in loose sheets of paper, most of it in your presence; the rest by sheets sent unto you as fast as they were done" (p. 57).

The scarcity of readers within the *Arcadia* itself may serve to remind us of what a comparatively rare commodity well-developed literacy was in Renaissance England, and how distinctive a quality was the Sidney family's sustained and wide-ranging literariness; and we can hardly fail to respond, even at this distance, to the excitement of this brief glimpse of the real-life relationship between the young Sidney, hard at work, and his devoted sister sitting and watching him in a room at Wilton. But even as we notice how closely comparable this is with the scene in which Parthenia similarly sits and watches Argalus in their parlor, we must also register a significant difference: the Countess of Pembroke is not Sidney's wife but his sister, and literally to confuse the two is taboo, however much that curious formulation "To my dear lady and sister" may seem to do so metaphorically.

Sidney, then, envisages his literary offspring as fundamentally a product of his own family situation, and indeed seems to have conceived of it originally as something intended primarily for consumption within that charmed circle. Ironically, of course, the work in question is actually centered on the need to look outside that family circle; Sidney leaves us in no doubt of the fact that Basilius is both misguided to attempt to keep his daughters unmarried and with him for ever and also will be unable to achieve it. At the same time as the romance preaches the need for exogamy, romance, and encounters with strangers, however, it never fails to register the potential pain they may cause. In the *Arcadia*, travel is dangerous, and love hurts. Even an initially successful exogamous marriage like that of Parthenia and Argalus comes swiftly to a fatal conclusion. And as the characters attempt to negotiate successfully this fraught territory of alliance and romance, moving on from one family group to the formation of another, so Sidney's definitions and codifications of love and desire begin to offer some rules of guidance which, by never losing sight of the dangers of the various possible extremes of behavior into which the young lover may fall, may perhaps suggest strategies for avoiding.

Notes

1. Margaret M. Sullivan, "Amazons and Aristocrats: The Function of Pyrocles' Amazon Role in Sidney's Revised *Arcadia*," in *Playing with Gender: A Renaissance Pursuit*, ed. Jean R. Brink, Maryanne C. Horowitz, and Allison P. Coudert (Urbana: University of Illinois Press, 1991), p. 62. On differences between the two versions' treatment of love see also Mark Rose, *Heroic Love: Studies in Sidney and Spenser* (Cambridge, Mass.: Harvard University Press, 1968), p. 37.
2. Victor Skretcowicz, "Categorising Redirection in Sidney's *New Arcadia*," in *Narrative Strategies in Early English Fiction*, ed. Wolfgang Görtschacher and Holger Klein (Lewiston, N.Y. and Salzburg: The Edwin Mellen Press, 1995), p. 139.
3. Clare Kinney, "The Masks of Love: Desire and Metamorphosis in Sidney's *New Arcadia*," *Criticism* 33 (1991): 461.
4. Sir Philip Sidney, *The Countess of Pembroke's Arcadia*, ed. Maurice Evans (Harmondsworth: Penguin, 1977), p. 201. Although I quote from an edition

of *The Countess of Pembroke's Arcadia*, I shall be discussing only the new *Arcadia*, since the revisions in the treatment of love in the reworked section are so extensive that passages in the old *Arcadia* cannot be taken as a guide to what would have happened in the new.

5. Katherine Duncan-Jones has recently argued that it is more appropriate to read Sidney in *homosexual* terms (see her review of Alan Stewart's *Philip Sidney—A Double Life*, *The Observer Review*, February 13, 2000, p. 12).
6. For a full documentation of Renaissance fears on this score, see Laura Levine, *Men in Women's Clothing: Anti-Theatricality and Effeminization, 1579–1642* (Cambridge: Cambridge University Press, 1994), though Levine does not specifically discuss the *Arcadia*.
7. For comment on Miso's narrative, on its similarities to the thought of the princes, and its movement from Dicus in the *Old Arcadia* to Miso in the new version, see e.g. Kinney, "The Masks of Love," pp. 466–69.
8. Anne Sussman, " 'Sweetly Ravished': Sidney's *Old Arcadia* and the Poetics of Sexual Violence," *Renaissance Papers* (1994): 55, 66.
9. Brenda Cantar, "Charmed Circles of Enchantment: Pre-Oedipal Fantasies in Sir Philip Sidney's *Arcadia*," *Sidney Newsletter & Journal* 12.1 (1992): 9.
10. John Ford, *The Broken Heart*, ed. Brian Morris (London: Ernest Benn, 1965), Prologue, ll.14–15. All further quotations from the play will be taken from this edition.
11. See e.g. S. P. Sherman, "Stella and *The Broken Heart*," *PMLA* 24 (1909), and, more recently, Verna Ann Foster and Stephen Foster, "Structure and History in *The Broken Heart*: Sparta, England, and the 'Truth,' " *English Literary Renaissance* 22 (1988): 305–28.
12. *The Broken Heart*, ed. Morris, introduction, p. xi.
13. On incest in the *Arcadia*, see also Cantar, "Charmed Circles of Enchantment," p. 8.

Chapter 4

The Thigh and the Sword: Gender, Genre, and Sexy Dressing in Sidney's *New Arcadia*

Steven Mentz

When you meet a human being, the first distinction you make is "male or female?" and you are accustomed to make this distinction with unhesitating certainty.

—*Sigmund Freud, "Femininity"*[1]
New Introductory Lectures on Psychoanalysis *(1933)*

While generally acknowledged to be the most influential work of prose fiction in the English Renaissance, Sidney's *Arcadia* is a strangely fractured work. Only since the discovery of a complete manuscript in 1907 has it been possible to read the tale in a coherent form, in a version now called the *Old Arcadia*.[2] Until then, only the partially revised text—the *New Arcadia*—was available to readers. The *New Arcadia* is a hybrid, combining Sidney's revised version of Books 1 to 3, which breaks off in the middle of a sentence, with Books 3 to 5 of the *Old* version. The resulting work, first published in the composite text of 1593, awkwardly marries a heroic romance to the happy pastoral tale of the earlier version.[3] Critics and readers since the sixteenth century have attempted to explain the generic and narrative hole at the work's center. Hugh Sanford, the secretary to the Countess of Pembroke, acknowledged in a prefatory letter to the *New* version that the book was "the conclusion, not the perfection of Arcadia."[4] Sidney himself, in a letter written for the *Old Arcadia* but published with the *New*, calls the work "a trifle, and that triflingly handled" (p. 57).[5] In part because of its structural fragmentation, the *New Arcadia* seems an extended experiment with the idea of coherence itself. Sidney's text hybridizes both genre and gender, and its manipulation of literary convention and sexual display provides a suggestive parallel to recent notions of the performativity of human sexual identity.[6] Sidney's portrait of Pyrocles/Zelmane explores the social mutability of gender and in particular its manipulation through the semiotics of clothing.

At their most ingenious, critical approaches to the genre of Sidney's work nearly reach Polonius's impossible categories: "pastoral-comical, historical-pastoral, tragical-historical, tragical-comical-historical pastoral" (2.2.396–99).[7] Sidney's sense of his own literary form relied on a variety of classical and early modern exemplars, especially Sannazzaro, Heliodorus, Montemayor, and *Amadis of Gaul*.[8] The *New Arcadia* defines in a self-consciously broad sense what Stephen Greenblatt has called "the mixed mode."[9] As Greenblatt notes, Sidney's modification of fixed generic codes appears to imply a flexible understanding of human character: "Sidney seemed instinctively to feel that for the world he wished to portray, there could be no unified, pure form with a single style, a uniform set of characters, and a fixed perspective."[10] Expanding Greenblatt's reading of Sidney's generic play to encompass his text's understanding of gender and sexuality reveals a pattern of heterodoxy in Sidney's thought. Sidney appears to be not only a "connoisseur of doubt," as Greenblatt calls him, but a connoisseur of how clothing changes sexual roles.[11] For Sidney, as for many contemporary theorists, gender roles are constructed by the intersection of clothes, bodies, and narrative context.

As foundational categories, genre and gender have important similarities. They share a common etymology, from, the Latin *generare*, to create or bring forth. They both rely on an audience's presumed knowledge of what elements should match each other. The desire to keep familiar things together motivates our efforts to classify new phenomena according to their gender or their genre. Both modes of classification operate through judgments that are made quickly and then color all subsequent interpretation. Literary criticism, which has been categorizing by genre since Aristotle, has become in the twentieth century increasingly concerned to explore gender roles. Especially since Freud and psychoanalytic criticism, gender has become an obsessive area of discussion for cultural and literary critics, although the connection between gender and genre has not always been emphasized.[12] Given early modern writers' interest in generic decorum, studies of this period have an opportunity to combine modern interest in gender studies with historically powerful generic categories.[13]

I intend to show that Sidney's *New Arcadia* consciously blurs the categories of gender in much the same way that the text has long been acknowledged to unsettle generic boundaries. The crucial emblem for unstable gender distinctions is the cross-dressing of Pyrocles, Prince of Macedon. Through Pyrocles/Zelmane's clothes, Sidney investigates the power, instability, and plasticity of gender categories. Gender—particularly femininity, but also, as I shall show, masculinity—appears something that can be created by placing a well-chosen costume in a particular narrative context. Sidney's concern with the details of the Zelmane costume is part of his critical investigation of the social codes of his sumptuary culture. His portrait reveals how the mixed motives of human actors strain against rigid categories of sexual expression. Zelmane's imaginative bisexuality does not create a neutral or utopic space beyond gender, but rather exposes the instability of erotic desire and gender construction. Sidney's heterodox hero/heroine and his hybrid text stop short of bringing his critiques of genre and gender to their explosive conclusions. Considering his treatment of the semiotics of clothing, however, connects the initial crisis in pastoral Arcadia to the violent struggles of Amphialus's rebellion. In each case, a certain kind of female clothing provokes both desire and violence.

Sidney's experiments in genre have been well documented.[14] Consideration of his treatment of gender, however, oscillates between historicist readings of Sidney as a spokesman for the masculinist pieties of his humanist teachers, and more sentimental portraits of him as a feminist *avant la lettre*.[15] I propose to examine Sidney's treatment of gender not through his idealized heroines, but through the cross-dressed Pyrocles. In the nearly immature Pyrocles, I believe, Sidney explores most deeply the relationship between masculine and feminine qualities. I shall begin by examining how critics have reacted to Pyrocles's costume, and then I shall suggest a new way to understand the cross-dressing, informed by modern understandings of the sexual semiotics of clothing. I shall then examine two moments in the *New Arcadia* during which the Zelmane costume affects the text: the moment in which Pyrocles appears to Musidorus dressed as an Amazon, and the final scene of the revision, in which Zelmane defends herself and the Arcadian princesses from Anaxius and his two brothers. These moments isolate the act of cross-dressing and the consequences of gender hybridism in Sidney's text.

PROVOCATION IN ARCADIA

The shock of seeing Pyrocles abandon armor for a dress early in the *New Arcadia* provokes a famous debate with his cousin Musidorus. Commenting on this scene has given rise to a continuing controversy in Sidney criticism, with critics taking the side of one or the other prince. Mark Rose epitomizes the once-standard reading that supports Musidorus against Pyrocles. He writes, "Sidney, I believe, intended his audience to find Pyrocles's disguise offensive."[16] Rose's reading relies on a normative understanding of sexuality in which the two genders are easily distinguished and completely separate. (Freud's maxim reminds us that on some level we expect gender to be this clear-cut.) The work of feminist criticism, especially since the 1970s, has significantly increased attention to moments of tension within the order of gender. Rose's position does, however, find some support in the humanist ideals that Sidney was taught. His education, as Richard Helgerson has noted, valued the public over the private, the male over the female, and reason over passion.[17] What remains unclear, however, is the extent to which Sidney—writing in the "prodigal" form of romance—accepted these humanist ideals uncritically.

The opposite camp's position is stated most directly by John Danby: "[Sidney] would seem to be insisting that man is capable of a synthesis of qualities that includes the womanly yet avoids the hermaphroditic."[18] Here Pyrocles/Zelmane embodies bi-gendered perfection. Some version of Danby's point of view typifies many recent reconsiderations of this scene, especially those influenced by feminist scholarship. Mary Ellen Lamb, for example, sees the cross-dressing as signifying "an inner change" in Pyrocles.[19] David Cressy shifts the emphasis slightly by arguing that cross-dressing per se was not "so transgressive."[20] Casey Charles sees the costume as part of the creation of "a new masculine social identity" within "the male lover who accepts himself as a sexual subject."[21] For all these critics, and for Rose as well, Pyrocles's costume epitomizes his unstable social status. Changing the clothes has changed the man.

The debate between the Rose and Danby camps centers on the emotional or psychological function of the Zelmane disguise. In Sidney's text, the debate between Pyrocles and Musidorus prefigures this critical controversy. Musidorus argues for reason, male clothing, and Rose; Pyrocles counters in favor of love, cross-dressing, and Danby. Most recent critics, especially feminists, hew to the Pyrocles/Danby side, although attention to Sidney's understanding of sexuality and the relationship between the princes has nuanced Danby's celebration.[22] Sidney's text does not conclude this debate so much as break it off, and critical readings of the work must grapple with his apparent sympathy with both Pyrocles and Musidorus.

I shall explore the consequences of Zelmane's cross-dressing by starting not with psychology but with the practical question of narrative function. What does her costume *do* in the *Arcadia*? What happens in Sidney's text that would not have happened had our hero not donned women's clothing? Since prose romance is a plot-centered genre, it is valuable to begin analyzing Zelmane's cross-dressing by considering how it changes the plot of the *New Arcadia*. Somewhat surprisingly, the costume matters quite a lot in Sidney's narrative, and not simply as a symbol of either Pyrocles's immaturity or his bi-gendered insight. Rather, the costume sets the main plot in motion. Basilius's retreat to the countryside may be initiated by his misreading of the Delphic oracle, but Zelmane keeps him waiting and hoping in pastoral Arcadia.

Above all, Zelmane's clothes provoke. They provoke incontinent desire in Basilius, and later Zoilus, a tortured surrender to passion in Gynecia, and a slightly more controlled passion in Philoclea. They further provoke Musidorus (and readers like Rose) to despair of the prince's reason. To understand how the Zelmane costume operates, and what its consequences are for Sidney's understanding of gender roles, I will employ the term "sexy dressing" in the sense that the critical legal theorist Duncan Kennedy has defined it. Kennedy's exploration of the links between female clothing and violence in modern America can also be used to describe the function of the Zelmane costume. Kennedy explains "sexy dressing" as a "provocative" or "exhibitionist" set of clothes that "has the two meanings of 'sex' and 'deviance.' "[23] When Musidorus first sees Zelmane, he reacts to exactly these two meanings of the costume: he fears her "womanish habit" because of its overt sexuality, and also because of the deviance that will arise as Pyrocles "frame[s] [his] behaviour" to these clothes (p. 133). "Sexiness," in Kennedy's specialized sense, unsettles Pyrocles's status as the hero of an up-to-then conventional prose romance.

Kennedy's theory of "sexy dressing" argues that clothing can become provocative speech by "implicitly affirm[ing] the ideas coded into it" (p. 186).[24] Kennedy continues, "Sexy dress is sexy *only* in terms of the dress codes that regulate virtually all social space. These codes pervasively regulate the degree of sexiness permitted in each setting" (p. 163). He goes on to enumerate how clothing norms change in different settings, so that a bikini is more sexy in the bedroom than on the beach but fully transgressive in an office (p. 163). According to Kennedy's analysis, clothing serves as a temporary generic marker; certain kinds of clothes imply certain narrative situations: "a costume or a particular item of dress produces its effect by making an allusion, or reference, that evokes a character in a narrative that is known to the audience" (p. 189). Draping female clothes on a male body unsettles Zelmane's narrative and generic contexts. Her clothes transgress doubly, since they evoke bedroom and battlefield stories simultaneously. These clothes, as much as Basilius's retreat, create crisis in Arcadia: they provoke King, Queen, and princess away from responsibility and self-control.[25]

Kennedy investigates sexy dressing to reveal how women's clothes distort the enforcement of sexual harassment and assault laws in modern America. His notion that provocative dress challenges rigid systems of interpretation, however, also applies to Sidney's text. Dismissed from court by his intransigent Queen, Sidney produced a text that explores conventions of gender and genre. Kennedy argues that sexy dressing in one view provokes abuse, but it can also be deployed by individuals as a defense against an abusive culture. He speculates that transgressive dressing might help create a "sexually autonomous woman" (p. 203) and contribute to the "utterly Utopian idea" of complete symmetry between the sexes (p. 208). He also laments the continuing connection between sexy dress and eroticized violence (pp. 127, 131). Kennedy's utopian gender symmetry, his critique of erotic violence, and his location of "pleasure/resistance" (p. 128) within sexy dressing are all relevant to Zelmane. Sidney's cross-dressed prince embodies a feminized masculinity, and the transgressive costume exposes both the "pleasure" of fuller sexual knowledge and some "resistance" to masculinist sexual hierarchy. Lamb's suggestion of "deep sexuality and even . . . effeminacy . . . at the core of Sir Philip Sidney's *Arcadia*" seems apposite here, although the provocation of the Zelmane costume might imply an aggressive, rather than passive, attempt at what Lamb calls "revaluing the feminine."[26]

Zelmane as sexy dresser contributes to the disruption of the generic expectations raised by pastoral Arcadia. She also, in the final scenes of the revision, challenges the place of martial valor in Sidney's heroic ideal. Her hybrid male–female heroism is neither the humanist ideal of Danby, for whom the decision to dress as an Amazon seems straightforwardly positive, nor Kennedy's hopeful egalitarianism, but rather a heroism on the far side of provocation and despair.[27] The ghostly image of the original Zelmane, a young woman who died for love of Pyrocles, hovers behind the costume to recall the cost of erotic attachment in Arcadia. Zelmane unsettles herself and the kingdom, creating chaos in Arcadia. As I shall show, the broken sentence of the revision's end can serve as a metaphor for the price, for author and character, of her experiment in costume.

"Nature Simply or Nature Helped by Cunning": Zelmane in Arcadia

Zelmane's appearance to Musidorus begins Sidney's use of the pronoun "she" to describe this character. The pronoun accents and repeats the provocation of the costume: each time Sidney uses the word "she" for a character we know is a "he," the frisson of blurred genders increases.[28] The two princes have been separated by shipwreck, and Musidorus finally discovers Zelmane in a "little wood" (130) after scouring Arcadia for the lost Pyrocles. Zelmane is thus the object of a semierotic quest before she is known to be (newly) feminine. Chance and a tired horse[29] lead Musidorus to a lady who banishes all thought of sleep: "It was . . . a lady who, because she walked with her side toward him, he could not perfectly see her face, but so much he might see of her that was a surety for the rest that all was excellent" (p. 130). This sentence previews the description that follows: Zelmane is partly hidden and not easy to see, but her visible parts incite desire for what is covered.

The motif of partial covering, of sexy dressing that reveals and conceals, dominates the description of Zelmane. A creature of paradox, she shows and hides, exposes and covers, and finding her in a wooded glen is itself an act of dis-covering:

> Well might [Musidorus] perceive the hanging of her hair in fairest quantity in locks, some curled and some as it were forgotten, with such a careless care and an art so hiding art that she seemed she would lay them for a pattern whether nature simply or nature helped by cunning be the more excellent: the rest whereof was drawn into a coronet of gold richly set with pearl, and so joined all over with gold wires and covered with feathers of divers colours that it was not unlike to an helmet, such a glittering show it bare, and so bravely it was held up from the head. Upon her body she ware a doublet of sky-colour satin, covered with plates of gold and, as it were, nailed with precious stones that in it she might seem armed. The nether part of her garment was so full of stuff and cut after such a fashion, that though the length of it reached to the ankles, yet in her going one might sometimes discern the small of her leg, which with the foot was dressed in a short pair of crimson velvet buskins, in some places open, as the ancient manner was, to show the fairness of the skin. (pp. 130–31)

The play between what is revealed, by carelessness or subtle art, and what is covered, by hair or helmet, coronet or armor, announces the arrival of

Zelmane as a provocative object. She mixes martial gear and soft, feminine garments, as the description shifts from curls to helmets, from doublets to armor, and finally to the small of her leg. The narrator's eye travels the length of Zelmane's body from head to toe and concludes by lingering on the "fairness of . . . skin" of her exposed foot. Even the Arcadian princesses, who have so far appeared only in paintings, would be hard-pressed to beat this entrance.

When Zelmane describes Philoclea a few pages later, she revives the narrator's descriptive style: "[Philoclea's] body (O sweet body!) covered with a light taffeta garment, so cut as the wrought smock came through it in many places, enough to have made your restrained imagination have thought what was under it" (p. 146). It appears that dressing in women's clothes has given Zelmane insight into how those clothes create sexiness. In fact, to the extent that Philoclea reminds the reader (and Musidorus) of Zelmane, it may be that feminine beauty is always cross-gendered in this text. The teasing eroticism of Sidney reading the early version of his text aloud to a roomful of "fair ladies" at Wilton highlights the provocation.

Musidorus sees Zelmane first, but the first attempt to interpret her is not his rational masculinist disgust, but rather Pyrocles's own choice of emblem. The device Pyrocles chooses expresses ambivalence and hope: "a Hercules? . . . with a distaff in his hand, as he once was by Omphale's commandment, with a word in Greek but thus to be interpreted, 'Never more valiant' " (p. 131). This motto splits critical response into its predictable camps; Rose insists that the Renaissance despised the distaff-spinning Hercules, while the Danby camp praises Pyrocles for showing himself never more valiant than when serving love.[30] Sidney had already written about the emblem, in his *Defence of Poesy* (ca. 1580), where he noted that the image "breedeth both delight and laughter: for the representing of so strange a power in love procureth delight, and the scornfulness of the action stirreth laughter."[31] This scornful laughter and delight, however, are not as simple as the "offensive[ness]" Rose imagines that the disguise will produce.

I suggest, reasonably, that Sidney intends the emblem to be ambiguous and provocative. Delight and scorn work together ironically, and the emblem's conscious irony reveals both vulnerability and instability. Zelmane, like Sidney, knows very well the dangers of her provocative disguise. Sidney suggests that Pyrocles can be admired for assuming the distaff, but that is not to say (with Danby) that he must be admired unconditionally. Scorn remains the risk of cross-dressing, and the laughter that the disguise creates is hard to interpret. The motto and costume remain mixed.

Sidney concludes Zelmane's description by turning to the sword on her thigh. This last glimpse of her body brings to a climax the intermingling of erotic and martial subtexts. The image unsettles Sidney's narrator, who cannot decide whether sword or thigh is more dangerous: "[O]n her thigh she ware a sword which, as it witnessed her to be an Amazon . . . so it seemed but a needless weapon, since her other forces were without withstanding" (p. 131). Zelmane unsettles the common metaphoric system in which love becomes a battlefield, as she is literally at home in both love and war. She wields sword and thigh, battlefield and bedroom, and this radical juxtaposition unsettles as it attracts.

As this sexy character strides through Basilius's kingdom, nearly all the people who see her are provoked to uncontrollable desire. Even Musidorus succumbs to her charms. Her transgressive costume inflames him before he recognizes his old friend. When he finally recognizes her as Pyrocles, Musidorus appears "as Apollo is painted when he saw Daphne suddenly turn into a laurel" (p. 132). The analogy seems clear; like Apollo, Musidorus is frozen exactly as he loses what he desires. This scene, notably, produces less delight and laughter than an eroticized pathos. Musidorus loses both a convenient shield for homosocial/sexual eros, and also a potential female object of desire. Casey Charles notes that Sidney's delicate touch allows "the unmentionable monstrosity of homosexual behavior...into discourse,"[32] but Sidney's blurring of genders puts both hetero- and homosexual feelings on display.

After Musidorus, the list of Zelmane's conquests comprises nearly everyone in the Arcadian royal family. With the constant provocation of her clothes and her body, she seduces Basilius, Gynecia, and Philoclea. Each of the three reads the relationship of clothing to body differently, and thus each succumbs to different charms. Basilius reads the clothing naively, accepts her as a woman, and offers his "doting love" (p. 149). Gynecia pierces the disguise but finds the male beauty irresistible; she inverts Basilius's understanding of the body–clothing relation and desires the Hercules beneath the dress. Philoclea, less worldly than her mother but shrewder than her father, does not attempt to resolve Zelmane's gender ambiguity, but rather accepts the costume and the feelings it provokes: "Away then all vain examinations of why and how. Thou lovest me, excellent Zelmane, and I love thee" (p. 244). These varied passions testify to Zelmane's provocative range, inciting desire in foolish old men, shrewd middle-aged women, and innocent young girls.

"This weak sex": Zelmane in Captivity

In the so-called Captivity Episode, which makes up the last part of Book 3 that Sidney revised, Zelmane and the two princesses are imprisoned by Amphialus and Cecropia. In this interior space, far from the pastoral fields of Arcadia, the logic of Zelmane's costume plays itself out. The prison gives Zelmane no space in which to act out the chivalric exploits that Amphialus and Musidorus undertake outside the castle. The episode presents a crisis of male virtue, in which typical heroic actions appear worthless. In this uncertain new space, new tactics must be discovered. It is here that Zelmane's disguise becomes useful and even heroic.

The capture of Zelmane and the princesses by Cecropia begins with another kind of sexy dressing. The pastoral maidens who entice them toward Cecropia's brigands wear clothes that recall Zelmane's, but leave less to the imagination: a "livery of scarlet petticoats...were tucked up almost to their knees... [leaving] their legs naked" (p. 441). Their upper garments also reveal "their breasts liberal to the eye" (p. 441). These clothes invert Zelmane's coy half-coverings, and remind the reader that not all feminine costumes are as finely constructed as Zelmane's.

Failing to understand the deceitful subtext of this display, Zelmane and the princesses are seduced by these clothes as Zelmane's clothes have seduced others. Zelmane's dazzling wardrobe has cut a swath through Arcadia, but now she gets hoist by her own sexy petard. Captured, she loses her sword (p. 443), and with it the martial half of her Amazon costume. Her doublet still looks like armor, but she has become all thigh and no sword. From this fully feminized position, Zelmane must reconstruct her hybrid gender and its potency.

Zelmane's final combat with Anaxius and his brothers is a key moment for cross-dressing in Sidney's text. It expands and, to some extent, concludes the inquiry into gender construction that began when Zelmane is first described. Zelmane's hypermasculine antagonists lust after their prisoners, so Zelmane opposes them not as a rival knight but as an assailed woman. Sexy dress now provokes violence as well as desire, creating in the brothers an "evil consort of love and force" (p. 588). Zelmane, implicitly defending the consort of love and force that her costume has represented, seduces them with her now-swordless costume.

At first Zelmane's sexiness forces Anaxius to listen to her, because "the excellency of her beauty and grace made him a little content to hear" (p. 582). She speaks, and he stares: "sometimes with bent brows looking upon the one side of her, sometimes of the other" (p. 582). Like Musidorus in the wood, Anaxius is transfixed by Zelmane's mixture of eroticism and force. Simply being stared at, however, does not give Zelmane any advantage.

Working within her generic and gendered confines, she attempts to defeat the brothers by using the tactics of both a pursued heroine and a chivalric hero. First, attempting to be a knight, she challenges Anaxius to "choose thee what arms thou likest" (p. 582). From a prisoner and a woman, the challenge brings a smile to Anaxius's face, all the more readily since his love for Pamela has begun to mellow his rage. Searching for a way back to anger and combat, Zelmane conjures by her male name, Pyrocles, whom Anaxius hates.[33] Like the disguised heroines of comic drama, Zelmane plays on her hidden identity: "I tell thee, no creature can be nearer of kin to [Pyrocles] than myself: and so well we love, that he would not be sorrier for his own death than for mine" (p. 583). This witticism, however, fails to bring Anaxius to combat.

Zelmane then turns to a "feminine" ruse, pretending to agree to an unwanted marriage proposal in order to buy time. Pamela refuses to go along, arguing that even this minor deception is "flatter[ing] adversity" (p. 584). She appears to see Zelmane's machinations as unwelcome distractions from her quest for martyrdom. Pamela continues, "Hope is the fawning traitor of the mind, while under colour of friendship it robs it of his chief force of resolution" (p. 585). Zelmane cannot argue against her resolve, so she reminds her that blind faith is not a practical tactic for mere mortals. She convinces Pamela to play along with her ruse by hoping for a last-minute reversal. "While that [time] may bring forth any good," Zelmane argues, "do not bar yourself thereof" (p. 585). Philoclea agrees with this plan easily, but convincing Pamela marks a clear victory for Zelmane.

The ruse gains a trip to the Delphic oracle, which appears for the moment to postpone the crisis. Unlike the tale's first oracle, however, the new oracle is not mysterious. It bluntly refuses to endorse the marriages, and this refusal drives Anaxius back to violence (pp. 586–88).[34] Even the journey to and from Delphi does not create much delay, as it occupies only two pages of text. Feminine tactics of delay, apparently, can do no more than a purely masculine direct challenge.

Having exhausted male and female tactics separately, Zelmane combines them in the final pages of the revision. Now that her costume is all thigh and no sword, Zelmane notably is not the most attractive woman in captivity; the elder brothers pursue Pamela and Philoclea, while youthful Zoilus lusts after Zelmane. Pursued by him, she plays the part of the coy Amazon who must engage her spouse in ritual combat before marriage. She emphasizes that this combat will be a formality, saying, "Therefore, before I make mine own desire serviceable to yours, you must vouchsafe to lend me armour and weapons, that at least with a blow or two of the sword I may not find myself perjured to myself" (p. 589). The word "perjured" highlights a complex game of identities: a man dressed as a woman asks for male gear in order to pretend to effect a womanly submission to male desire. Zelmane's request, notably, is for the rest of her disguise. She wants to complete her Amazon garb by rearming herself, and she emphasizes the sword's place in an eroticized costume. Inflamed by her sexuality, Zoilus loses control and assaults her, so that "she should quickly know what a man of arms he was" (p. 588). This phrase demonizes Zoilus as one who believes rape to be the ultimate expression of masculinity, but it also uncomfortably echoes Zelmane's earlier defense of female clothing: "there is nothing I desire more than fully to prove myself a man in this enterprise" (p. 136). Proof of masculinity appears in the loss of control created by feminine clothes.

In embracing Zelmane, however, Zoilus plays into her hands. The physical contact crosses the boundaries of the disguise, and he ends up wrestling with a better warrior than himself. Having seduced him into her embrace, Zelmane emerges from it with Zoilus's sword in her hands. Her thigh has gotten her a new sword. Now fully dressed as an Amazon, she can play a martial part again. From this point until the revision ends, Zelmane the Amazon returns to her double role as the dominant hero/heroine.

Zelmane's warrior role will be significantly altered by her status as pursued woman. Her ensuing martial exploits are undercut by her unchivalric slaughter of the two younger brothers. She exerts power in and through female clothes, but when she takes up the sword she nearly debases her masculine identity. Sidney's narrator mirrors her potential slip back into masculinity by calling her "Pyrocles" four times (pp. 593–94) before returning to

"Zelmane" on the final pages. In her first re-masculinized action, she attacks Zoilus, who flees back to his brothers. Zelmane kills him "even as he came to throw himself into their arms for succour" (p. 590). Even more than Amphialus's slaughter of Argalus and Parthenia, this killing does not seem a chivalric act.

Lycurgus, Zelmane's next opponent, falls before her in unequal combat. She steals his sword in addition to Zoilus's, and thus doubly masculinized—"two swords against one shield" (p. 591)—she drives him to his knees. His plea for mercy starts to work on her "repressed" (p. 591) emotions, but Lycurgus gets betrayed by an article of clothing. Here the darker half of Kennedy's theory applies, and eroticized clothes activate male violence. Zelmane notices on Lycurgus's arm "a garter with a jewel which... [Zelmane] had [previously] presented to Philoclea" (p. 592). This garter, ripped off Philoclea's arm, acts as a "cypher" (p. 592) for Zelmane's jealousy and rage. It incites her to deny mercy and butcher the kneeling Lycurgus. Once again, the juxtaposition of a male body and intimate female clothing—this time Lycurgus's arm and Philoclea's garter—provokes a loss of self-control.

The final combat—in a sense the "end" of the revised text—matches the heroic Anaxius against Pyrocles/Zelmane, who now wears both sexual identities at once. In a crucial moment of generic self-consciousness, Sidney links Anaxius to Achilles. Anaxius wields "a huge shield, such, perchance, as Achilles showed to the pale walls of Troy" (p. 594). Anaxius, previously described as a knight without courtesy,[35] is the last opponent for Zelmane as cross-dressing tactician. At first the pair's martial prowess links them via the chivalric trope of brothers in arms: "So that they both, prepared in hearts and able in hands, did honour solitariness there with such a combat as might have demanded, as a right of fortune, whole armies of beholders" (p. 593). The word "fortune" intrudes on this image to remind the reader that the *New Arcadia* is not an epic but a romance, dedicated not to martial combat but to the indirect ways of fortune.

The status of fortune in the final combat recalls the generic hybridity of the *New Arcadia*. Anaxius appears to be a character out of Homer's *Iliad*—Ajax if not Achilles—but Sidney's primary classical model is not Homer but Heliodorus, and not epic but romance.[36] In this episode, Sidney downplays the place of martial exploits in the heroic ideal, as Heliodorus does throughout the *Aethiopian History*.[37] Unlike his classical exemplar, however, Sidney manages to de-emphasize martial valor in the midst of a bloody swordfight.

The link between the two combatants continues in an extended simile that brings the battle under the sign of romance:

> But like two contrary tides, either of which are able to carry worlds of ships and men upon them with such swiftness as nothing seems able to withstand them, yet meeting one another, with mingling their watery forces and struggling together, it is long to say whether stream gets the victory; so between these, if Pallas had been there, she could scarcely have told whether she had nursed better in the feats of arms. The Irish greyhound against the English mastiff; the

> sword-fish against the whale; the rhinoceros against the elephant, might be models, and but models, of this combat. (p. 593)

This simile moves Sidney's text from the epic *Iliad* to the romance of the *New Arcadia*. Even Pallas, goddess of war and patron of Odysseus, cannot interpret the scene. The "contrary tides" move the warriors from the battlefield to the sea, where what looks like chaos recedes to reveal a Providential plan. The models suggested for the two combatants, greyhounds and mastiffs, sword-fish and whales, rhinoceros and elephants, remain "but models" because the sea itself is the dominant metaphor. In generic terms, the tides represent epic (Anaxius) and romance (Zelmane), and in the presumed triumph of Zelmane, romance may indeed defeat epic. The combat, moreover, parodies the heroic ideal since Zelmane has neither armor nor shield. The tides snatch final agency away from the two heroes and place it where it belongs, above them, in divine hands.

The final exchange reveals that mere force of arms cannot win the day. For the epic hero Anaxius, this realization comes as a shock. Raging against his fate, Anaxius despises the gods who will not let him overcome a woman: " 'I think,' said he, 'what a spiteful god it should be who, envying my glory, hath brought me to such a wayward case' " (p. 594). This reference to supernatural control allows Zelmane to demonstrate her superior knowledge of her gender and her genre. She replies that the gods who have devised this fate for Anaxius are just: " 'Thou dost well indeed,' said Zelmane, 'to impute thy case to the heavenly providence, which will have thy pride find itself, even in that whereof thou art most proud, punished by the weak sex which thou most contemnest' " (p. 594). The distinction between Anaxius's "spiteful god" and Zelmane's "heavenly providence" could not be clearer. Zelmane revels in her identity as "this weak sex." Her speech, the last speech in the revision, shows Zelmane in the midst of a heroic battle recalling her feminine nature. She has inverted her own emblem, so that the spinning Hercules now fights as well. Although Pyrocles presumably would have shed his Amazonian mask had Sidney lived to complete the revision, at this crucial juncture he wields both identities together.

A few lines later, the revision breaks off in mid-sentence. We cannot know how Sidney intended to conclude Book 3, but the combat in progress when the rupture occurs merits special scrutiny. I suggest that Sidney broke the text here so as not to upstage a moment that is both Zelmane's triumph and her fall, her acceptance of a mutually intertwined male and female nature. Her combination of seduction and warfare, of being both an object of lust (from Zoilus) and herself incited to excessive desire (by Philoclea's garter), personalizes the provocation of her cross-dressing. Given the new complexity of her character, a martial triumph cannot but be anticlimactic. She is violent and unsettling, neither a passive woman nor a chivalric man but an unstable mixture. She has become her costume, and Sidney has written himself into a corner. He has combined martial and erotic values, but his plot still needs each separately: Zelmane's sword to end the Captivity Episode, and her seductive dress to entice the Arcadian royal family. Sidney may have been reluctant to return separately to either arms or eroticism. In the teeth of this dilemma, I speculate, Sidney laid down his pen, and the war in Holland prevented him from taking it up again. Zelmane's sexy dress had become so central to the author's intentions that he could not bring himself to write the scenes where she would have to lay it aside.

NOTES

1. Sigmund Freud, "Femininity," *New Introductory Lectures on Psychoanalysis* (1933), *The Standard Edition of the Complete Psychological Works of Sigmund Freud*, James Strachey, ed. (London: Hogarth Press, 1964) 22:113.
2. See Katharine Duncan-Jones, *Sir Philip Sidney: Courtier-Poet* (New Haven: Yale University Press, 1991), p. xxiii.
3. An earlier edition of the *Arcadia*, published 1590, included only the revised books, and breaks off in the middle of Book 3. On the circumstances of the publication of the 1590 *Arcadia*, see my "Selling Sidney: William Ponsonby, Thomas Nashe, and the Boundaries of Elizabethan Print and Manuscript Cultures," *TEXT* 13 (2000): 124–46.
4. Sir Philip Sidney, *The Countess of Pembroke's Arcadia*, Maurice Evans, ed. (New York: Penguin, 1977), p. 59. All further citations from the *New Arcadia* are from this edition and are given in the text.
5. Many recent critics have emphasized the structurally coherent *Old Arcadia*, but in terms of literary history, the composite *New* text has priority. As C. S. Lewis writes, "it, and it alone, is the book which lived; Shakespeare's book, Charles I's book, Milton's book, Lamb's book." See C. S. Lewis, *English Literature in the Sixteenth Century* (Oxford: Clarendon Press, 1954), p. 333.
6. For probably the most influential formulation of the contingency and performativity of gender, see Judith Butler, *Gender Trouble: Feminism and the Subversion of Identity* (New York: Routledge, 1990).
7. William Shakespeare, *Hamlet, The Riverside Shakespeare*, G. Blakemore Evans and J. J. M. Tobin, eds., 2nd ed. (Boston: Houghton Mifflin, 1997).
8. See A. C. Hamilton, "Sidney's *Arcadia* as Prose Fiction: Its Relation to Its Sources," *English Literary Renaissance* 2 (1972): 29–60.
9. Stephen Greenblatt, "Sidney's *Arcadia* and the Mixed Mode," *Studies in Philology* 70 (1973): 269–78.
10. Greenblatt, "Sidney's *Arcadia* and the Mixed Mode," p. 271.
11. Greenblatt, "Sidney's *Arcadia* and the Mixed Mode," p. 274.
12. For a complementary analysis of both categories, see Mary Gerhart, *Genre Choices, Gender Questions* (Norman: University of Oklahoma Press, 1992).
13. On early modern writers and generic form, see, e.g., Rosalie Colie, *The Resources of Kind: Genre-Theory in the Renaissance*, Barbara K. Lewalski, ed. (Berkeley: University of California Press, 1973); and Claudio Guillén, *Literature as System: Essays Toward the Theory of Literary History* (Princeton: Princeton University Press, 1971).
14. See, e.g., Hamilton, "Sidney's *Arcadia* as Prose Fiction"; Arthur Kinney, *Humanist Poetics: Thought, Rhetoric, and Fiction in Sixteenth-Century England* (Amherst: University of Massachusetts Press, 1986); and Nancy Lindheim, *The Structures of Sidney's Arcadia* (Toronto: University of Toronto Press, 1982).

15. Katharine Duncan-Jones opens her excellent biography of Sidney by placing herself firmly in the latter camp. "In Sidney's work," she writes, "misogyny is never allowed to stand uncorrected" (*Courtier-Poet*, p. 2). While I believe this statement exaggerates somewhat, it does distinguish Sidney from many of his Elizabethan peers.
16. Mark Rose, "Sidney's Womanish Man," *Review of English Studies* n.s. 15 (1964): 354
17. See Richard Helgerson, *The Elizabethan Prodigals* (Berkeley: University of California Press, 1976).
18. John F. Danby, *Poets on Fortune's Hill: Studies in Sidney, Shakespeare, Beaumont and Fletcher* (London: Faber & Faber, 1952), p. 57.
19. Mary Ellen Lamb, "Exhibiting Class and Displaying the Body in Sidney's *Countess of Pembroke's Arcadia*," *Studies in English Literature* 37 (1997): 63.
20. David Cressy, "Gender Trouble and Cross-Dressing in Early Modern England," *Journal of British Studies* 35 (1996): 439.
21. Casey Charles, "Heroes as Lovers: Erotic Attraction between Men in Sidney's *New Arcadia*," *Criticism* 34 (1992): 479–80.
22. Winfried Schleiner and John O'Connor place the cross-dressing in the context of its source in *Amadis of Gaul*. Schleiner suggests that the trope provides both a "vehicle for discussing male homosexuality" (p. 619) and also explores the possibility of a "convergence of genders" (p. 615). See Winfried Schleiner, "Male Cross-Dressing and Transvestitism in Renaissance Romance," *Sixteenth-Century Journal* 19 (1988): 605–19; John O'Connor, *Amadis de Gaule and Its Influence on Elizabethan Literature* (New Brunswick: Rutgers University Press, 1970).
23. Duncan Kennedy, "Sexual Abuse, Sexy Dressing, and the Eroticization of Domination," *Sexy Dressing, Etc.: Essays on the Power and Politics of Cultural Identity* (Cambridge: Harvard University Press, 1993), pp. 162, 164. Further citations in the text.
24. For a broader reading of how clothes operate as symbols in art and culture, see Anne Hollander, *Seeing Through Clothes* (New York: Viking, 1978). For a reading of cross-dressing in modern culture, see Marjorie Garber, *Vested Interests: Cross-Dressing and Cultural Anxiety* (New York: Harper Collins, 1993).
25. Musidorus and Pamela comprise the only love not caused by the Zelmane costume—although Musidorus does fall in love only after he has seen Zelmane.
26. See Lamb, "Exhibiting Class," pp. 56, 68.
27. While Pyrocles does cross-dress in the *Old Arcadia* (under the name Cleophila) the *New* version's emphasis on recovering heroic values within a pastoral space places greater tension on the trope, especially on the connection between erotic desire and martial rage.
28. I follow Sidney by calling the cross-dressed hero "she" and "Zelmane" throughout.
29. The tired horse might allegorically indicate a weakness of the flesh, the very weakness Musidorus will deny in his debate with Zelmane.
30. Rose, "Sidney's Womanish Man," p. 361. Rose cites the opposing viewpoint from Samuel L. Wolff, *The Greek Romances in Elizabethan Prose Fiction* (New York: Columbia University Press, 1912), p. 338.

31. Sir Philip Sidney, "Defence of Poesy," *Sir Philip Sidney*, Katharine Duncan-Jones, ed. (Oxford: Oxford University Press, 1989), p. 245.
32. Charles, "Heroes as Lovers," p. 478.
33. Pyrocles killed Anaxius's uncle Euardes in Book 2.
34. For the second Oracle's un-Delphic tone, see Michael McCanles, "Oracular Prediction and the Fore-conceit of Sidney's *Arcadia*," *ELH* 50 (1983): 240–43.
35. When Anaxius joins Amphialus, he has no patience for his fellow knight's courtly lifestyle: "But Anaxius . . . told Amphialus that for his part he liked no music but the neighing of horses, the sound of trumpets, and the cries of yielding persons" (p. 524).
36. On the influence of Heliodorus on Sidney, see Kinney, *Humanist Poetics*; Lindheim, *The Structure of Sidney's Arcadia*; Hamilton, "Sidney's *Arcadia* as Prose Fiction"; Wolff, *Greek Romances in Elizabethan Prose Fiction*.
37. Heliodorus's hero, Theagenes, is a lineal descendent of Achilles, but the tale describes little armed combat.

Chapter 5

Prisoners of Love: Cross-Cultural and Supernatural Desires in Lady Mary Wroth's *Urania*

Sheila T. Cavanagh

Lady Mary Wroth's *The Countess of Montgomery's Urania*[1] is filled with innumerable characters who undergo countless romantic and political adventures. Dominated by episodes involving the royal offspring of the Kings of Morea, Naples, and Romania, this voluminous romance covers significant geographical and intellectual territory. In the printed text, the central characters come of age, both personally and professionally. Many of them inherit thrones and establish knightly reputations, at the same time that they become embroiled in complex romantic entanglements that conclude with a number of marriages and a host of broken hearts. The manuscript *Urania* continues to follow most of these characters, as well as many of their children, spouses, and confederates. The sequel also expands the geographical scope of the narrative and introduces characters from beyond the western regions that predominate in part one. Most notable among these newcomers is Rodomandro, the dark skinned King of Tartaria, who marries Queen Pamphilia, the central female figure in the story. In addition, the manuscript continues Wroth's examination of other exotic territories, such as the realm of the occult.

As I argue elsewhere,[2] Wroth creates a global vision in the *Urania* that demonstrates her considerable interest in both geographic and spiritual spaces. Since there are countless romantic escapades during the course of this lengthy narrative, this apparent fascination with other places often intersects with the narrative's representation of fulfilled and thwarted sexual encounters. At the same time, Wroth's text frequently pushes against the boundaries of sanctioned early modern sexual practices while its characters explore the world outside familiar territories. Wroth's narrative acknowledges a panoply of erotic desires that do not conform to conventional patterns. As a result, we now enjoy access to a significant early modern literary text that provides numerous examinations of the potential pleasures and perils emanating from sexual unions outside traditional parameters. Since even licit heterosexual couplings between Western European courtiers commonly fall prey to the complications of unrequited love, infidelity, and other barriers, the *Urania*'s readers should not be surprised to discover that still greater obstacles impede those with less conventional desires or involvements, even though the text does not tend to criticize those embroiled in such entanglements. Although Wroth's *Urania* represents a noteworthy range of sexual possibilities, it simultaneously provides its audience with cautionary portraits of these lovers' experiences.

These literary romantic warnings begin early in the printed text, when Allimarlus, the King of Romania's page, repeats a story he heard from an unnamed duke, whose passion for another man led to his impoverishment and despair (1, 34–37).[3] According to the chastened duke, he spent considerable time as the "mightiest, richest, ancientest, and sometimes happiest of these parts" (1, 34) before becoming enamoured of an unscrupulous young man. Abandoning his domestic responsibilities, the duke names his beloved as heir, which puts a tragic set of events into motion. Impatient for his inheritance, the young man contracts for the duke's death and upon believing this goal achieved, murders the hired killer, displaces the ostensible widow after seizing her assets, and takes over as ruler of the duke's estates. The sadder but wiser duke then reconciles with his wife, but makes no attempt to regain his rightful place. He also resists efforts by Parselius and Amphilanthus to rectify the situation,[4] insisting that "my affection could not so much alter it selfe as to hate where once so earnestly I affected, or seeke revenge on him, whose good I ever wished" (1, p. 36). The will of Amphilanthus prevails, however, and the deposed duke regains his rightful position after his lover is tortured until he "burst and dyed" (1, p. 37). The sorrowing ruler then receives permission to turn the dukedom over to his daughter before embracing the life of a hermit, whereby he proclaims, "those steepie woody hilles, and the Cave I rest in, shall bee all the Courts or Pallaces that these old eyes shall ever now behold" (1, p. 37). The contrite man is slated to end his days in rustic isolation, since his wife dies, apparently from happiness, when the dukedom is restored: "my wife thinking she had seen enough when I was my selfe againe, departing this life with joy and content" (1, p. 37). Even though the duke's desire itself is not derided, therefore, its inappropriateness in this context is still made clear by the woeful man's sad history.

Unlike the couplings that will be discussed below, the union that leads to this duke's downfall does not seem to involve a supernatural lover or a partner from abroad.[5] Nonetheless, it shares an important attribute with several of those other relationships in that it highlights the illicit affair's effect upon reproduction. In general, the narrative of the *Urania* seems most concerned with the consequences rather than the objects of sexual desire. In this episode, for example, the treacherous deeds of the beloved and the situation's impact upon the duke's marriage attract censure and remorse, but the sex of the two partners receives no comment from anyone involved in the incident. In all respects, the tale resembles similar stories told about adulterous heterosexual liaisons. As Josephine Roberts remarks, Wroth's nonchalance about this kind of erotic exchange is noteworthy: "In her frank treatment of homosexuality, Wroth addressed a subject that few of her contemporaries dared mention" (1, lxvii).[6] However much tribulation is caused by the duke's indiscretion, therefore, it does not seem to result from the sex of the two participants.

Although the lover's sex receives no comment in this episode, however, the most prominent result of this alliance is clearly announced: "my wives company in respect of his, was unpleasing to me. Long time this continued, which continuance made me issue-les" (1, p. 34). It is this lack of a child that prompts the duke to designate his lover as heir, thereby precipitating the ensuing disaster.[7] The transfer of power and authority to an untrustworthy lover thus appears to wreak far more havoc than the homosexual behavior, a suggestion that is furthered by the duke's account of reuniting with his wife. Despite her husband's considerable betrayal, the duke's wife apparently welcomes him back without hesitation, as the errant husband recounts: "she bought a little house in a thick and desart wood, where she was not long before I came unto her, discovering my selfe to both our equall passions of joy and sorrow. Privatly we there continued many years" (1, p. 36). This brief rendition of the couple's reconciliation intimates that the abandoned woman harbors no ill-will or resentment for her treatment, particularly since she resumes sexual relations with her spouse and finally produces the child she was denied earlier. As the duke announces: "God in our poverty giving us an unexpected blessing, which was a daughter" (1, p. 36).[8] Eventually, as noted, the daughter inherits, the wife and lover both die, and the remorseful duke commits himself to a hermit's calling. Since the wife is said to depart "this life with joy and content" (1, p. 37), the tale ends with the evildoer punished, the innocent rewarded, and the perpetrator choosing perpetual penance. In short, order has been restored and no further consideration of the situation is needed, since female rulers do not generally cause distress in the narrative. The reader, moreover, can easily imagine a different situation in the romance where partners of the same sex would live as happily as any of the couples do in the *Urania*.

This emphasis upon the personal qualities of one's lover and the relationship's impact upon inheritance accords with the views typically presented in the *Urania*. Extramarital desires provoke minimal condemnation in this narrative, with the consequences rather than the fact of sexual longings again receiving the most attention.[9] Desires, whether or not they can be fulfilled lawfully, tend to receive a sympathetic narratorial reception unless they interfere with civic or familial responsibilities.[10] Since the text tends to be pessimistic about the possibility of happily fulfilled desires, these unions often fail, but they still provide varied imaginings about the diversity to be found within the worlds of love and lust. Primary among these conceptualizations is Wroth's representation of the relationship and marriage between Pamphilia and Rodomandro, which is depicted at length in the manuscript *Urania*. Pamphilia's thwarted desire for Amphilanthus fills much of the complete romance, although there is never any reason given for the couple's failure to wed permanently. The mystery behind Pamphilia's unsatisfied yearning for Amphilanthus is deepened, moreover, by the queen's wedding to the King of Tartaria, whose appearance in the text prompts fearful suspicions in the unfaithful emperor, and whose ethnic background broadens the erotic domain of the romance for several of the characters.[11]

Rodomandro enters the narrative after Pamphilia and Amphilanthus have been involved in a frustrating romance for hundreds of pages. Although the couple continually profess love for each other, they never get married permanently, possibly because their relationship is punctuated by Amphilanthus's consistent infidelity. Although all of their closest friends have settled down and begun families by the end of the printed *Urania*, these prominent characters continue to engage in an erratic, emotionally painful courtship. At the point that Rodomandro appears, there is no indication that Pamphilia and Amphilanthus will ever break out of the destructive pattern they have established for their relationship.

Everything changes, however, when the attractive King of Tartaria seeks refuge from a shipwreck at the court of the Morean king. Everyone except Amphilanthus is delighted to greet the newcomer and welcomes him with open arms (2, pp. 42–43). The emperor, however, immediately conceives an overwhelming jealousy, "fearing his coming had binn to bee his rival" (2, p. 44). As a preemptive strike against this intruder into his romantic domain, Amphilanthus promptly "marries" Pamphilia,[12] setting aside whatever reasons have kept him from taking this step previously. Although this union does not prevent either partner from subsequently marrying other people, it calms the emperor's immediate fears and he soon develops a close friendship with the shipwrecked visitor.

Rodomandro's inclusion into the intimate spheres of these royal families facilitates the narrative's exploration of desire across ethnic divides. Tartaria during this period covered an enormous territory that stretched across Asia and included parts of China and India;[13] thus, Rodomandro's position as "The Great Cham" establishes him as holding the eastern equivalent of Amphilanthus's political position. As King of Tartaria, Rodomandro represents most of Asia in his subsequent courtship of Pamphilia.[14] Territorial expansion is only rarely mentioned as a motive for romantic entanglements;[15] nevertheless, marriage to Rodomandro offers Pamphilia the opportunity to increase the geographical sphere of her influence greatly.

Although Pamphilia takes seriously her expanded responsibilities after this marriage, and refers to "Asia, which is my husbands country and mine" (2, p. 378), she gives no indication that the prospect of becoming Queen of Tartaria attracts her. In fact, she professes reluctance to wed even up to the moment of her vows (2, p. 276), and later expresses dissatisfaction and frustration with her spouse as often as she demonstrates affection toward him.[16] Despite this vexed portrait of their courtship and marriage, however, the lengthy and lawful union between Pamphilia and Rodomandro offers an unusual early modern representation of a sanctioned, even lauded, interracial sexual partnership that eventually helps promulgate similar erotically charged encounters between other characters. However perplexing this marital coupling often appears to be, therefore, it holds a prominent place within the *Urania*'s speculations about unconventional erotic possibilities.

This union between Pamphilia and Rodomandro offers an especially intriguing portrait of intercultural relationships because the narrative's conceptualization of Tartaria runs counter to standard ancient and early modern descriptions of this land and its inhabitants. As Robert Cawley demonstrates, derogatory accounts of Tartarian appearance, behavior, and heathenism recur in early modern literature, including references in plays by writers such as Shakespeare, Dekker, Marlowe, Fletcher, and Massinger (pp. 188–207).[17] Such portraits correspond with most written accounts offered about Tartarians for hundreds of years; thus, Wroth would have been cognizant of her marked deviation from these conventions, when she presents Rodomandro as a brave and praiseworthy man: "This brave Prince, entering the roome of Presence, came with soe brave a countenance and yett soe sivile a demeanor as made all eyes subject to his sweetnes" (2, p. 42). This emphasis upon Rodomandro's graciousness and bravery is further underscored by the company's response to him. The King of Morea, for instance, urges the Tartarian to "freely make your owne wellcome by commaunding mee as your humble servant" (2, p. 43). Despite Amphilanthus's concerns over Rodomandro's romantic agenda, therefore, the foreign king is welcomed with joy by the Moreans, with no mention made of the purported ancient enmity between the two countries (2, p. 73).

The disparity between common understandings of Tartaria and Wroth's reconfiguration of these representations is also marked by her consistent labeling of this important character as "The Great Cham."[18] This historically accurate title denotes the king's place in a non-Christian lineage stretching from Ghengis Khan through Kublai Khan. In addition, many contemporary writers, such as Peter Heylyn, assert that the Great Cham was designated by his followers as the "sonne of the immortal God" (sig. Xx2).[19] While Wroth goes to great lengths to establish Rodomandro's acceptable religious convictions, her use of this title would make it difficult for her original readers to miss his barbaric origins. This labeling also keeps his conflicted background prominent during the often confusing episodes that perplex many current readers.

Not surprisingly, therefore, responses to the marriage between Rodomandro and Pamphilia vary. For instance, while there is certainly much evidence to support Kim Hall's assertion that "Rodomandro's status as Pamphilia's husband/lover is always contingent, always qualified by Pamphilia's and the reader's knowledge that Amphilanthus is her destined mate" (p. 206),[20] none of the characters in the narrative ever question this union. In fact, the King of

Morea offers approval of the couple's presumptive engagement even before Rodomandro has had an opportunity to propose (2, p. 260). Even though Pamphilia demonstrates considerable hesitation up to the moment of the ceremony (2, pp. 274–76), therefore, her willing participation in the nuptials and the enthusiastic endorsement of her family and friends suggest that Rodomandro's exotic origins do not disqualify him from participation in the erotic schema of the romance. While Pamphilia herself continues to yearn for Amphilanthus and exchanges some passionate kisses with him after they both are wed to other people (2, p. 283), Rodomandro still becomes enmeshed in the tightly knit relationships that lie at the core of the narrative's concerns and his adventures remain central to the action. Despite Pamphilia's ambivalence, therefore, Rodomandro quickly becomes a key player in what Gary Waller terms "the family romance" of the *Urania*.[21]

As suggested, Rodomandro's entry into the family introduces a number of important issues regarding unions between those of different ethnic backgrounds. The narrative's insistence upon Rodomandro's Christianity, for instance, implies that however acceptable a black man might be within this community, marrying Pamphilia off to a Tartarian infidel would be unimaginable. References to the king's Christianity abound, therefore, correcting any readers who might assume that "The Great Cham" in this tale upholds his historical counterpart's religious affiliation. Thus, he is made general of the Christian forces protecting Pamphilia, for instance (2, pp. 115, 117). At the same time, however, as Hall notes (p. 208), the son Pamphilia bears dies unnamed and in infancy, indicating that the Pamphilian queen will not participate in the continuation of the Tartarian lineage.[22]

Once again, therefore, the issue of progeny inserts itself into the *Urania*'s consideration of nonconventional erotic relationships. In this case, the unnamed infant fulfills at least two important functions, even though he only appears during the announcement of his death. Like the daughter of the repentant duke described earlier, this child confirms the existence of sexual relations between a hitherto estranged or emotionally distant couple. Just as the duke's daughter helps verify the reconciliation between her parents, Pamphilia's motherhood tangibly establishes that her marriage with Rodomandro has been consummated. This point is particularly important in the *Urania*, where sexual intercourse between married partners cannot be assumed. Amphilanthus, for example, resists consummating his marriage to the Princess of Slavonia until the bride's impatient parents force the issue (2, p. 323).

Verification of Pamphilia's sexual involvement with Rodomandro is also significant given the uncertainty surrounding her physical relationship with Amphilanthus. Many scholars have speculated about the parentage of the Knight of the Faire Designe, a character who plays a prominent role in the manuscript. Amphilanthus is commonly thought to be the young man's father, but this is never stated explicitly in the text.[23] The emperor's potential paternity inevitably, then, raises questions about the knight's mother, but the narrative also never provides information about her. Amphilanthus, of course, has many romantic conquests in the romance, and at least one knight in the narrative expresses surprise to discover that he has a grown son (2, p. 289). Given this sexual environment, Faire Designe could be the son of Pamphilia and Amphilanthus; he could be the offspring of Amphilanthus without the emperor's knowledge; or Wroth could be providing a red herring to tantalize her audience. In any event, although intimations of sexual activity between the renowned couple can certainly be read between the lines, particularly after their "marriage" (2, p. 45), there is no definite physical evidence that it ever occurs.

Although Pamphilia's unnamed son will never rule Tartaria, therefore, even after his death he confirms his parents' physical relationship in a way that Pamphilia's intimacy with Amphilanthus cannot be verified. Thus, however vexed the interracial marriage between Pamphilia and Rodomandro often appears to be, the brief existence of an heir solidifies the acceptability of the Tartarian king as a sexual partner for Pamphilia, even while it circumvents potential concerns about the advisability of permanent issue from such unconventional relations. Once again, therefore, Wroth's text acknowledges sexual desires outside traditional patterns, even while it represents the personal and communal difficulties that can accompany the enactment of such desires.

As previously alluded to, Rodomandro's ready acceptance into Pamphilia's circle of family and friends facilitates at least two other erotic encounters in the narrative. Although the king arrives with a group of princes from his native land, these royal companions never appear in any of the subsequent love stories. Two women claiming real or fabricated familial ties to the Tartarian king attract romantic attention from members of the *Urania*'s inner circles, however. These connections with Rodomandro suggest that this king and his family pass muster in the romantic world of this narrative in ways that other exotic natives do not.[24] Although most of Wroth's characters spend an inordinate amount of time traveling to foreign lands, only a limited range of countries seems to produce sanctioned marital or sexual partners. The pair of stories involving Rodomandro's "sisters," moreover, hint that being related to this king offers an inside track into a world that does not always readily accept unknown others. Rodomandro, therefore, may represent an exemplary exception to an unstated rule suggesting that while exotic figures may be appealing, they often remain suspect.[25]

Both ostensible sisters appear fairly early in the manuscript, although only one claims an indisputably legitimate place in the Tartarian royal family. Readers receive just a segment of this bona fide sister's story, but the song introducing her suggests that she has recently fallen in love: "Stay holy fires / Of my desire / Flame nott soe fast; / My loves but young" (2, p. 74). Further details of her amorous involvement never follow, however. Instead, she attracts the attention of Licandro, the young prince of Athens, who has recently triumphed over a malevolent giant, and in the process, obtained the freedom of many people, including this princess of Tartaria.

One of the most striking attributes of this unnamed princess becomes evident as soon as Licandro begins to describe the object of his newly discovered love. Unlike her brother, whose skin color instigates so much discussion when he arrives at the Morean court,[26] the princess clearly possesses white skin and blue eyes, as Licandro reveals in his comments on her beauty: "her cheekes of Roses damaske, her forhead, chinn, neck, and hands of purest snowe" (2, p. 76).[27] This considerable discrepancy between the physical characteristics of the two siblings receives no comment in the narrative, however, even though this woman's position as "the King of Tartarias sister and his onely one" (2, p. 76) is never questioned. Nevertheless, in all respects, the young eastern princess appears to possess the same kind of physical qualities as those displayed by the many western ladies. Additionally, her personal situation implies that she may function in part as an avatar of Pamphilia, since the princess is said to be traveling to the home of her uncle, described as "a great prince who intends to make her his hiere" (2, p. 76), a circumstance that parallels Pamphilia's own inheritance of her uncle's throne. By erasing her potentially problematic race and by aligning the young woman with Pamphilia, the narrative seems to present the Tartarian princess as a perfect romantic match for Licandro—if the reader sets aside the love she already claims for herself as expeditiously as the prince does. Since Rodomandro's skin color does not bar him from Pamphilia, his sister could presumably be considered desirable even with a dark complexion, but this possibility is never explored.

The narrative conundrum accompanying the damask cheeks of the princess is intensified as this episode continues, first by an amusing tale of cultural difference, then by the unexpected introduction of the occult into this romantic imbroglio. While Rodomandro's sister generally seems undifferentiated from the other ladies of Licandro's acquaintance and her virtue remains unquestioned, the couple's truncated romance keeps questions of racial incompatibility alive. Although the reasons for Licandro's immediate attraction toward the beautiful and gracious princess are never questioned, he is almost immediately denied the opportunity to court her. Instead, he encounters both cultural and spiritual obstacles.

Licandro receives nothing but praise in the text, being billed as "above most men discreete, and of any as of the bravest sort" (2, p. 74). Nonetheless, the knight's objectionable manners create the first site of estrangement between the young couple in a comic scene that seems to invert contemporary accounts of Tartaria's barbarousness. Apparently overcome with the princess's beauty, Licandro forgets his manners upon leaving the lady's company. Instead of a formal parting, the knight "kissed her hand, butt soe fervently as if his lips wowld have dwelt there" (2, p. 77). Reacting with horror, the princess makes her displeasure clear:

> She, never used to such moist salutes, tooke her hand away, somewhat more neere snatching then courtious taking itt, and with a fro[w]ne, able (from such a heavenlike beauty) to kill then please, turned away, which made a bashfull blush rise in the prince. (2, p. 78)

Although the princess's appalled response is not attributed directly to her cultural background, it seems plausible that Licandro's amusing gaffe affronts Tartarian sensibilities, since Rodomandro's impeccable manners are always highlighted.[28] The Athenian prince, therefore, fails to meet Tartarian expectations for civility.

Whatever the reason for Licandro's mistake, he immediately offers to correct it: "lett mee kis that hand againe. You shall see I will doe itt courtly" (2, p. 78). After a pause, the princess agrees, and "smiling to se how her corrections [were] wrought, gave him her hand to kis, which he did most cerimoniously" (2, p. 78). Although this interlude ends happily, the princess's initial hesitation is noteworthy. Apparently, Licandro's sloppy kiss not only raises concerns about his decorum, it also prompts the princess to question his background and identity more broadly: "I ame nott satisfied who you are" (2, p. 78). She is quickly assured of his "nobleness" (2, p. 78), but in the context of her dismay at Licandro's habits, this query once again suggests that her Tartarian lineage and courtesy here overshadow western attributes and appearances. As an unobtainable object of desire, the princess appears to overturn conventional western cultural evaluations. Even though Licandro's worthiness is not completely undermined, his failure to win this lady raises numerous questions about the relative value being assigned to Athenian and Tartarian royalty in this episode.

The narrative's presentation of this thwarted romance becomes even more complicated before its conclusion. Separating from his love interest after this initial misstep, Licandro still harbors hope that he will win the lady's heart. These desires cause him to spend a restless night, whereby "Hee tumbled, hee tossed up and downe every wher" (2, p. 78), and finally abandons any hope of sleep in favor of penning a "woefull" poetic tribute to the object of his affection (2, p. 79). In the meantime, his friend Ollymander is visited by a dream concerning the lovelorn prince.[29] According to Ollymander's account of this vision, fate has not reserved the Tartarian princess for the young Athenian: "This Lady is nott for you, butt as great an one is, and one you shall with just eyes acknowledg fitter for you, and from whom you shall receive parpetuall comfort" (2, p. 80). Lest Licandro doubt this second-hand visitation from the spirit world, Ollymander has received a ring that he offers to his young friend. When the prince places the jewel upon his hand, his lovesickness evaporates: "no sooner on butt all olde pasions abandoned, and he was as free as ever" (2, p. 81). Like the Sapphic leaps in the printed text that liberate numerous characters from their fruitless affections, this ring leaves Licandro ready to meet and marry his destined mate. At the same time, it provides the reader with more speculation regarding the cultural propriety of his former affections and the apparent need for divine intervention to separate Licandro from his initial romantic choice.

Some of these lingering issues result from the language accompanying Licandro's miraculous transformation. Here, even as the tale reaches its culmination, the reader is given reason to reevaluate the relationship. In noting that the princess will no longer be subject to Licandro's protestations of love, for example, the narrator remarks, "The Tartarian Princes[s] need *fear* noe more...for now hee is as cerimonious as ever, butt discreete and carefull now" (2, p. 81; emphasis added). While the use of "fear" in this context can easily accommodate an innocent reading, it also introduces hitherto unarticulated doubts about the prince's intentions, although I do not find sufficient evidence to support Jocelyn Catty's contention that Licandro intends to rape the princess (pp. 210–11).[30] It is striking, however, that after announcing Licandro's revived courtesy, the narrator proclaims that the young man has abandoned his "foulish loving" (2, p. 81). While Wroth's spelling is frequently unconventional, this dual invocation of "foolish" and "foul" is hard to ignore in this setting, particularly since it follows an unusual, if not unprecedented, mode of spiritual intervention into human romantic affairs.[31] Clearly, some unspecified agent of fate perceives the need to inhibit this potential romantic relationship. The rationale for this otherworldly involvement remains unarticulated, however, and the reader cannot easily determine whether it is Licandro or the Tartarian princess who makes this loving "foulish." The narrator shifts the scene before the prince and princess exchange their respective stories (2, p. 81) and neither character reappears, so the curtailment of their possible romance remains unexplained. Accordingly, just as Rodomandro's marriage to Pamphilia enables the expansion of this community's erotic world, but does not provide an unambiguous portrait of international or interracial conjunction, the story of Licandro and the Tartarian princess offers another vexed glimpse of love across ethnic divides. As Rodomandro's sister, the princess seems suited for an enviable place in the marital structures of the romance, but the narrative leaves her story and her fate unresolved. It is certainly possible that the issue of cross-cultural procreation plays a role in these decisions, but that aspect of their interrupted courtship remains unspoken.

Although the Tartarian princess who catches Licandro's eye is billed as being Rodomandro's "onely" sister (2, p. 76), a mysterious other "sister" appears somewhat earlier in the manuscript. While this female initially presents herself plausibly as a human member of the Tartarian royal family, it soon becomes clear that she is a spirit who has come with evil intent. Her two journeys into the lives of the *Urania*'s central families introduce several significant questions about the world portrayed in the text, including further queries about the role of ethnic differences, familial connections, and spiritual configurations in this narrative's construction of sexual desire. This mysterious figure disrupts many of the text's established expectations and provides readers with an alternative perspective on the domestic and sexual patterns presented elsewhere.

This calculating intruder appears at the beginning of the manuscript *Urania*, which opens with an extended tale of Selarinus's grief over the loss of his wife Philistella in childbirth.[32] As he travels in pursuit of comfort, the sorrowing widower encounters the seer Melissea's niece Saphalina, who is accompanied by Parselius's lost children. The lady reports that she has been sent to bring the forlorn Selarinus to the dwelling of her aunt's sister.

Reluctant to forgo courtesy, despite his private sorrow, the grieving knight joins her party. Since Melissea has provided significant solace and support to many of the main characters, Selarinus's willingness to enter the seer's care appears to signal the beginning of his recovery.

Such an optimistic interpretation of Selarinus's ensuing fate seems to be supported by Saphalina's presentation to the woeful man:

> knowing your distress and the danger your sadnes might bring you into, [Melissea] hath appointed a course more safe and fitting for you, then your dollors it may bee wowld have let you to . . . she will come, though most unusuall to leave her Island, and conduct you whether your better starrs have directed you. (2, p. 5)

Far from being comforted by the knowledge that Melissea will be joining him, however, Selarinus responds by bemoaning his current status. This further despair prompts a sharp rebuke from Saphalina, who informs him that Philistella is "displeased" (2, p. 5) at his grieving and that she much prefers heaven to "this dull lump whereon we live" (2, p. 5). Chastened by his companion's outburst, Selarinus resigns himself to her guidance: "for hee now resolving to bee directed by this Lady and her advise, settled him self ther till she showld dispose of him" (2, pp. 5–6).

Based on the previous adventures of his family and friends, Selarinus ought to be able to relax at this point. Despite losing his beloved Philistella, he has been assured that he will be taken care of and he has received word of Philistella's posthumous happiness. Up to this point, Melissea's counsel has been unassailable and no one who has accepted her assistance has been harmed. Many of the key characters risked death, for instance, when Melissea told them to jump into the sea and they did so without hesitation or ill-effect (1, pp. 230–31). Placing supreme faith in Melissea and her nieces has henceforth been a choice that no one has regretted.

Fate, however, appears not to have sent Selarinus to Melissea for protection.[33] Although the seeming glitch in the seer's support structure is never explained (or criticized), Selarinus meets the source of his eventual downfall after he entrusts himself to the care of Melissea and her family. While still adjusting to the idea that recovery from his debilitating grief might be possible, the king thinks he hears some "whispering" (2, p. 6), and the sound lures him into the company of "the rarest creature to his immagination that ever eye beeheld since Philistella died" (2, p. 6). From this point onward, his life will be different. The bedazzled king announces to the alluring woman that "my coming hether was by fortune, and soe blessed I account it" (2, p. 8), not yet realizing that fortune offers a rocky path at this point.

As noted, this adept spirit uses what appears to be a forged lineage to establish her romantic credentials. Claiming to be "daughter to the King of Tartaria" (2, p. 9),[34] she concocts an elaborate tale of her fraught marriage to the younger son of the King of Frigia. She also announces that this union produced two children who "are safe, and inchanted, wher alsoe many more are" (2, p. 9).[35] Within a few lines, therefore, the lady claims familial links with both Rodomandro and with Urania's sister-in-law Veralinda. She also places herself in the company of those numerous central characters whose children spend most of the manuscript under enchantment. In short, she offers Selarinus a tale designed to demonstrate her rightful position within the tightly knit circles that represent his primary familial and social environment.

Once again, however, the issue of the woman's "race" is bypassed, apart from the brief comment that "her face, neck, and hands [are] of the rarest and cleerest complexion" (2, p. 7).[36] Although the spirit uses Rodomandro's royal and personal stature to convince Selarinus that she is a worthy, though unknown woman, she does not make any obvious attempt to present herself in the likeness of a Tartarian, unless one surmises that she fashions herself after Rodomandro's actual fair-skinned sister. Her sexual allure, therefore, is sanctioned by her relationship with a renowned king, while her skin tone does not initially warrant mention and seems not to factor significantly into the story. The spirit's physical manifestation quickly becomes a moot point, however. Almost immediately after recounting her history, the woman urges Selarinus "to beleeve this butt a fiction" (2, p. 10): "Thus I have related my story to you. I beeseech you, onely pitty mee and forgett all this, deeming itt a dreame, unles I shall demaund your ayde" (2, p. 10). After offering the surprising information that Melissea's sister is often "deluded by us vaine spiritts heere, who delight in our selves onely in abusing mortalls" (2, p. 10), the female figure vanishes and the story quickly leaves Selarinus behind. Apart from learning that beautiful women cannot always be trusted, Selarinus escapes relatively unscathed from this encounter.

Much later in the story, when the knight next encounters the lady, the consequences are less benign, however. While the untrustworthy lady claims that the poor man's prophetic dream of their meeting represents the work of "destiny" (2, p. 304), Selarinus responsibly proclaims that the ensuing problems emanate from "his owne acte and folly" (2, p. 304).[37] After "taking resolution to adventure with her" (2, p. 304), Selarinus almost immediately forgets "all things but his love for the Lady, which increased soe Violently as hee was allmost wild for want of her sight" (2, p. 304). The knight remains enthralled for a considerable time, although his desire keeps him content for much of this period: "In this pleasing delight to him (att that time) she held him somme yeeres till she had tow children by him" (2, p. 305). Eventually, the spirit tires of Selarinus and lets him go, though "soe weake, soe tottered, soe torne, as certainly hee was nott able to have lived" (2, p. 397). Fortunately, Melissea happens—"by chance"—to find his predicament written in her books (2, p. 397) and she arranges first his rescue, then the fostering of his children (2, p. 401). Newly unencumbered, Selarinus obeys a vision from his departed wife, who urges him to join his brother Parselius, who is also widowed and perplexed. Attempting to follow these instructions, Selarinus does not vanish, but his adventures become much less suspect for the rest of the romance.

Selarinus's placement within the familial structures of the *Urania* makes this saga a particularly interesting contribution to the romance's representation of issues involving sex, ethnicity, and progeny. Unlike the fruitless couplings discussed earlier, the sexual involvement between Selarinus and the spirit produces children. Given Selarinus's genealogy, this means that the royal lines of Albania and Epirus now include two descendants with supernatural origins and that Pamphilia is the aunt of fairy children. This situation prompts remarkably little distress, however.[38] The children are sent off to be raised in the desert (2, p. 401) and no further notice is taken of them. Even in this romance, where adultery and illegitimacy generally provoke minimal concern, this blasé attitude toward half-human children seems noteworthy. Apart from the woman who asks to undertake their care, however, no one, including the two parents, pays any attention to these offsprings. Unlike the many purported succubi who sought human seed in order to breed on the devil's behalf,[39] this spirit seems focused upon Selarinus's degradation and upon sexual gratification. The children's presence marks the amount of time that Selarinus has served as a prisoner to desire; they do not seem to have been the object of the exercise. Since the romance ends not long after they have been safely stowed with a benevolent keeper, the kind of problems the children's existence may eventually cause never intrudes into the lives being portrayed.

Until the children are born, moreover, the story clearly focuses upon the pleasures of supernatural sexual congress. While the king's family and friends are said to seek Selarinus everywhere and mourn his absence (2, p. 305), the text does not present a very compelling argument to suggest that the man was unhappy "to bee servile, and in the power of such a deadly Hellhound" (2, p. 305). Although Selarinus is near death after the spirit "had her desire and ends of him" (2, p. 397), there is little evidence to suggest that he did not enjoy the sex that he initially instigates: "[he] told her her mantle would soone bee layd of if itt pleased her, and his bed wowld bee a farr more easy seate" (2, p. 305).[40] While the narrative voices outrage against the "develish spiritt" (2, p. 305) who entraps the king and pardons Selarinus by suggesting that he was helpless: "Butt who can avoide Charmes" (2, p. 305), these protestations are never very convincing and the reader is left with the impression that while Selarinus may be embarrassed by his sexual escapades, he willingly engaged in them.

Selarinus thus enables the text to present a multiplicity of sexual experiences. Initially attracted to a purported Tartarian, who may or may not have dark skin, the king spends several years in sexual bondage to a supernatural being. Accordingly, Selarinus facilitates the narrative's further examination of desire outside of national and supernatural boundaries. Whether or not he desires a "Tartarian" specifically remains indeterminate; nevertheless, he models a western courtier's fulfillment of exotic sexual attractions. He also produces a pair of textual loose ends, which leave questions remaining about the color of their skin and about the implications of their existence. As Urania's brother-in-law, Selarinus holds a significant place in the genealogical network of the romance. His sexual aberrations, therefore, bring such illicit desires straight into the center of narrative's concerns. Moreover, since the narrative once again seems more concerned with the knight's ill-treatment than with the implications or results of his supernatural sexual involvement, the adventures of Selarinus provide another opportunity for a nonjudgmental examination of atypical human erotic desires.

As this brief overview of some of the *Urania*'s depictions of nonconventional sexual practices suggests, Lady Mary Wroth did not feel overly constrained by standard propriety when composing her romance.[41] While she generally attaches cautionary tales or some indicator of ambivalence to these representations of desire, she still portrays a diverse assortment of sexual possibilities within her text. Although most of the major characters follow fairly uneventful patterns of courtship, marriage, and procreation after their youthful passions have been cleansed, other figures provide less predictable erotic narratives. As a result, modern readers are presented with a voluminous romance that demonstrates part of the breadth of one early modern writer's sexual imagination. Notable for the relative absence of negative narratorial commentary on these various desires, the *Urania*'s representations continually press against the boundaries of sanctioned sexual involvement. Just as her own extramarital experiences do not seem to have ended happily,[42] most of these stories contain sorrowful consequences. Nevertheless, the existence of these desires is generally treated dispassionately or sympathetically, as the *Urania* continually hints at the possibility of a revised sexual landscape.

NOTES

1. The *Urania, part one*, was published in 1621 and became accessible to current audiences with the publication of Josephine Roberts' exemplary edition in 1995. Until recently, the *Urania*, part two existed solely in a holograph manuscript in Chicago's Newberry Library; thankfully, Suzanne Gossett and Janel Mueller completed the modern edition of this work after Professor Roberts' tragic death and it is now generally available for the first time since its composition. The complete romance consists of approximately 600,000 words, with part one being divided into four sections and part two divided into two. Since the second part remained unpublished until 2000, I will refer to it as the manuscript *Urania* to distinguish it from the 1621 printed text. We do not know whether Wroth intended publication of either part of her romance. I will cite from the *Urania* using volume and page numbers from the recent printed editions of both texts. For example, citations from part one will be designated as 1, p. 10 and part two will be referenced as 2, p. 22 etc. See, *Mary Wroth: The First Part of the Countess of Montgomery's Urania*, ed. Josephine A. Roberts, Medieval & Renaissance Texts & Studies, Vol. 140 (Binghamton, N.Y.: Center for Medieval and Early Renaissance Studies State University of New York at Binghamton, 1995) and *Mary Wroth: The Secound Part of the Countess of Montgomery's Urania*, ed. Josephine A. Roberts; completed by Suzanne Gossett and Janel Mueller, *Medieval and Renaissance*

Texts & Studies, Vol. 211 (Tempe, Ariz.: Arizona Center for Medieval and Renaissance Studies, 1999).

2. In *Cherished Torment: The Emotional Geography of Lady Mary Wroth's "Urania"* (Pittsburgh: Duquesne University Press, 2001), I discuss Wroth's literary presentation of a kinetic universe, wherein physical, emotional, spiritual, and geographical spaces coexist and interact with each other.
3. Ellis Hanson argues that this story represents Wroth's portrayal of the relationship between James Stuart and Robert Carr. This plausible suggestion could contribute to some of the understatement that characterizes the episode. See Ellis Hanson, "Sodomy and Kingcraft in *Urania* and *Antony and Cleopatra*," in *Homosexuality in Renaissance and Enlightenment England: Literary Representations in Historical Context* (Harrington Park, N.Y.: Haworth Press, 1992), pp. 135–51.
4. Parselius and Amphilanthus play major roles throughout both parts of the *Urania*. Parselius is Pamphilia's brother, who marries Dalinea, Princess of Achaya, after first wooing Urania, Princess of Naples. Amphilanthus, Urania's brother and Pamphilia's inconstant lover, begins the narrative as son to the King of Naples. Over the course of the romance, he inherits his father's throne, then becomes King of the Romans and Holy Roman Emperor.
5. We are, in fact, given little information about this "young man" except for his behavior, so I am assuming that he is meant to represent a local, nonsupernatural person. Jonathan Goldberg analyzes many early modern literary representations that link sodomy with other practices engaged in by "foreign" persons, but the *Urania* does not offer such parallels. See Jonathan Goldberg, *Sodometries: Renaissance Texts, Modern Sexualities* (Stanford: Stanford University Press, 1992).
6. Ellis Hanson argues, "same-sex friendships in *Urania* are almost always an escape from the miseries of marriage and the inconstancy of love" (p. 138). It remains unclear whether this explanation holds true in this instance.
7. Valerie Traub offers an insightful account of a similar concern in Shakespeare's sonnets. See Valerie Treaub, "Sex Without Issue: Sodomy, Reproduction, and Signification in Shakespeare's Sonnets," in *Shakespeare's Sonnets: Critical Essays*, ed. James Schiffer (New York: Garland, 1999), pp. 431–52.
8. It is interesting to note that the duke's first joy in the child is her performance as a servant for her parents (1, p. 36).
9. The apparent relationship between Wroth and her cousin William Herbert, in conjunction with the birth of two children after the death of her husband, suggest that Wroth's own desires did not correlate with societal norms and expectations. Josephine Roberts, among others, offers an account of the Wroth/Herbert liaison (1, lxxxvi–lxxxix).
10. The story of adulterous lovers Salamino and Celia, e.g., generally receives a sympathetic reading despite the bloodshed it causes (2, pp. 15–20).
11. By the time that Pamphilia marries Rodomandro, Amphilanthus has wed the Princess of Slavonia, but this also appears to be a vexed union.
12. Although several of the main characters attend the ceremony uniting Pamphilia and Amphilanthus, no one mentions it as an impediment to the subsequent nuptials of the emperor to the Princess of Slavonia or to the wedding of Pamphilia and Rodomandro. Josephine Roberts offers a historical explanation of the union. See Josephine Roberts, " 'The knott never to bee untide': The controversy regarding marriage in Mary Wroth's *Urania*," in *Reading*

Mary Wroth: Representing Alternatives in Early Modern England, ed. Naomi Miller and Gary Waller (Knoxville: University of Tennessee Press, 1991), pp. 109–32.

13. Giovanni Botero notes that Tartaria was the largest empire in the history of the world (sig. O3). See Giovanni Botero, *The trauellers breuiat, or, An historicall description of the most famous kingdomes in the world*, ed. Robert Johnson (London, 1601).
14. In a prophetic remark in the printed *Urania*, the narrator notes that Amphilanthus was "Monarch of her [Pamphilia's] heart before shee knew Asia" (1, p. 568).
15. The malicious Queen of Candia hopes to persuade Amphilanthus to marry "the Dallmation ore Natolian Lady" arguing that "by this mairiage hee may inlarge his Empire" (2, pp. 132, 133), but this is an unusual moment.
16. When Faire Designe rescues Rodomandro from captivity, e.g., the king immediately sets off to reconcile with Pamphilia after an unexplained estrangement (2, p. 329).
17. Robert Ralston Cawley, *The Voyagers and Elizabethan Drama* (Boston: D. C. Heath and Company, 1938). Roberts similarly alludes to a common early modern association between Hades and Tartaria (2, p. 484).
18. In *Cherished Torment*, I offer an expanded discussion of Tartaria and the Great Cham.
19. Peter Heyleyn, *Microcosmus, or A little description of the great world* (Oxford, 1621).
20. Hall offers a fascinating reading of Rodomandro that often corresponds with my argument here. See Kim F. Hall, *Things of Darkness: Economies of Race and Gender in Early Modern England* (Ithaca, N.Y.: Cornell University Press, 1995), pp. 206–08. I suggest more strongly than she does, however, that the text remains ambivalent about the relationship between the king's skin color and his inability to win Pamphilia's love unequivocally. All of the other characters see him as eminently suitable and the text omits reference to the era's abundant negative literature about Tartaria. Since Pamphilia abandons her original determination to remain unmarried (1, p. 262), while leaving her reasons for accepting Rodomandro tantalizingly opaque, it is hard to determine how much of what transpires between them is attributable to his darkness. As I argue in my book, early modern geographical and historical writings about Tartaria provide valuable insights into the complicated relationship between Pamphilia and Rodomandro.
21. See Gary Waller, *The Sidney Family Romance: Mary Wroth, William Herbert, and the Early Modern Construction of Gender* (Detroit: Wayne State University Press, 1993).
22. As this discussion indicates, I disagree with Barbara Lewalski, who claims a dynastic rationale for Pamphilia's marriage to Rodomandro (p. 288). See Barbara Kiefer Lewalski, *Writing Women in Jacobean England* (Cambridge: Harvard University Press, 1993).
23. Roberts, e.g., alludes to this relationship (2, p. 530).
24. Since there is a missing bifolio sheet in the manuscript *Urania*, we do not have the complete story of another important dark-skinned character known as Follietto. This choleric figure does not seem destined for romantic success, however, since the text includes a prophecy that he will be "the greatest slave to love and loving follys that yett ever lived" (2, p. 60).

25. As I discuss at length in *Cherished Torment*, Rodomandro's position as king of Tartaria gives him special status in the geographical and political scheme of the romance.
26. The narrator describes him thus: "his face of curious and exact features, butt for the colour of itt, itt plainely shewed the sunn had either liked itt to much and so had too hard kissed itt, ore in fury of his delicasy, had made his beames to strongly to burn him" (2, p. 42).
27. Licandro mentions the lady's blue eyes in the poem he writes in her honor (2, p. 79), even though he claims in his blazon that they are indescribable (2, p. 76).
28. When he enters the story, e.g., Rodomandro is described thus: "His words answerable every way to his most princely fashion, rather respective then unsivile, nay humble then bold, yett princely" (2, pp. 42–43).
29. Ollymander was the captive jailor at the castle of the giant who enslaved the Tartarian princess and others. Licandro was saved from captivity by Ollymander's resourceful daughter Cliantè, who orchestrated the defeat of the giant (2, pp. 64–73).
30. See Jocelyn Catty, *Writing Rape, Writing Women in Early Modern England* (New York: St. Martin's Press, 1999).
31. Ollymander's role in the story is particularly striking, since characters more commonly have their own prophetic dreams or receive instructions from Melissea. Roberts offers "man-destroyer" as the etymological basis of Ollymander's name (2, p. 491), but the text does not explain this designation.
32. Selarinus is Prince of Albania at the start of the romance and is later crowned King of Epirus. His wife Philistella is Pamphilia's sister and his brother Steriamus marries Urania.
33. Notably, Selarinus does not believe himself worthy of fate's attention (2, p. 5).
34. The recently published version of the manuscript designates this spirit as Rodomandro's daughter, not his sister (2, pp. 7–9). I am presuming that she is taking the role of sister because she claims that her brother is arming in defense of Pamphilia (2, p. 10), but my argument does not depend upon a particular familial relationship.
35. Since the stories of the lost children are often confusing, her claim to have children enchanted with the others cannot be challenged easily.
36. When the spirit reappears, however, she is said to be a "delicate browne beautie" (2, p. 303). Since the manuscript was never revised for publication, it is possible that Wroth was initially thinking of a fair-skinned spirit, then made her "brown" to match her more closely with Rodomandro. Such discrepancies in the text are common.
37. Selarinus may be too hard on himself here. The text indicates that after being held captive for many years at Saphalina's house, the spirit immediately sought Selarinus when she was freed (2, p. 305).
38. The progeny from this coupling marks another departure from contemporary standards. Shakespeare flirts with the possibility of issue from similar unions, e.g., but Titania and Miranda never bear half-human offspring.
39. Succubi received considerable attention in contemporary literature and James Stuart's concern about witches is well known. See *Malleus Malleficarum*, a major treatise on witchcraft, for a description of succubitic practices (pp. 117–22), *Malleus Maleficarum*, ed. Montague Summers (New York: Benjamin Blom, 1928).

40. Although the spirits' fairy helpers apparently drug Selarinus, he continually appears to be a voluntary participant in the subsequent sexual encounters.
41. As many critics have explained, Wroth's depiction of illicit sexual activities did not pass unremarked. Most famously, Wroth offended Edward Denny, who protested the apparent unflattering fictive portrait of his family life (1, cv–cvi).
42. As Roberts notes, e.g., William Herbert bequeathed his estate to his nephew, not to the children he had with Wroth (2, xxii).

Part II

Queer Fictions

CHAPTER 6

SAME DIFFERENCE: HOMO AND ALLO IN LYLY'S *EUPHUES*

Stephen Guy-Bray

One result of the work on the history of sexuality in the last few decades has been the reluctance to apply our current sexual taxonomy to the lives and texts of the past. While this has led to many cumbersome locutions, most scholars would agree that the gain in subtlety has been enormous. Still, although we no longer feel comfortable using our contemporary terms to describe people in the past, our taxonomy is still dominated by binary thinking: in other words, we still tend to describe past sexualities as binary systems and the only change is that we use different binary oppositions. My problem is not with binaries *per se*, but rather with the narrow way in which they are used. As a rule, all that is at issue in any given binary taxonomy is whether two things or people are the same as each other or different from each other; furthermore, the tendency is to consider only one aspect with each pair: male or female; big or small; black or white; and so on. In this essay, I want to begin by looking at our use of sexual binaries to describe the sexualities of the past; I shall then discuss the first section of John Lyly's *Euphues* (1578), a text that holds out the possibility of subtler classifications of human relationships. What I see in this text is an awareness that an individual will often be both the same as and different from another individual and thus any assigning of labels can never be the whole story.

Although recent attempts to classify the sexuality of the past with due regard for historical accuracy are not primarily based on gender differences, they are still premised on the belief that sexuality is either one thing or one other thing. Two systems that have been proposed—one from ancient Greece and one from sixteenth-century England—are useful to my discussion, however, because they suggest ways in which we can expand our thinking. David M. Halperin has said that ancient Greek sexuality was also conceptualized as a binary system but that the difference was not one of gender:

> Sex is portrayed in Athenian documents not as a mutual enterprise in which two or more persons jointly engage but as an action performed by a social superior upon a social inferior. Consisting as it was held to do in an asymmetrical gesture-the penetration of the body of one person by the body (and, specifically, the phallus) of another-sex effectively divided and distributed its participants into radically distinct and incommensurable categories ("penetrator" versus "penetrated"), categories which in turn were wholly congruent with superordinate and subordinate social categories.[1]

In this binary system, one of the positions can only be occupied by a male, while the other can be occupied by either a male or a female. The importance of this system to my argument lies chiefly in that it provides this dual way of conceptualizing a man's sexual experience with another man. Rather than being entirely subsumed under the category of sameness, male homosexual experience can itself be seen as a binary system that contains both sameness and difference. Furthermore, ancient Greek sexual practice meant that many upper-class males would pass from one position to the other, and from this fact we can infer that what we would now call a sexual orientation is not necessarily fixed.[2]

The system used to classify sexual relationships between men in Renaissance England is somewhat different as the emphasis is on the relationship between the male couple and their social context. We owe our sense of this distinction to Alan Bray, who described one of his essays as "a commentary on two images.... One is the image of the masculine friend. The other is the figure called the sodomite."[3] Bray is too optimistic about the ease with which these images can be distinguished. For instance, he cites *Euphues* as an example of masculine friendship but goes on to say that in the relationship between Euphues and Philautus "[t]here was no suggestion at all... of the possible signs of a sodomitical relationship."[4] Yet Bray also says that one of the differences between a sodomitical relationship and a masculine friendship is that the latter has "behind it a web of social relations."[5] While we see Philautus as someone who is at home and who has various kinds of connections with other characters in Naples, Euphues is a foreigner among people he does not know and thus without any social relations except for those he can create and his actions clearly lead to the sort of rupture of the social fabric often seen in early modern England as the sign of the sodomite. As well, Alan Stewart's recent work on the connections between sodomy and humanism, an enterprise carried out largely through masculine friendships also serves to make drawing a distinction very difficult.[6] The binary oppositions that we use to organize sexual experience are thus not only subject to change over time, but are also liable to break down in practice. Nevertheless, however difficult it may be for us to distinguish between masculine friendship and sodomy, the distinction was obviously of great importance in the sixteenth century and as I see it, the narrative that occupies the first section of *Euphues* is increasingly concerned with establishing that Euphues and Philautus are just good friends.

Both binary systems offer ways of thinking about sexuality that stress the social context of sexual activity and relationships. In contrast, our present system of sexuality concentrates almost exclusively on gender difference, and is premised on the opposition between a preference for that which is different and a preference for that which is the same. There are many possible objections to this system, one of which is that the classification of people as being most importantly like or unlike ourselves insofar as their gender is the same as ours or not is much too narrow and another is that we may well feel that men and women are not particularly different. Nevertheless, the tendency is to regard the information that a person is sexually attracted to members of the same sex or of the opposite sex as important knowledge about that person—perhaps even the most important knowledge there is. This classification of sexuality is particularly unsuitable for periods like the Renaissance, in which one of the most important things to know about people's sexuality was how it reinforced or interfered with their class position. The narrowness of our system is intensified by the fact that the Greek prefixes we use might lead us to believe that we only have two choices: *heteros* means the other when there are only two, as opposed to *allos*, which means a potentially infinite number of other people and of other differences. As the subtitle of this essay indicates, I want to use a more broadly conceived binary system than is currently in place, one that uses allo rather than hetero, and thus does not limit the possible number of differences, and one that uses only the prefixes so as not to specify in advance what sort of difference is at issue.

I

Most critics writing on John Lyly's *Euphues: The Anatomy of Wit* have concentrated on the text's style almost to the exclusion of its content. Indeed, it has been suggested that *Euphues* has style rather than (or at the expense of) content. For instance, the *Oxford Companion to English Literature* says that euphuism is characterized by "the excessive use of antithesis, which is pursued regardless of sense."[7] Recent studies are more likely to argue that the book's style and its content are connected in important ways; one of the first of these studies (and perhaps still the most influential) was published in 1956 by Jonas A. Barish. Writing about parison, Barish says that "is, one might almost say, an instrument of thought whereby Lyly apprehends the world."[8] His analysis allows us to realize that the separation of *Euphues*'s style from its content is itself an "antithesis pursued regardless of sense." I want to argue that in order to understand Lyly's use of antithesis we should also consider his use of figures of sameness: we need to analyze the text's dependence on both difference and sameness and to see difference and sameness as related, rather than as the opposite poles of an antithesis.

In her analysis of his style, Janel M. Mueller has pointed out, "Lyly's actual sentences . . . contain a third element of difference."[9] Furthermore, although many of Lyly's sentences could be cited as examples of antithesis, that term is too narrow to describe the consistent, thematically significant use of this structure. Here, I follow the distinction made by Quintilian in his discussion of *mutatio*: "if this is what Rutilius calls alloiosis, [it] shows the differences among men and things and deeds: if used more broadly, it is not a figure; if more narrowly, it falls under antithesis."[10] In the passage to which Quintilian refers, Rutilius says that "in [alloiosis] there is division and separation of people and things, and a description of how much they differ."[11] Antithesis is best seen as a device that functions on the syntactic level and a writer's use of antithetical structure to make important points on a philosophical or sociological scale is properly called alloiosis.

I would make a similar point about Lyly's use of figures of sameness. The prevalence of these devices and their connection to what is happening on the level of the plot suggest that Lyly's use of them is more than a purely decorative or stylistic strategy. As in my discussion of antithesis and alloiosis, I would like to distinguish between the uses of figures of sameness on the level of the sentence and the use of sameness as a constitutive element in a text. In this case, however, the term I propose to use does not come from classical rhetoric. In a recent article on Renaissance romantic comedies, Laurie Shannon discusses the presence of what she calls "homonormativity . . . an almost philosophical preference for likeness or a structure of thinking based on resemblance."[12] On the level of the plot, *Euphues* is concerned with both alloiosis and homonormativity and this concern is also visible on the level of the sentence: "As therefore the sweetest Rose hath his prickel, the finest veluet his brack, the fairest flowre his bran, so the sharpest witte hath his wanton will, and the holiest heade his wicked waye."[13] This sentence actually has two antitheses, one relating to mental qualities and one to spiritual, and three comparisons from nature.[14] Only the first of these is drawn entirely from nature, since velvet and flour are both produced by humans, although in different ways: flour is a human refinement of something that grows naturally; velvet is produced from silk, which is itself manufactured (although not by humans). Furthermore, flour is a basic food, while velvet is a luxury good. As a plant, the rose can be compared to the wheat from which flour is made; as a symbol of love and beauty, the rose might better be compared to velvet. And, of course, Lyly's play on words (flour/flower), emphasized by the Renaissance spelling, further complicates the matter.

More could be said about this sentence; I have given this brief account to show that Lyly presents us with several kinds of sameness and differences, adumbrates possible relations among them, and complicates the simple opposition—Euphues has both bad and good qualities—that is the ostensible point of the sentence. Lyly relies on figures of difference and sameness because the first section of *Euphues* is to a great extent a reflection on the meaning and importance of both difference and sameness in human relationships. The text oscillates between alloiosis and homonormativity in its examination of personal relations. In Rutilius's formulation, Lyly attempts to show "division and separation of people . . . and a description of how much they differ," but he also attempts to show how much they are the same. Furthermore, in the relationships that Lyly depicts in *Euphues* the important difference between one character and another is not gender or social status or age or sexual role, although these differences—with the exception of the last—play a part in the text. The Renaissance distinction between those relationships that could be accommodated within the social system and those that were disruptive is more useful, but even this system turns out to be difficult to apply. *Euphues* begins by presenting us with a number of relationships that appear not to fit into any of the categories of whatever period that we could use to classify relationships. What is more, the binaries we might expect to use in thinking about the text's relationships (in particular, male/female and native/foreign) turn out to be less relevant than we might have thought.

II

The first example of Lyly's juxtaposition of sameness and difference on the level of personal relations comes in the dialogue between Euphues and Eubulus, an old Neapolitan. This might seem a fairly obvious contrast if we think of the connotations of the two cities (Athens represents the life of the mind and Naples the life of the body), but as soon as Lyly introduces this contrast he makes it problematic. Rather than acting as a spokesman for hedonism, Eubulus is the voice of sober wisdom while Euphues is presented as pleasure-loving. This opposition is stressed by the age difference between the two men and reflected in their names. Euphues's name comes from a Greek adjective (*eu* and *phues*) meaning handsome or of good disposition, while Eubulus (*eu* and *boulos*) means good counsel. The Greek man has a name that reminds us of his physicality (the root of the second part of his name is the verb *phuo*, to grow); the Italian has a name that indicates mental qualities. On the other hand, the fact that both names are Greek and begin with the same element suggests that we might want to see the two men as similar. The use of Greek names should remind us that Naples was founded by the Greeks and the difference between the cities may be less than we thought. Finally, this first section of the text is a small part of *Euphues* as a whole; for most of the book (and its sequels) Euphues sits in Athens and dispenses advice, which is one way of saying that he becomes Eubulus. What we might have understood as an opposition between an Athenian and a Neapolitan and between youth and age can now be read as two parts of one process, just as Athens and Naples represent different stages of Greek history. The dialogue may be taken to suggest that the difference between what we perceive as opposite things might be a different difference altogether and that there might not even be a difference. It is typical of the text that alloiosis is always becoming homonormativity and that the distinction between them is often difficult or even impossible to make.

Lyly's emphasis on the male couple is signalled by the fact that the first dialogue we read in *Euphues* is between a male couple or, at least, a potential couple as Eubulus quickly vanishes. The important male couple in the text is formed when Euphues meets a young Neapolitan called Philautus and falls in love: "*Euphues* showed such entyre loue towards him, that he seemed to make small accompt of any others" (pp. 196–97). In this separation of the two men from the society around them we can see the sign of homoerotic desire, as opposed to a masculine friendship that would situate the friends in "a web of social relations." Euphues's knowledge of friendship is theoretical rather than practical: "I haue red (saith he) and well I beleeue it, that a friend is in prosperitie a pleasure, a solace in aduersitie, in griefe a comfort, in ioy a merrye companion, at all times an other I, in all places ye expresse Image of mine owne person" (p. 197). Despite the fact that he and Philautus are from different countries and are virtually unknown to each other, Euphues presents this friendship as a relationship based on sameness. Twice by this early point in the narrative, then, masculine relationships that might have seemed to be characterized by difference (youth versus age in the case of Euphues and Eubulus; Greece versus Naples in both cases, to say nothing of the fact that these men do not know each other) have turned out to be characterized by sameness.

Euphues's summary of the benefits of friendship is chiefly cribbed from Cicero's *De Amicitia*, but it is noteworthy that he refers to the friend as "an other I." As Shannon points out, the expression Cicero uses is "*alter idem*."[15] Both Cicero's and Lyly's discussions have their source in Aristotle's discussion of friendship in the *Ethica Nicomachea* VIII and IX. Analyses of the role of friendship in *Euphues* have been hampered by because almost no one has considered the possibility that Lyly knew Aristotle—even the very famous passages on friendship.[16] The first point to make about Aristotle's discussion is that the expression Cicero translates as "*alter idem*" appears as "*heteros autos*."[17] The Latin means "another who is the same," while the Greek means "another self."[18] The difference may not seem great, and clearly both refer to a relationship in which one who is supposed to be different because he is, after all, another person, is really the same. Nevertheless, Aristotle first uses the term in a way that reveals that he is thinking about difference as well: "They say that the truly happy are self-sufficient and do not need friends, for they have what is good and being self-sufficient they do not need another person, while a friend, being another self [*heteron auton*] provides that which is impossible for us [to provide]."[19] Whatever else "*heteron auton*" may mean, it does not mean absolute sameness. For Aristotle, the other self may still be different from oneself, while for Cicero, the friend is someone who is the same. In the *Ethica Nicomachea*, friendship is both alloiosis and homonormativity.

Aristotle's discussion of self-love (*philautia*) and the fact that he frequently uses the term the self-lover (*ho philautus*) seem to me to confirm Lyly's indebtedness.[20] The name of Euphues's friend appears to indicate that this example of masculine love is self-centred, but a closer examination of what the *Ethica Nicomachea* has to say about friendship suggests that the situation is not so straightforward. Aristotle begins his discussion by considering how friendship arises: "Some claim that it has to do with resemblance and that we love those who resemble us."[21] He goes on to say that there have been other opinions, gives the example of Euripides, who speaks of friendship as a union of opposites like the earth and the rain, and ends by citing Heraclitus and Empedocles, who feel that friendship is a matter of resemblance. Aristotle's citation of two writers on the resemblance side and one on the difference side, as well as the fact that he concludes with a quotation from Empedocles ("like looks for like"),[22] may indicate that he favors this view but he refrains from making a pronouncement. As well, even if friendship starts with resemblance, those people may turn out to be different from us: what we initially perceive as homonormativity may turn out to be alloiosis.

These considerations do not occur to Euphues himself at this point, who instantly considers Philautus as his mirror image. In what may be an allusion to the passage from Empedocles, Euphues asks "Is it not a by woord, like will to like" (p.197) and concludes by insisting on sameness as the basis of the relationship: "I will therefore haue *Philautus* for my pheere, and by so much the more I make my selfe sure to haue *Philautus*, by how much the more I view in him the liuely Image of *Euphues*" (p. 197). I want to comment on two aspects of this sentence, the first of which is the use of the word "pheere." This word has the basic meaning of companion and can be used to mean friend or lover or mate. For modern readers, the word is a useful reminder that two relationships that we see as different (friend and lover) did not appear so different in the sixteenth century.[23] The second significant aspect is the description of Philautus as a "liuely Image of *Euphues*". Lyly's formulation returns us to the idea that a friend is "another I" and indicates that Euphues takes this statement literally. Furthermore, the use "Image" hints that this sameness is at least partly physical, and the emphasis in this passage is thus on how Philautus looks like Euphues, rather than on how he acts or thinks like him. This is yet another kind of sameness and Lyly may intend us to think of the passage in which Aristotle says that goodwill "seems to be the beginning of friendly love, just as the pleasure of [seeing] the face is of romantic love."[24] Euphues's love for Philautus is indeed a kind of *philautia* or self-love, but it is also romantic love.

Philautus accepts Euphues's offer of friendship in a speech that makes extensive use of Euphues's own words and emphasizes sameness—"seeing we resemble (as you say) each other in qualities, it cannot be that the one should differ from ye other in curtesie" (p. 198). The two quickly become inseparable:

> they vsed not onely one boord, but one bedde, one booke (if so be it they thought not one to many.) Their friendship augmented euery day, insomuch y^t the one could not refraine ye company of ye other one minute, all things went in co[m]mon betweene them, which all men accompted co[m]mendable. (p. 199)

The description of this relationship is similar to other descriptions of masculine friendship from the sixteenth and seventeenth centuries: for instance, the sharing of bed and board follows the conventions of early modern friendship.[25] That Euphues and Philautus share a book would seem to place their friendship under the aegis of humanism, but as Stewart has suggested, they appear to see this as a purely formal observance: "their disregard for the 'booke' as nothing more than an unwarranted convention guarantees the superficiality of their 'hot loue.' "[26] Their inability to refrain from seeing each other all the time appears to point to an excessive quality, but we are told that this relationship is "accompted co[m]mendable." Where we would tend to see difference, then, their contemporaries would see the resemblance between Euphues and Philautus and acceptable male couples: as Lyly implies, what is common is commendable. This passage does not clearly indicate that their relationship should be considered masculine friendship rather than sodomy, but rather that the distinction is difficult to make. Once again, Lyly presents us with a situation that cannot readily be classified either as alloiosis or as homonormativity.

Our sense of Euphues and Philautus as being in love should simultaneously make us more cautious about our ability to distinguish between the sodomite and the masculine friend and more likely to wonder whether what initially appears as an antithesis between the main character's initial homo bond with Philautus and his subsequent hetero bond with Lucilla is really an example of isocolon at a narrative level. In other words, in presenting us first with a bond between men and then with a bond between a man and a woman, is Lyly giving us alloiosis or homonormativity? After all, when Euphues first sees Lucilla, we are told that "at the firste sight [he] was so kyndled with desyre, that almost he was lyke to burn to coales" (p. 201). Euphues falls in love with Lucilla faster and harder than he did with Philautus, but Lyly presents these as differences of degree rather than of kind. The similarity between these relationships (the most important relationships in the text) underlines the inadequacy of our sexual system: if Euphues's relationship with Lucilla is not very different from his relationship with Philautus, the fact that the former is a woman and the latter a man may not be important. What does matter is how each relationship can be accommodated in the web of social relations to which Bray refers. As he suggests, it is this consideration that separates the friend from the sodomite; I would add that this is the case whether the relationship has a sexual component or not. As a result, neither our own habit of foregrounding gender difference nor what is assumed to be the Renaissance habit of distinguishing between masculine friendships on the basis of whether or not the friendship can be accommodated by the social order seems particularly helpful in making sense of Lyly's text.

III

The friendship between Euphues and Philautus seems to exist outside of society, and it is only with the introduction of Lucilla that Lyly situates the two men in a social context. Lyly begins by telling us about her father: "*Philautus* being a towne borne childe, both for his owne continuance, & the great countenaunce whiche his Father had whyle he liued, crepte into credite with *Don Ferardo* one of the chief gouernours of the citie" (p. 199). One of the effects of this sentence is to situate both Philautus and Lucilla in a network of social, economic, and familial relations. The difference between them and Euphues is not only nationality, but also the contrast between people connected to those around them both by class and by family and people who are apparently without any such connections. From this point of view, Philautus and Lucilla are the same and Euphues is different from either of them. Their resemblance is emphasized by their impending marriage: Philautus "wanne hir by right of loue, and should haue worne hir by right of lawe, had not *Euphues* by straunge destenie broken the bondes of marriage" (p. 199). To return to the binary, I would characterize the bond between Philautus and Lucilla at this point in the narrative as homo and the bond between Euphues and either of the first two as allo: the distinction between homo and hetero is not helpful in this case.

These relationships are allo both because of Euphues's foreignness and because the relationships are situated outside the social context in which the narrative is set. In contrast, in the speech in which he summarizes to Lucilla his plans for her marriage, Ferardo stresses that he sees this marriage as socially and economically significant: "Mine onely care hath bene hetherto to match thee with such an one, as shoulde be of good wealth able to maynteine thee, of great worship able to compare with thee in birth, of honest conditions to deserue thy loue, and an *Italian* borne to enioye my landes" (p. 227). Thus in his relationship with Lucilla—a relationship that destroys the alliance Ferardo has planned—Euphues could be called a sodomite insofar as he recalls E. K.'s nearly exact contemporaneous characterization of sodomy as "disorderly loue."[27] Euphues's love for Lucilla is disorderly in several ways: it disorders his relationship with Philautus, the relationship between Philautus and Lucilla, the relationship between Lucilla and Ferardo, the relationship between Philautus and Ferardo, and, most generally, the system of using women to reinforce bonds between and among men. From this point of view, his love for Philautus would not be sodomitical as it does not interfere with what Lyly presents as the status quo: it is the heteroerotic relationship that is sodomitical here rather than the one between men. What is more, our sense of which relationship to characterize as disruptive is complicated by the fact that is difficult to say which of Philautus's relationships is prior to the other and thus which of the two, Euphues or Lucilla, should be seen as the interloper. In the story as it would have taken place in real life, Lucilla has prior claim; in the story as it is told, however, Euphues was first, and his claim is strengthened by the onomastic connection between him and Philautus and, I would argue, by the fact that this view of the text is true to the experience of reading it.

In her disruption of various alliances (between herself and Philautus, between her father and Philautus, between Euphues and Philautus, then between herself and Euphues, and ultimately between herself and each of the men who follows him), Lucilla is a transgressive figure both on a personal and on a social level. This transgression can be seen not only in what Lucilla does, but even in the fact that she does so much. As Katharine Wilson has remarked, "The agency in the tale belongs to Lucilla, and the others can only react."[28] If it were not for Lucilla, *Euphues* would hardly qualify as a tale at all: there is a sense in which *Euphues: The Anatomy of Wit* is really the story of Lucilla rather than of the eponymous character. As we have seen, the introduction of Lucilla Lyly presents the personal relationships depicted in his text as taking place to a certain extent in public. Consequently, we can see that Lucilla's disruptions may expand beyond the sphere of the personal and into the web of social relations that underpins the state. While all men consider the friendship of Euphues and Philautus "co[m]mendable," the public judgment passed on Lucilla will, as her father tells her, be very different: "As thy beautie hath made thee blaze of *Italy*, so will thy lyghtnes make thee the bye word of ye world" (p. 244). The sodomite in the text is not Euphues, the headstrong foreigner who arrives in Naples without ties to anyone and who quickly forms a passionate attachment to another man, but Lucilla, whose "disorderly loue" threatens to destroy that attachment.

But while we seem to be encouraged to consider Lucilla as egregious, this is only one possible reading of the text. In a conversation with Euphues, Lucilla cites precedents for her behaviour: "did not *Helen* ye pearle of *Greece* thy countriwoman first take *Menelaus*, then *Theseus*, and last of all *Paris*" (p. 239). As her connection of Euphues and Helen suggests, this should strike us as a precedent that applies to Euphues as much as it does to Lucilla: he should accept the validity of the precedent because he too has abandoned Philautus, to whom he promised to be faithful, for someone else. The fact that both Lucilla and Euphues have betrayed Philautus is the most obvious similarity between them. I would also point out that Lucilla's "lyghtnes" should remind us of Euphues's own inability to govern himself, which Lyly was careful to establish at the beginning of the text and that aroused Eubulus's concern. As Richard A. McCabe remarks, Lucilla "emerges in the course of the work as exactly the sort of person Euphues initially threatens to become."[29] Although a summary of the plot might lead us to think of the two as enemies, although this is certainly how Euphues would see it, and although this turns out to be the result of the events of this section of the text, the experience of reading the text suggests that the two are similar: in one sense, Lucilla is Euphues's "other I."

The resemblance between Lucilla and Euphues is crucial to Lyly's presentation of relationships, as in this sense their relationship is homo and the relationship each has with Philautus is allo. Euphues refuses the identification, and in his answer to Lucilla, he refers to Helen as "my countriewoman borne, but thine by profession" (p. 240). The situation in which Lucilla and Euphues find themselves here illustrates homonormativity—"a structure of thinking based on resemblance," but Euphues sees it as illustrating alloiosis—"division and separation of people and things, and a description of how much they differ." I return to the wording of the definitions because Euphues's refusal of identification is the narrative's major turning point. Until this point, *Euphues* has taken place in a world of blurred binaries. There has always been a sense that it is important to divide and separate both individuals and the relationships among them, but it has proved surprisingly difficult to define and to keep distinct the classifications by which this division and separation would be performed and characters have seemed to belong now to one category and now to another. Although Lyly could hardly be said to depict a world of polymorphous play, he has given us reasons to question rigid systems of classification. Any space for questioning is quickly closed off, however. It is the female character who is pivotal in this regard, although less in her actions than in the conclusions men draw from them. Euphues and Philautus have seemed to be indeterminate and to resist easy classification, but Lucilla is associated with what comes to seem a dangerous indeterminacy. She begins as a figure whose behavior parallels Euphues's and her decision to love him rather than Philautus is not, on the face of it, unreasonable. In choosing Curio, however, she chooses as a man who, as she confesses to Euphues, is "neither to be compared to *Philautus* in wealth, nor to thee in wit, neither in birth to the worst of you both" (p. 238). After rejecting first Philautus and then Euphues, Lucilla rejects Curio; eventually, we learn that she rejects the other men who take Curio's place, going from bad to worse until she dies "in great beggerie in the streetes" (p. 312). The news of this event produces a flood of moralizing on Euphues's part in which, among other things, he returns to the precedents she cited: "I durst sweare that for beastlines she was the *Helen* of *Greece*" (p. 312). Lucilla comes to stand for the dangers of change, and with her demonization the positive implications of change and of indeterminacy in general are negated.[30]

By the end of the narrative portion of the book, Euphues has come to represent stability. This development hardly seems probable given the stress on Euphues's instability at the beginning of the text, but the point is that Lyly can now use Lucilla to show alloiosis: Euphues is stable because he is different both from her and from his earlier self. As Wilson notes, Lucilla does have agency, but her agency turns out to be employed in the service of a narrative of masculine development. This shift from change to stability (a change that is only possible because of Lucilla) is demonstrated most obviously by Euphues's misogynistic sententiousness. In response to the news that Lucilla now loves Curio, Euphues delivers a long soliloquy in which he shores up many of the binary oppositions that had come under question. After lamenting his personal losses, he proceeds to make generalizations: "I had thought that women had bene as we men, that is true, faithfull, zealous, constant, but I perceiue they be rather woe vnto men, by their falshood, gelousie, inconstancie" (p. 241). Although this characterization of men cannot be supported by Euphues's behavior, it turns out to be the statement on which his conclusions are based. Lyly presents the belief that men and women are inherently different and that men are better than women as the form of alloiosis that underwrites all the others. As the speech progresses,

Euphues returns to some of the oppositions (in particular, the opposition between Naples as the city of the body and Athens as the city of the mind) that the text itself has led us to question—"I will to *Athens* ther to tosse my bookes, no more in *Naples* to lyue with faire lookes" (p. 241)—and resolves to devote himself to scholarship: "The *Axiomaes* of *Aristotle*, the *Maxims* of *Iustinian*, the *Aphorismes* of *Galen*, haue sodaynelye made such a breache into my minde that I seeme only to desire them which did onely earst detest them" (p. 241). Euphues's study plan might seem to parallel Lucilla's sudden change from man to man (to man), but the hundreds of pages that follow this declaration indicate that Lyly wants us to think that he is sincere in his declaration.

Euphues ends his speech by returning to his identification of Naples with women and with romantic love and his generalizations about all women on the basis of Lucilla's behavior:

> As therefore I gaue a farewell to *Lucilla*, a farewell to *Naples*, a farewell to woemen, so now doe I giue a farewell to the world, meaning rather to macerate my selfe with melancholye then pine in follye, rather choosinge to dye in my studye amiddest my bookes, than to courte it in *Italy*, in the company of Ladyes. (p. 242)

His desire to renounce everything is partly based on the fact that he sees his friendship with Philautus as irrecoverable—a reasonable assumption given the unpleasant letters they exchanged after Lucilla rejected Philautus for Euphues. Still, Euphues begins his speech with a binary opposition between Lucilla and Philautus in which the loss of the latter emerges as the more important loss: "I haue lost *Philautus*, I haue lost *Lucilla*, I haue lost that which I shall hardlye finde againe, a faythfull friende" (pp. 240–41). In some ways, the narrative could suitably end here, with Euphues having lost both his chances for human relationships and about to devote himself to the life of the mind, but then the problem would be that the difference between men and women (which is, as I have said, the alloiosis that underwrites all the others) would only be affirmed in speech and not in action.

The narrative must end with a return to masculine friendship, but this friendship must be constituted on more solid grounds than the sudden infatuation based on resemblance that initially united the two. The first step in this process is Philautus's change of heart: "hauing intelligence of *Euphues* his successe, and the falshoode of *Lucilla*, although he began to reioyce at the miserye of his fellowe, yet seeinge hir ficklenesse coulde not but lamente hir follye, and pittie his friendes misfortune" (p. 245). When the two men first meet again, they begin by "casting discourtesie in the teeth each of the other," but soon they proceed to "noting disloyaltie in the demeanor of *Lucilla* [and] after much talke renewed their old friendship both abandoning *Lucilla* as most abhominable" (p. 245).[31] Their condemnation of Lucilla provides the solid ground for renewed friendship. While the text can be interpreted as linking masculine friendship and masculine love for women, it ends by presenting them as linked only because they are opposites. What appeared as resemblance can now only be perceived as difference. The narrative has progressed in two ways in its depiction of masculine friendship: this friendship is now seen to be unlike the love of women, and—as the rest of the paragraph informs us—this friendship is cleared of any suspicions that it might be sodomitical since it can only exist at a distance:

> *Philautus* was earnest to haue *Euphues* tarrie in *Naples*, and *Euphues* desirous to haue *Philautus* to *Athens*, but the one was so addicted to the court, the other so wedded to the vniuersitie, that each refused ye offer of the other, yet this they agreed betweene themselues that though their bodyes were by distaunce of place seuered, yet the coniunction of their mindes should neither bee seperated, by the length of time, nor alienated by chaunge of soyle. (pp. 245–46)

The friendship between Euphues and Philautus has been re-created in such a way that no further progression is possible. This shift from movement to stasis is reflected in the book itself, as the rest of Lyly's writings about Euphues contain virtually no narrative movement, and also in the change from the blurred and frequently indistinguishable binaries that characterized the first part of the text to the fixed binaries—men are constant while women are inconstant, Naples represents the courtier's life while Athens represents the scholar's life—that characterize the rest of the work. The book's subtitle could be said to have pointed to a union of oppositions as it combines the body (*The Anatomy*) and the mind (*of Wit*), but the shift from narrative to epistolary mode indicates that combinations—including masculine friendship—are now only possible if they are textual. The first example of the new mode comes in the paragraph that concludes the first section of the text: "that he might bridell the ouerlashing affections of *Philautus*, [Euphues] conuayed into his studye, a certeyne pamphlet which hee termed a coolinge carde for *Philautus*, yet generallye to be applyed to all louers" (p. 246). Lyly does not end his story with the reunion between the two men or even with their separation, but rather—and crucially—by stressing the difference between the two. We can see this as the final attempt to separate masculine friendship from sodomy. The fact that the two men will henceforth be separated by hundreds of miles might be thought to clear them of suspicion, but their separation turns out to consist not only of geography but also of the difference between a disciplined scholar and a man with "ouerlashing affections." Although Philautus will remain someone to whom things happen—someone who is part of a narrative—Euphues himself is very different. Lyly concludes his text by focusing on alloiosis rather than on homonormativity and by limiting the space in which masculine friendship can exist in a way that might remind us of the depressing conclusion of Book IX of the *Ethica Nicomachea*: "And so this is all the treatment of friendship; now we shall go on to pleasure."[32]

NOTES

1. "Is There a History of Sexuality?" in *The Lesbian and Gay Studies Reader*, ed. Henry Abelove, Michèle Aina Barale, and David M. Halperin (New York: Routledge, 1993), p. 418.
2. In this system women cannot have sexual orientation at all, although they may be the object of a man's sexual orientation.
3. "Homosexuality and the Signs of Male Friendship in Elizabethan England," in *Queering the Renaissance*, ed. Jonathan Goldberg (Durham NC: Duke University Press, 1994), p. 40.
4. Bray, "Homosexuality and the Signs of Male Friendship," p. 46. He supports his claim by quoting a passage from *Euphues and his Ephoebus*, a treatise on education that is one of the many texts added to *Euphues: The Anatomy of Wit*. He says that in this passage Lyly calls the sodomite "a most dangerous and infectious beast" (p. 46). A careful reading of the passage reveals that although Lyly does describe a man who will value the boy he is teaching "for his comely countenaunce" in this way, the passage as a whole begins with a reference to "*Socrates, Plato, Xenophon, Eschines, Sæbetes*, and all those that so much commende the loue of men" (I.280). Surely any clear distinction between the masculine friend and the sodomite is impossible given this context.
5. "Homosexuality and the Signs of Male Friendship," p. 42.
6. *Close Readers: Humanism and Sodomy in Early Modern England* (Princeton: Princeton University Press, 1997). See especially pp. 148–60.
7. See, e.g., the *Oxford Companion to English Literature*, ed. Margaret Drabble (Oxford: Oxford University Press, 1985), s.v. *Euphues*. For a similar view expressed sympathetically, see Shimon Sandbank's "Euphuistic Symmetry and the Image," *SEL* 11 (1971): 1–13.
8. "The Prose Style of John Lyly," *ELH* 23 (1956): 16. For a good example of this approach since Barish, see Judith Rice Henderson, "Euphues and his Erasmus," *ELR* 12 (1982): 135–61.
9. *The Native Tongue and the Word: Developments in English Prose Style 1380–1580* (Chicago: University of Chicago Press, 1984), p. 390. Mueller is speaking of Lyly's dedication to Lord Delaware, but her point is true of many of *Euphues's* sentences.
10. *Institutionis Oratoriae*, ed. M. Winterbottom, 2 vols. (Oxford: Clarendon Press, 1970), 9.3.92; II.533. All translations from classical texts are my own.
11. *Figuris Sententiarum et Elocutionis*, ed. Edward Brooks, Jr (Leiden: E. J. Brill, 1970), II.2; 27.
12. Laurie Shannon "Nature's Bias: Renaissance Homonormativity and Elizabethan Comic Likeness," *Modern Philology* 98 (2000–01): 191–92.
13. *Euphues: The Anatomy of Wit, The Complete Works of John Lyly*, 3 vols, ed. R. Warwick Bond (Oxford: Clarendon Press, 1902), I.184. All references to Lyly's works are to the first volume of this edition and will appear in the text.
14. For an analysis of Lyly's use of examples from the natural world, see Raymond Stephanson, "John Lyly's Prose Fiction: Irony, Humor, and Anti-Humanism," *ELR* 11 (1981): 3–21.
15. Shannon, "Nature's Bias," p.189.
16. In his discussion of Lyly, Arthur F. Kinney refers briefly to Aristotle's discussion of friendship before turning to Cicero. See *Humanist Poetics: Thought, Rhetoric,*

and Fiction in Sixteenth-Century England (Amherst: University of Massachusetts Press, 1986), pp. 169 et seq.

17. *Ethica Nicomachea*, ed. J. Bywater (Oxford: Clarendon Press, 1894), IX.9, 1169b and IX.9, 1170b.
18. Forms of the word "autos" can have three meanings: the self (myself, yourself, himself, and so on); him or her or it; the same. In Aristotle's first use of the expression—*ton de philon, heteron auton* onta—the word is in the accusative case and we could say either "while the friend, being another self" or "while the friend, being another him." In the second—*heteros gar autos ho philos* estin—we could only say "the friend is another self."
19. *Ethica Nicomachea*, IX.9, 1169b.
20. Aristotle unsurprisingly disapproves of self-love for the most part, but see IX.8, 1169a for the suggestion that a good man should be a self-lover (*tov men agathon dei philauton einai*).
21. *Ethica Nicomachea*, VIII.1, 1155b.
22. *Ethica Nicomachea*, VIII.1, 1155b.
23. The use of this word in this context can be taken to suggest that our contemporary distinction between homosexual and homosocial might not have occurred to Lyly or to his contemporary readers. For a discussion of the importance of the word "fere" with specific reference to the poetry of the Earl of Surrey, see my *Homoerotic Space: The Poetics of Loss in Renaissance Literature* (Toronto: University of Toronto Press, 2002), pp. 105–06.
24. *Ethica Nicomachea*, IX.5, 1167a.
25. Compare, e.g., John Aubrey's description of Beaumont and Fletcher: "They lived together in the Banke side, not far from the Play-House, both batchelors; lay together; had one Wench in the house between them, which they did so admire; the same cloathes and cloake, &c.; between them" (*Aubrey's Brief Lives*, ed. Oliver Lawson Dick [London: Secker and Warburg, 1950], p. 21).
26. Stewart, *Close Readers*, p. 153. For a perceptive discussion of the role of humanism in the text, see Joan Pong Linton, "The Humanist in the Market: Gendering Exchange and Authorship in Lyly's *Euphues* Romances," in Constance C. Relihan, ed., *Framing Elizabethan Fictions: Contemporary Approaches to Early Modern Narrative Prose* (Kent, OH: Kent State University Press, 1996), 73–97.
27. Edmund Spenser, *Shepheardes Calender, Poetical Works*, ed. J. C. Smith and E. de Selincourt (Oxford: Oxford University Press, 1912), "Januarye," gloss on "Hobbinol."
28. " 'An ensample to all women of lightnesse': Lyly's Lucilla and her Influence," *Imaginaires* 2 (1997): 33.
29. "Wit, Eloquence, and Wisdom in *Euphues: The Anatomy of Wit" Studies in Philology* 81 (1984): 306.
30. For a more optimistic view of this topic, see the article by Wilson, "An ensample to all women of lightnesse."
31. The common sixteenth-century spelling "abhominable" underscores the point I have been making. This spelling supported the false etymology that the word came from Latin "ab" and "homo" and thus referred to something not suitable for men. The word actually derives from the Latin verb "abominor," whose roots are "ab" and "omen."
32. *Ethica Nicomachea*, IX.12, 1172a.

Chapter 7

Rogue-Sirens: Urban Seduction and the Collapse of *Amicitia*

Morgan Holmes

In his 1630 courtesy treatise, *The English Gentleman*, Richard Brathwaite observes that "the life of man . . . is a *continuall temptation*"—there is "neither time, place, sexe nor condition exempted from temptation."[1] According to Brathwaite the impulse to stray from gentlemanly decorum must be resisted if civilization is to survive the changes he and many others imagined infecting the realm. The chapbook literature of roguery, which appeared in England from roughly the mid-sixteenth century through the first two decades of the seventeenth, directly engaged with (and likely help to foment) this perceived crisis. These popular narrative accounts of the criminal underworld repeatedly emphasize that for the young man about town, illicit temptation is immensely difficult to resist. Especially in London, one is constantly at risk of falling prey to the seductive dexterity of Machiavellian rogues who are able to take a "cony" (the term, in cant parlance, for a hapless victim) and lay him "upon the Anvil of their wits, till they have wrought him like wax."[2] Malleable to seductive tempters, conies can be reshaped or "versed"[3]—that is, emotionally and physically turned from the upstanding life they once knew—to a host of debased desires and practices.

Such potentially disturbing metamorphosis can be considered in light of Jean Baudrillard's distinction between *eros* and seduction. The former, Baudrillard suggests, is "the force of attraction, of fusion, of conjugation"; the latter, meanwhile, is the "more radical figure of disjunction, distraction, illusion and diversion, a figure that alters essence and meaning, alters identity and the subject."[4] Temptation through eroticized seduction occupies an important place in the early modern literature of roguery. These representations of metamorphic seductions tell us much about the mutating of traditional identities and relationships among, for the most part, non-aristocratic people, particularly in London, one of Europe's preeminent transformative urban environments.

While the study of eroticism in literary roguery has, to date, mostly been concerned with cross-gender desire and behavior, in this essay I focus on homoerotic relations between men.[5] Many of the chapbook tales of rogues' schemes and adventures, I endeavor to show, offer untapped opportunities to deepen our understanding of the changing nature of male homoeroticism in early modern England. That said, I am the first to admit that digging up a few more 400-year-old literary manifestations of homoeroticism is, on its own, not a terribly exciting undertaking after twenty-odd years of similar scholarly pursuits. Instead, the more important critical work I hope this chapter accomplishes is an illumination of the way the literature of roguery represents what I believe was a turning point in cultural history. Certain of these roistering chapbooks strongly suggest that between about the mid-sixteenth century and the first two decades of the next, English society witnessed the debasement of the long-standing ethical and cultural value of male homoeroticism and its replacement by attitudes more in keeping with modern Western attitudes.

One of my key terms in this study is *amicitia*, a centuries-old, homoerotically vectored manifestation of intense male bonding associated with supreme masculine virtue, especially within society's more elevated ranks. My central point is that the tempting performances of homoerotic seduction and friendship found in roguery narratives mark the disintegration of *amicitia* and its usurpation by decidedly modern, urban, and instrumental alliances geared toward financial gain. *Amicitia* certainly did not vanish entirely from England in or around 1620; but if we credit the literature of roguery with some degree of evidentiary veracity, its cultural authority was severely undermined and the way was paved for its relegation to the cabinet of ancient curiosities.

In order to establish the main moral and historical contexts for this discussion, I begin by addressing the perceived threat that roguery and vagabondage posed to social stability. I then explore the cultural valence of homoerotic male friendship and its seductive simulations by London's rogues (a.k.a. "cony-catchers"). A major part of my close textual analysis focuses on Gilbert Walker's 1552 chapbook, *A Manifest Detection of the Most Vile and Detestable Use of Diceplay*. More than any other, this pamphlet influenced the form and content of subsequent sixteenth- and seventeenth-century rogue writings. Walker's work both clarifies the importance of homoeroticism to metropolitan roguery and establishes the concerns that, as I show in the final section of the essay, animate the wickedly ribald accounts by Robert Greene and Thomas Dekker of *amicitia*'s translation into aggressive self-interest.

THE PERILS OF ROGUERY

The orthodox early modern conceptualization of roguery took it to be a source of great danger to England's security. Vehemently denounced by Parliament and the Established Church, perfidious rogues and vagabonds were the *bêtes noires* of upstanding community relations.[6] The Elizabethan homily "Against Idlenesse," for instance, warns that if left unchecked by England's "good and godly lawes," an unwholesome bevy of "idle vagabonds and loitering runnagates . . . deuoure the sweet fruits of other mens labour, being common lyers, drunkardes, swearers, theeues, whooremasters, and murderers, refusing all honest labour, and giue themselues to nothing else, but to inuent and doe mischiefe." Motivated by such attitudes, successive Tudor and Stuart laws mandated grisly punishments for those men and women discovered to be rogues.[7] The chapbook literature of roguery picked up on (and at times even helped to fuel) these normative evaluations, not infrequently labeling rogues as "caterpillars" who stealthily munch away on the green leaves of the commonwealth. As Thomas Dekker's vigilant Belman even more hysterically observes, "those Monsters" are "More dangerous . . . to a State, then a *Ciuill Warre*, because their villanies are more subtile and more enduring."[8]

In many early modern chapbooks, rogue toxicity is based on a cunning misappropriation of civility's material and performative signifiers. Rogue writings are peppered with references to "gentlemen-foists"; men who "go commonly well apparelled . . . [and] bear the port of right good gentlemen"; villains who "carry[ ] the shew of Gentlemen";[9] and others who are "apparelled like honest civil Gentlemen, or good fellows, with a smooth face, as if butter would not melt in their mouths."[10] In a tone of utter exasperation, Dekker's Belman asks: "Who would imagine that Birds so fair in shew and so sweet in voice should be so dangerous in condition?"[11]

Anxiety over these adroit performances makes cultural sense given what Katharine Eisaman Maus argues was a deep interest in early modern England with the potentially dangerous disjuncture between inward, private belief and outward, public appearance.[12] Francis Bacon's skeptical regard for the opacity of the human heart provides us with a contemporary insight into this hazardous gap. Despite his conviction that a completely open relationship with another man is possible and laudable, Bacon recognized that for the most part people do not fully reveal their desires and intentions to others. In keeping with his long-standing concern over the powers of human judgment and the difficulties entailed in the accurate discernment of truth, in his Tacitean essay "Of Simulation and Dissimulation" Bacon anatomizes the various means employed for the "hiding and veiling of a man's self." Of the three methods—"Closeness," "Dissimulation," and "Simulation"—the latter most precisely characterizes rogue performances for, as Bacon puts it, simulation exists "when a man industriously and expressly feigns and pretends to be that he is not." Along similar lines, when describing the London underworld's dangerous horde of rogues, one of Gilbert Walker's speakers concludes: "the foundation of all those sorts of people is nothing else but mere simulation."[13] Highly mobile thespians of the street, London's cony-catching rogues (or at least their literary avatars) aggressively and treacherously capitalized on the relative ease of simulating respectable identities in their relentless pursuit of illicit pleasures and filthy lucre.

SIRENIC SIMULATION

In *The English Gentleman*, Richard Brathwait condemns the "insinuating *Sharkes*" who simulate virtuous companionship, warning his readers: "So dangerous are these *Syrenian* friends, that like the *Sicilian* shelves, they menace shipwracke to the inconsiderate sailer." Nicholas Breton, in his character book *The Good and the Badde*, describes a "Knaue" as a roguish fellow who, because of his "Sirens tongue," is "the hurt of Amity" and "a Traytor to Affiance."[14] Employing near-identical terminology to describe cony-catchers, Robert Greene complains that "these caterpillars resemble the Sirens" who "... sound out most heavenly melody in such pleasing chords, that whoso listens to their harmony, lends his ear unto his own bane and ruin."[15]

Thomas Dekker evokes the power and the danger of these sirenic wiles in his portrayal of the demon Pamersiel who is sent to our world to recruit people to fight under Lucifer's "dismal and black Colors." As we will soon see, the instructions Pamersiel receives strongly resemble the seductive practices of human rogues: "Creep into bosoms that are buttoned up in satin," Satan instructs his minion, "and there spread the wings of thine infection. Make every head thy pillow to lean upon, or use it like a Mill, only to grind mischief."[16] Satan's imagery of bosoms and pillows neatly captures the overheated and eroticized component of rogue-sirens' uncivil seductions.

A complete understanding of these encounters between rogue-sirens and their male conies needs to take account of the idealized homoerotic relationship they perversely imitate. One of the hallmarks of early modern gentlemanliness was *amicitia*, a virtuous friendship between two men rooted in centuries of tradition and honor. It is important to recognize that *amicitia* was not a culturally eccentric phenomenon. In his study of the moral and, especially, literary representation of homosexual desire during the sixteenth and early seventeenth centuries, Bruce Smith underscores the importance for this period of perfectly symmetrical, classically inspired bonding to emotional and political ties between men. Masculine same-gender desire was not marginal to common social experience, Smith contends; early modern people acknowledged a "*potential* for erotic feeling in male relationships of all kinds," whether age-graded, gender-marked, or egalitarian. He also observes that "homosexuality" was an important "symbolic way[] in which males could enact and affirm the patriarchal power that dominated the entire culture." Jeffrey Masten similarly remarks that in this era homoerotic friendship between men was "not only sanctioned but also *constitutive* of power relations."[17]

The cultural basis for *amicitia*'s value was well entrenched. In his essay "On Having Many Friends," for instance, Plutarch draws on Aristotle and Cicero to maintain: "in our friendship's consonance and harmony there must be no element unlike, uneven, or unequal, but all must be alike to engender agreement in words, counsels, opinions, and feelings, and it must be as if one soul were apportioned among two or more bodies."[18] Francis Bacon's 1612 essay, "Of Friendship," articulates a similar understanding current in early modern Europe: "It is friendship, when a man can say to himselfe, I loue this man without respect of vtility. I am open hearted to him, I single him from the generality of those with whom I liue; I make him a portion of my owne wishes." Bacon likewise concludes in his discourse "Of Love" that "Nuptial love maketh mankind; friendly love perfecteth it."[19] Brathwait also describes masculine friendship as "two hearts . . . so individually united, as neither from other can well be severed." Of all commentators, Michel de Montaigne glosses *amicitia* the most movingly in his explanation of why he adored his friend Étienne: "Because it was he, because it was my selfe."[20]

Given the cultural importance of *amicitia*, it is not surprising that in the literature of roguery the masquerade of homoerotic companionship is a prime strategy of seduction for roguish men who sought to destabilize normative power arrangements and allocations of symbolic value and material wealth. Again, there is an abundance of anxious commentary on such behavior. One must beware crafty imitations of friendly likeness because, Plutarch counsels, "flattery which blends itself with every emotion, every movement, need, and habit, is hard to separate from friendship"; on this account, sirenic devils shape themselves to whatever is agreeable to a man in order to gain his trust and so achieve their foul ends. Darkening Plutarch's picture, Brathwait warns that camaraderie is easily simulated by men who possess "a Heart outward, and a Heart inward; outwardly pretending, and inwardly plotting."

Drawing on such pragmatic assessments of the difficulty of knowing whether or not the signifiers of *amicitia* are genuine or mere facsimiles, Robert Greene associates with counterfeit friendship that which Thomas Harman (an earlier pamphleteer) refers to as rogues' "double demeanor in each degree."[21] Greene therefore advises his readers that a "Taker-up"—one of the four men necessary to carry out the "Barnard's Law" of cony-catching—has "a thousand policies to insinuate himself into a man's acquaintance."[22] It is this eerie power of simulation as it revels in this shady hollow between an external image of love and an internal, "pollitick" corruption that so intrigues Greene and other creative recorders of the urban underworld. In their writings, criminal simulations of *amicitia* are windows onto an erotically perverse community of rogues, perverse not because they exhibit homoerotic traits or perhaps even indulge in homoerotic activities, but because they manipulate friendship's commendable social charge to achieve wicked, destructive ends.

DICEPLAY AND DESIRE IN THE URBAN WILDS

Sirenic rogue eroticism is nowhere more amply attested to than in Gilbert Walker's influential chapbook, *A Manifest Detection of the Most Vile and Detestable Use of Diceplay*, a work Arthur Kinney describes as "marvellously integrated" and "poetically realized." The fact that this octavo pamphlet survives today in only three copies and is probably a second edition of a lost, shorter version written or printed around 1545, is material indication of the text's popularity. Walker's text was not only instrumental in establishing the popularity of rogue literature in England, but it also provided a foundational text on which successive generations drew for inspiration, language, concepts, and plots.[23] Understanding homoerotic rogue seductions in *A Manifest Detection* therefore provides a framework for comprehending this dimension of subsequent rogue writings.

A Manifest Detection is written in dialogue form and comprises a discussion between two "Interlocuters" known simply as "R" and "M," the former man a victim of gentleman cony-catchers and the latter a worldier sort who deciphers the seductive deceits that have been practiced on his friend. With *A Manifest Detection* we enter a world of addictive vice memorably condemned by the Tudor anti-theatricalist, John Northbrooke. Diceplay—the Devil's "alectiue"—Northbrooke vigorously admonishes, is

> a doore and windowe into all theft, murder, whoredome, swearing, blaspheming, banketting, dauncing, rioting, drunkennesse, pryde, couetousnesse, craft, deceyt, lying, brawling, fighting, prodigalitie, night-watchings, ydlenesse, beggerie, pouertie, bankrupting, miserie, prisonment, hanging, &c. and what not.[24]

The Puritan moralist Philip Stubbes similarly fulminates that cony-catching through gambling is "worser than open theft" because "this being a craftie pollitick theft, and commonly don vnder pretence of Freendship, few, or none at all can beware of it."[25] Clearly, from a normative moral perspective "friendly" cony-catching gamblers such as those who appear in *A Manifest Detection* inhabit a realm of sinful iniquity that threatens the foundations of civilization.

In Walker's urban wilds, a dangerous belt of perverse affection cinches ever tighter around moral society. The preface to *A Manifest Detection* plainly sets out Walker's principal anxiety regarding society's vulnerability to dissolution: "under color and cloak of friendship, many young Gentlemen be drawn to their undoing" (p. 65). This "undoing" of a gentleman through false *amicitia* begins at the level of simulation. Roaming about in St. Paul's Cathedral (a center point in the criminal as well as the socially upstanding geography of early modern London[26]), "R" reports that he noted that "there walked up and down by me in the body of the Church a gentleman, fair dressed in Silks, Gold, and Jewels, with three or four servants in gay liveries" (p. 66). As "R" explains, he and the man quickly caught each other's fancy:

> I advised him well, as one that pleased me much, for his proper personage and more for the wearing of his gear and he again at each check made in our walking cast earnest looks upon me . . . [which signified] that he noted in me something that liked him well, and could be content to take some occasion to embrace my acquaintance.

Given the homoerotic potential in early modern friendship's passionate "embraces," the "earnest looks" and non-aural communication of interest and desire that radiate between the two men during their watchful St. Paul's encounter suggestively parallel the behavior known today among gay men as "cruising." In his narrative, Walker also ambiguates the distinction between courtship as political attendance in the halls of power, and courtship as an erotic game, presenting the successful seduction of "R"—"but a raw Courtier"—by a rogue-siren who himself claims to be " 'too old a courtier' " (p. 67). By drawing together the two types of courting, Walker in fact merely illuminates the fact that, as Tudor and Stuart social-climbers well knew, political "courting" was itself an eroticized economy of patronage and friendship circulating, primarily, among men.[27]

The seduction of one man by another, Walker's story demonstrates, is an intoxicating ritual that demands interpretation; yet, it is all too easy to be mistaken in one's evaluations. "R" explains to his friend that he attempted (as Plutarch and other theorists of *amicitia* said one must) to "understand" the gentleman's "behavior, and what sort he was of (for man's nature, as ye know, is in those things curious, specially in such as profess courting)" (p. 66). For this tender youth, however, the sirenic "grammar" (to use Walker's term) of simulated friendly seduction was too "curious" to decipher correctly, and therefore he was unable to resist the rogue's advances:

> therefore, lay all excuses aside, and shape yourself to keep me company for one dinner, while your man and mine shall walk here together till twelve of the clock, and if your friends happen to come hither, he shall bring them home to us. I love to see Gentlemen swarm and cleave together like Burrs. (p. 67)

Walker's text seems again to leap across the centuries to the present day when, upon hearing this tale, "M" breathlessly asks: "How, then? Went ye home together?" "What else?" "R" responds: "Would ye have me forsake so gentle a friend, and so necessary acquaintance?" (p. 67). Entirely enmeshed in an enticing fiction of *amicitia*, "R" is powerless to resist the masculine swarming and cleaving that the well-dressed and courteous rogue so deftly promises.

Walker ensures that his readers are made well aware of the shocking perils that await trusting gamblers. Explaining to his friend the methodology of rogues, "M" reports that once the leader of the "gay gamesters" has "sucked [his] needy companion so dry that there remaineth no hope to press any drop of further gain from him," he then attempts to convert his new young friend to a life of cony-catching by using "necessity for a great part of persuasion" (p. 74). Playing the part of a wise and caring partner, this elder rogue informs his novice that he wishes "to help you to maintain yourself like a gentleman, as hitherto of yourself ye have been able." In order to assure cooperation, the arch-swindler says to his poor cony: "Neither can ye forget ... how friendly I have entertained you in every condition, making my house, my Servants, my Horses, mine apparel, and other things whatsoever I had, rather common to us both than private to myself" (p. 73). Set within the context of a culture steeped in the theory of ideal male bonding and mutuality, the rogue's words shimmer in a seductive simulation of *amicitia*'s codified rhetoric.

A crucial point to be noted in this conversion ritual is that Walker's censuring of cony-catchers is not based on homophobia, but rather on a far more material anxiety that their actions will lead to the economic and moral ruin not just of isolated individuals but quite possibly of an entire stratum of society. This frightening potential of widespread disintegration is indeed what one of Walker's earliest readers gleaned from the text. The anonymous author of one of the first English courtesy treatises, *The Institucion of a Gentleman*, warns of diceplay that for

> noble men and gentlemen, yet doth it vngentle them both by the thyng it self (as hassardors are accompted vnhonest men) and also for that it vnricheth lordes, & maketh the*m* poore gentleme*n*: it putteth oftimes a Castle into a capcase, of old ma*n*ers it byldeth newe Cotagis, it torneth fee simple to fee single, with other infinite like properties.[28]

As we have seen, the principal irony that rogue narratives point to in such scenarios of degeneration is that the "ungentling" process is carried out by men who look and act like true, amicable gentlemen.

Having noted "sparks" of "fidelity and secretness" in the youth's "nature," and having convinced his cony that the only salvation is to turn rogue himself, Walker's rogue-siren then draws his new acolyte into a "closet" where he instructs him in the "privy way" of crooked diceplay so that he too may cozen the unwary (pp. 74–75). But not just any dupes will do; specifically, the professor rogue wants his recruit to capitalize on his "acquaintance" with "such as be rich and full of money," for "better it is that each man of them smart a little than you to live in lack" (p. 74). In order to survive his tumble from fiscal stability, the young gentleman will be forced into a life of roguery, thereby sacrificing his former companions for and through a perverse simulation of *amicitia*. From what we can glean of roguish pursuits, however, it is unlikely that these new conies will suffer only "a little"; more probably, they too will endure a downward spiral to absolute penury and thereupon be compelled to cony-catch their own uninitiated friends. This likelihood of an incremental domino-effect "undoing" among the gentry—a rampant practice of "spoiling Gentlemen of their inheritance"[29]—warrants a fear that Thomas Dekker later raises when he claims the underworld aims at nothing less than destroying "*Law*, *Iustice*, *Order*, *Ceremonie*, *Religion*, *Peace*, and that honourable title of *Goodnesse*."[30] At this rate, Walker's story prompts readers to ask, how soon will it be before true *amicitia* has vanished because all gentlemen have metamorphosed into siren-rogues?

In *A Manifest Detection* and a host of other such publications, the debasement of *amicitia* and gentlemanliness is the result of a wicked, often rank-jumping contamination of intimate, trustworthy male partnership. In its role as a cautionary tale for young gallants visiting the big city, however, Walker's chapbook attempts to rescue ideal male friendship by juxtaposing the true solidarity of "R" and "M" (whose wise counsel aims to save his companion from more misery) and the malice of simulated gentlemen. As conclusive evidence of the great gulf that separates true and false camaraderie, Walker asserts that even among rogues themselves, solidarity is a fleeting chimera:

> *R*. Is there no more fidelity among them? Can they not be content, one false knave to be true to his fellow, though they conspire to rob all other men?
>
> *M*. Nothing less! Did not I warn you in the beginning that the end of the science is mere deceit? And would ye have themselves against their kind, to work contrary to their profession? . . .
>
> *R*. . . . And if there cannot be one faithful couple found in the whole band, how might I hope, that am but a stranger, to win an unfeigned friend amongst them? (p. 78)

The "science" of roguish anti-friendship is diametrically opposed to the "faithful couple" ideal set out by Brathwait and others for whom perfect masculine friendship is embodied in the relations of "a faithfull *Damon* or a *Pythias*; a *Pylades* or *Orestes*; a *Bitias* or a *Pandarus*; a *Nisus* or *Euryalus*."[31] These examples of long-term, trustworthy *amicitia*, though, seem to be little match for knavish seducers for whom "falsehood in fellowship" (*Detection*, p. 84) is central to their dangerously seductive way of life.

GREENE, DEKKER, AND METROPOLITAN WILES

A Manifest Detection was followed by a number of other related chapbooks such as John Awdeley's *The Fraternity of Vagabonds* (1561) and Thomas Harman's *A Caveat for Common Cursitors* (1566, 1568, 1573), texts that rather earnestly purport to warn honest folk against the wicked ruses of England's vagabonds and sturdy beggars. By and large, though, it was not until forty years had passed before prose writers again began to produce popular narrative accounts of urban, cony-catching rogues. The stories that Robert Greene and Thomas Dekker put forth in, respectively, the early 1590s and the first two decades of the seventeenth century, follow in a number of respects (sometimes to the point of plagiarism) the themes and stories Walker had pioneered, including the exploitative simulation of homoerotic friendship. Examined in company with Walker's work, however, certain tales by Greene and Dekker provide us with a purchase on comprehending the gathering disintegration of *amicitia*'s ethical and cultural value in English society.

In order to understand this transformation it is vital to acknowledge that the literature of roguery that sprang from the pens of Walker, Greene, and Dekker is probably the most metropolitan of all genres to have appeared in early modern England. Its authors have their fingers on the pulse of what Satan, in Dekker's *Lantern and Candlelight*, calls "the great and populous

City in the West" (p. 225). Lawrence Manley has identified the ways in which Greene's cony-catching pamphlets evince a "low-life 'roughing up' of monological structures that yields a more heterogeneous urbanism." Dekker too, Manley argues, injects into his prose the spirit and issues that constituted London's "savage turmoil." Not unlike Constance Relihan who reasons that Greene's fictions destabilize normative attitudes toward legality and morality, Manley concludes that professional writers such as Greene and Dekker, their "heteroglot readership," and the cony-catchers who populate their chapbooks, share an awareness of the "power of the city" to "reconstitute classes, estates, and professions."[32] If we credit the literature of roguery with even a modicum of documentary truth-telling, it seems clear that gentlemanly *amicitia* did not go unscathed by the metropolis's metamorphic power. Two hundred years before Percy Shelley penned the famous verdict that "HELL is a city much like London," guidebooks to the capital's underworld exposed the dark arts of seduction practised under cloak of virtue.[33]

The homoerotic seductions woven into chapbooks by Greene and Dekker appear on the surface to be much like the one recounted at length in *A Manifest Detection*. Greene's last published work, *The Black Book's Messenger*, for instance, offers the witty antihero Ned Browne an opportunity to recount his exploits among the London citizenry. Like other cozeners who animate roguery's chapbooks, this rogue was "in outward shew a Gentlemanlike companion, attired very brave"; Browne mirthfully recalls that he once "walk[ed] up and down Smithfield, very quaintly attired in a fustian doublet and buff hose, both laid down with gold lace, a silk stocking and a new Cloak."[34] Midway through his memoir, Browne describes a still-potent method of cozening that basks in the glow of devoted *amicitia*: "a number of my companions yet living in England who, being men for all companies, will by once conversing with a man, so draw him to them that he shall think nothing in the world too dear for them, and never be able to part from them, until he hath spent all he hath" (p. 200). Friendly rogues like Browne provided these young men—fellows who were clearly possessed of more money than discretion—with ample temptations to forfeit all they had. For a "lasciviously addicted" cony, London's sirens "have *Aretine's* Tables at their fingers' ends, to feed him on with new kind of filthiness"; those who are "covetously bent" will be tempted by alchemical trickery; men who yearn to travel abroad will be set "on fire" with tales of European capitals and the promise of a joint adventure. This last temptation, Browne tells his readers, instills such a love that "you will rather consent to rob all your friends than be severed from him one hour" (pp. 200–01).[35] Of course, all these seductive promises are merely the means to purloin hapless gents of their overstuffed purses.

In the third chapter of Dekker's *Lantern and Candlelight*, we learn about a similar practice known as "gull-groping," whereby gentlemen are cheated at "ordinaries" (i.e., taverns). Instructed by Pride that "he must put himself in good clothes" because in London men are "looked upon for their outsides," Satan's errand-demon, Pamersiel, is "translated into an accomplished gallant" so that he can mingle undetected among rogues and their conies (pp. 226–27). One of the most homoerotic hoodwinking practices of which Pamersiel hears is the pursuit and conquest of young men who have recently come to the capital after inheriting their fathers' estates. Once the rogues have discovered such a man's lodging, they appoint a particularly intelligent member of the company to entice their prey:

> after some four or five days spent in Compliment, our heir to seven hundred a year is drawn to an Ordinary, into which he no sooner enters but all the old-ones in that Nest flutter about him, embrace, protest, kiss the hand, *Congée* to the very garter, and, in the end, to shew that he is no small fool, but that he knows his father left him not so much money for nothing, the young Cub suffers himself to be drawn to the stake. (p. 230)

Painting a scene of exaggerated courtliness likely intended to produce mirth in his nonaristocratic readership, Dekker shows how easily *amicitia* may be performed for wicked ends: "For even they that seem dearest to his bosom shall first be ready and be the foremost to enter with the other Leaders into conspiracy how to make spoil of his golden bags" (p. 230).

These two examples illustrate the continued currency of homoerotic friendship in tales of rogue seductions. Yet, Greene and Dekker do not piously reproduce this motif in exactly Walker's mid-sixteenth-century terms. For instance, while the gull-groping rogues at the tavern are clearly up to no good, Dekker's satirical tone makes it quite uncertain whether we are supposed to sympathize wholeheartedly with the young innocent who gets fleeced of all his money. As with Greene, there is something too in Dekker's enthusiastic tone and effort to amuse that differentiates his tale of *amicitia*'s subversion from Walker's much more earnest, morally scandalized delivery. Finally, while in Walker's rendition homoerotic temptation lies at the heart of cozenage, in narratives by Greene and Dekker it is but one glittering tile in a whole complicated mosaic of deceit; as a result, false friendship experiences an equalizing loss of place as the preeminent underworld treachery.

Greene and Dekker's representations of homoerotically spiced criminality conform to their representation of a city that dissolves moral and social difference through a sheer abundance of people, pleasures, and pursuits. During his late-night excursions *en ville*, Pamersiel discovers that "ordinaries" are aptly named places in which a radical leveling of rank occurs: "it was a school where they were all fellows of one Form, and [where] a country gentleman was of as great reckoning as the proudest Justice that sat there on the bench above him" (p. 227). This tavern might be taken as a microcosm of Greene and Dekker's metropolitan vision. Living up to its early modern name, everyone here is truly *ordinary*—that is, their public stations may differ but their desires and many of their devices are the same. In the context of an increasingly heterogeneous urban environment, Greene and Dekker transform Walker's nostalgic concern that classical *amicitia* is a threatened phenomenon into a blackly humorous proposition that at least in London the market and self-interest govern human relations.

In *A Manifest Detection*, "M" tells his friend that once a rogue has robbed a cony of all his money, he will endeavor to convert him to a life of crime by delivering a lecture on the pervasiveness of cozenage in all areas of human intercourse:

> no man is able to live an honest man unless he have some privy way to help himself withal, more than the world is witness of. Think you that noble men could do as they do if in this hard world they should maintain so great a port only upon their rent? Think you the lawyers could be such purchasers if their pleas were short and all their judgments, justice, and conscience?... Could merchants, without lies, false making their wares and selling them by a crooked light to deceive the chapman in the thread or color, grow so soon rich, and to a baron's possessions, and make all their posterity gentlemen?... Whoso hath not some anchorward way to help himself, but followeth his nose, as they say, always straightforward, may well hold up the head for a year or two but the third he must needs sink and gather the wind into beggars' haven. (p. 74)

As we have seen, Walker's story attempts to refute the rogue-siren's advocacy of an "anchorward way" by offering the example of the honorable friendship between "M" and "R." The sneaking suspicion that worldly success depends on following a "privy way" of deceit does, however, vividly resurface in later writings that lack *A Manifest Detection*'s conservative moral containment.

In Greene's *Notable Discovery*, for instance, a swindler argues: "I am sure you are not so ignorant, but you know that few men can live uprightly, unless [they] have some pretty way (more than the world is witness to) to help [themselves] withal" (p. 174).[36] The universality of this "pretty way" underpins *The Defence of Cony-Catching*'s entire sardonic apology: "There is no mystery nor science almost, wherein a man may thrive, without it be linked to this famous art of cony-catching... What trade can maintain his traffic, what science uphold itself, what man live, unless he grow into the nature of a cony-catcher?" (pp. 356–57). Cuthbert Cony-Catcher—the text's putative author—even lashes out at none other than Robert Greene, noting that he is "a scholar, and a Master of Arts, and a cony-catcher in his kind" (p. 343). Given that Greene himself likely wrote *The Defence*, this accusation carries an ironic deflation of moral pretence. As *The Belman*'s rogue commissar bluntly puts it: "Alas, Alas, Silly Animals, if all men should haue that which they deserue, we should doe nothing but play the *Executioners* and tormenters one of another" (sig. C2^{v}).[37]

In the metropolitan literature of roguery by Greene and Dekker, socially leveling claims for the ubiquity of cozenage merge with a desanctification of *amicitia*. Here, friendship between men sheds its virtuous patina and transforms into merely another means to achieve ignoble, antisocial ends. Whereas Walker's "M" was certain that rogues never form true partnerships, later books represent things rather differently. In Awdeley's significantly titled *Fraternity of Vagabonds*, for instance, the first line testifies that England does, contrary to the opinion of certain doubters, contain a "brotherhood of Vagabonds." Writing not long after Awdeley, Harman casts doubt on *amicitia* as an aristocratic preserve when he recounts: "There was not long sithence two Rogues that always did associate themselves together and would never separate themselves unless it were for some special causes, for they were sworn brothers and were both of one age and much like of favor."[38]

For their part, Greene's elaborations of rogue alliances reflect what Manley identifies as the author's "deepening recognition that the structures, beliefs, and practices which govern social interaction are themselves constituted by mutual investment, confidence, and credit."[39] In his *Second Part of Cony-Catching*, Greene speaks of "nips" and "foists" who "have a kind of fraternity or brotherhood amongst them"; in addition, each one of these crooks "hath some trusty friend whom he calleth his treasurer" (p. 214). Meanwhile, in *The Third and Last Part of Cony-Catching*, Greene describes a "crew of mates"; later, he elaborates the tricks practiced by two "crafty copesmates."[40] What Manley calls Greene's "outlaw point of view"[41] can also be found in Dekker's treatment of rogue fidelity. Indeed, Dekker went so far as to discuss men who had fulfilled Walker's anxiety by devolving, through penury, from upstanding gentlemen into gentleman-rogues. In *Lantern and Candlelight* we are given the example of four "loose-fortuned gallants . . . tied in one knot" who turn to cony-catching in order to support their sensual indulgences (p. 232). Coming together in this way is not purely for monetary gain, however, for as Dekker soon after notes, "sometimes Knaves tie themselves in a knot, because they may be more merry" (p. 239). In *O per se O*, Dekker even spells out a roguish echelon's ten demonic anti-commandments, beginning with: "Thou shalt my true Brother be, keeping thy faith to thy Brothers (as to my selfe) if any such you haue" (sig. N2^{v}). Such claims and directives certainly give one pause to wonder whether *amicitia* had not all along been a rather less artless and pure alliance than its aristocratic and gentlemanly apologists had for centuries made it out to be.

In any event, the late-sixteenth- and early-seventeenth-century shift to a model of merry solidarity among rogues was likely intended, in part, to intensify readers' anxieties over the threat posed by a well-organized and hostile urban underworld, as well as to provide a certain pleasurable *frisson* of dread. More politically, considered in the context of Walker's portrayal of cozening through simulated *amicitia*, these partnerships and networks also indicate a transgressive parody of élite-culture friendship. Second-generation rogue literature—particularly that written by Greene and Dekker—enters into a dissident, corrosive relationship with the orthodox expression of homoeroticism between men as it figures in philosophical disquisitions, courtesy treatises, and Walker's popular narrative. In the chaotic metropolis Greene and Dekker so vividly paint, gentlemen are themselves guilty of underhanded efforts to get ahead in the world. *Amicitia*, that glowing hallmark of gentle breeding, collapses in the urban wilds to become yet another mechanism of deception and profit.

A Manifest Detection raises the suspicion that Plutarchan bonding is an endangered creature; a brutal, concupiscent future seems to lurk just around the temporal bend. While Walker's "M" successfully hauls his friend "R" back from the brink of this brutal *locus infelicis*, however, just a few decades later Greene and Dekker graphically represented this new version of male relations as a virtually inescapable reality that had come to saturate almost all of London's social intercourse.

HERE WE ARE

One of the reasons early modern literature of roguery is so important to cultural history is because it reflects and probably participated in a profound alteration of the ways in which men in Anglophone cultures were and are conventionally permitted to think of their relations with one another. In addition, sirenic rogue seductions illuminate the role of the city in establishing the recognizably modern primacy in male homosocial relations of de-eroticized, instrumental alliances. As even Francis Bacon, the erstwhile proponent of *amicitia*, sighed in a 1625 essay, "There is little friendship in the world, and least of all between equals, which was wont to be magnified."[42]

Just as today the urban space often serves as a crucible in which traditional beliefs, morals, and identities are dissolved and transformed, so too did the London of Gilbert Walker and, especially, of Robert Greene and Thomas Dekker, function as a zone of cultural metamorphosis. As English society became evermore metropolitan in character and outlook, the long-standing privileging of homoerotic male friendship above all other relationships receded into an otherworldly domain that later writers such as John Milton, Thomas Gray, Alfred Tennyson, and E. M. Forster could describe only in the ember terms of youthful reminiscence and nostalgia.

NOTES

The author would like to thank Bruce Smith for his scholarly mentorship and the staff of the Folger Shakespeare Library for their research assistance. Goran Stanivukovic deserves my gratitude for his friendship and our years-long conversation about all things early modern and strange. Preparation of this essay was aided by a fellowship from the Social Sciences and Humanities Research Council of Canada.

1. Richard Brathwait, *The English Gentleman* (1630; Facs. rpt. Amsterdam, 1975), p. 235.
2. Thomas Dekker, *Lantern and Candle-light* (1608), reprinted in *Rogues, Vagabonds, and Sturdy Beggars*, ed. Arthur F. Kinney (1973; rpt. Amherst: The University of Massachusetts Press, 1990), p. 232 (hereafter cited in the text).
3. Robert Greene, *A Notable Discovery of Cozenage* (1591), reprinted in Kinney, p. 179 (hereafter cited in the text).
4. Jean Baudrillard, *The Transparency of Evil: Essays on Extreme Phenomena*, trans. James Benedict (London: Verso, 1993), p. 141.

5. Insightful explorations of cross-gender eroticism among rogues, vagabonds, and beggars can be found in William Carroll's *Fat King, Lean Beggar: Representations of Poverty in the Age of Shakespeare* (Ithaca: Cornell University Press, 1996), passim.
6. A. L. Beier argues that new negative attitudes (such as the ones encountered in the literature of roguery) toward vagrancy emerged in the context of, and in part as a response to, an "emerging bourgeois world of discipline," population migration, landlessness, and destitution (*Masterless Men: The Vagrancy Problem in England, 1560–1640* [London: Methuen, 1985], xxi, pp. 14–28). In the introduction to his anthology of rogue writings, Kinney also addresses the historical causes of vagabondage and anxieties over its perceived proliferation, citing the effects of unemployment, enclosure, industrial expansion, population growth, the disbanding of army and navy units, and monastic dissolution (pp. 19–24).
7. *Certaine Sermons or Homilies Appointed to be Read in Churches In the Time of Queen Elizabeth I* (1623; Facs. rpt. Gainesville, FL, 1968), II.253 (cited by volume and page number). Frequently renewed legal statutes gave cruel force to these demonizing moral views of rogue and vagabond sinfulness. The main Tudor/Stuart statutes legislating against rogues and vagabonds are 22 Hen. VIII.c.12 and 27 Hen.VIII.c.25 (3); 1 Edw.VI.c.3 and 3&4 Edw.VI.c.16 (4.1); 14 Eliz.c.5 (4.1) and 39 Eliz.c.4 (4.2); 1 Jac.I.c.7 and 7 Jac.I.c.4 (4.2), in *Statutes of the Realm* (1817; Facs. rpt. London, 1963, 1967) (cited by volume and part number). The following Royal Proclamations outlaw rogues and vagabonds: 622, 637, 692, 736, 762, 779, 796, 800 in *Tudor Royal Proclamations*, vols. 2 and 3, ed. Paul L. Hughes and James F. Larkin (New Haven: Yale University Press, 1969); and 27, 158, 161, 173, 179 in *Stuart Royal Proclamations*, vol. 1, ed. James F. Larkin and Paul L. Hughes (Oxford: Oxford University Press, 1973). See also Paul Slack's *The English Poor Law 1531–1782* (Cambridge: Cambridge University Press, 1995). For more on the whipping, ear-boring, ear-clipping, branding, carting, imprisonment, compulsory labor, enslavement, banishment, and hanging of rogues, see Beier, *Masterless Men*, pp. 158–64; on the bridewell houses of correction, see Beier, *Masterless Men*, pp. 164–69.
8. Robert Greene, *A Disputation, Betweene a Hee Conny-catcher, and a Shee Conny-catcher* (1592), reprinted in *Cony-Catchers and Bawdy Baskets: An Anthology of Elizabethan Low Life*, ed. Gamini Salgado (Harmondsworth: Penguin, 1972), p. 269; Thomas Dekker, *The Belman of London* (1608; Facs. rpt. Amsterdam, 1973), sig. A3^r (hereafter cited in the text). Evidence of literature's influence on more conventionally political works appears in William Harrison's *The Description of England*, ed. Georges Edelen (1587; Ithaca, NY: Published for the Folger Shakespeare Library by Cornell University Press, 1968), pp. 184–85, which draws on Thomas Harman's *A Caveat or Warning for Common Cursitors* for evidence that England is threatened by a voracious plague of rogues and vagabonds. In general, early modern discussions of the underworld pay little heed to the formal boundaries between history, sociology, and what has come to be thought of as literature. For varying responses to the English literature of roguery's historical accuracy, see Bryan Reynolds, *Becoming Criminal: Transversal Performance and Cultural Dissidence in Early Modern England* (Baltimore: Johns Hopkins University Press, 2002), 1, p. 22;

Ian Archer, *The Pursuit of Stability: Social Relations in Elizabethan London* (Cambridge: Cambridge University Press, 1991), pp. 208–15, pp. 231–33; Frank Aydelotte, *Elizabethan Rogues and Vagabonds* (Oxford: Oxford University Press, 1913), pp. 77, 101, 137; Carroll, *Fat King*, pp. 6–15; Kinney, *Rogues, Vagabonds*, pp. 1–6, 13–19, 32–41; and Salgado, *Cony-Catchers*, p. 15, and *The Elizabethan Underworld* (1977; rpt. New York: St. Martin's Press, 1992), p. 33.

9. Dekker, *Lantern*, p. 240.
10. Greene, *A Notable Discovery*, p. 167. Robert Greene, *The Second Part of Conny-Catching* (1592), reprinted in Salgado, *Cony-Catchers*, p. 217; John Awdeley, *The Fraternity of Vagabonds* (1561), reprinted in Kinney, *Rogues, Vagabonds*, p. 95.
11. Dekker, *Lantern*, p. 243.
12. Maus briefly but suggestively addresses the counterfeiting of acquaintance and respectability by rogues in Greene's *Notable Discovery of Cozenage* (*Inwardness and the Theater in the English Renaissance* [Chicago: University of Chicago Press, 1995], pp. 24–26). In his discussion of a Foucauldian "penal semiotics," Carroll also touches on the relations between official concerns and literary representations of rogues' mastery of "the codes of civil society" (p. 45).
13. Bacon, *A Selection of His Works*, ed. Sidney Warhaft (New York: Macmillan, 1965), pp. 58–59. Gilbert Walker, *A Manifest Detection of the Most Vile and Detestable Use of Diceplay, and Other Practices Like the Same* (1552), reprinted in Kinney, *Rogues, Vagabonds*, p. 73. Carroll discusses dissimulation and simulation through recourse to Baudrillard (p. 46).
14. Brathwait, *The English Gentleman*, pp. 253–54; Nicholas Breton, *The Goode and the Badde, Or Descriptions of the Worthies, and Vnworthies of this Age* (London, 1616), p. 24.
15. Greene, *Second*, pp. 207–08.
16. Dekker, *Lantern*, pp. 225–26.
17. Bruce R. Smith, *Homosexual Desire in Shakespeare's England: A Cultural Poetics* (Chicago: University of Chicago Press, 1991), pp. 76, 75. Throughout his book, Smith illuminates the connections between male friendship and homoeroticism in a wide variety of Classical and Renaissance moral treatises and literary texts; see esp. pp. 33–41, 55–77. Jeffrey Masten, *Textual Intercourse: Collaboration, Authorship, and Sexualities in Renaissance Drama* (Cambridge: Cambridge University Press, 1997), p. 37.
18. Plutarch, "On Having Many Friends," in *Plutarch's Moralia*, vol. 2, trans. Frank Cole Babbitt (London: Heinemann and Cambridge, MA: Harvard University Press, 1928), p. 67. Despite his allowance here of "two or more bodies," throughout his essay Plutarch makes clear that a loving male couple is the optimum basis for an ideal friendship (cf. pp. 49–51).
19. Bacon, *Selection*, pp. 41, 70. In the enlarged versions of Bacon's essay "Of Friendship" that appeared after the edition of 1612, the homoerotic connotations are significantly diminished and are replaced, e.g. in the 1632 text, with a utilitarian focus on the ways in which a friend can aid in one's worldly endeavors ("Of Friendship," in *The Essayes or Covnsels, Civill and Morall* [London, 1632], pp. 149–63).
20. Brathwait, *The English Gentleman*, pp. 243, 279. For more on Brathwait's visual and verbal homoerotic twinning in the context of Renaissance textual

collaboration between men, see chapter two of Masten's study. Michel de Montaigne, *Montaigne's Essays*, vol. 1, trans. John Florio (1603; London, 1965), p. 201.

21. Plutarch, "How to Tell a Flatterer from a Friend," in *Plutarch's Moralia*, vol. 1, trans. Frank Cole Babbitt (London: Heinemann and Cambridge, MA: Harvard University Press, 1949), pp. 275, 271; Brathwait, *The English Gentleman*, p. 237; Thomas Harman, *A Caveat for Common Cursitors, Vulgarly Called Vagabonds* (1566), reprinted in Kinney, *Rogues, Vagabonds*, p. 153.
22. Greene, *A Notable Discovery*, p. 165.
23. Kinney, *Rogues, Vagabonds*, pp. 61, 245. On Walker's influence, see Aydelotte, pp. 120–21; and Kinney, *Rogues Vagabonds*, pp. 61–62. Walker's text was largely plagiarized in the anonymous *Mihil Mumchance, His Discouerie of the Art of Cheating in False Dyce Play, and Other Vnlawfull Games* (London, 1597).
24. John Northbrooke, *A Treatise Against Dicing, Dancing, Plays, and Interludes* (1577; New York, 1971), pp. 117, 119.
25. Philip Stubbes, *The Anatomie of Abuses* (London, 1583), sig. O7^{v}.
26. As a meeting place for men and rogues, Saint Paul's joined other homosocial locales such as pubs, taverns, alehouses, ordinaries, and theaters. In his seventeenth-century survey of London, Donald Lupton presents Saint Paul's in a similar light as Walker, commenting on the "Company of *Hungarians*" (his word for cony-catchers) who stroll the "middle Ile" of the cathedral waiting for a wealthy "yonker." When they locate one, in order to fleece their prey of his money these rogues "neuer leaue flatring him in his own words and sticke as close to him, as a Bur vppon a Trauailers cloake; and neuer leaue him til he and they haue saluted the greene Dragon, or the Swanne behind the Shambles" (*London and the Covntrey Carbonadoed and Quartered into Seuerall Characters* [London, 1632], p. 12). Reynolds discusses Saint Paul's in connection with London's criminal subculture, and in so doing also makes brief reference to Walker's tale (pp. 109–13).
27. As Bray shows, the "subtle bonds" uniting patrons, clients, suitors, and friends engaged in ritualized political courtship were "virtually entirely" composed of the "conventions" of homoerotic male comradeship ("Homosexuality and the Signs of Male Friendship in Elizabethan England," *History Workshop* 29 [1990]: 3–8). See also Robert Shephard's discussion of eroticized courting (and subsequent appraisals of it) at the courts of Elizabeth and James ("Sexual Rumours in English Politics: The Cases of Elizabeth I and James I," in *Desire and Discipline: Sex and Sexuality in the Premodern West*, ed. Jacqueline Murray and Konrad Eisenbichler [Toronto: University of Toronto Press, 1996], pp. 101–22).
28. *The Institucion of a Gentleman* (1555; Facs. rpt. Amsterdam, 1974), sig. Hviii^{r}–Hviii^{v}. Slightly earlier in this text the author bases his chapter-long condemnation of dicing among gentlemen on information and opinions that he gleaned from "a little boke called the deteccion of dicepley" (sig. Hvii^{r}). In all likelihood this text is one of the editions of Walker's *Manifest Detection*. Northbrooke offers a similar condemnation of diceplay as the catalyst of gentility's destruction (p. 141).
29. Walker, *A Manifest Detection*, p. 71.
30. Dekker, *O per se O. Or a New Cryer of Lanthorne and Candle-light* (London, 1612), sig. A2^{r} (hereafter cited in the text).

31. Brathwait's catalogue of archetypal companions echoes Plutarch's "On Having Many Friends" (pp. 49–51).
32. Lawrence Manley, *Literature and Culture in Early Modern London* (Cambridge, 1995), pp. 346, 361, 347. Constance C. Relihan, *Fashioning Authority: The Development of Elizabethan Novelistic Discourse* (Kent, OH and London: Kent State University Press, 1994), p. 69. My thoughts on London as a principle locus of heterogeneity and transformation, particularly with regard to sexuality, find intriguing cross-cultural parallels in a recent article by N. S. Davidson on unauthorized sexual practices in early modern Venice, another heterogeneous metropolitan space undergoing rapid and sometimes startling social change (see "Sodomy in Early Modern Venice," in *Sodomy in Early Modern Europe*, ed. Tom Betteridge [Manchester: Manchester University Press, 2002], pp. 65–81).
33. Percy Bysshe Shelley, "Peter Bell the Third," in *The Complete Poetical Works of Percy Bysshe Shelley*, ed. Thomas Hutchinson (London: Oxford University Press, 1905), l, p. 146.
34. Robert Greene, *The Black Book's Messenger* (1592), reprinted in Kinney, *Rogues, Vagabonds*, pp. 193, 199 (hereafter cited in the text).
35. *Aretine's Tables* no doubt refers to Raimondi's salacious engravings published along with 16 of Pietro Aretino's bawdy sonnets (Kinney, *Rogues, Vagabonds*, p. 303, n.12). Ian Moulton discusses the reputation Aretino (a known bisexual sodomite) and his texts had for sexual and moral depravity capable of infecting English minds and bodies (*Before Pornography: Erotic Writing in Early Modern England* [Oxford: Oxford University Press, 2000], 119–57). Greene had written of this Aretine seduction by Italianate pseudo-travellers in his earlier pamphlet, *The Defence of Cony-Catching* (1592), reprinted in Salgado; there, the rogues are dressed to kill in either "*la mode de France*," or "*à l'espagnol*" (pp. 358–59 [hereafter cited in the text]).
36. The brackets have been introduced by the text's editor.
37. In *The Belman*, Dekker's chief rogue parodies a traditional Christian humility *topos* when he provides a theoretical underpinning for omnipresent deception: "doe we not all come into the world like arrant *Beggers*, without a rag vpon vs? doe we not all goe out of the world like *Beggers*, sauing onely an old sheete to couer vs? & shall we not walk vp & down in the world like *Beggers*, with old blankets pind about vs?" (sig. C2^{v}).
38. Awdeley, *The Fraternity of Vagabonds*, p. 91; Harman, *A Caveat for Common Cursitors*, p. 121.
39. Manley, *Literature and Culture in Early Modern London*, p. 343.
40. Greene, *The Third and Last Part of Cony-Catching* (1592), reprinted in Salgado, *Cony-Catchers*, pp. 242, 245.
41. Manley, *Literature and Culture in Early Modern London*, p. 343.
42. Bacon, *Selection*, p. 172.

Chapter 8

Gelding Gascoigne

Alan Stewart

A Hundreth sundrie Flowres bounde vp in one small Poesie (1573) has come to carry a lot of critical baggage.[1] As readers have warmed to its playing with both manuscript and print conventions, it has been appropriated as some kind of transitional work, invoked to show the continuities of "manuscript culture" and "print culture," but then just as surely employed to prise them apart. Often these earnest readings fail to deal with the volume's most salient feature—its ironic, erotic humor, which is part and parcel of its strange straddling of manuscript and print. Rather than being a truly transitional work (if such a thing could exist), *A Hundreth sundrie Flowres*, coming almost a full century after Caxton opened his printing press, positions itself deliberately on an *imagined* line between manuscript and print, two contemporaneous media, playing with and mocking readers' complacent expectations of both. With sometimes outrageous wit, it demonstrates why it is too reductive to regard manuscript transmission, as one critical tradition has it, as belonging "to a culture that valued personal intimacy, sociality, and participation, if not also intellectual and social exclusivity—all features that generally distinguished it from print transmission."[2] But it also shows how manuscript transmission is willfully *projected* as belonging to such a culture; how in print, manuscripts and the traffic in manuscripts come to *signal* intellectual and social exclusivity, secrecy, privacy, intimacy, and—as I shall argue here—a particular brand of erotic male sociality that print culture threatens to "geld."

My starting point is a reference in the first document in *The Posies of George Gascoigne Esquire. Corrected, perfected, and augmented by the Authour* (1575), in which George Gascoigne formally laid authorial claim to *A Hundreth sundrie Flowres.*[3] In a dedicatory epistle "to the reuerend Diuines" of the Court of High Commission, the body charged with authorizing printed publication, Gascoigne presents "this seconde edition, my Poemes gelded from all filthie phrases, corrected in all erronious places, and beautified with addition of many moral examples" (¶.iiij^{r}). It has been argued that Gascoigne's lament of censorship may have been exaggerated, for as Richard McCoy has argued, the "gelding" metaphor "is a disturbing one but deceptively hyperbolical for his revisions were slight and superficial."[4] Whatever the reality, the metaphor is important. It figures this "gelding" as a move from pagan classical models (including one presumably fictitious classic) to the Calvinist doctrine of Théodore de Bèze (Beza):

> I neither take example of wanton Ouid, doting Nigidius, nor foolish Samocratius. But I delight to thinke that the reuerend father Theodore Beza, whose life is worthily become a lanterne to the whole world, did not yet disdaine too suffer the continued publication of such Poemes as he wrote in youth. And as he termed them at last *Poëmata castrata*, So shal your reuerend iudgements beholde in this seconde edition, my Poemes gelded . . . (¶.iiij^{r})

As Richard Helgerson has influentially argued, Gascoigne and several of his contemporaries appropriated the myth of the prodigal not only as a *topos* in their fiction but as a trope with which to fashion literary careers; recent work by Richard McCoy, Wendy Wall, and Lorna Hutson has developed that hypothesis.[5] Théodore Beza, however, is an intriguing choice. By 1575, Beza was the living cornerstone of reformed Genevan morality, the acknowledged successor to Calvin, who died in his arms. But Beza's present piety was blotted (or in the prodigal narrative, vouchsafed) by a youthful aberration: a volume of *Poemata*, early Latin experiments written between 1535 and 1540 in the style of classical authors, published in Paris by Conrad Badius in 1548. As an iconic Protestant prodigal, then, Beza fits the bill: but Gascoigne's invocation is, like so many of his allusions, steeped in irony. According to Gascoigne, Beza "did not yet disdaine too suffer the continued publication of such Poemes as he wrote in youth" (¶.iiij^{r})—and indeed, Beza had overseen and authorized a second edition of his *Poemata* in 1569, printed by Henri Estienne in Geneva.[6] But the point of this second edition was not to endorse "continued publication," but precisely to purge the volume of its now embarrassing components.

Gone are witty epitaphs on youthful friends, and in come earnest eulogies on the great and good of European Reformation thought—Melanchthon, Gessner, Luther, Zwingli, Œcolampadius, Calvin. A series of sometimes lascivious love epigrams to one "Candida" disappears. And gone is one poem that more than any other had dogged Beza on his path from Paris to Geneva: "Theodorvs Beza de sva in Candidam & Audebertum beneuolentia,"[7] in which Beza, in Vezelai, pushes himself to choose between the loves [amores] of Candida in Paris, and the charmes [lepores] of his male friend and fellow poet Germain Audebert in Orléans. In the sequence of poems preceding this, Candida has been established as an emphatically physical lover. Now, the attractions of Candida and Audebert are presented in exact, strict counterpoint and ultimately, Beza chooses the man:

> But if I must choose one,
> I will give you priority, Audebert:
> And if Candida starts making a fuss,
> What then? I"ll shut her up with a kiss.[8]

It may well be, as some critics have vehemently argued, that this was a *fantaisie d'étudiant* indulged in by Beza and Audebert, a playful aping of Horace and Catullus.[9] But it became dynamite as evidence when Beza's Catholic detractors claimed that he fled Paris to escape the threat of clamp-down on sodomites.[10] One allegedly quipped, "Instead of your Audebert, now you have embraced Calvin, and so have substituted a spiritual male-whore for a carnal one; thus being still what you were—a sodomist."[11] Two decades after its 1548 publication, the poem was still a talking point in weighty learned commentaries: in his 1567 *Responsio ad Bezam Vezeliam Eceboliam*, Gabriel Fabricius called for readers to remember Beza's obscene verses;[12] in the same year, Claude de Sainctes devoted a long passage to the Audebert verse;[13] and from Poland, Cardinal Stanislas Hosius added his voice.[14] In 1582, the poem was given new life in a muckraking biography of Beza by the anti-Calvinist Jerome Bolsec.[15] We know, too, that the message spread to another English reader: in 1586 when Anthony Bacon was investigated on charges of sodomy in Montauban, France, his young male servant testified that Bacon had talked him into sex by saying there was nothing evil about the practice—indeed, the Genevan minister Beza enjoyed it (and this from Bacon, an ardent Calvinist, who had spent time in Beza's house in Geneva).[16] The poem was still being gleefully cited and lampooned in England as late as 1633, by Benjamin Carrier.[17]

Beza's 1569 revision of his *Poemata* was designed explicitly to rebut the recent attacks by Hosius, Fabricius, and de Sainctes. In a lengthy dedicatory epistle addressed to the Hungarian scholar Andreas Dudith, Beza alludes specifically to the Audebert poem: "these damned men [istos perditos] are not ashamed to transform into an Adonis a man [Audebert] whose life is so exemplary and worthy, and to impute to me a crime against which I am convinced I need not defend myself to any honest man."[18] He claims that his opponents "write that Beza has drunk since his infancy all the lewdness and impudence of the poets; that he has devoted his entire life to satisyfing his passions, and fulfilling his desires; to describing his loves (you remember, reader, the exaggerated rhetorical flourish [δεινωσιν] of an orator from the Sorbonne [Claude de Sainctes]); finally, to avenging himself on his rivals. They go so far as to turn him into a courtesan [meretricem], a bawd [lenam], a sodomite [cinædum]."[19]

So what does it mean that Gascoigne chooses Beza as his prodigal model? In the model provided by the "Audebertus versus Candida" verse, Beza's sexual relations with a woman are inexorably linked with his sexualized relations with a man and friendly versifier—a model that is also, I contend, a central structuring conceit of *A Hundreth sundrie Flowres*. With this allusion Gascoigne provides a strategy for reading *A Hundreth sundrie Flowres*, but, as I shall suggest, it backfires—for it is a strategy that draws attention not only to the volume's faux-manuscript anthology presentation, but also to what Goran Stanivukovic has called "the complex issue of the relationship between the producer, the consumer, and the textual circulation of sodomy" faced with the new demands and possibilities of an expanding print market.[20] Ultimately, Gascoigne gets "gelded" in a way he did not foresee.

§

A Hundreth sundrie Flowres is supposedly a collection of writings by various gentlemen previously in friendly circulation in manuscript, made public in print through the intervention of friends. However, it implies a single author by rehearsing the standard apologia with which many writers (allegedly anxious about a perceived "stigma of print")[21] safeguarded the publication of their works: and indeed, while works by many writers are supposedly included, only "George Gascoigne" is named repeatedly.[22] "Gascoigne" is thus effectively cast within what Gillian Austen has called "a fictive literary circle,"[23] paradoxically employing print to advertise, in Wendy Wall's words, a "manuscript collectivity" which "impersonate[s] the textuality of elite amateurism";[24] throughout, however, as Richard McCoy notes, "the prominence of Gascoigne's name in the table of contents renders this thin veil of anonymity fairly transparent."[25]

This complex apology-cum-identification is established by means of a confected correspondence between the printer, the publisher (in the sense of the one who makes the work public), and the collector/editor—respectively A. B., H. W., and G. T. The naming of A. B.—distinguished from the stationer Richard Smith named on the title page, and bearing initials that might denote the early modern "John Doe"—already alerts the reader to the suspicion that there is less to the publication of *A Hundreth sundrie Flowres* than meets the eye. Even as A. B. refers the reader to prefatory letters by H. W. and G. T., he expresses his doubt that "I feare very muche (all these words notwithsta*n*ding) that these two gentlemen were of one assent compact to haue it imprinted" (sig. Aij^{r}). The printer is happy enough, since he can find "nothing therein amisse" except "two or three wanton places passed ouer in the discourse of an amorous enterprise," and even there, "the words are cleanly (although the thing ment be somewhat naturall)" (sig. Aij^{r-v}). The reader is immediately made aware that this is a volume where "the words" and "the thing ment" may be—and probably are—distinct.

This opening letter refers the reader to the prefatory epistles attached to "A discourse of the aduentures passed by Master F. I."—indicating that despite the volume's variety of materials, this discourse is central. (It also suggests that something went awry with the book's complex, shared printing, since it refers the reader to materials that appear only well into the book—*after* Gascoigne's englishing of Ariosto's *Supposes*.)[26] In two letters, presented in reverse chronological order, the story unfolds. G. T. had taken "a number of *Sonets*, layes, letters, Ballades, Rondlets, verlayes and verses, the workes of your friend and myne Master *F.I.* and diuers others," and had "with long trauayle confusedly gathered [them] together" and "reduce[d] them into some good order . . . in this written Booke" (sig. Aij^{v}). In August 1572, G. T. passed the "written Booke" to his friend H. W., and "charged" H. W. that he "should vse them onely for mine owne particuler commoditie, and eftsones safely deliuer the originall copie to him againe." While H. W. did indeed return the volume, he also "entreated my friend *A.B.* to emprint" it, "[a]nd further haue presumed of my selfe to christen it by the name of *A hundreth sundrie Flowers*" (sig. Ai^{r}).

A Hundreth sundrie Flowres is thus presented to the reader as an anthology—literally, a gathering of flowers, "*one small Poesie*," drawing self-consciously on the printed "manuscript"—popularized in Richard Tottel's 1557 *Songs and sonettes*, and we are thus cast as voyeurs of what Wendy Wall has described as "a surreptitiously printed commonplace book."[27] But crucially, I would add, we are privy to the process of its becoming a "commonplace book," via what G. T. describes as a "register" (sig. Aiii^{r}) compiled from loose papers. Thus we are given the several metamorphoses of this book: from loose papers (conveyed from writers to editor G. T.), to written "register" (lent to H. W. and leaked to A. B.), to (printed) commonplace book. It is the material implications of this first shift—from handwritten loose papers to copied written register—that is at stake, as the written book becomes a printed book, by no means uniquely: after all, as Jeffrey Masten, Peter Stallybrass, and Nancy Vickers have argued, "the era of the printed book is accompanied from the first by a nostalgia for handwriting."[28] But my point is that this "nostalgia" is mobilized to particular ends—and not with perfect success.

The materiality of the process is highlighted from the start. The volume runs directly into the anthologized papers, interspersed with G. T.'s editorial notes, starting:

> When I had with no small entreatie obteyned of Master *F.J.* and sundry other toward young gentlemen, the sundry copies of these sundry matters, then aswell for that the number of them was great, as also for that I found none of them, so barreyne, but that (in my iudgme*n*t) had in it *Aliquid Salis* [something salty, i.e. witty, and especially being considered by the very proper occasion whereuppon it was written (as they them selues did alwayes with the verse reherse vnto me the cause y^{t} then moued them to write) I did with more labour gather them into some order, and so placed them in this register. Wherein as neare as I could gesse, I haue set in the first places those which Master *F.J.* did compyle. And to begin with this his history that ensueth, it was (as he declared vnto me) written vppon this occasio*n*. The said *F.J.* chaunced once in the north partes of this Realme to fall in company of a very fayre gentlewoman whose name was Mistresse *Elinor*, vnto whom bearinge a hotte affection, he first aduentured to write this letter following . . . (sig. Aiij^{r})

G. T.'s interventions here point to the inherent impossibility of his editorial project. For, in order to tell the story, to create a "discourse," G. T. has to have access not merely to the loose papers, the textual traces that he presents to the reader, but also to a firsthand account of the occasion for their composition: the writers "them selues did alwayes with the verse reherse vnto me the cause y^t then moued them to write." The papers by themselves will not tell the story—and G. T.'s "discourse," while appearing to tell the story, in fact introduces more questions than it answers.

F. J.'s first epistle is a straightforward loveletter, couched in standard "fire in frost" Petrarchan paradoxes:

> Mistresse I pray you vnderstand that being altogether a straunger in these parties, my good hap hath bene to behold you to my (no small) contentation, and my euill happ accompanies the same, with such imperfection of my deserts, as that I finde alwayes a readie repulse in mine owne frowardnes. So that consideringe the naturall clymate of the countrie, I must say that I haue found fire in frost. And yet comparing the inequalitie of my deserts, with the least part of your worthines, I feele a continuall frost, in my most feruent fire. Such is then the extremitie of my passions, the which I could neuer haue bene content to committe vnto this telltale paper, weare it not that I am destitute of all other helpe. Accept therfore I beseeke you, the earnest good will of a more trustie (than worthy) seruaunt, who being therby encouraged, may supplie the defects of his abilitie with readie triall of duetifull loyalty. And let this poore paper (besprent with salt teares, and blown ouer with skalding sighes) be saued of you as a safegarde for your sampler, or a bottome to wind your sowing silke, that when the last nedelfull is wrought, you maye returne to readinge therof, and consider the care of hym who is
>
> More youres than his owne. F. I. (sig. Aiij^{r–v})

From his first communication, F. J. insists on the paper-ness of his letters. More than the vehicle that spills his secrets to his beloved, it is a "telltale *paper*," a "poore *paper*" that carries the physical signs of his unrequited passion: besprent [sprinkled] with salt tears, blown over with scalding sighs. And beyond the immediate moment of its reading, it can (if the recipient sees fit) endure and serve another purpose—as a protection for her needlework, or as a "bottom" onto which she can wind her silk.[29] The latter use vouchsafes the letter's rereading, when it becomes visible again as the silk runs out, and the reader's reimagining of its sender, F. J. ("consider the care of hym who is More youres than his owne").

The incorporation of F. J.'s letter into Elinor's sewing works on several levels. The representation of a woman sewing, as Lena Cowen Orlin has argued, signifies "a badge of virtue" for a woman, giving her "an invisibility that in this respect paralleled that of the man of good fame."[30] However, as Jonathan Goldberg and Jennifer Summit have pointed out, a women's needlework is also often figured in problematic relation, both analagous and in opposition to, a man's writing.[31] Playing on those meanings, F. J. is hoping through his writing to enter a supposedly virtuous women's space that he holds and hopes to be sexually suspect: for, as Richard Hyrde writes, "where in all handiworks that men say be more meet for a woman, the body may be busy in one place, and the mind walking in another: and while they sit sewing and spinning with their fingers, may cast and compass many peevish fancies in their minds."[32] Here, F. J. trusts that those "peevish fancies" will center on his letter, a material part of the "sewing," directly held in Elinor's fingers.

Throughout the narrative, letters and verses are importantly material. Elinor responds with a letter: F. J., mistakenly believing it to be his own, rips it into shreds, and has to reassemble it in order to read it (sig. Aiiij^{r-v}). F. J. writes verses to Elinor and "priuily lost them in hir chamber" (sig. B^{r}); later again, "tarying a while in the chamber [he] found oportunitie to loose his sequence neere to his desired Mistres," who has to prise them away from a curious maid (sig. Biij^{v}–Biiij^{r}), and so on. But what is remarkable about these material letters is their heavy eroticization—which surpasses the more obvious physical interaction between the couple. In the case of the first letter, it is only after we read it, with its conceits of how it might remain close to Elinor's person, that we discover that the letter in fact reached Elinor by F. J. stuffing it into her bosom—an act of physical intimacy that we might expect to preempt the epistolary foreplay. Partly this makes for bathetic comic effect; but partly also, I would suggest, it urges the reader to invest in an economy where the traffic in letters is considerably more erotic than its declared goal of simple physical contact. At precisely the moment when the letters move from G. T.'s "register" into A. B.'s printed book, when their material nature is denied, those letters take on a new and dangerous eroticism.

"The aduentures of Master F. I." plays repeatedly on this mismatch between the raw materials of G. T.'s anthology, G. T.'s narrative of events, and the events themselves. Modern critics have often complained of *non sequiturs* in the story, an effect brought about by its trademark lapses in temporal narrative: its habit of providing the reader with pertinent facts only *after* they have ceased to be pertinent, and not at what we might perceive as the "proper" stage of the story. Thus we learn only retrospectively that Dame Frances is F. J.'s kinswoman, that the lord of the house is Elinor's father, and—most crucially—that Elinor has a husband. Conversely, we are told *before we need to be told* that letters supposedly from Elinor are composed by her male secretary—a denial of the punchline we might anticipate. Moreover, the letters and poems—supposedly the materials on which the story is constructed—do not always have a place in that story. Letters are written but not sent; poems are composed but not written down. Time and again we are made aware of the power that these written traces have to mislead the reader. One effect is to produce the reader as cynical but alert, always on the lookout for clues. An overarching conceit of *A Hundreth sundrie Flowres* is that its materials prompt "doubts," "conjectures," and "supposes"—the last played out in Gascoigne's englishing of Ariosto's *I suppositi.* From the outset, we're told by A. B. that "the case seemeth doubtful," and he "will disclose [his] coniecture": immediate signs that the reader needs to start interpreting. This reading strategy is also one that the characters need to adopt—and they do so to a greater or lesser extent.

The heterosexual imperative of F. J.'s "aduentures" drives to produce this alert "learned Reader" as emphatically male. Lorna Hutson argues that the new prose fiction of the 1560s and 1570s, deriving from Bandello, "produced, through its very privileging of exemplary reading as a basis for masculine social agency, a gendered split in its educative orientation toward readers. Women were offered examples of conduct to imitate, or take warning by, while men were asked to identify with male protagonists who used such examples flexibly and pragmatically, as resources for the emplotment of prudent undertakings and persuasive discourses."[33] "The aduentures of Master F. I." can be made to fit this model with frightening ease. Read this way, F. J.'s skill lies not only in his production of letters, sonnets, and riddles, but in his ability to read texts and situations (and then produce his texts *ex tempore*). Elinor, on the other hand, is rendered humorously ridiculous for her inability to read situations, her reductive misunderstanding of basic poetic conceits (she is jealously enraged when F. J. addresses a poem to her as "Helen"), and her comic willingness to make herself sexually vulnerable.

Within the logic of this economy, Elinor is not able by herself to continue the epistolary foreplay initiated by F. J. But after he has delivered his first letter, Elinor responds with the following:

> Your sodeyn departure, from our pastime yesterday, did enforce me for lacke of chosen co*m*pany to return vnto my worke, wherein I did so long continew, till at the last the bare bottome did drawe vnto my remembraunce your straunge request. And although I founde therin no iust cause to credite your coloured woordes, yet haue I thought good hereby to requite you with like curtesie, so that at least you shall not condemne me for vngratefull. But as to the matter therin conteyned, if I could perswade my selfe, that there were in mee any coales to kyndle such sparkes of fire, I might yet peraduenture bee drawen to beleue that your minde were frosen with like feare. But as no smoke ariseth, where no cole is kindled, so without cause of affection the passion is easie to be cured. This is all I vnderstand of your darke letters. And of much as I meane to aunsweare. (sig. Aiiij^{v})

Once again, the material nature of the letter is prioritized. F. J. at first believes it to be a letter from her, when he espies "(*in Romaine*) these letters *SHE.*" Roman or italic hands were and are routinely identified with (usually élite) early modern women, because as writing master Martin Billingsley puts it, it "is conceiued to be the easiest hand that is written with Pen, and to be taught in the shortest time: Therefore it is vsually taught to women, for as much as they (hauing not the patience to take any great paines, besides phantasticall and humorsome) must be taught that which they may instantly learne."[34] However, such an identification is reductive: both women and men are known to have practiced different hands—indeed, as Jonathan Goldberg notes, "one sign of high literacy in the period has precisely to do with the ability to manage several hands."[35] F. J. himself writes "in counterfait" (sig. B^{r}), and it follows that a recognizably "female" hand can be faked by a literate man, in order to give the impression of a woman writing.[36] And sure enough, reading beyond the hand, moving from form to content, suspicions grow. As G. T. reports, "My friend *F. J.* hath tolde me diuers times, that imediately vppon receit hereof, he grew in ielosy, that the same was not her owne deuise." G. T. "allowed his [F. J.'s] iudgment": "For as by the stile this letter of hirs bewrayeth that it was not penned by a womans capacitie, so the sequell of hir doings may discipher, that she had no ready clearkes then trustie seruants in store" (sig. Aiiij^{v}). Here again, the proleptic relevation of "the sequell of hir doings," with its hints of "ready clearkes," undercuts the linear narrative. The reader is told, because "he" needs to know at this point, that the letter was "not penned by a womans capacitie" but by the capacity of a "ready clearke." Later, G. T. informs the reader explicitly of what he has already hinted: "so may you nowe vnderstand the cause. Shee had in the house a friend, a seruaunt, a Secretary: what should I name him? such one as shee esteemed in time past more than was cause in tyme present" (sig. Biiij^{r}).

Elinor would not be unusual in not writing all her own letters: in his recent study of some 2,500 English letters written between 1540 and 1603 ostensibly by women, James Daybell has detected more than a quarter that show evidence of involvement by men in addition to the named female author—by secretaries, amanuenses, and family members.[37] But within F. J.'s "fictive literary circle," Elinor's use of a secretary gives rise instantly to suspicions. G.T. has notable difficulty in defining the Secretary: he is a member of the household, "a friend, a seruaunt, a Secretary"—placed troublingly in several, mutually exclusive categories. Later, he attempts it again, this time calling into question (through a series of rank-based epithets) the Secretary's masculinity: "This manling, this minion, this slaue, this secretary." Angel Day's *The English Secretary* (1599) also tells of the difficulty of placing the secretary socially: "hee is in one degree in place of a *seruant*, so is he in another degree in place of a *friend*."[38] Day himself was anxious on this point, revising the passage extensively between different editions in the 1590s, attempting to answer his own dilemma noting: "The limits of *Friendshippe* (as it might bee obiected) are streight, and there can bee no *Friend* where an inequality remayneth. Twixt the party commanded & him that commaundeth, there is no societie, and therfore no *Friendship* where resteth a *Superiority*."[39] He evades his own conundrum by invoking "affection": "[B]y all common likelihood it is assuredlie to be coniectured, that no one personage of estate, laieth choice vpon such a one to serue so neer about him, and to be in place of so great trust as appertaineth to a man of that reckonning, but ere he long haue vsed him, he bindeth vnto him at least some good part of his affection."[40] But this undefined "affection" inevitably leaves the relationship open to accusation: according to Sir Robert Cecil, himself a principal secretary of state, the Secretary is the object of envy because of his "most easie and free access to Princes," an access that he renders as an amorous encounter: "As longe as any matter of what weight is handled onely between ye Prince and ye Secretary, those Councells are compared to ye mutual affection of two lovers."[41] Day and Cecil are writing of the relationship between a male master and a male secretary, who can in the rhetoric of the period, replace each other or become one; or share the space of a man's closet. But how is this impossible relationship inflected when the master is a lady?

Renaissance literature contains several women with literate male servants, penmen, and secretaries, and their relations are often represented as suspect.[42] In Shakespeare's *King Lear*, Goneril relies on her steward Oswald not only to write letters to her sister, but also to "add such reasons of your owne, as may compact it more": their textual intimacy causes Regan to assert to Oswald that she knows he is "of her [Goneril's] bosome in vnderstanding." *Twelfth Night* rehearses the ridiculousness of the steward/mistress relationship through Malvolio's comicly lecherous courting of Olivia, while simultaneously displaying the erotic possibilities granted by Cesario's textual skills displayed in "his" courting of Olivia. John Webster's Duchess of Malfi takes as her lover her secretarially skilled Antonio, a move that leads inexorably to her death. In Samuel Daniel's *Cleopatra*, the heroine is betrayed by her secretary Seleucus who reveals all her secrets to Caesar, only to find himself unemployable: proved a false secretary to Cleopatra, why should Caesar trust him? "For how could hee imagine I would be/Faithfull to him, being false vnto mine owne?" In Dekker and Webster's *Westward Hoe*, Signor Justiano disguises himself as "a wryting Mecanicall Pedant" to gain access to, and seduce, Mistress Honysuckle.[43]

Here that suspicion is developed at length. G. T.'s de-manning of the Secretary ("manling," "minion") is bolstered by a startlingly unflattering description (courtesy "by report of my very good friend *F.J.*"):

> Hee was in height, the proportion of twoo *Pigmeys*, in bredth the thicknesse of two bacon hogges, of presumption a *Gyant*, of power a Gnat, Apishly wytted, Knauishly mannerd, & crabbedly fauord, what was there in him then to drawe a fayre Ladies liking? (sig. $Biiij^{r-v}$)

What indeed? Secretarial skills, available on demand, writes G. T.: "Marry sir euen all in all, a well lyned purse, wherwith he could at euery call, prouide such pretie conceytes as pleased hir peeuish fantasie, and by that meanes he had throughly (long before) insinuated him selfe with this amorous dame." When the Secretary rides to London—his absence leaving Elinor with "a disfurnishing of eloquence" (sig. $Biiij^{v}$)—F. J. is at liberty to move in, as provider of pretty conceits and of sex. His departure

> was yet vnto *F.J.* an opertunitie of good aduau*n*tage, for when he perceiued the change of hir stile, and therby grew in some suspicion that the same proceded by absence of hir chiefe Chauncellor, he thought good now to smyte while the

> yron was hotte, and to lend his Mistresse such a penne in his Secretaries absence, as he should neuer be able at his returne to amende the well writing thereof, wherfore according to hir commaund he repayred once euery daye to hir chamber, at the least, whereas he guided him selfe so wel, and could deuise such store of sundry pleasures and pastymes, that he grew in fauour not onely with his desired, but also with the rest of the gentlewomen. . . . (sig. Biiij^{v})

F. J. replaces the Secretary as the pen Elinor uses, hoping to replace him as the penis that he supposes Elinor uses.[44] And, of course, F. J. (being an astute reader) supposes correctly. In time, Dame Frances takes it on herself to apprise F. J. of Elinor's promiscuity as "the most vnconstant woman lyuing," having "of long time ben yeelded to the Mynion *Secretary*," despite there being "(quod shee) no one point of worthynesse, yit shameth she [Elinor] not to vse him as hir dearest friend, or rather hir holyest Idoll" (sig. Diii^{r}).

With the introduction of the Secretary, the narrative draws once again on the specific material practices of early modern letter writing, playing on a real and acute anxiety about correspondence: letters are "assuring" many personal and professional transactions, but how to authenticate the signatory? A typical comic witness is Samuel Rowlands's verse "To the Deuils Secretarie":

> But roome for one that thinkes his art far better,
> The deuils secretarie with his letter,
> And tels you he is sent from such a friend,
> For certaine mony he entreats you lend,
> And for assurance, shews the parties hand,
> Whereby his meaning you may vnderstand.
> Or with acquittance, else to you he's sent
> From such a Lord or Lady, for some rent,
> Hauing their hands so cunning counterfait,
> Many are wronged with most false deceit.[45]

The evil power of the devil's secretary lies in his skill of counterfeiting "hands" by which meanings are understood and transactions are assured. And therein lies the paradox of the penman-secretary. His assurance comes from his master or employer whose hand, in effect, he is paid to counterfeit: the danger lies at the moment when he uses that skill to counterfeit for his own benefit.[46]

While most early modern treatments of suspect penmen are, like Rowlands's, concerned with potential fraud or treason, "Master F.J." plays on the erotic and sodomitical possibilities of this "faking" of letters. Introducing the male secretary, a third character, into the erotic sparring of Elinor and F. J. produces a variation on the archetypal homosocial triangle influentially developed by Eve Kosofsky Sedgwick.[47] Here, this third character is required in order to facilitate the (supposedly) two-way correspondence between the couple. F. J. and the Secretary are rivals for Elinor's sexual favors, both using their "pens" to bid for her attention. But those pens are also the providers of love letters: much of the erotic epistolary friction between F. J. and Elinor is, in fact, between F. J. and the Secretary. After the first narrative hint that Elinor has a "ready clearke," it is not long before G. T. becomes more explicit. On the following day, F. J. "thought better to replie, either vpon hir, *or vpon hir Secretary*" (sig. B^{r}, my emphasis) with a letter that includes the following passage:

> The cause of myne affection, I suppose you behold dayly. For (self loue auoyded) euery wight may iudge of themselues as much as reason perswadeth: the which if it be in your good nature suppressed with bashfulnes, then mighty loue graunt, you may once behold my wan cheeks wasshed in woe, that therein my salt teares may be a myrrour to represent your owne shadow, and that like vnto Narcissus you may bee constrayned to kisse the cold waues, wherein your cou*n*terfait is so liuely portrayed. For if aboundance of other matters fayled to drawe my gazing eyes in contemplacion of so rare excellency, yet might these your letters both frame in me an admiration of such diuine esprit, and a confusion to my dull vnderstanding, which so rashly presumed to wander in this endles Laberinthe. Such I esteeme you, and thereby am become such, and Euen
>
> *HE. F. I.*

Read by Elinor, this is a bland call for her to witness F. J.'s woes, a praise of her "rare excellency." Read by, and written to, her Secretary, the letter suddenly comes alive. F. J. supposes that "you [the Secretary] behold dayly. . . The cause of mine affection [Elinor]." The strange parenthetical reference to "self loue" is illuminated by the reference to Narcissus: looking into F. J.'s tears, the Secretary will see another man, another himself, "your owne shadow," his "counterfait"—or in a mirror, the Secretary will see himself, Elinor's "counterfait," her counterfeit hand. And that image may "constrayn" the Secretary "to kiss the cold waues" of F. J.'s tears, to kiss F. J.'s face. What draws F. J.'s admiration and confusion (and again, his "gazing eyes") is not the "aboundance of other" unspecified "matters," but the "rare excellency" specifically of "these your letters." What makes F. J. "HE" is his correspondence with the "SHE" that is the Secretary.

It is no accident that immediately after F. J. writes this to the Secretary, the reader receives news of the first physical contact between F. J. and Elinor: "This letter finished and fayre written ouer, his chau*n*ce was to meete hir alone in a Gallery of the same house: where (as I haue heard him declare) his manhood in this kind of combat was first tried" (sig. B$^{r–v}$). Even here, in a sentence describing their first physical encounter, we have to wait first to hear the detail of the letter's production—"finished" but then "fayre written ouer"—so its apparent spontaneity is revealed for the studied composition it really is. In narrative terms, and for the reader, this letter *produces* the first erotic encounter between F. J. and Elinor. In "real" terms, however, the letter is not transacted: F. J. meets Elinor in the gallery, she repels him, he protests, and it is at that point F. J. refers to the letter, still in his hand: "being by lack of oportunitie constreined to co*m*mit my welfare vnto these blabbing leaues of bewraying paper (shewing y^{t} in his hand) I am here reco*m*forted w^{t} happy view of my desired ioye" (sig. B^{v}). Only some time later, is she "contented to accept his proferd seruice" (sig. Bij[r]). The letter is lost, even to G. T., who remembers it only at the last minute: "y[t] thus they departed: sauing I had forgotten this, shee required of him the last rehearsed letter, saying that his first was lost, & now she lacked a new bottome for her silke, the which I warra*n*t you, he grau*n*ted: ..." (sig. Bij[r]). In the narrative, then, the letter (to the man) takes priority over the physical (with the woman): the erotic encounter is enacted between F. J. and the Secretary, and for the reader, within the letter.

When the Secretary is away, Elinor's letters take a different form, writing "with hir own hand & head" (sig. Biiii[r]), and the foreplay is interrupted. G. T. vouches for its authenticity ("This letter I haue seene, of hir own hand writing"—ironically, of course, given the abundance of counterfeited hands)—but the difference is all too apparent from the "great difference of Style":

> Good seruant, I am out of al doubt much beholding vnto you, and I haue great comfort by your meanes in the stenching of my bloud [F. J. cured her nose-bleed], and I take great co*m*fort to reade your letters, and I haue found in my chamber diuers songs which I think to be of your making, and I promise you, they are excellently made, and I assure you that I wilbe ready to doe for you any pleasure that I can, during my lyfe: wherefore I pray you come to my chamber once in a day, till I come abroad again, and I wilbe glad of your company, and for because that you haue promised to bee my HE: I will take vpon me of this name, your SHE. (sig. Biiii[r])

Whereas the Secretary dealt in balanced equivocation, in her breathlessly unpunctuated letter Elinor makes herself overly complimentary ("I promise you, they [diuers songs] are excellent made"), emotionally vulnerable ("I take great comfort to reade your letters"), socially indebted to F. J. ("out of al doubt much beholding vnto you"), and inevitably, sexually available to him: "I assure you that I wilbe ready to doe for you any pleasure that I can . . . come to my chamber once in a day . . . I will take vpon me of this name, your SHE" (sig. Biiii[r]). Later, such inability to write becomes broadly comical: when she and F. J. have consummated their relationship, Elinor appears at dinner "onely in hir night gowne gyrt to hir" wearing "a little cap crosssed ouer the crowne with two bends of yellowe Sarcanet or Cipresse, in the middest whereof she had placed . . . in paper this word, *Contented.*" The word, betraying her sexual infidelity, is, of course, "of hir owne hand writing" (sig. Eiij[v]).

Elinor's writing is explicitly sexual, but only throws into relief the more erotic nature of the correspondence between men. Although Fraunces reveals Elinor's affairs with two other houseguests, H. D. and H. K. (Diii[r]), the Secretary is the only rival whom F. J. takes seriously. When Elinor's husband returns (the first we've heard of him), he loses his horn while out riding, and F. J. ostentatiously lends him his bugle—an endearingly heavy-handed figure of cuckoldry, with an accompanying sonnet that perhaps even Elinor would be able to read correctly (sig. Fiiij[r–v]). But when "the vnhappy

Secretary" returns from London, F. J. is devastated: "on who*m* *F. I.* had no sooner cast his eyes, but immediately he fel into a great passion of mynd, which might be compared vnto a feauer" (sig. G^{r}). F. J. is torn "betwene the remembraunce of his forepassed pleasure, and the present sight of this monster whom before (for lack of like instruction [i..e Fraunces' revelations]) he had not so throughly marked and beheld" (sig. G^{v}). At first, F. J.'s illness is enough to maintain Elinor's attention, but eventually the Secretary is able "to renew his accustomed consultations" (sig. Jiiii^{v}) with her. This time G. T. allows the implied textual/sexual pen/penis analogy its full force, larding it with a musical conceit:

> in very deed, it fell out that the *Secretary* hauing bin of long time abse*n*t, & therby his quils & pe*n*nes not worn so neer as they were wont to be, did now prick such faire large notes, y^{t} his Mistres liked better to sing faburden vnder him, tha*n* to descant any longer vppon *F. J.* playne song: and thus they continued in good accorde, vntill it fortuned that Dame *Fraunces* came into hir chamber vppon such sodeyn as shee had like to haue marred all the musick. Wel their co*n*ueied their clifs as closely as they could, but yit not altogither w^{t}out some suspicio*n* giuen to ye said dame *Fraunces* . . . (sig. Jiiii^{v})

From this point, the Secretary has almost constant access to Elinor's presence: at dinner, where "attired in a night kerchief" Elinor "loked very drowsely vpon all folkes, vnlesse it were hir secretary, vnto whom she designed sometime to lend a freendly glaunce" [sig. K^{v}]) or in her chamber ("who had there assembled hir secretary, Dam *Pergo*, and the rest" [sig. Kij^{v}–Kiij^{r}]).

F. J.'s relationship with the Secretary, a prerequisite of his relationship with Elinor, is forged on the same grounds as his relationship with G. T., and G. T.'s with H. W. And it is these relationships that are lost in the revised 1575 *Posies*. Despite claims to full-scale gelding, it is in fact only "The aduentures of Master F. I." that sustains major changes to its content, once again suggesting that this "discourse" is central to the volume. Gone are the prefatory editorial maneuvers, gone the English setting and the titillating use of initials. Instead, F. J. is blandly identified as Ferdinando Jeronimo, and the entire story becomes a first-person narrative, supposedly translated from the Bandello-esque Bartello. The lost scandalous components include some love scenes, and the verse celebrating F. J.'s "horning" of Elinor's husband. The letters remain intact, as does a narrative explanation of them—although that explanation is now the preserve of an omniscient narrator, rather than a self-conscious editor.[48] Most importantly, we lose F. J.'s "fictive literary circle," which governs not only the organization of the volume but the revelation of the narrative, necessarily involving the (male) reader as a newly initiated member of that circle.

Which takes us back to Beza. Beza's *Poemata* put into print the verses that circulated between him and his fellow young male poets, verses in which they traded the physical delights of Candida. But Candida only exists in the context of that literary exchange. When Gascoigne invokes Beza in 1575 he is not merely appropriating Beza's piety or prodigality. He is laying claim to the milieu of poetic exchanges that governed Beza's early life, a milieu that provides sexual intercourse with women through textual intercourse with men. When Beza boasts in the punchline of his poem that even by choosing his fellow poet Audebert over Candida, he can still stop her mouth with a kiss, he simultaneously admits the converse—that only in putting the man first, his fellow poet and reader, does the poet get the woman.

§

But to read *A Hundreth sundrie Flowres* in this way is to read it through Gascoigne's characterization of it in the *Posies*, as a pre-"gelded" text. What does it mean that Gascoigne "gelds" his text in 1575? When the printer of George Pettie's *A petite Pallace of Pettie his pleasure* introduces his volume the following year, he similarly states that he has "put the same in print vsing my discretion in omitting sutch matter as in the Aucthours iudgement might seeme offenciue, and yet I trust not leauing imperfection in the discourse, wherof if I haue not gelded to mutch, I thinke I have deserued the lesse blame."[49] Pettie's text is "gelded," ameliorated in the gardening senses of "pruned," "cut," or "removed." But that husbandry pruning is never fully separable (despite the *OED*'s insistence) on a more violent cutting out and damaging of the gelded object. Thus William Fulke mocks Thomas Heskins's use of a scriptural passage "which he hath so often repeated, and yet mangled and gelded, least the true sense might be gathered out of it," and attacks Gregory Martin's omissions in his reading of Saint Basil: "Thus you vse to gelde the Doctors sayings, when you rehearse them."[50] William Watreman, writing on Egypt, places text-gelding as a counterfeiting crime comparable to false coining, tampering with weights, and forgery: "And who so clipped the coigne or counterfacted it, or chaunged the sta*m*pe or diminisshed the weighte: or in lettres and writinges, shoulde adde any thing, by entrelinyng, or otherwise: or should guelde out any thyng, or bryng a forged euidence, Obligacion or Bille, bothe his handes ware cutte of."[51]

Gascoigne's "gelded" draws on both the ameliorative pruning and the mutilating sense of the verb, the latter confirmed by the gloss of Beza's "*Poëmata castrata*," a phrase not apparent in Beza's writings and presumably, typically, another invention of Gascoigne's. He is clearly implying that what has been lost is masculine potency. Wendy Wall follows this through, noting: "When promising a sexual purification of his work, a chastening of its taint of lust, Gascoigne associates masculinity with the previous illicit and scandalous text." Wall takes this as a starting point to argue that this distancing from masculinity is part of a "re-dressing" undertaken by Gascoigne, a progressive "casting himself as a hermaphroditic combination of male writer and female subject."[52] But does Gascoigne really "geld" anything at all?

Stephanie Jed has shown how the correcting of ancient texts, described as "castigating," "making chaste," was a central activity of humanist philology: "a text made chaste or castigated by a philologist is, by definition, a contaminated text, a text that has suffered the wounds of being handled or touched. Philological thought . . . has tended to obscure the history and politics of this contradiction."[53] By contrast, and suspiciously, Gascoigne is at pains to bring this process to the reader's attention, simultaneously advertising the illicit nature, the "filthie phrases" of his original version, and the sexualized but desexualizing process of "gelding" the text for revision. I suggest that the process Gascoigne claims for 1575 was in fact already in place in 1573: the true "gelding" of the text, the "un-manning" and emasculatory maneuvers, are made not by his later amendments, but by the very process of moving into print.

In order to appreciate this, we have to resist what Gascoigne provides for us, namely a privileged and flattering perspective whereby we, as "learned Readers," decode the literate clues, and successfully anticipate the turns of the narrative. By aligning ourselves with F. J. and G. T. (but believing ourselves more astute) we necessarily enter into the male humor of their circle, where Elinor becomes effectively illiterate, *and therefore* sexual prey. But as Susan C. Staub notes in an important essay, not all the women in the "Aduentures" are unable to read. Lady Frances is placed crucially as a voyeur of the sexual encounter between F. J. and Elinor, "in the place usually occupied by the male poet-lover . . . [where he] sees his mistress in the arms of a rival";[54] as a voyeur, "Frances serves as a kind of stand-in for the reader" (p. 43). Her intrusion "begins to undermine Gascoigne's carefully constructed male readership and effectively inverts the power relations implied in the commonplace masculine spectator/feminine spectacle paradigm. Thus he deprivileges the male gendered gaze, creating a site of potential gender anxiety" (pp. 41–42). Then, predictably, Frances proves to be an emasculator: seeing F. J.'s "naked sworde glistring vnder the skyrt of his night gowne" (sig. E^{v}–Eij^{r}) after his first night spent with Elinor, she steals it and renders him impotent. Staub continues:

> The fear of emasculation is inextricably linked to anxieties about publishing and censorship . . . [In "The Aduentures of Master F. I."] the pen and the sword, both symbols of phallic power, are conflated. The stealing of the sword metaphorically enacts the writer's greatest fear, the confiscation of his pen. Gascoigne's choice of imagery, then, suggests what happens when literary power is suppressed. Paradoxically, the man who loses generative literary power becomes like a woman. (p. 44)

Staub concludes: "I would argue that Frances's gaze represents Gascoigne's own anxiety about the inability to control his readers after publishing his work. The power no longer resides in the author but in the reader. That this reader is figured as female makes her all the more terrifying" (p. 51)—hence those *poemata castrata*. Of course, the figure through which the reader should be controlled is not "Gascoigne," but G. T.—and significantly, G. T. also refers to his controlling editorial endeavors in terms of "gelded" ability: "I haue done [the ordering of papers] according to my barreyne skill" (sig. Aij^{v}).

This might make us think twice about Gascoigne's prodigal claims in his letter "to the reuerend Diuines." Despite its elaborately produced appearance of a "literary circle" sustained by "elite amateurism," the printed *Flowres* betrays its true nature. As Staub has pointed out, while insisting on its educative value, the printer A. B. twice employs the term "commodity" in describing the volume—ostensibly promising the reader an abstract virtuous "commodity,"[55] but also hinting that the printed book, unlike the loose papers or the manuscript anthology, is a commercial commodity. Even more tellingly, H. W. utters the word *three* times: he is charged by G. T. "that I should vse them onely for mine owne particuler commoditie"; while he admits that "I my selfe haue repeated this commoditie, to sit and smile at the fond deuises," he then goes on to title and make public the work "to please a number by common commoditie" (sig. Ai^{r}). Describing his editorial endeavors in mixed figures of prostitution and merchandizing, he "has procured for these trifles this day of publication" (sig. Ai^{v}) claiming that he is, as Staub shows, "but halfe a marchant" (sig. Ai^{r}) because he has redelivered the volume to G. T.[56] His claim to semi-merchant status is of course disingenuous, not to say nonsensical: there is no such thing as half a merchant, no halfway compromise between manuscript and print, and by allowing "particuler commoditie" to become "common commoditie," H. W. has, effectively, gone merchant. But I would argue that the claim to prior "particuler commoditie" and "elite amateurism" is always an illusion, because the "fictive literary circle" is never what it appears. As the printer A. B. introduces the story of Master F. J., he expands the titillating initials, "whome the reader may name Freeman Iones, for the better vnderstanding of the same" (sig. Aiij^{r})—that is, not the country gentlemen we might expect from the story's remote northern setting, but a freeman of the city like A. B. himself—and perhaps like the Secretary too who, we recall, leaves Elinor's service—and why?—"by occasion rydden to London forsothe" (sig. Biiij^{v}).

A Hundreth sundrie Flowres presents itself as a voyeuristic entry into the elite male amateurism of manuscript culture. As Gascoigne himself tells the "Reader":

> I thought good to aduertise thee, that the most part of [these Posies] were written for other men. And out of all doubt, if euer I wrote lyne for my selfe in causes of loue, I haue written tenne for other men in layes of lust. . . . [I]n wanton delightes I helped all men, though in sad earnest I neuer furthered my selfe any kinde of way. (¶¶¶^{v}–¶¶¶.ij^{r})

He is here speaking not only of the men in his narrative, but also of the men who will read *Posies* for their own "commoditie"—indeed he writes "To al yong Gentlemen, and generally to the youth of England" (¶¶.ij^{r}), "it is your vsing (my lustie Gallants) or misvsing of these Posies that may make me praysed or dispraysed for publishing of the same" (¶¶.iij^{v}). Just as F. J. offers

Elinor his pen in the Secretary's absence, Gascoigne offers his pen to his male readers—both to serve them sexually, and to service them sexually. The placing of the "manuscript anthology" to print is therefore supposed to involve the print "learned Reader" in a highly eroticized homosocial literary exchange, previously the (always supposed) domain of the élite amateur literary circle. But in truth the book is a printed commodity whose circulation cannot be controlled, whose readers are not all men invested in fantasies of literate country-house retreats providing illicit sex with married women. At the moment as print is restructuring "the relationship between the producer, the consumer, and the textual circulation of sodomy," Gascoigne produces a nostalgic manuscript fantasy that both insists on and denies its material form: where loose papers (their "commoditie" personally available to the reader) appear to circulate between men and seduce desirable married women, but where in fact they are petrified in a print narrative, providing "common commoditie" for all, and "particular commoditie" for no man.

NOTES

Lorna Hutson first introduced me to "Master F. J." at Queen Mary and Westfield College, University of London: what follows remains indebted to her teaching. I am grateful to James Daybell, Goran Stanivukovic, and an anonymous reader for their comments on an earlier draft, and to Tyler Smith for urging me to resist Gascoigne's wit. This essay was written with the generous support of a Short-Term Fellowship from the Folger Shakespeare Library.

1. *A Hundreth sundrie Flowres bounde vp in one small Poesie* (London: Richarde Smith [1573]). Further references are in the main text.
2. Michael D. Bristol and Arthur F. Marotti, "Introduction" to *Print, Manuscript, and Performance: The Changing Relations of the Media in Early Modern England* (Columbus: Ohio State University Press, 2000), pp. 1–29 at p. 13; see also Harold Love, *Scribal Publication in Seventeenth- Century England* (Oxford: Clarendon Press, 1993); Arthur F. Marotti, *Manuscript, Print and the English Renaissance Lyric* (Ithaca: Cornell University Press, 1995).
3. *The Posies of George Gascoigne Esquire* (London: H. Bynneman for Richard Smith, 1575). Further references are in the main text.
4. This letter is the only "evidence" that *A Hundreth sundrie Flowres* was in any way "banned," since the Stationers' Company records for the pertinent period are missing. Intriguingly, however, the 1575 *Posies* did run into trouble with the Court of High Commission—on August 13, 1576, "by appointment of the Q. M. Commissioners," Richard Smith returned "half a hundred of Gascoignes poesies" to the Stationers' Hall—although perhaps only because Gascoigne was provocatively toying with them in this letter? See C. T. Prouty, *George Gascoigne: Elizabethan Courtier, Soldier, and Poet* (New York: Columbia University Press, 1942), pp. 78–79; *Records of the Court of the Stationers' Company 1576 to 1602 from Register B*, ed. W. W. Greg and E. Boswell (London: The Bibliographical Society, 1930), pp. 86–87. For the debate over whether to take the censorship claims seriously, see Richard C. McCoy, "Gascoigne's 'Poëmata castrata': The Wages of Courtly Success," *Criticism: A Quarterly*

for Literature and the Arts 27 (1985), pp. 29–56 at pp. 32–33, and Cyndia Susan Clegg, *Press Censorship in Elizabethan England* (Cambridge: Cambridge University Press, 1997), ch. 5.

5. Richard Helgerson, *The Elizabethan Prodigals* (Berkeley: University of California Press, 1976); McCoy, "Gascoigne's 'Poëmata castrata,'" pp. 32–33; Wendy Wall, *The Imprint of Gender: Authorship and Publication in the English Renaissance* (Ithaca: Cornell University Press, 1993); Lorna Hutson, *The Usurer's Daughter: Male Friendship and the Representation of Women in Early Modern England* (London: Routledge, 1994).
6. Théodore de Bèze, *Poemata editio secunda ab eo recognita* ([Geneva:] Henri Estienne, 1569). For bibliographical details see Frédéric Gardy with Alain Dufour, *Bibliographie des œuvres théologiques, littéraires, historiques et juridiques de Théodore de Bèze* (Geneva: E. Droz, 1960), pp. 4–6 (item 5). See also Paul-F. Geisendorf, *Théodore de Bèze* (Geneva: Labor et Fides, 1949), pp. 280–81.
7. *Theodori Bezæ Vezelii poemata* (Paris: Conrad Badius, 1548), f.vii.^{v}–f.viii.^{r}; see Gardy with Dufour, *Bibliographie de Théodore de Bèze*, pp. 1–2 (item 1).
8.

   Sed postquam tamen alterum necesse est,
   Priores tibi defero, Audeberte:
   Quòd si Candida forte conqueratur,
   Quid tum? basiolo tacebit imo. (Beza, *Poemata*, f.viii.^{r})

9. Geisendorf, *Théodore de Bèze*, p. 23.
10. "'De Bèze a fui Paris moins qu'un arrêt du Parlement, l'invitant à se purger d'une accusation de Sodomie....' Ainsi s'exclaimaient à l'unisson les ennemis de Bèze." Alexandre Machard, "Recherches sur la querelle des 'Juvenilia,'" in his ed., *Les Juvenilia de Théodore de Bèze* (Paris: Isidore Lisieux, 1879), XIII–LXXIV at XVII–XVIII.
11. See Noel I. Garde, *The Homosexual in History* (New York: Vantage Press, 1964), p. 298.
12. "et meminimus obscoeni carminis, quo amatorem cum venatore comparas." Gabriel Fabricius, *Responsio ad Bezam Vezeliam Eceboliam* (Paris: Claude Frémy, 1567), fo. 20, cit. *Correspondance de Théodore de Bèze*, ed. Hippolyte Aubert, Alain Dufour, Claire Chimelli, and Béatrice Nicollier, vol. 10 (1569) (Geneva: Droz, 1980), p. 96, n. 12.
13. Claude de Sainctes, *Responsio... ad Apologiam Theodori Bezæ editam contra Examen Doctrinæ Caluinianae* (Paris: Claude Frémy, 1567), sig. X.iiij.$^{r-v}$.
14. Stanislas Hosius, *Catholici cvivsdam et orthodoxi ivdicivm et censvra, de iudicio & censura ministrorum Tygurinorum & Heydelbergensium, de dogmate contra adorandam Trinitatem in Polonia nuper sparso* (Cologne: apud Maternum Cholinum, 1565), sig. M6^{r-v}.
15. Hierosme Bolsec, *Histoire de la vie, movers, doctrine, et deportements, de Theodore de Beze* (Paris: Guillaume Chaudiere, 1582), sig. Eij^{v}–Eiiij^{v}.
16. Lisa Jardine and Alan Stewart, *Hostage to Fortune: The Troubled Life of Francis Bacon 1561–1626* (London: Victor Gollancz, 1998), pp. 108, 82–84, drawing on Joyce Freedman, "Anthony Bacon and His World, 1558–1601" (unpublished Ph.D. dissertation, Temple University, 1979), pp. 104–06.
17. [Benjamin Carrier], *Pvritanisme The Mother, Sinne The Davghter* (St. Omer: English College Press, 1633), sig. E4^{v}–E7^{r}. My attention was drawn to this piece by Goran V. Stanivukovic, "Between Men in Early Modern England"

(forthcoming in Katherine O'Donell and Michael O'Rourke, eds. *Siting Queer Masculinities*).

18. "At istos perditos non pudet . . . illum quidem ea tum autoritate tum dignitate viru*m* in Adonidem transformare: mihi verò id sceleris impingere, ad quod depellendum nulla me indigere apud que*m*quam honestum hominem defensione mihi persuasi." Beza to Andreas Dudith, May 14, 1569, Geneva. *Poemata* (1569 edn.), *.vi^{r-v}.
19. "Bezam à pueritia imbibisse vatum impudicitiam & impudentiam, totamque ætatem ex plendis suis libidinibus & cupiditatibus, ac describendis suis amoribus (agnoscis, lector sorbonici oratoris δεινωσν) denique vlciscendis riualibus suis, exercuisse; quem etia*m* in meretricem, in lenam, in cinædum denique tra*n*sformant." Bèze, *Poemata* (1569 edn.), *.v^{r-v}. Later in the letter, he launches a counterattack on the sodomy of the Roman Catholic Church.
20. This essay is prompted by Stanivukovic's call for work on the impact of new understandings of early modern sodomy on readings of the prose fiction of the period. "For if in any study of sodomy the issue at stake is not only the recognition of somatic experience but also its circulation in and the impact on the social sphere, then the availability of textualised discourses of sodomy increased with the expansion of the early modern print market. This in turn raises the complex issue of the relationship between the producer, the consumer, and the textual circulation of sodomy." Goran V. Stanivukovic, review article in *Textual Practice* 12 (1998), pp. 349–55, at p. 353.
21. The classic statement is J. W. Saunders, "The Stigma of Print: A Note on the Social Bases of Tudor Poetry," *Essays in Criticism* 1 (1951), pp. 139–64; see more recent interventions by Helgerson, *Elizabethan Prodigals*; Arthur Marotti, "Patronage, Poetry, and Print," *Yearbook of English Studies* 21 (1991), pp. 1–26; and Wall, *Imprint of Gender*. The narrative here is highly reminiscent of Barnabe Googe's detailed excuses presented in the dedicatory epistle to William Lovelace in his *Eglogs, Epytaphes, and Sonettes* (London: Thomas Colwell, 1563), sig. a.v^{r}–a.vij^{r}, discussed in Marotti, "Patronage, Poetry, and Print," pp. 5–6.
22. As G. W. Pigman III notes, "the headnote to the first poem in the avowedly Gascoigne section of 'The devises of sundrie Gentlemen' " reads " 'I will now deliver unto you *so many more* of Master Gascoignes Poems as have come to my hands, who hath never beene dayntie of his doings, and therfore I conceale not his name' " (Pigman's emphasis). Pigman, "Editing revised texts: Gascoigne's *A Hundreth Sundrie Flowres* and *The Posies*" in *New ways of looking at old texts, II: Papers of the Renaissance English Text Society, 1992–1996*, ed. W. Speed Hill (Tempe: Medieval & Renaissance Texts & Studies/ Renaissance English Text Society, 1998), pp. 1–10 at p. 3, n. 5.
23. Gillian Austen, "Gascoigne's *Master FJ* and its Revision, or, 'You Ain't Heard Nothin' Yet!' " in *Narrative Strategies in Early English Fiction*, ed. Wolfgang Görtchacher and Holger Klein (Lewiston and Salzburg: The Edwin Mellen Press [Elizabethan and Renaissance Studies 118], 1995), pp. 67–85 at p. 75.
24. Wall, *Imprint of Gender*, here at pp. 244, 242, 232; for her reading of Gascoigne, see pp. 243–250. See also Richard McCoy, "Gascoigne's 'Poëmata castrata': The Wages of Courtly Success," *Criticism* 27 (1985) pp. 29–55; Marotti, "Patronage, Poetry, and Print," pp. 9–15.
25. McCoy, "Gascoigne's 'Poëmata castrata,' " p. 33.

26. For the fullest account of this, see Adrian Weiss, "Shared Printing, Printer's Copy, and the Text(s) of Gascoigne's *A Hundreth Sundrie Flowres*," *Studies in Bibliography* 45 (1992), pp. 71–104. Weiss concludes (from H. W.'s letter) that "Gascoigne intended that 'The adventures of Master F.J.' appear first in the book," but "his directions for the sequence of texts" was not implemented during the lengthy process of printing (p. 99).
27. Wall, *Imprint of Gender*, p. 244.
28. Jeffrey Masten, Peter Stallybrass, and Nancy Vickers, "Introduction: Language Machines" in *Language Machines: Technologies of Literary and Cultural Production*, ed. Masten, Stallybrass, and Vickers (New York: Routledge, 1997), pp. 1–14 at p. 7.
29. In a 1645 letter, James Howell writes: "I will twist up what I know upon as narrow a bottom as may be shut up within the compass of this letter." Howell, *Epistolæ Ho-Elianæ: familiar letters domestic and forren* (1650 edn.), 1:267, as cited. *OED* s.v. bottom sb., 15 (2: 434).
30. Lena Cowen Orlin, "Three Ways to Be Invisible in the Renaissance: Sex, Reputation, and Stitchery" in *Renaissance Culture and the Everyday*, ed. Patricia Fumerton and Simon Hunt (Philadelphia: University of Pennsylvania Press, 1999), pp. 183–203, here at 199, 185–87.
31. Jonathan Goldberg, *Writing Matter: From the Hands of the English Renaissance* (Stanford: Stanford University Press, 1990), p. 141; Jennifer Summit, *Lost Property: The Woman Writer and English Literary History 1380–1589* (Chicago: University of Chicago Press, 2000), p. 168.
32. Richard Hyrde, dedicatory epistle to *A devout treatise upon the Paternoster made fyrst in latyn by the moost famous doctour mayster Erasmus Rotorodamus* quoted in *Vives and the Renascence Education of Women*, ed. Foster Watson (London: Edward Arnold, 1912), pp. 166–67, cit. Goldberg, *Writing Matter*, p. 141.
33. Hutson, *Usurer's Daughter*, p. 115. Hutson does not attempt a reading of "Master F.J." through this paradigm.
34. Martin Billingsley, *The Pens Excellencie or The Secretaries Delight* (London: J. Sudbury & G. Humble, 1618), sig. C4^{r}. I am grateful to James Daybell for drawing this passage to my attention.
35. Jonathan Goldberg, *Desiring Women Writing: English Renaissance Examples* (Stanford: Stanford University Press, 1997), pp. 144–63 at p. 145. See also James Daybell, "Women's Letters and Letter Writing in England, 1540–1603: An Introduction to the Issues of Authorship and Construction," *Shakespeare Studies* 27 (1999), pp. 161–86.
36. It may be that only the signature "SHE" is in Roman, in which case the Secretary did "pen" it in both senses.
37. Daybell, "Women's Letters," pp. 162, 164. Daybell adds the caveat: "It is important to note that, in this respect, the writing of women's letters did not differ significantly from men's letters" (pp. 164–65).
38. Angel Day, *The English Secretary, or Methode of Writing of Epistles and Letters... Now Newly Reuised* (London: C. Burbie, 1599), sig. Nn3^{v}, discussed in Goldberg, *Writing Matter*, p. 268. Goldberg's suggestive work on secretaries is taken up in Richard Rambuss, *Spenser's Secret Career* (Cambridge: Cambridge University Press, 1993); Alan Stewart, *Close Readers: Humanism and Sodomy in Early Modern England* (Princeton: Princeton University Press, 1997), pp. 161–87.

39. Day, *The English Secretorie* (London: Richard Iones, 1592), sig. R^{v} (second sequence). For Day's anxious revision of this passage see Stewart, *Close Readers*, pp. 175–76.
40. Day, *English Secretary* (1599 edn.), pp. 112–13.
41. Robert Cecil, "The State and Dignitie of a Secretarie of State," Bodleian Library, Oxford, Ashmole MS 826, fo. 29.
42. This paragraph is based on Stewart, *Close Readers*, pp. 177–78.
43. William Shakespeare, *The Chronicle Historie of the Life and Death of King Lear and His Three Daughters* (London: N. Buttrer, 1608), sig. D2^{v}, I2^{v}; idem., *Twelfe Night, or What You Will* in *Comedies, Histories, & Tragedies. Published According to the True Originall Copies* (London: Isaac Jaggard and ed. Blount, 1623), sig. Y2^{r}–Z5^{r}; John Webster, *The Tragedy of the Dutchesse of Malfy* (London: J. Waterson, 1623); Samuel Daniel, *Delia and Rosamund Augmented. Cleopatra* (London: Simon Waterson, 1594), sig. L4^{v}; Thomas Dekker and John Webster, *West-ward Hoe. As it hath beene diuers times Acted by the Children of Paules* (London: Iohn Hodgets, 1607), sig. B3^{v}.
44. Compare *West-ward Hoe*: Mistress Honysuckle asks her writing master for "a new pen" because "my old one [her husband's] is stark naught, and wil cast no inck." *West-ward Hoe*, sig. C^{r}.
45. Samuel Rowlands, *More Knaues yet? The Knaues of Spades and Diamonds* (London: Iohn Tap, n.d.), sig. E2^{v}–E3^{v}.
46. See also Goldberg, *Writing Matter*, ch. 5.
47. Eve Kosofsky Sedgwick, *Between Men: English Literature and Male Homosocial Desire* (New York: Columbia University Press, 1985).
48. It is this shift to "modernity" that prompts Wolfgang G. Müller to regard the 1575 version as "an outstanding work of English narrative art which can lay claim to be regarded as the first English novel." Müller, "The Modernity of the Second Version of George Gascoigne's *Master F. J.*," in *Narrative Strategies in Early English Fiction*, ed. Görtchacher and Klein, pp. 87–102 at p. 87.
49. George Pettie, *A Petite Pallace of Pettie His Pleasure*, ed. Herbert Hartman (London: Oxford University Press, 1938), p. 9; I owe this reference to Wall, *Imprint of Gender*, p. 260, n. 34.
50. William Fulke, *D. Heskins, D. Sanders, and M. Rastel... ouerthrowne, and detected of their seuerall blasphemous heresies* (London: Henrie Middleton for George Bishop, 1579), sig. Y^{v}; idem., *A Defense of the Sincere and True Translations of the Holie Scriptures into the English Tong* (London: Henrie Bynneman for George Bishop, 1583), sig. Zij^{v}.
51. William Watreman, trans., *The Fardle of facions conteining the aunciente maners, customes, and Lawes, of the peoples enhabiting the two partes of the earth, called Affrike and Asie* (London: Jhon Kingstone and Henry Datton, 1555), sig. E.j.^{r}. As Will Fisher notes, counterfeiting is often associated with sodomy—and the punishment is a literal "gelding": see Fisher, "Queer Money," *ELH* 66 (1999), pp. 1–23, esp. p. 10.
52. Wall, *Imprint of Gender*, pp. 260, 261.
53. Stephanie H. Jed, *Chaste Thinking: The Rape of Lucretia and the Birth of Humanism* (Bloomington and Indianapolis: Indiana University Press, 1989), p. 33.
54. Susan C. Staub, "The Lady Frances Did Watch: Gascoigne's Voyeuristic Narrative," in *Framing Elizabethan Fictions: Contemporary Approaches to*

Early Modern Narrative Prose, ed. Constance C. Relihan (Kent: Kent State University Press, 1996), pp. 41–54 at p. 41.

55. "the well minded ma*n* may reape some commoditie out of the most friulous works that are written"; "it [the volume] hath with this fault [some unpleasant savors] a greater commoditie than common poesies haue ben accustomed to present" (both sig. Aij^{v}).
56. This account is based on Staub, "The Lady Frances Did Watch," pp. 45–46.

Chapter 9

"Knights in Armes": The Homoerotics of the English Renaissance Prose Romances

Goran V. Stanivukovic

In a 1563 German edition of Ovid's *Metamorphoses*, there is a curious engraving (figure 9.1).[1] Preceding the Latin text of Book I, entitled the Golden Age. III. (Aetas aurea. III.), this engraving depicts, in the forefront, three scantily clad couples. Two male–female ones (courting?) on the right of the tree are in a state that suggests, ambiguously, rest and weariness, intimacy and detachment. On the left of the tree, however, with their backs turned to the viewer, two men sit close to, and look at each other. The one on the far left, seemingly older than the other, is holding the younger around his waist, tight to his body, intimately, casually slipping his hand down toward the younger man's groin. The apparent age difference suggests one of the most conventional ways in which male same-sex eroticism was culturally manifested in the Renaissance.

The curious aspect of this scene of Golden Age, which, as Ovid says, "sine militus usu / mollia securae peragebant otia gentes" ("was such that souldiers helpe might easly be forborne"), is that it provides us with a rare image of the homosocial and erotic coupling of two men in the Renaissance art of Ovidian engravings.[2] Except for the tranquility that has overtaken the world of the Golden Age in which Saturn reigns ("Aurem . . . in quo regnanet Saturno, rerum omnium plena fuir tranquillitas"),[3] the text below the engraving implies there is nothing either in Ovid or in the text of the German edition in Latin that would have inspired the engraver to insert this male couple, except that the Ovidian Golden Age was an age of unrestrained passion.[4] The intimate male bond might then suggest that in an age of peace, "where no sword nor helmet [was] worn" (sig. B2v) ("non galeae, non ensis

Figure 9.1 The Golden Age in *Metamorphoses Ovidii*, Francoforti, 1563. The Newberry Library, Chicago (Case Y 672. O 9456).

erat" [I, 99]), soldiers have become lovers of women and other men. The Golden Age of plenitude, fertility, and maternity, an age removed from the demands of masculine pursuit, is one of the legendary topics of pastoral art and literature. The inscription of homoeroticism in the archetype of the Golden Age, then, is the artistic license. It enables the engraver to accommodate in the emblematic ideal of freedom and sensuality the kind of eroticism that is reviled in early modern culture. Yet the age of the eternal spring, represented in the Golden Age archetype, in the words of Stephen Hinds, "is what will disappear . . . from the earth as a whole, as a result of the rape of Proserpine."[5] The Golden Age *topos*, then, reminds us of a double transgression: rape and homeroticism, both of which bring an end to procreation and human happiness. The reminder of bareness and decay in the Golden Age *locus amoenus*, therefore, is most significantly and symbolically implied by the only couple incapable of procreation on its own: the embracing male couple.

Similarly remote from the familiar (and civilized) world of England, or from the European West, is the world of Renaissance romances. The narratives of romances, which burgeoned on the print market of Renaissance England between 1580 and 1620, are typically set in the fantastical lands of literary imagination, or in the geographically ambivalent countries of the mythical Natolia (Asia Minor); they are set in the lands in which the chivalric plots of romances nostalgically echo the times of heroic chivalry. Removed from the cultural constraints of the West, where homoeroticism is a horrifying crime, romances, like the *topos* of the Golden Age in the German engraving, act as conduits for much that is imagined and desired (which is not necessarily of erotic nature)[6] but that is either suppressed, unrealized, or past. The romances that I am going to discuss here are vehicles for the spectacles of pleasure against the background of romanticized chivalry, anti-Turkish sentiments, and the orientalism of the East.[7] In the fantastical and imagined lands of romances, nonnormative sexuality represents part of the world in which agency is represented in chivalric combat and courtship. When it enters that world, as in the German engraving, homoeroticism does not disturb it, but is made part of it. In both the engraving and the romances, it is the placement of the desiring, erotic body within a specific space—the Golden Age pastoral or the fictional land—that enables homoeroticism, and conditions our reading and understanding of the homoerotic subject and sexuality, prompting us to ask new questions about the role of fiction in representing sex and gender in early modern England.

The blissfully presented male couple in the landscape of the Golden Age (hetero)erotics in the engraving acts, in my project of rethinking the historicization of Renaissance homoeroticism, as an example of transformations that new historicism has helped bring about, that is, "the discovery of unexpected discursive contexts for literary works by pursuing their 'supplements' rather than their overt thematics."[8] Such unexpected moments of homoerotic identification complicate conventional—heteroerotic and heroic—forms of masculine identification in popular romances of the sixteenth and the seventeenth centuries. Similar moments in romances also reveal rhetorical strategies employed to express homoeroticism at the heart of a genre that endorses the socially validated heteroerotic courtship, matrimonial felicity, man-to-man combat, heroic friendship, militant masculinity, chivalric success, and imperial conquest. Yet episodic digressions from the normative narratives of courtship and chivalry direct us to where we might want to look for what appear to be the ambiguous signs of homoerotic desire in the archives of Renaissance literature. In turn those digressions also prompt us to rethink the relationship between the printed text and its readership in the formation of both print culture and subjectivities in the English Renaissance.

The relationship between romance and male sexuality has frequently been the subject of criticism, which has treated cross-dressing, one of the staple features in romances, as a sign of sexual transgression, a fissure in the representation of a stable heteroerotic masculinity. Thus critics have typically resorted to Philip Sidney's *Arcadia* and have interpreted Pyrocles's disguise as Amazon Zelmane in Book I as an example either of the parody of masculinity, or of the inscription of homoerotic desire into the romantic narrative of courtship and chivalric adventure. The androgyny Zelmane acts as a sort of check of patriarchal culture against transgressive behavior. Yet, although Zelmane's androgyny attracts the naïve and young Philoclea, it neither prevents her attraction to develop into a physical desire, nor does it allow Basilius to complete his seduction of Pyrocles-Zelmane. Zelmane's androgyny turns Basilius into, as Constance Jordan argues, a "parodic version of the prospective husband of treatises on the conventional marriage."[9] On the one hand, cross-dressing may prevent "lesbian" desire by laughing it out of the realm of possibility, for Philoclea's passion for Zelmane is, after all, desire for man, not a woman. On the other hand, androgyny appears to parody masculinity, but only as a narrative trick and not to make it an object of desire, thus reminding us that masculinity is not at stake here, since Basilius does not succeed in courting Zelmane. Yet in both cases, cross-dressing prevents the blurring of the boundaries between textual actions in which a body might be seen as an object of desire and the cultural context that surrounds that body and on which that body has an effect. Whether cross-dressing and homoeroticism are linked in prose fiction, or whether cross-dressed body is a sign of cultural disruption regardless of whether it does or does not carry the connotation of sexual desire has been for a while at the center of *Arcadia* criticism. Thus Gregory Bredbeck sets out to show that cross-dressing and homoeroticism are intricately connected, though only as "potentiality, not . . . intentionality," and that in Sidney's romance it "becomes an index of the sort of male panic that resides beneath the surface of the entire text."[10] In *The Old Arcadia*, Bredbeck argues, homoeroticism is "an indicator of everything that the romance's high artifice of heteroeroticism fails to capture."[11] Yet Bredbeck's assertion that homoeroticism effected by drag is a sort of undercurrent that runs counter to the heteroerotic narrative in *The Old Arcadia*, resonates with an optimism that all those who engage in the archaeology of Renaissance homoeroticism would want to show.

If cross-dressing indeed allowed us to link with homoerotics, the picture of Renaissance (male) homoerotics would look brighter given the number of cross-dressed male bodies in the romances. Yet if we look beyond the *Arcadia*, at romances that are influenced by it but that also depart in some significant ways from the *Arcadia*, we see that clothes are not crucial in determining gender identity. In those romances the cross-dressed body is used textually in ways other than as an object of desire (e.g., to enable social mobility, sneak out of the paternal household, conceal identity in order to test the beloved's loyalty, avoid dangers in the strange lands, escape rape by pirates and renegades). Romances such as Henry Robarts's *Pheander, the Mayden Knight* (1595) and Emanuel Ford's *Ornatus and Artesia* (?1599), for instance, suggest the opposite to what the critics of the *Arcadia* have argued. In *Ornatus and Artesia*, for example, cross-dressing is not associated with gender anxiety nor, specifically, to homoeroticism. Furthermore, in these texts, cross-dressing is related neither to parody of masculinity nor to sexual panic. Rather, drag is a sign of the main hero's adolescence, and is culturally and textually best related to youth, freshness, and sexual inexperience (especially in *Pheander*). In Ford's romance, cross-dressing features as a disguise and the author is very conscious of the gender under it. When Ornatus cross-dresses he renames himself "Sylvian" (note the masculine form of the female name Sylvia), but Ford uses the masculine pronoun to refer to that cross-dressed body. That skirts do not incur anxiety over masculine prowess is quite clear in the episode in which Ornatus takes them off, deflowers Artesia, and then, spurred by his new self-image, the result of his lovemaking, bravely goes off to war (sig. Q2^{r-v}). Writing about transvestism in Renaissance romances, Winfried Schleiner argues that drag and disguise are both pleasurable and fetishistic, but not problematic, and that cross-dressing "allowed the narrator to write about sex while hiding behind distancing *as it were* or *ut ita dicam*."[12] According to Schleiner, cross-dressing is a relative stratagem of fiction's plot, and something that is part of fiction's structure, rather than a sign of gender ideology that fiction makes its topic.

Recent social history has argued that cross-dressing has little to do with transgression and sexual confusion. Thus David Cressy draws our attention to the need to distinguish clearly between the "occasional deployment of items of cross-gender," which men used during various folk festivals, charivaris, and May games, and "gender-bending transvestism, while recognizing... that divine wrath knew no such discrimination."[13] Although not denying that cross-dressing "clearly touched a raw nerve and produced, in these reformers [contemporary moralists who attacked theatrical cross-dressing] a recirculating rhetoric of anxiety and fear," Cressy's work on various cultural, especially folkloristic, cross-dressing, shows the nonthreatening nature of cross-dressing, at least in the social realm.[14] Thus Cressy argues, "[c]ross-dressing... was not so transgressive as critics and scholars have suggested, nor was it necessarily symptomatic of a sex-gender system in distress."[15] Cressy's arguments about the nonthreatening transvestism in the social sphere of Renaissance England remind us that cultural cross-dressing was different from the pronouncements against it in the anti-theatricalists' pamphlets. Looking at it alongside drag in prose fiction, it also helps us see cross-dressing in romances as different from that in the theater. If male characters wearing female clothes in romances (as my examples of Ford and Roberts suggest) and society were not signs of sexual transgression, we might want to look for examples of homoerotics in fiction in different textual actions and rhetorical strategies. Narrative and eloquence, more than cross-dressing, are also central to our understanding of what is always at stake in the homosocial bonds among men in early modern prose fiction.

Witness this example from Sir Philip Sidney's *The Countesse of Pembrokes Arcadia*, in which Pyrocles and Musidorus find themselves in the country of Pontus. Sidney says:

> They [Pyrocles and Musidorus] were brought to the king of that countrey, a Tyrant also, not through suspition, greedinesse, or reuengefulness, as he of *Phrygia*, but... of a wanton cruelty: inconstant in his choise of friends, or rather neuer hauing a friend but a playfellow; of whom when he was wearie, he could not otherwise rid himselfe then by killing them; giuing sometimes prodigally, not because he loued them to whom he gaue, but because he lusted to giue: punishing, not so much for hate or anger, as because he felt not the smart of punishment: delighted to be flattered, at first for those vertues which were not in him, at length making his vices vertues worthy the flattering: with like iudgement glorying, when he had happened to do a thing well, as when he had perfourmed some notable mischiefe.[16]

This passage illustrates one of the frequent models of representing male homoerotics in early modern romances: the conflation of aggressiveness and violation of courtly comportment that includes a disparity between men. For example, in the third part of *Palmerin of England*, the implication of homoerotics gives rise to homophobic violence. Soboco, an Indian pagan, lashes out, verbally and militantly, at Florendos, a knight, who inquired about his abducted wife and niece among Soboco's knights. After implying that Florendos might be a sodomite—" Thou shouldst be some pretty youthfull Ganimede, that demaundest for women among Knightes in Armes"—Soboco fights Florendos.[17] The anxiety over effeminacy is here articulated as the anxiety over sodomy, and the ensuing aggression suggests an attempt to erase both sorts of fears from the heroic narrative. The Tyrant's "wanton cruelty," which mixes lust and brutality (he kills his minions as soon as he has had enough enjoying them), resonates with the frequent association of monstrosity with sodomy in the Renaissance, an accusation that can be traced back to the Bible. Thomas Lodge, for example, says: "the very night Christ was born, [the] sodomitical crue perished" and that "God should be thanked [the] monsters are banished."[18] The tyrant's lack of courtly comportment—he likes to be flattered; lacks virtue; he is prone to violent behavior, especially as he likes punishing; and he turns vices into virtue—further suggests the ways in which sodomy was thought to manifest itself as a social practice and in which it was imagined, as Lodge does, in Christian discourses against corporeal vices. Sidney's Tyrant thus echoes Lodge (himself echoing Augustine) on the sodomite "as an enemie to vertue, . . . [who] consumeth wealth, & louing pleasure."[19] Tyrant's destructive sexuality is represented as deviant courtliness that is fatal to men. Sidney says:

> He [Tyrant] chaunced at that time (for indeed long time none lasted with him) to haue next in vse about him, a man of the most enuious disposition, that (I thinke) euer infected the aire with his breath; whose eyes could not looke right vpon anie happei man, nor eares beare the burthen of any bodies praise: contrarie to the natures of all other plagues, plagued with other well being; making happinesse the ground of his vnhappinesse, & good newes the argument of his sorow: in sum, a man whose fauour no man could winne, but by being miserable.[20]

Tyrant's behavior is represented here as sodomitical because the only kind of bond that he has with other people is neither friendship nor knightly homosociality. Nor is he engaged in heteroerotic courtship, but in a deviant use of other men's bodies for his short-lasting pleasure.

Yet there are other aspects of Tyrant's homoeroticism, culturally more important for Sidney's humanist fiction; they are philologically implied by the word playfellow. "Playfellow" is described in the *OED* as "a companion in play or amusement; a companion generally, or in any action or course." The term is childish, but Tyrant's "wanton cruelty" adds a rather macabre dimension, a kind of sadism mixed with excessive behavior, to the childish sporting of Tyrant and his fellow.[21] "Playfellow" resonates ambivalently with meanings that suggest innocence, friendship, and love. In that sense, for example, it is used in *A Midsummer Night's Dream*, when Hermia calls Helena "sweet playfellow" ("farewell, sweet playfellow, pray thou for us," 1.1.220). This speech not only "establishes their friendship," as the Oxford Shakespeare editor glosses it, but it also provides the first of several speeches in this play in which the rhetoric of female friendship is progressively more explicitly mixed with the language of romantic love.[22] In another instance, "playfellow" is oddly used in Thomas More's *Richard III*. The young prince's mother sarcastically mocks Richard the Protector's attempt to get Edward V's younger brother out of her custody and back with his brother. She says:

> Troweth the protector (I pray god he may proue a protectour) troweth he that I perceiue not whereunto his painted processe draweth? It is not honorable that the duke bide here: it were comfortable for them both that he wer with his brother, because the king lacketh a playfelowye, be ye sure. I pray God send them both better playfelowes than hym, that maketh so high a matter vpon such a trifling pretext: as though they coulde none be founden to play with the kyng, but if his brother, that hath no lust to play for sickness, come out of sanctuary, out of hys sauegarde, to play with him.[23]

Again, "playfellow" is a childish term, one that describes the relationship in which parity is not a requirement, as in humanist friendship. Thus More's use of "playfellow" helps to clarify the distinction between Shakespeare's and Sidney's uses of that term as an artifice that complicates friendship. If Helena and Hermia are playfellows indeed, then their friendship should not be allowed to continue, for it would be considered childish and superficial. But since that friendship does continue (despite their feud in Act 3), it seems that in Shakespeare "playfellow," with its implied meanings of childishness and innocence, only masks the amorous and erotic implications of the friendship between Helena and Hermia. If in Shakespeare "playfellow" becomes a signifier that enables the romantic and potentially erotic nature of female friendship to continue unchecked, in Sidney, however, the term suggests failed friendship, one that has not been allowed to develop into a positive force. Sidney's attempt to set off failed friendship based on inequality from the culturally recognized friendship based on equality is clearly marked in the narrative, since the Tyrant episode follows immediately after the "enterchange" of the true friends, Musidorus and Pyrocles. As Robert Parry, another writer of romances, says of Moderatus and Priscus, two friends in *Moderatus, or the Black Knight*, "nothing is to be expected in amitie and friendship, more than equalitie."[24] On the subject of friendship based on equality, Sidney says:

> And so vpon securitie of both sides, they [Pyrocles and Musidorus] were enterchanged. Where I may not omit the worke of friendship in *Pyrocles*, who both in speech [and] countena[*n*]ce to *Musidorus*, well shewed, that he thoughts himselfe iniured, and not relieued by him: asking him what he had euer seene

> in him, why he could bot beare the extremities of mortall accidents as well as any man? And why he should enuy him the glorie of suffering death for his friends cause, and (as it were) rob him of his owne possession?[25]

Contrasting true and failed friendship is an attempt to highlight *amicitia* as a positive form of male bonding.[26] The juxtaposition of true with failed friendship might also be seen as an attempt to evacuate true friendship of all its anxieties, which, for example, Alan Bray sees as an inherent nature of friendship. It allows him to reroute those anxieties and violence into failed friendship, a bond that does not belong to the humanist narrative of virtue.[27] These two episodes also illustrate how Renaissance fiction helps us "inquire into the valence of the specific terms in which . . . friendship is constructed" not only in classical literature, to which David Halperin's view applies, but in Renaissance prose fiction as well.[28] While Sidney represents true friendship based on power equality in terms that make it a socially acceptable and normative form of male alliance, he represents failed friendship in terms that make it a potential site of other, nonnormative kinds of male bonding that do not belong to the realm of *amicitia*. If in Sidney's *Arcadia* the bond between equal friends features as a site of true friendship, one that is free of erotic charge so that other forms of friendship, which might include love and eroticism, can be kept in check, in other texts, true friendship and eroticism are privileged over other forms of erotic and romantic bonding, especially heteroeroticism.

The blurring of the boundaries between friendship and desire fills the pages of *The second part of the first Booke of the Myrrour of Knighthood*, printed in 1585 and translated by Robert Parry. This romance constituted one of the parts in the highly popular romance cycle by the Spanish writer, Diego Ortuñez de Calahorra, cycle which circulated in adapted translations in the English print market of the 1580s. On his way to protect Princess Lyndabrides, Rosicler, a knight, comes across a strange procession. On a one hundred foot long chariot on twelve wheels of ivory there is a mounted tent with two compartments: chamber and a closet. The chariot is pulled by giants and is accompanied by a procession of twenty young women (followed by more giants) dressed in sumptuous clothes and adorned with "verie faire and gallant bunch of feathers" (sig. L1^r). They are riding unicorns, all "betrapped with cloth of gold" (sig. L1^r). In the closet sits a beautiful damsel; in the tent, a melancholy knight "of a high stature and well made, his face was verie faire and of a good and gentle proportion" (sig. L1^v). His armor is covered with gold and precious stones, and the scales of Atlantic fish; he is dressed in silk robes covered with feather, fish scales, and diamonds. He looks like a parody of a lavishly dressed courtier and a New World Indian, or the female allegory of America in Adrien Collaert's engraving of personified America (See figure 9.2).

The knight's sword is of fine gold, he carries a scepter made of emerald, and on his head he wears a hat of green silk covered with rubies. Rosicler ignores the lady in the front chamber but fixes his gaze on the knight in the

Figure 9.2 Collaert, A., after M. de Vos. America (Allegory). Netherlandish, sixteenth-century engraving. The Metropolitan Museum of Art, Estate of James Hazen Hyde, 1959 (59.654.10).

closet, feeling "within himself a great weakness" (sig. K8^r). Rosicler's weakness, his (sudden) deficiency of strength and power, is represented by his fixation on the "wrong" sight: the knight in the closet (the knight is himself weakened, emasculated, by the clothing), not the beautiful damsel, as would befit a knight in a romance. The knight's closet is in fact an ambiguous space, which provides a site not only for the redefinition of friendship but also for the sublimated exotic homoeroticism of prose romances. The fantastical and exotic pageant, whose appearance weakens Rosicler's heroic masculinity, and in which the woman in the first compartment disappears from the narrative at the expense of the resplendent knight in the closet, thus ends up being a spectacle for and about men. The narrative's focus on men, and the erasure of a woman, privileges male bonding over heteroerotic courtship, by making Rosicler's fascination with the knight in the closet a source of ocular pleasure of the romance's male readers. As a prelude to the romance's longest homosocial narrative of male, here queered, friendship, the pageant episode suggests that in the culture where homoerotic attractions between men was considered one (most horrible) of the sins of the flesh, fantasy and exoticism have became conduits for desire shared between men. The uninhibited spectacle of ocular pleasure is enabled by the narrative that takes place somewhere in Greece, in the eastern Mediterranean, in the region on the borders of Christianity, that is conveniently far away from the corporeal limitations of England. In this and other examples we see how the chivalric world of romances enables both homoerotic desire and heroic valor to coexist without compromising either the marital or heroic contexts.

Weakened by the sight of the knight in the closet and spurned by a desire to defend the Princess Lyndabrides, Rosicler, the knight of Sun, leaves his paternal home, against his father's wish that he "remain and lodge within the pallace."[29] Yet Rosicler does so because he is torn between Claridiana and Lyndabrides, two princesses he has had a clandestine affair with. Before he set out, however, he "went out of the Pallace with great desire to speake with two Princes Brandizel and Claueryondo" (sig. P5[r]) who were to make him company and who had just emerged in Greece after their separation from Floriandus, knight of the Sun, at sea. At this point, the narrative slips into a most unusual digression:

> when he came into the place, he went straight vnto them and lead them into a secret chamber within the Chariot, whereas they made themselues knowen to the one vnto the other, where they embraced the one the other with great delight, as those which loued together like vnto perfect friends. And with the greate desire they had to see one another, they remained a great while embracing before anie of them could speake, but after that they were somewhat quieted, the two Princes Brandizel and Claueryndo did giue the knight of the Sunne to understand of all that euer they had passed, after such time as they were departed at the sea.... Wherein they passed all that daie till night drew on.[30]

Since display of affection and trust among "perfect friends" was common and expected, one wonders what is the purpose of the "secret chamber" where that amicable intimacy is displayed? There is no doubt that a "secret chamber" in the chariot signals privacy and provides a space for the illicit attraction between men. It is a space in which friends share embraces and stories until they remain breathless, a clearly not just homosocial but queer space that is safely detached from the public eye. It is also a space in which friendship offers an opportunity to free oneself from the normativity of the rhetoric of courtship and moderation that the knight displays in his subsequent meeting with Lyndabrides. The secret chamber, thus, opens to the reader the content of Rosicler's private closet. In a lucid discussion of the technology and social organization of the early modern closet that focuses primarily on the potentially eroticized relationship between the master and his secretary, Alan Stewart asserts: "the early modern closet...is often associated with the construction of a new modern subjectivity."[31]

The new subjectivity that we see emerging here is, I would argue, one that redefines two formulations of masculinity in early modern literature and culture: friend and knight. The secrecy of the chamber, within which the reunion of long separated knight-friends takes place, erases the boundaries that separate intimacy and passion from socially acknowledged transactions between men. That the closet eroticizes friendship at a time (at the end of the sixteenth century) when, in prose fiction, romantic masculinity has started to replace militant masculinity, is also signaled at the end of this episode when yet another nocturnal reunion of friends becomes an alternative for the heteroerotic dilemma. After he has eventually spent one whole day in "amorous conuersation" (sig. P6[r]) with the Princess Lyndabrides, fearing that the memory of her "would haue troubled him" (sig. P6[r]) were he to return to Claridiana at this point, he returned "vnto his friends, & and there lodged all four together in one chamber, in foure beds" (sig. P6^{r}). (The fourth friend, who joins them in the chamber, is Floriandus.) It was not uncommon in the Renaissance (and in Renaissance romances) for friends, male or female, to share the same bed. Talking about Moderatus and Priscius, Parry, the translator of *Myrrour* (Book I, Part II), says that "one chamber was common unto them both."[32] The separation of bedfellow-friends raises doubt and increases longing in the waiting friend. Even though the separation puts the waiting friend in the position of shared loyalty to the friend and the beloved, it nonetheless does not compromise the longing for the woman. As Parry says of Priscius waiting for Moderatus in his (their) chamber: "The absence of his friend Moderatus also greatly troubled him, both for that he longed to understand his successe with Florida, and also much maruelled, why he came not to bed vnto him the night before, as his manner was."[33] In Parry, Priscius's romantic yearning for Florida (and his recollection of the previous night spent with her) is not compromised by his amicable longing for Moderatus. It is only so because the friendship of Moderatus and Priscius's friendship is developed in Parry's romance without being complicated by homoerotic desire. Alone in his chamber, Priscius's "frivolous and vaine thoughtes"[34] are directed to Florida only. But the *Myrrour* romance presents other possibilities for both friends. It privileges homosociality in the context of erotics over heteroerotic romance without excluding the possibility that either of those options may be the end of chivalric quest.

The temporary rejection of women (both of the lady in the chamber and the two princesses in Rosicler's life) from the narrative of courtship, and the substitution of this narrative with the one in which male friendship is represented in romantic terms suggests the extent to which the narrative of courtship is troubled and it signals that marriage may not be the only goal in that narrative. Desire inscribed in both the chamber, where the four friends spend a night, and the closet, with its exotic-looking knight, does not destabilize but solidify the male alliances at the heart of the romance's privileged world of heroic masculinity. The example from *The Myrrour of Knighthood* is an instance of what Mario DiGangi calls "the homoerotics of masculinity," of heroic masculinity, I would add. In this, and other examples that I will discuss, we see how the chivalric world of romances enables both homoerotics and heroics to coexist, without compromising either marital or heroic context. The homoerotics of heroic masculinity in romances are thus different from those of early modern, especially tragicomedies of the Caroline period, in which the form of homoerotic desire "may well differ within marital or peacetime contexts."[35] If in tragicomedies, as DiGangi suggests, heroic pursuit precludes homoerotic desire in war time but enables it in peacetime, in romances, homoerotic desire circulates within both heroic and romantic contexts in which marriage is, but may not necessarily be, the only end to courtship. As the example from *The Myrrour of Knighthood* suggests, leaving the woman's chamber at night in order not to compromise her chastity and honor becomes a pretext for wishing to spend a night with friends. The idea of the wandering knight, whose continent Christian body becomes an inviting and powerful temptation to shake the normativity of (hetero) sexual attraction, appealed greatly to the writers of romances.[36]

In Richard Johnson's romance, *The Most Famovs History of the Seuen Champions of Christendome* (first published in 1596), traveling and transgressions constitute the fabric of the narrative. One of the seven knights, Sir Anthony of Italy, has spent too much time in Lady Rossalinde's chamber, and, irked by the urge to prove his masculinity in combat, he is about to abandon her, saying:

> for thy sake Ile stand as Champion against all knights in the world: But to impare the honour of my Knighthood, and to liue like a carpet dancer in the laps of Ladies I will not: though I can tune a Lute in a Princes Chamber, I can sound as well a fierce alarum in the field: honour calles mee foorth, deare Roassalinde, and fame intends to buckle on my armour, which now lies rusting in the idle court of Thrace. Therefore I am constrayned (though most unwilling) to leaue the comfortable sight of thy beautie, and commit my fortune to a longer trauell.[37]

The passage evokes the familiar Renaissance ideology of love as an emasculating force, one that turns a hero into a "carpet dancer": an effeminized (perhaps orientalized) pleaser indulging in luxury and passion. At the moment when the narrative is about to restore Sir Anthony's heroic masculinity by sending him on his way to combat, it takes another twist that suggests the opposite; it emasculates him with a homoerotic context. Rossalinda does not want to share the fate of many a romantic damsel, that of an abandoned woman, evoked both explicitly and implicitly, through references to the abandoned women in classical myths, Camma and Alcyone; she requests that Sir Anthony of Italy take her with him ("forsake me not, deare knight of Christendome" [sig. J1^{v}]). At this point at the end of the chapter, Sir Anthony makes Rossalinda his page, and has her cross-dress (the episode echoes Rosalind's cross-dressing into a page in Shakespeare's *As You Like It*):

> her rapier was a Turkish blade, and her ponyard of the finest fashone, the which shee wore at her backe tyed with a Orenge tawny coloured scarfe, beautified with tassels of unwoven silke, her buskins of the smoothest kiddes skinnes, her spurres of the purest Lidian steele. In which when the noble and beautifiell Lady was attyred, she seemed in stature like the god of loue, when he sate dandied vpon Didos lap, or rather Ganimede, loues minion, or Adonis, when Venus shewed her siluer skinne to intrap his eyes to her unchaste desires.[38]

The humor of this episode is hard to miss, for what starts off as the rejection of emasculation and a recuperation of chivalric comportment, turns into a scene whose homoeroticism undoes the heroic intention through a serious of comparisons that suggest erotic transgressions. Johnson's comparisons evoke, first, one of the causes of Juno's rage against Aeneas's honor paid to ravished Ganymede (the image is a variation of the opening of Christopher Marlowe's play *Dido, Queen of Carthage*, where Jupiter is dandling Ganymede on his knee), echoing Virgil's suggestion of Ganymede's ravished honor (*rapti Ganymedis honores, Aeneid* I. 28), who symbolizes homoeroticism in Renaissance literature and art.[39] The reference to Adonis and Venus resonates not only with unbridled desire but with homoeroticism as well. Jonathan Bate reminds us that "[t]he Venus and Adonis story must be seen in the broader context of the Orphic series of narratives concerning destructive passion, female desire . . . and homoerotic charm."[40] What starts as a narrative of heroic quest is quickly turned into a parody of heroic and masculine ambition. Johnson's attempt to write homoerotics out of the chivalric narrative becomes a way of speaking about it, by relegating homoerotic desire to a woman's cross-dressed body. Yet it is not Rossalinda's cross-dressed body that itself suggests homoeroticism. Rather, it is that body's visual connections to the cultural signifiers (the mythological figures it was compared to) associated with homoeroticism that attribute erotic meaning to it. In turn, the body of Rossalinda and its sartorial blazon become the conduit for homoeroticism within the chivalric fiction, for the kind of Renaissance masculinity Rossalinda performs is already queer.

The fiction's playfulness with homoerotics at the end of the chapter describing the heroic adventures of the Italian champion has greater cultural implications. We see how fiction acts as a medium to promote heroic and masculine ideals of other champions. Anthony of Italy is the only Christian champion in Johnson's fiction imagined by its author within the context of emasculation and homoeroticism. The parody of Sir Anthony's heroic masculinity through the emasculating and homoerotic contexts within which it is imagined is meant neither to deprecate nor to compromise heroic masculinity.[41] The parody of heroic masculinity in Johnson becomes a vehicle for imagining homoerotic desire within the narrative of heroic quest. Rather than separate homoerotic from heroic masculinity, and not censor homoerotic desire, this episode makes the two manifestations of masculinity coexisting. By making both a hero and woman-page agents in this comic episode, Johnson's narrative disturbs the rigid gender divisions and expected sexual roles promoted by romantic love fictions.

Looking for signs of homoeroticism in prose romances—a literary genre scorned in the Renaissance because of its explicit display of violence, lewdness, and pornography—yields mostly examples of nongenital homosexual actions. Everywhere one looks in the romances of the Renaissance, one finds examples of masculine friendship and other forms of homosocial bonds, especially between knights; but explicitly homoerotic or perilously sodomitical episodes are conspicuously absent from romances. Sidney's Tyrant, who uses and discards playfellows at a high rate, is a rare case of a sodomitical character represented as a failed friend. The division between sodomy (excluded from romances) and homoeroticism (inscribed in them) suggests that prose romances distinguished between threatening and nonthreatening discourses of nonnormative desire. This division implies, then, that homoeroticism is not excluded as a possibility in the formation of Christian subjectivity in the fiction of romances. That is already a step beyond the culturally organized realm of male sexuality, which exclusively promoted self-control, courtship, and marital sex whose goal is procreation.

The relative invisibility of the homoerotic body in prose romances points out to the fact that male same-sex representation in fiction may be sought within a number of ways in which male–male desire is manifested. This includes passion, intimacy (enabled by touch, embrace, wish to share time and space away from the gaze of other characters, secretly), oaths of loyalty, and different transactions between men that assure their alliances outside the realm of the public and normative sphere within which masculinity was realized: chivalry. Narratives that privilege (with a touch of campy indulgence in humor and excess) homoeroticism over courtship in romances also suggest popular literature's resistance to homophobia, typically mediated in theological discourses, that swept early modern English culture like a bush fire. Both Catholic and Protestant preachers, for example, considered sodomy a sexual sin and used it defamatorily in their tracts against each other. Benjamin Carrier, a Catholic priest, a convert from Protestantism, writes:

> In the yeare 1632, there was discouered in London a Society of certaine Sodomites, to the number of forty, or fifty; all of them being earnest and boate Puritans, who had their common appointed meeting-place, for their abominable Impiety; of which number diuers of them (and such as were good temporall estates and meanes) were apprehended, and the rest instantly fled.[42]

Carrier's fantasy of what looks like a raid of a group of Puritan mollies, represented here as a community of self-identified homosexuals, is symptomatic of homophobia in early modern London. With their treatment of homoeroticism as an inflection of chivalric masculinity and a kind of desire that exists alongside other kinds of erotic charge, romances are not only diametrically opposite from the cultural paranoia exhibited in Carrier's treatise, but they also stand in opposition to theological (both Catholic and Protestant) discourses against sexual pleasure in general and homoeroticism in particular. This is why I think we should look at popular romances as texts that, implicitly, in their narratives, questioned other normative, primarily theological, discourses of sexuality. I would argue that we should look at romances not as texts that only reflected contemporary ideas of sex, but as agents that helped shape a new culture of sexuality. I would like, therefore, to make a point that even mere fragments of homoerotic representation in romances become a factor in the way in which the othering of the queer circulates in Renaissance literature, especially fiction. As Valerie Traub reminds us "[h]istorically, embodiments of desire rise and fall into an out of representation: at particular moments, and in relation to social, political, and economic forces, certain ways of conceptualizing gender and eroticism will be especially salient; at other moments they will occasion little concern."[43] A small number of homoerotic episodes from prose-fiction, therefore, should not be taken as the genre's reaction against corporeal transgression. On the contrary, the romance is a genre whose success on the print market partially depended on its shock effect primarily based on either violations of the body or excesses of behavior.[44] Rape, abductions, the Christians' aggression over, and by the Turks and Moors, and male violence against both men and women are some of the most frequent manifestations of subverted normative behavior in romances. In a genre that aestheticizes excess[45] and that proliferated at the time (in the last two decades of the sixteenth and the first half of the seventeenth century) when the theme of forging the nation became central to both cultural and literary representations of masculinity, representations of physical violence would have been considered the most threatening to Protestant nationalism and most destructive of the reproductive ideal promoted by romances. Reading homoeroticism in romances requires, using Valerie Traub's term, "cracking the code" of the practices of representation and conceptualization of erotically desiring men as conceptualized in early modern romances.[46] Homoeroticism is in fact mediated through the rhetoric and episodes of masculine friendship, and it is represented in the structuring of narrative that tests masculine friendship. What these fictions show, then, is that homoeroticism is represented as a public and political, though close and almost intimate, alliance between men. This separates it from sodomy, which, as Alan Stewart has reminded us recently, was considered "a household crime" in the Renaissance.[47]

The question of homoeroticism in prose romances, then, is probably best posited in the way in which Eve Sedgwick discusses the relationship between homosexuality and homosociality: it is the question of "the *structure* of men's relations with other men,"[48] and it is that structure primarily, not love or sexuality, that, according to Sedgwick, one might call desire. The kind of desire that I have called homoerotic emerges out of the structure of masculine friendship, one that is always already, both in classical and humanist discourses of *amicitia*, exclusive of women, potentially intimate, but based on the need to establish alliances, upon which the state rests, within the masculine realm. The structure of this desire in Renaissance prose fiction, however, is different from the homosocial and potentially homoerotic structures of relationships Sedgwick highlights. In romances, the structures of friendship suggest a nongenital form of bonding between men, whose purpose is to solidify, not subvert, the very fabric of the nationalist Protestant English state. The link between this kind of homoeroticism, politics, and power, therefore, opens up a new way of looking at queer relations in Renaissance fiction, especially romances. Because it is, in its most frequent manifestations subsumed into masculine friendship, romance homoeroticism is constructed in romances less as an erotic pleasure but more as a confirmation of masculine bonds within the social and political spheres of power they occupy. This form of homoeroticism is neither explicitly somatic (as, e.g., Edward's and Gaveston's is)—it is not sodomitical—nor is it politically inflected (as, e.g., the barons' aggression in Christopher Marlowe's play *Edward II*). Because the bonding between close friends occurs between equal men, there is neither power nor status disparity to separate homoerotic desire from any other kind of male relationships in romances. If the erasure of power among equal friends enables nongenital homoerotic desire to go unchecked, in other situations where there is an imbalance of power sexual, but non-homoerotic desire, the male–male bond is quite clearly constructed as threatening. The peril of romance narrative does not come from the homoeroticized body, but from the body of the incontinent woman, from female sexuality outside marriage that threatens to subordinate and seduce men. (This is, e.g., what distinguishes the romance structure of desire from Sedgwick's nineteenth-century examples.) Here is, for example, how Parismenos has been seduced by Angelica:

> Parismenos had no sooner seated himselfe, but Angelica sate downe on his left knee, clasping her right arme about his necke, with a kinde and sweete gesture, hiding her other in his manlie bosome, which was unbuttoned by reason of the heate, first, making many kisses a Prologue to her speech.[49]

Angelica's prologue is directed not so much to her speech, in which she expresses desire for Parismenos, but it is a prelude to the satisfaction of her sexual urge in the night to come. In a culture in which premarital sexuality threatens woman's honor, and in the genre that emphases male continence and the preserving of female chastity, the narrative of woman's seduction of men is as disturbing as sodomy.

The division between the relative occlusion of homoeroticism in romance narratives and the representation of homoeroticism as nonthreatening, may also be the result of the role romances played in the culture of new emerging subjectivity in early modern England. Yet what this division also tells us is that in their fictions, romance writers did not consider heteroerotic desire to be the only desire available to men. This new subjectivity constituted part of the conflicting discourses of sexuality and marriage, discourses that were part of the new morality that saw the family as a micro commonwealth, as a symbolic nucleus of the Renaissance state whose power was growing. Martin Ingram identifies this push toward stabilizing both micro and macro commonwealth as part of "the quest for order" in Renaissance England, one that involved the consolidation of both civic discipline and sexual morality.[50] Because the "new" humanist family dependent on the control of pleasure and an assurance of reproductive economy, both literary and nonliterary humanist discourses of sexuality emphasized continence and marriage. Achieving this ideal of "an ordered society," therefore, depended on new humanist discourses featuring oaths of love and friendship, and feelings of mutuality, between men and women, but between friends as well.[51] The purpose of these oaths was either to endorse marriage as a moral and social ideal or to cement male friendship as one of the pillars of the new commonwealth. Sexual discipline as the ideal of sexual morality remained central to this "new" family, but it existed together with the emerging freedom to choose future marriage partners, a move one might call a push toward the changing nature of patriarchy. These values also emerged at the time when, as Christopher Hill suggests, "[m]arriage was delayed longer than in any other known [Renaissance] society."[52] While the behavior of young women was described (or, rather, prescribed) in the conduct books written by puritan preachers, popular romances were, in a manner of speaking, fictional conduct books for a male youth who, caught in the period between puberty and marriage, had to discipline his burning desires. Produced against this culture of control in the process of the shaping of the new subject, romances, like other literature, promoted new ideals of marriage and heroism.

Yet the push toward a redefinition of marriage, love, and courtship, coupled with the shift from heroic to romantic masculinity, also provided Renaissance fiction with possibilities to fantasize about different scenarios of this delayed route to marriage. Thus in those romantic fictions we encounter the representation of what Frances E. Dolan's has described as a broadening perspective in the early modern discourses of gender and sexuality, one that includes "a whole range of relations between the sexes for which marriage and heterosex cannot account."[53] As Andrew Hadfield argues, "in the sixteenth century it was not obvious to many writers of 'literature' what it was they were attempting to achieve. 'Literature' was not clear and distinctly identifiable category of writing which would be employed to deal with certain themes in a particular way."[54] It is precisely in this ambiguous status of romance, one that celebrates some of the social ideals while at the same time remains open to spectacles of pleasure of other kinds, that we should see the role romances play in the dissemination of the discourses of illicit sexuality in Renaissance England.

Even the isolated homoerotic narratives, embedded in the longer fictions of amorous and chivalrous conquests, contributed in the Renaissance to the textualizing of homoerotics, to the culture in which the circulation of texts and discourses shaped and affected, pleased and troubled, the readers, agents upon whom the society relied for its stability and power. That even one book about illicit sexuality, a book buried in a big library of illustrious titles and topics can disturb the cultural establishment, is illustrated in what is most likely an imagined scenario that Thomas Coryate, a seventeenth-century traveler in Europe, says he witnessed on a trip to Switzerland. In *Coryats Crudities*, he says that in Zurich he met Henry Bullinger, "the nephew of that famous preacher and writer of godly memory Henry Bullinger [the older?], the successor of Zuiunglius."[55] In a tract that, in this part at least, echoes with the Puritan disdain for Catholics, the younger Bullinger showed Coryate the library in his study:

> He led me into his studie, which is exceedingly well furnished with diunitie bookes, and much augmented with many of his grandfathers.... he shewed me most execrable booke written by an Italian, one *Ioannes Casa* Bishop of Beneuentum in Italy, in praise of that vnnaturall sinne of Sodomy. This booke is written in the Italian tongue, and printed in Venice. It came first to the hands of this mans grandfather aforesaid, who kept it as a monument of

> the abhominable impurity of a papistical Bishop, to which end this mans also that received it from his grandfather, keepeth it to this day.[56]

Besides being yet another example of the use of sodomy as a defamatory gesture toward Catholics, this episode works in a meta-literary way as well. In that sense it suggests how, on the one hand, under the guise of deprecation, homoerotic discourses and texts are said, by the speaker, to have been circulated and to have been preserved from disappearance. Yet in doing so, on the other hand, Coryate's text itself becomes a channel through which discourses of sodomy circulated among contemporary readers. If in their individual narratives prose romances offer only brief episodes of homoeroticism buried in a mass of heteroerotic and heroic plots, their contribution to a dissemination of the Renaissance discourses of homoerotics should be sought in the cumulative effect those romance discourses shared with other printed discourses of homoeroticism, like the engraving in the German edition of *Metamorphoses* or Coryat's text, which circulated in the print market of the Renaissance and among its consumers.

Notes

I am grateful to the Newberry, Folger, and Huntington libraries, and the Social Sciences and Humanities Federation of Canada, for funds that supported my work on this essay. I thank Natasha Hurley and Alan Stewart for their criticism and help with earlier drafts of this essay.

1. *Metamorphoses Ovidii, argvmentis quidem soluta oratione, enarrationibus autem & allegorijs elegiaco uersu occuratissimè expositae*, illustrated by M. Iohan, [Frankfurt], 1563, sig. A3^r. The Newberry Library, Chicago, Case Y 672 O 09456.
2. Unless otherwise stated, throughout the essay I quote the Latin original from *Ovid, Metamorphoses*, Books I–VIII, with an English translation by Frank Justus Miller, revised by G. P. Goold (Cambridge, MA and London: Harvard University Press, 1994), I. pp. 99–100. The references are to book and line numbers. I quote the English translation from Arthur Golding's *The. XV. Bookes of P. Ouidius Naso, Entytuled Metamorphosis* (London: Willyam Seres, 1567), sig. B2^v, STC 18956.
3. *Metamorphoses Ovidii*, sig. A3^r.
4. In the Golden Age, Ovid says, "[t]here was no feare of punishment, there was no threatning lawe / In brazen tables nayled up, to keepe the folke in lawe" ("poena metusque aberant, nec verba minantia fixo / aere legebantur" I. pp. 91–92).
5. Stephen Hinds, "Landscape with Figures: Aesthetics of Place in the *Metamorphoses* and Its Tradition," in *The Cambridge Companion to Ovid*, ed. Philip Hardie (Cambridge: Cambridge University Press, 2002), p. 124.
6. The English colonization of the eastern Mediterranean, especially the Levant, was one of those failed political ambitions turned into literary fantasies.
7. In addition to literary (ancient and Renaissance romances) and cultural (mercantile exchange between East and West) influences, romances may also have come out of the fictions of the East. We find this eastern or oriental

connection in romances, e.g., in Fynes Moryson's travel account in Turkey, where he compares a group of armed horsemen that he came upon to the characters of romances. He says: "They [the horsemen] were armed with Launces, Shields, and short broad Swords, so as a man would haue said, they had been the Knights of *Amadis de Gaule*. Neither is it vnprobable, that those fictions came from the horsemen of *Asia*, since wee did see some mile from *Tripoli*, a Bridge called the Bridge of *Rodomont*, and a Fountaine neere *Scandarona*, called the Amazons Fountaine, and many like monuments in these parts." See Fynes Moryson, *An Itinerary Written By Fynes Moryson Gent. First in the Latine Tongue, and then Translated By him into English. Containing his Ten Yeeres Travell Through the Twelve Domjnions of Germany, Bohmerland, Sweitzerland, Netherland, Denmarke, Poland, Jtaly, Turkey, France, England, Scotland, and Ireland* (London: by John Beale, 1617), sig. X3v, STC 18205.

8. Catherine Gallagher and Stephen Greenblatt, *Practicing New Historicism* (Chicago and London: University of Chicago Press, 2000), p. 17.
9. Constance Jordan, *Renaissance Feminism: Literary Texts and Political Models* (Ithaca and London: Cornell University Press, 1990), p. 229.
10. Gregory W. Bredbeck, *Sodomy and Interpretation: Marlowe to Milton* (Ithaca and London: Cornell University Press, 1991), p. 108.
11. Bredbeck, *Sodomy and Interpretation*, p. 107.
12. Winfried Schleiner, "Male Cross-Dressing and Transvestism in Renaissance Romances," *Sixteenth Century Journal* 29(4) (1988): 612.
13. David Cressy, "Gender Trouble and Cross-Dressing in Early Modern England," *Journal of British Studies* 35(4) (1996): 451; reprinted in his book *Travesties and Transgressions in Tudor and Stuart England* (Oxford: University Press, 2000), pp. 92–115.
14. Cressy, "Gender Trouble," p. 443.
15. Cressy, "Gender Trouble," p. 439.
16. Sir Philip Sidney, *The Countesse of Pembrokes Arcadia* (London: for William Ponsonbie, 1598), sig. L6r, STC 22541.
17. *The third and last part of Palmerin of England* (London: for William Leake, 1602), sig. Gg4r, STC 19165.
18. Thomas Lodge, *Wits miserie, and the worlds madnesse: discouering the deuils incarnat of this age* (London: A. Islip, 1596), sig. H3r, STC 16677.
19. Lodge, *Wits miserie*.
20. Sidney, *The Countesse of Pembrokes*, sig. L6r.
21. Interestingly, one of the earlier meanings of the word "play," according to the *OED* (6C) is "amorous disport, dalliance, sexual indulgence." It first occurs in this context in 1425 in "Cursor Mundi," a narrative poem that describes a providential view ("course") of scriptural history mixed with romance, written in Middle English so that common folk could understand it. Curiously, the situation in which "play" is used erotically involves only men, Mathan and Jacob, and Jacob and Joseph, in the context of the Fifth Age of the World and the family of Virgin Mary. Here is the poet of "Cursor Mundi": "Mathan gat Iacob in pleye, / Iacob Ioseph soth to seye / Of that syde is to telle no mo." That the "Cursor Mundi" poet does not want to tell the full story of the four-men play suggests the improper (to say the least) nature of that play. Quoted from "Cursor Mundi," Trinity College, Cambridge, MS. R.3.8. (588), ed. Richard Morris, Early English Text Society (1875), part II (London, New York, and Toronto: Oxford University Press, reprinted, 1966), lines 9247–48.

22. Quoted from William Shakespeare, *A Midsummer Night's Dream*, the Oxford Shakespeare, ed. Peter Holland (Oxford and New York: Oxford University Press, 1995). I am indebted to Alan Stewart for drawing my attention to this use of "playfellow."
23. *More's History of King Richard III*, ed. J. Rawson Lumby, facsimile of the 1513 original (Cambridge: Cambridge University Press, 1883), p. 36. I am indebted to Alan Stewart for drawing my attention to this passage and for sharing his thoughts on this passage with me.
24. Robert Parry, *Moderatus, The Most Delectable and Famous Historie of the Blacke Knight* (London: R. Jhones, 1595), sig. C1^{r}, STC 19337.
25. Sidney, *The Countesse of Pembrokes*, sig. L5^{r}.
26. Pyrocles's and Musidorus's friendship, based on equality, moderation, and virtue, is also an attempt to counter male youth's libertinism that Sidney suggests have engulfed city life. He says: "[Y]oung men [are] verie fault-finding, but verie faultie: and so to newfanglenesse both of manner, apparell, and each thingels [*sic*], by the custome of selfe-guiltie euill, glad to change though oft for worse; merchandise abused, and to townes decaied for want of iust and naturall libertie." Sidney, *The Countesse of Pembroke*, sig. L1^{r}.
27. I am referring to Alan Bray's article "Homosexuality and the Signs of Male Friendship in Elizabethan England," *History Workshop Journal* 29 (1990): 1–19.
28. David M. Halperin, *One Hundred Years of Homosexuality: And Other Essays on Greek Love* (New York and London: Routledge, 1990), p. 77.
29. *The second part of the first booke of the Myrrour of Knighthood*, translated by R[obert] P[arry] (London: by Thomas Este, 1585), sig. P4^{r}.
30. *The second part of the first booke of the Myrrour of Knighthood*, sig. P5^{r}.
31. Alan Stewart, *Close Readers: Humanism and Sodomy in Early Modern England* (Princeton: Princeton University Press, 1997), p. 162.
32. Parry, *Moderatus*, sig. C1^{r}.
33. Parry, *Moderatus*, sig. K1^{r}.
34. Parry, *Moderatus*, sig. C2^{r}.
35. See Mario DiGangi, "The Homoerotics of Masculinity in Tragicomedy," *The Homoerotics of Early Modern Drama* (Cambridge: Cambridge University Press, 1997), pp. 134–54.
36. This idea goes back to the narratives of saints' wanderings in the eastern Mediterranean, narratives described in the *Apocryphal Acts*. See Peter Brown, *The Body and Society: Men, Women, and Sexual Renunciation in Early Christianity* (New York: Columbia University Press, 1988), p. 197.
37. Richard Johnson, *The Most Famovs History of the Seuen Champions of Christendome* (London: for Elizabeth Burbie, 1608), sig. J1^{r}, STC 14679.
38. Johnson, *The Most Famovs History of the Seuen Champions of Christendome*, sig. J1^{v}–J2^{r}.
39. See James M. Saslow, *Ganymede in the Renaissance: Homosexuality in Art and Society* (New Haven: Yale University Press, 1986).
40. Jonathan Bate, *Shakespeare and Ovid* (Oxford: Clarendon Press, 1994), p. 54. In his anti-Puritan tract, *PVRITANISME The Mother, SINNE THE DAUGHTER* (St. Omer: English College Press, 1633, STC 4264), Benjamin Carrier, a Catholic priest, links Adonis to sodomy in his defamation of Theodore Beza, a Reformed theologian and Calvinist, as a sodomite who kept "a boy *Andebertus* (which Beza kept as his *Adonis*, or *Ganimede*, by abusing the boys body)" (sig. E4^{v}).

41. What we may be seeing here is that Italy was no longer considered a hotbed of sodomy, as its reputation indicated in earlier times. As William Thomas, a Tudor traveller in Italy, writes upon visiting Florence in the middle of the sixteenth century: "they [Florentines] haue been much burdeined with Sodomie in time past. I can not perceiue there is any such thing now." See William Thomas, *The History of Italye* (London: Thomas Marshe, 1561), sig. Nn4[v], STC 24018. Although Thomas's view was not shared by many who associated Italy with sodomy in the Renaissance, his statement may be corroborated by evidence in some recent scholarship on homosexuality in Renaissance Italy. Both Michael Rocke, writing on Florence, (*Forbidden Friendships: Homosexuality and Male Culture in Renaissance Florence* [New York and Oxford: Oxford University Press, 1996]) and Guido Ruggiero, writing on Venice, ("Sodom and Venice," *The Boundaries of Eros: Sex Crime and Sexuality in Renaissance Venice* [New York and Oxford: Oxford University Press, 1985], pp. 109–45), offer evidence suggesting that at least the number of reported cases of sodomy in Florence and Venice was higher in the fourteenth and the fifteenth centuries, but that it dropped in the sixteenth.
42. If we entertain the possibility that the described raid of homosexuals is not Carrier's fantasy (though it is difficult to prove that it is not), but the account of an incident in a molly house of sorts, then we are dealing with an identified homosexual subculture. See B[enjamin] C[arrier], *PVRITANISME*, fol. 1[v].
43. Valerie Traub, "The Perversion of 'Lesbian' Desire," *History Workshop Journal* 41 (1996): 25.
44. Charles Mish shows that between 1576 and 1620 more fiction appeared than drama. See Charles C. Mish, "Comparative Popularity of Early Fiction and Drama," *Notes and Queries* 197 (June 21, 1952): 269.
45. In the Epistle to the Reader, in the seventeenth-century edition of *The Famous History of Palmendos, Son of the Most Renowned Palmerin D'Oliva* (London: E. Alsop, 1653, STC 18064), presumably the printer describes the genre of romance ("quintaessence of Romancy"), suggesting that it "hath joyned Art to abundance, and mingled mildnesse with Majesty" (sig. A4[r]). This epistle is not in the first edition of this work, printed by J. Charlewood for S. Watersonne in 1589.
46. Valerie Traub, "The (In)Significance of 'Lesbian' Desire in Early Modern England," in *Queering the Renaissance*, ed. Jonathan Goldberg (Durham and London: Duke University Press, 1994), p. 65.
47. Alan Stewart, "Bribery, Buggery, and the Fall of Lord Chancellor Bacon," in *Rhetoric and Law in Early Modern Europe*, ed. Victoria Kahn and Lorna Hutson (New Haven and London: Yale University Press, 2001), p. 138. For sodomy as a domestic crime within an aristocratic household, see also Cynthia Herrup, *A House in Gross Disorder: Sex, Law, and the 2nd Earl of Castelhaven* (New York: Oxford University Press, 1999).
48. Eve Kosofsky Sedgwick, *Between Men: English Literature and Male Homosocial Desire* (New York: Columbia University Press, 1985), p. 2.
49. *Parismenos: The Second Part of the Most Famous, Delectable, and Pleasant Historie of Parismus, the Renowned Prince of Bohemia* (London: Thomas Creede, 1599), sig. Bb1[r].
50. Martin Ingram, "Sex and Marriage: Laws, Ideals and Popular Practice," *Church Courts, Sex and Marriage in England, 1570–1640* (Cambridge: Cambridge University Press, 1987), p. 126.

51. I borrow the phrase "ordered society" from the title of Susan Dwyer Amussen's book *An Ordered Society: Gender and Class in Early Modern England* (Oxford: Basil Blackwell, 1988). For the formation of this new subjectivity in romance fiction under the influence of changing ideology of self and literature in the Renaissance, see also Lawrence Manley, *Literature and Culture in Early Modern London* (Cambridge: Cambridge University Press, 1995).
52. Christopher Hill, "Sex, Marriage, and the Family in England." *The Economic History Review*, Second Series, 31 (1978): 455.
53. Frances E. Dolan, *Whores of Babylon: Catholicism, Gender, and Seventeenth-Century Print Culture* (Ithaca and London: Cornell University Press, 1999), p. 93.
54. Andrew Hadfield, *Literature, Politics and National Identity: Reformation to Renaissance* (Cambridge: Cambridge University Press, 1994), p. 1
55. Thomas Coryate, *Coryat's Crudities* (London: W.S., 1611), sig. Ff7^{v}–Ff8^{r}, STC 5808.
56. Coryate, *Coryat's Crudities*, sig. Ff8^{r}.

Part III

Textuality and Desire

Chapter 10

Emasculating Romance: Historical Fiction in the Protectorate

Elizabeth Sauer

> *The common Occurrances of the World, do not arrive alwayes at a pitch high enough for example, to stir up the appetite of the Reader, which things feigned may do under the notion of a Romance.*
>
> —*Sir Percy Herbert,* The Princess Cloria *(1661), sig. A2*^{v}

This essay examines the rewriting of the English romance tradition in relation to seventeenth-century political culture and strained gender relations, which lay at the heart of the "crisis of order" in the period.[1] The Renaissance witnessed the Golden Age of romance fiction and drama, culminating in the production of Sir Philip Sidney's *Arcadia* and Edmund Spenser's *Faerie Queene.* In a pejorative sense, a "romance" was an imaginary, flighty story featuring extraordinary adventures presented episodically and involving low-class, stereotypical characters; when used favorably, the term referred to what John Milton described as "those lofty fables and Romances, which recount in solemne canto's the deeds of Knighthood founded by our victorious Kings; & from hence had in over all Christendome."[2] Romance also became identified with works of popular fiction with historical or topical references; such texts included Sidney's *Arcadia* (1580–90) and John Barclay's *Barclay his Argenis* (1621, Lat.; 1623, Engl.).[3] Following the death of Elizabeth, the feminized romance tradition—which was hybrid and experimental from the start—underwent various metamorphoses in response to the growing disenchantment with courtly life and the escalation of civil and political tensions that affected cultural expression and literary tastes. Renaissance romances could sustain criticisms of political authority, but the overlay of governmental affairs and sexual politics in later romances transformed the genre. When it emerged from the furnace in the seventeenth century, the arcadianisms of the traditional romance were notably suppressed or emasculated. No longer distanced from historical realities, a new kind of romance developed, one that was neither pastoral nor chivalric. Though literary critics, cultural critics, and historians have generally devoted scant attention to the romances of the civil war and interregnum period, the genre is a valuable expression of royalist literary and political culture. Royalist writers, the main producers of romances, are known for retreating in the civil war and Interregnum years; and yet, as Robert Wilcher, Susan Wiseman, Dale Randall, Lois Potter, and others have observed, they did turn to satire, closet dramas, and historical fiction to register their response to current events and thus to engage that world.[4]

At a time when governmental authority was understood and legitimized in terms of hierarchical gender relations, growing political instability provoked James's reaction against his predecessor's androgyny—"a weak woman's body" and "the heart of a king"[5]—and justified his reinforcement of established social ranks, sexual distinctions, and traditional codes of conduct. Male-authored writings from high and popular culture, ranging from imaginative literature to political treatises and domestic conduct manuals, likewise promoted the ideology of male primacy. Stereotypes of insolent, duplicitous, sexually permissive women and the rhetoric of feminized waywardness and tyranny served as popular devices for discrediting "uxorious" opponents.[6]

Writers and political commentators frequently cited the disruption of hierarchical gender relations as one of the factors contributing to the fragmentation of the body politic, and it is this subtext that I consider in my analysis of the mid-century historical romance. When kings retreat or become uxorious and women perform the role of courtiers, anarchy erupts, undermining the political order.[7] A review of the romance tradition and its adaptation by seventeenth-century writers from both sides of the political divide establishes a context for interpreting Richard Brathwaite's *Panthalia: or the Royal Romance*, a historical romance often neglected in studies of early modern royalist literary culture.[8] Despite its late Interregnum publication date, *Panthalia* offers broad coverage of early modern political history, while providing revealing insights into the corresponding emasculation of the romance tradition. The relationship of Brathwaite's interset story—the arcadian tale of Panthalia—to the enveloping historical account is especially valuable for what it can teach us about the "notion of a *Romance*" (Herbert, *The Princess Cloria* [1661]) in the changing political and literary culture of the period.

I

The genealogy of *Panthalia* includes the influential and best-loved romance of the period, Sir Philip Sidney's *Arcadia*, whose complex publication history spans centuries. The earlier old *Arcadia* contained five books and was circulated in manuscript in 1580; it was not actually published until 1912 when Albert Feuillerat produced his edition of Sidney's prose works. Dissatisfied with the form of the old *Arcadia*, Sidney added several new stories, which he dovetailed with the principal one, in imitation of Spanish romances. Left incomplete at the time of Sidney's death in 1586, the manuscript was printed and published in a quarto volume in 1590 by Ponsonby. Three years later, the folio edition of Mary Herbert appeared as a modification of the quarto version. It also concluded the narrative from the old *Arcadia*, and in the final sentence of the fifth book of *Arcadia* invited its readers to join in the romance: "But the solemnities of these marriages, with the *Arcadian* pastorals, full of many comicall advantures, hapning to those rurall lovers . . . may awake some other spirite to exercise his pen in that, wherewith mine is already dulled."[9] The seventeenth century gave rise to many more editions of *Arcadia*, which in turn influenced dramas like Beaumont and Fletcher's *Cupid's Revenge* (1612), Henry Glapthorne's *Argalus and Parthenia* (1639), and Shirley's *A Pastoral Called the Arcadia* (1640), as well as prose fiction of the period: Gervase Markham's *English Arcadia* (1607, 1613), Barclay's *Argenis*, Anne Weamys's *A Continuation of Sir Philip Sidney's Arcadia* (1651), and Brathwaite's *Panthalia*.

In composing the *Arcadia*, Sidney drew on the newly fashionable pastoral, Sannazaro's *Arcadia* (1504) and Jorge de Montemayor's *Diana enamorada* (1559), of which seventeen editions and two continuations appeared in the Renaissance. *Arcadia* was also indebted to the chivalric romance *Amadis de Gaule*, despite its declining popularity in the early modern period. In his critique of Charles's romanticized "autobiography" in *Eikon Basilike*, John Milton names these forerunners of Sidney's *Arcadia* in condemning the frivolous nature of the Sidneian tradition and its literary and political inheritance. While Charles's selection from the romance was spiritual rather than political in nature, the reception history of *Arcadia* does expose a political subtext. William Dugard, for example, who printed the March 1649 edition of *Eikon Basilike* that included the notorious Pamela Prayer that Charles cited, wrote in a preface to the 1655 edition of *Arcadia* that Sidney had been "shadowing moral and politick results under the plain and easie emblems of Lovers."[10]

Certainly Dugard's interpretation is validated by the example of Sidney's Basilius, the duke of Arcadia, whose abdication of responsibility, retirement to the forests of Arcadia, and misguided passion for Pyrocles (disguised as the masculine Amazon, Zelmane), disrupt the idyllic world of Arcadia. In the seventeenth century, the received tradition of *Arcadia* identified Basilius with King James. Despite Basilius's compromised authority and Pyrocles's own confessions to Philoclea about his ineffectual rule, Sidney's romance did not lose its appeal. In spite of the political critique of monarchy that it sustained, the romance as a genre maintained its popularity among royalists. John Barclay's *Argenis*, a fictional account of European history in the sixteenth century, is the most obvious derivative of *Arcadia*, and it too includes weak rulers, like King Meleander and Nicompompus. Yet among the translators of Barclay were defenders of the court, including Ben Jonson, who produced an English version of *Argenis* in 1623, and Robert Le Grys and Thomas May who did the same in 1628 and 1629.

But in the latter half of Charles's reign, the romance was abandoned when royalist politics turned tragic. Thomas May, who was known for his contribution to the life and literature of courtly culture in the 1620s and 1630s, including his translation of Lucan's *Pharsalia* (1627), became secretary to Parliament and produced the influential *History of the Parliament of England* (1647) on the outbreak of civil war. Moving rapidly through the reigns of Elizabeth and James, May focuses in his *History* on Charles I's dispute with foreign and domestic powers. The calling on November 3, 1640 of what became the Long Parliament is immediately followed by an account of the arraignment of the archbishop of Canterbury and then of the trial and execution of the earl of Strafford. The effeminacy of the post-Elizabethan governments is one of the subtexts of May's historical narrative. In the account of Strafford's trial, for example, the effeminate courtiers earlier associated with James's government now defend the cause of Strafford in a mock-courtroom drama:

> The courtiers cried [Strafford] up, and the ladies (whose voices will carry much with some parts of the state) were exceedingly on his side.
>
> It seemed a very pleasant object, to see so many Sempronias (all the chief court-ladies filling the galleries at the triall) with pen, ink, and paper in their hands, noting the passages, and discoursing upon the grounds of law and state. They were all of his side; whether moved by pity, proper to their sex, or by ambition of being thought able to judge of the parts of the prisoner.[11]

May's account influenced the great champion of the parliamentary cause, John Milton, who was commissioned to write *Eikonoklastes* to counteract the effects of *Eikon Basilike*. "None were [Strafford's] Friends but Courtiers, and Clergimen," Milton chides, "the worst at that time, and most corrupted sort of men; and Court Ladies, not the best of Women; who when they grow to that insolence as to appeare active in State affaires, are the certain sign of a dissolute, degenerat, and pusillanimous Common-wealth" (*CPW*, 3:370).

The execution of Strafford set the stage for Laud's and ultimately Charles's beheading. Parliamentary defenses of the proposed regicide consistently invoke the king's submission to a female ruler as the cause of his demise. Henrietta Maria's lead role in court masques—including Walter Montague's *The Shepherds Paradise*, which was performed in January 1633 by an all-female cast that included the queen; and *Salmacida Spolia* (1640), in which Henrietta Maria played an Amazon—anticipated her major part on the English stage in a performance that "eclipsed" the king himself. According to the prophet Eleanor Douglas, the "over-mastred" king, cast in the role of the tragic Samson, had in "*great Imbecillitie [subjected] himself to a Woman's waywardnesse.*"[12] Political and satirical prints and woodcuts also exposed the sexual politics underlying the king's domestic affairs. *The Sussex Picture, or, An Answer to the Sea-Gull*, written in the same strain as that in

The Great Eclipse of the Sun, satirizes the relationship of the king to the foreign queen and to Catholic forces by depicting Henrietta Maria and her husband on either side of a bishop. The title refers to a picture—purportedly taken from a Flemish ship on the Sussex coast and sent to Parliament by Colonel Morley—which represents the submission of the crown to the distaff and the crosier.[13] Deceiving both the English court and clergy, Charles had cultivated the image of the sovereign ruler only to be outperformed by his wife and the Catholics she procured, May accuses: "the queen's power did by degrees give privilege to papists (and, among them, [to] the most witty and Jesuited) to converse, under the name of civility and courtship, not only with inferiour courtiers, but with the King himself, and to sow their seed in what ground they thought best" (p. 22). By this time, Parliament had impeached the queen for her "performances with her popish army."[14]

In *The History of Britain*, Milton rehearsed Tacitus's story of Cartismandua's betrayal of Venutius and of the British who fall under the "Subjection to the Monarchie of a Woeman, a peece of manhood not every day to be found among *Britans*." Venutius, the first husband of the adulteress, loses his political power, having been deprived of "the autority of ruling his own Houshold" by succumbing to the trickery of his wife (*CPW*, 5, 1:73–74). The relevance of this particular story for Milton's historical account is evidenced in his list of proposed British tragedies, headed by the reference to Venutius and Cartismandua.[15] Charles's fall into tyranny and effeminacy, then, added one more tragedy to Britain's political history.

The seizure of Charles's correspondence at Naseby on June 14, 1645 first unsettled the conjunction of his private and public identity, and furnished Parliament with evidence of the king's behind-the-scenes negotiations and machinations. The editor of the king's correspondence announces the publication of the letters in *The King's Cabinet Opened* as a revelation of the truth: "now by Gods good providence the traverse Curtain is drawn, and the King writing to *Ormond* and the Queen, what they must not disclose is presented upon the stage."[16] Henrietta Maria's letters to her husband characterize her role as a female warrior and even betray an "ironic awareness"[17] of the part she performed in the court: "In case of descant, I must act the captain, though a little low in stature, myself."[18] The correspondence demonstrates in turn Charles's deference to his "manly" wife not only in his private affairs but also in "his endeavours to bring in forren Forces, Irish, French, Dutch, Lorrainers, and our old Invaders the Danes upon us, besides his suttleties and mysterious *arts in treating*: to sumn up all, they shewd him govern'd by a Woman" (Milton, *Eikonoklastes, CPW*, 3:538). England's political history, then, is scarred by internal strife represented both by the civil war and by the tyrannical rule of self-divided kings rendered impotent by female treacheries.

Shortly thereafter the king, however, succeeded in recuperating the romance tradition in *Eikon Basilike*, the bestseller of the seventeenth century, which presumably exposed the inner chamber of his heart and soul.

The Princely Pellican captures *Eikon Basilike*'s strategic negotiation between the private and public spaces as the king "ingenuously laid Himself open" "in a private addresse for the Publick interest."[19] Casting himself as a penitent sinner as well as a national martyr, the king established the authenticity of his tragic narrative for seventeenth-century readers and reignited the public's romance with kingship. The production of *Eikon Basilike* reconciled Charles, God, Henrietta Maria, and the people. On one level, the text operates as ritual and prayer to present what Charles described as "the soul's more immediate converse with the Divine Majesty."[20] On another, it reunites the married couple in a transcendent love: the queen's "sympathy with me in my afflictions will make her virtues shine with greater luster, as stars in the darkest nights, and assure the envious world that she loves me, not my fortunes" (*EB*, 31). That *Eikon Basilike* was read as romance is recognized by Sir Percy Herbert in *The Princess Cloria*, which represents Charles as Euarchus (Sidney's king of Macedonia from *Arcadia*), speaking in a dignified style characteristic of romance: "You may behold also a liberty extraordinary given to these men, rather by violence to execute what they please, then justly to proceed in what they should... O you Gods, it is the Sword onely (that never was ordained for Government, but Execution) by which *Euarchus* must fall: Alas, alas, my friends, (said he) to what a pass are your Rights come, when the Father of them all must perish, because he desires still to make them good to your posterity?"[21]

While presenting a lively portraiture, *Eikon Basilike* also assumed a life of its own in the print culture and political culture of the period. Richard Royston, for whom John Grismond and Roger Norton printed the first edition, and the forementioned William Dugard, who printed the edition that first contained the King's Prayers, were summoned before the Council of State and arrested soon after the appearance of their respective editions. Thereafter the publisher, John Williams, defied the ban on publication by producing pocket-size editions, which enabled *Eikon Basilike* readers to carry the image of the king with them—literally and not just figuratively. The controversy about the inclusion of Pamela's prayer only increased the number of editions that were produced.

A critical reader and judge of the monarch's words and deeds, Milton in *Eikonoklastes* reconstructs the history of Charles's reign and arraigns him and his supporters. In chastising Charles for his earlier reluctance to carry out the "just act" of prosecuting the earl of Strafford, Milton accuses the king of "knit[ting] contradictions as close as words can lye together" (*CPW*, 3:372–73). The use of the word "lye" emphasizes the king's deceit evidenced in his building of "many faire and pious conclusions upon false and wicked premises" and in his "Scolastic flourishes," which are "beneath the decencie of a King" (*CPW*, 3:372–73). However, the words "lye together" also evoke images of a lascivious monarch and, by implication, an incestuous court.

Charles's own "lying" words and, in particular, his authorship of *Eikon Basilike*—contested since its first appearance (*CPW*, 3:150 ff.)—reinforced his treachery, according to Milton whose attacks on Charles are also laced with the rhetoric of effeminacy. "Examples are not farr to seek," Milton accuses in his account of Henrietta Maria's departure, "how great mischeif and dishonour hath befall'n to Nations under the Goverment of effeminate and Uxorious Magistrates. Who being themselves govern'd and overswaid at home under a Feminine usurpation, cannot but be farr short of spirit and autority without dores, to govern a whole Nation" (*Eikonoklastes, CPW*, 3:421). Moreover, as a political actor, Charles was an imitator of female performances. From the example of his Catholic grandmother, Mary Queen of Scots, who was executed at Fotheringay Castle in 1587, he learned "as it were by heart, or els by kind, that which is thought by his admirers to be the most vertuous, most manly, most Christian, and most Martyr-like both of his words and speeches heer, and of his answers and behaviour at his Tryall" (*Eikonoklastes, CPW*, 3:597).

On March 15, 1649 the printer William Dugard brought out an edition of *Eikon Basilike* with certain addenda, including four prayers attributed to the king. The supplementary matter proved immensely popular, and was inserted into unsold copies of *Eikon Basilike* as well. Following his efforts at discrediting Charles's stage performances that masquerade as piety—Shakespeare being "the Closet Companion of these his solitudes" (*Eikonoklastes, CPW*, 3:361), Milton links monarchy to the heathen romance tradition of *Arcadia*: Charles had "so little care of truth" "as immediately before his death to popp into the hand of that grave Bishop who attended him . . . a Prayer stol'n word for word from the mouth of a Heathen fiction praying to a heathen God; & that in no serious Book, but the vain amatorious Poem of Sir Philip Sidneys *Arcadia*; a Book in that kind full of worth and witt, but among religious thoughts, and duties not worthy to be nam'd; nor to be read at any time without good caution" (*Eikonoklastes, CPW*, 3:362). The "Poem" refers to Sidney's intricately wrought, interminable romance. The first prayer by Charles, "A Prayer in Time of Captivity" (*EB*, pp. 183–85), differs from Pamela's only in the final sentence in which the king asks for his reward through the "merits of Thy Son, our alone Saviour, Jesus Christ" (*EB*, p. 185), while Pamela pleads for the preservation of "the vertuous *Musidorus*."[22] Milton was not alone in his condemnation of the king's prayer, which testified to Charles's insincerity: the anonymous *None-Such Charles His Character* (1651) regrets that Charles's

> "soule was more fixt on *Bens* verses, and other Romances, during the time of his imprisonment, then on those Holy Writs, wherein salvation is to be sought for the soul, as well as for the body. Yet some men of these times, will be gulled, and made beleeve that he who could never speak nor write but like a Tyrant, could at last write like a Divine."[23]

In his 1650 edition of *Eikonoklastes*, Milton advances his case against Charles by expanding the passage: "For he certainly whose mind could serve him to seek a Christian prayer out of a Pagan Legend, and assume it for his own, might gather up the rest God knows from whence; one perhaps out of the French *Astraea*, another out of the Spanish *Diana*; *Amadis* and

Palmerin could hardly scape him... so long as such sweet *rapsodies* of Heathenism and Knighterrantry could yeild him prayers" (*Eikonoklastes, CPW*, 3:366–67). Leading Charles (and the reader) down the slippery slope of "pagan" romances from Catholic countries, Milton specifically refers to the *Astrée* of Honoré d'Urfé, which was first published in 1620 and established a new fashion in French fiction and drama. As mentioned earlier, Jorge de Montemayor's *Diana* influenced Sidney's *Arcadia*. Composed in the fourteenth century, either in Spanish or Portuguese, *Amadis* is famous for having been saved, together with *Palmerin of England*, from the fire that destroyed Don Quixote's library of chivalric romances. *Palmerin*, a 1500s Portuguese work by Francesco Moraes, was first printed in Spanish by Luis Hurtado. The litany of romances is often recited in attacks on royalists; John Hall's anti-royalist *Mercurius Britanicus* (1648), for example, denounces royalist conspiracies as "rash, heady and desperate adventures, which are as improbablye as any thing we have read of in *Bevis, Amadis, Palmerin*, or *the Knight of the Sun*."[24]

II

When history changed to tragedy with the outbreak of civil war, royalist romance writers and actors were driven underground. The main performer on the tragic stage, Charles I, reinforced the tragic nature of the age. Yet at the same time, he paradoxically conditioned the imaginative possibility for a romantic/comedic end to seventeenth-century royalist history. In the meantime (the Interregnum), literary culture reflected the complex negotiations of history, tragedy, comedy, and romance. Edmund Gayton's *Pleasant Notes on Don Quixote*, a valuable source of information on the period, uses the language of the stage-play world to work out these relationships. In a defense of plays and romances, Gayton observes: "For want of these chimera's (which had no more harm in them, than their impossibility) reall phantasmes, and strong delusions have succeeded and possessed not a few, who transported with their own imaginations, doe not write Romances, but act them, and fill the world with substantial Tragedies."[25] Heroic poems, whether Davenant's *Gondibert* or Cowley's *Davideis*, fell short of what was needed to capture the tumultuous age; and though we "sense intermittent political pressures" in these works, they offer no detailed correspondence between politics and fiction.[26] My concern in the second half of this essay is with the emergence of genre that did achieve such a correspondence: historical/allegorical prose fiction, which materialized in a romance form that was no longer pastoral or chivalric.[27]

In 1653, Sir Percy Herbert remarked disapprovingly in *Cloria and Narcissus. A Delightfull and New Romance, Imbellished with divers Politicall Notions, and singular Remarks of Moderne Transactions* on the dearth of romances in England: "since for many years past, not any one Romance hath been written in the English tongue; when as daily from other Nations so many of all sorts fly into the World, whether out of any diffidence in apprehension, or for other secret causes, I cannot tell."[28] Published in two parts in 1653 and 1654 and in five parts in 1661 as *The Princess Cloria: Or, The Royal Romance*,[29] *Cloria and Narcissus* is among only five extant political romances of this period. The others are: Sir William Sales's *Theophania, or several modern histories presented by way of romance* written in 1645 but published in 1655; Richard Brathwaite's *Panthalia: or the Royal Romance* (1659); *Aretina: or the serious romance* by Sir George Mackenzie, published in 1660; and *Don Juan Lamberto*, possibly by John Phillips or Thomas Flatman, published in 1661. For its Protectorate publication date, its historicizing of the romance form, and for its intriguing overlay of sexual politics and governmental affairs, *Panthalia* is the primary focus of the remainder of this chapter.

Panthalia: or the Royal Romance was published under a pseudonym in August 1659. It exhibits the characteristics of the romance as a hybrid genre structured on diversity. In the opening dedication to his sister in *Arcadia*, Sidney described his intricately woven, labyrinthine text as a wild conception. Correspondingly, in "The Opinion of a Native Candiot touching this ROYAL ROMANCE"—which forms part of the front matter of *Panthalia*—"FLORENCIO TRIBACCIO" recommends *Panthalia* as "a Directory to every equal and sinewy *Author*" (sig. A2^{v}). Itself a composite creation, *Panthalia* resembles not only Sidney's *Arcadia* but also Barclay's popular *Argenis* in which historical events are presented in romance form. One of the poems in the front matter to *Panthalia* is by "AMADIN BARCLAY" (sig. A4). And like the even more complex romance by Sir Percy Herbert, *Panthalia* appeared in the London market in a revised version to account for recent changes in English politics. Brathwaite's Prologue identifies the Royal Romance's political/romantic subject matter as "State-Stories intervein'd with amorous Tales, / Rare loyal love breath'd on with prosperous Gales" (sig. A4^{v}). Embedded in the sinewy *Panthalia* are accounts from histories, journals, letters, and speeches that further unsettle the distinction between history and romance. Brathwaite feminizes the genre of romance and directs the work in part at female readers.[30] At the same time, *Panthalia* defiantly announces in "An Advertisement to the judicious Reader" its intention to perform in a manner characteristically unfeminine for the time:

> "this Royal Romance, has taken upon her the spirit to shew her self to the world . . . such is her confidence grounded on the strength of Reason, and judicious Opinion, she stands at defiance against all corky and unballanc'd judgments. And having now got the boldness to speak Loyalty, and with the resolution of *Hiero* and *Leæna*, to spit in the face of Treason: she blusheth not in coming abroad into the world, being equipag'd with the livery of Loyalty"

(sig. A3^{v}). Though *Panthalia* was probably completed in the summer of 1658, this Advertisement in the front matter and the Postscript at the end of the text were added in 1659 to reflect changes on the national stage, including Richard Cromwell's departure from Whitehall in July 1659. Brathwaite's muse Thalia presides over both the pastoral and comedy, though the subtitle anticipates *Panthalia*'s engagement with politics: "A DISCOURSE

Stored with infinite variety in relation to STATE-GOVERNMENT...And presented on a *Theatre* of Tragical and Comical *State*, in a successive continuation to these Times."

In *Panthalia*, Sidney's Arcadia is replaced by Brathwaite's Candy (Crete). Like Mildmay Fane's *Candy Restored*, which appeared on the eve of the revolution in 1641, *Panthalia* in the aftermath of war looks ahead to Candy's return to order. The plot of Brathwaite's romance depicts the exemplary reign of Bellingeria (Elizabeth), followed by the turbulent years of the rule of Basilius (James) and Rosicles (Charles I). Charicles (Charles II) enters the narrative after the battle of Worcester, and Brathwaite continues his history through the Protectorate to the death of Climenes (Cromwell). The fictional tale of the character, Panthalia, the "pretty peddler," appears at the midpoint of the romance ("*Pleasant Passages*," p. 146), and complicates the relationship between history and fiction while emasculating the romance genre.

Though a conservative and wealthy Anglican royalist, Brathwaite was not reticent in exposing the failings of his own culture and society. In *A Survey of History: or, A Nursery for Gentry* (1638, 1651), Brathwaite criticizes romances, identifying them as "histories" characterized by "sensuality" and the depiction of "light love (though they be dangerous familiars to haunt ladies)" (p. 275). In contrast to romantic and classical tales, which serve as inducements to lust, is Brathwaite's account of refined love in his 1640 prose romance, *The Two Lancashire Lovers: or the Excellent History of Philocles and Doriclea*.[31] In *Panthalia*, Brathwaite politicizes the dangers associated with female dominance by satirizing male complacence and effeminacy, thus targeting uxorious male readers. He names the character Basilius, who makes "the Wild Forrest the Place of his solace and recreation" (p. 40), after Sidney's famous duke of Arcadia who retreats to the pastoral world. Brathwaite thus invokes the received tradition of *Arcadia*, which associated Basilius's negligence with that of James who contributed to the national effeminacy that fuelled civil and political unrest. After Basilius insists that Ismenia, his consort, sever her ties with the Platonic cult, the court is converted into a theater in which Ismenia and her female companions "play the Platonick Courtiers" (p. 40). In *Panthalia*, we are led not only into the luxurious court but also into the interior world of Basilius, who becomes tainted by his surroundings. As a royalist supporter, Brathwaite nevertheless accounts for Basilius's unmanly conduct without diminishing his integrity: "Neither did this indifferency to Feminine Objects, nor his affection to the contrary Sex, proceed (as some weakly conceipted) from frigidity of Nature: nor any inordinate degeneracy: but rather from the gust of those active recreations and exercises which he affected" (p. 41). Again the fault lies in the king's liberal lifestyle, which Brathwaite labels as "noxious" (p. 41). In Basilius's court, women play masculine parts while courtiers are rendered effeminate: "For those virile & masculine spirits, which formerly proclaimed the Heirs of Honour, were become now strangers to actions & exploits of valor" (p. 42); "And indeed what by the effeminacy of that present State, whose long peace and security had brought most of the Nobility to that delicacy; that as their Spirits were averse from the Exercises of Arms; so were their intellectual parts and inward abilities so weakned" (p. 43). Later in the interset story of Panthalia, the lead character will excuse her rash decision to undertake her perilous journey by explaining that "[t]he most virile and Masculine spirits have not at all times their wits near them: well then may our resolvs arising from the weakness of our Sexe, receive excuse" (p. 202).

In his account of their relationship in Arcadia, Sidney underscores Basilius's folly in ministering to the manly Zelmane, who "so would have it" (p. 72). The criticisms about Basilius's ignoble love and ineffectual governance in *Arcadia* are transferred to *Panthalia*, in which the courts of Basilius and Rosicles (James and Charles) fall prey to the rulers' lack of restraint and submission to women. Brathwaite's description of Rosicles's relationship to Irina resembles that of Basilius and Zelmane in Sidney's romance, and that of Brathwaite's Basilius and Ismenia: Rosicles becomes "a Subject to his Queens Command: and she to the pursuit of her own pleasure"; he became in turn a "Compleat Courtier: not so much out of a love that he bore to that Change, as the satisfaction of his Choice: seeing *Irina* would have it so" (p. 98). As in his account of Basilius, Brathwaite attacks the unrestrained liberty of (feminized) entertainments in Rosicles's court.

Brathwaite deploys the language of effeminacy in the descriptions of the lead figures in the ensuing civil war, whom he identifies with false rhetoric, unchecked flights of the imagination, and feminine influences. One of the many scenes in *Panthalia* involving an exchange of letters that enables readers to enter the private world of lovers/spouses features the Fairfaxes—Sir Thomas Fairfax having served as a Puritan General in Cromwell's government. Brathwaite's Lady Verona, Sir Thomas Fairfax's wife, "excite[s] her weak Consort" through her letters and various other forms of persuasion (p. 105). Her words incite rebellion in Bellonius (Thomas Fairfax) who is urged to denounce the corruption of Rosicles's government, which, like Verona's own household, is managed by a woman: "*Is not the Court become by the sensuall liberty of a* Ferrara *Lady; who courts her endeered Favorite* Claridamus, *as if he were her espoused Consort, a Roman Suburra? Do not our Publick Streets and Stages Eccho with Scens of their dishonour*?" (p. 106). Bewitched by the rhetoric of the mad Verona, who is portrayed throughout the episode as a Puritan shrew, Bellonius is led off by "Ambition," which "now begun strongly to work upon him" (p. 107).

The revolutionary leader, Climens (Oliver Cromwell), likewise courts Ambition—"his Minion" (p. 116)—while simultaneously pursuing the wife of the Puritan general, John Lambert, Brathwaite's Lamachus. Not even his allies are immune to his exploits, Brathwaite reports in his indictment of Climens: "even *Fania's* honour, *Lamachus* his endeered Consort (a Lady of approved continence) by his too much freedom, became suspected: and by the aspersive pen of a Satyrizing Pamphleter basely traduced" (p. 120). Among the satires that spread the rumors of Cromwell's licentiousness was *The Famous Tragedie of King Charles I*.[32] In Act 4 of this play-pamphlet, Cromwell returns from chasing the Scots (at Preston in August 1648) to woo the wife of John Lambert. Frances Lambert was known for her letters and petitions, for the intimacy between her household and Cromwells's, and consequently for her representation as a satiric butt in royalist lampoons and satires.[33] In the *Famous Tragedie*, Cromwell calls for a masque, and he and Mrs. Lambert proceed to dance with allegorized parliamentarian figures: Ambition, Treason, Lust, Revenge, Perjury, and Sacrilege. *Panthalia* further develops the Lambert–Cromwell relationship by creating a love triangle as Lamachus falls in love with the barbarian witch, Climens/Cromwell; Lamachus's extraction was good, Brathwaite maintains, in accordance with popular sentiment, "but his actions inlarged his fame. Which had climb'd to an higher Story, had he not with *Medæa* taken the worser part" (p. 121).

Muratus and Mazinella (Sir William Waller and his wife) are featured in the following episode in *Panthalia.* Thomas May, who celebrates Waller's achievements in his *History of the Parliament*, observes that his "name was grown to be a great terror to his enemies" (p. 310). Brathwaite, however, elevates Waller ultimately in order to diminish him even more. Muratus's pride increased his fame, for which he served as "a singular *Amanuensis*" (p. 122). Mazinella becomes so transported by the reports of her husband's reputation that she subjects Muratus to a relentless onslaught of "fantastick Letters" (p. 122) that commend his heroism. Brathwaite emphasizes the flighty, trivial nature of Mazinella's conduct as an exercise in "venting strange Imaginary whimsies, such as her airy brain conceited of her Muratus" (p. 129). In extolling her warrior, Mazinella proudly acknowledges her reliance on hyperbole: "*I shall infinitly taxe the Poets, my invincible Muratus, for feigning Atlas to be the Worlds Supporter, when my imaginary eye represents to my Fancy the Sinewey Shouldiers of my* Herculean Muratus" (p. 122). "The perusall of this Letter begot a thousand imaginary Conceipts in *Muratus*," we are told, thus reinforcing the connections between fancy and femininity (p. 124). But fickleness, the companion of fortune, is the other member of the triangle: "So inconstantly had Fortune turn'd her wheele; and lay'd this great *Hannibals* honour in the dust: causing his Fame and Fidelity to perish both together: a just reward for his immeriting service" (p. 127). History before too long checked Waller's romantic/heroic flights when Charles defeated him at Cropredy Bridge in June 1644. That Waller would lead an uprising on the king's behalf in 1649 remained unknown by Brathwaite.

Up until the mid-century—and at the midpoint of Brathwaite's historical romance—English politics is dominated and eclipsed by malignant female influences. An account of the correspondence between Charles and Henrietta Maria follows the epistolary episodes narrated thus far, but is devoid of satire; rather the letter exchanges romanticize the royal couple, while anticipating the historical tragedy soon to take place on the scaffold. In a rewriting of the 1645 event of Parliament's seizure of the king's letters, Brathwaite stages a melodramatic scene of a betrayed, imprisoned king, who, deprived of his liberty and all outlets for expressing melancholy, reflects piously on the unjustly exiled queen. The implied dialogue between Charles and God in the 1649 bestseller *Eikon Basilike* is represented in this Royal

Romance through the correspondence between Rosicles and Irina. In their exchange, king and queen are portrayed as tragic heroes nobly confronting defeat. They also defend themselves against accusations directed at the historical Charles and Henrietta Maria when the Cabinet was opened to reveal Charles's affair with foreign powers and Henrietta Maria's affair with one of her favorites, Charidamus Henry Jermyn.[34] As the author of his history and destiny, Charles asserts control over his image again. In choosing to become "his own *Amanuensis*" (p. 136), he reminds us of Waller; but Charles writes in self-defense to counter "the *Gazetta's* of the time; which usually delude their Hearers either by abridging or exceeding truth in their Narrations" (p. 136). Moreover, he develops a romantic ending for his tragic historical narrative by envisioning a rising sun and a reconciliation with his wife and with God: "Mean time, let us anchor our hopes in this, that the Superiour Powers...will afford us more chearful beams of reviving Comfort; by crowning our Cloudy day with a Clear Evening: and so re-unite us, or by a gladsome Translation impose a period to our suffering: and joyntly eternize us" (p. 140). Here in Brathwaite's romance, it is fitting that Rosicles include his beloved in the plea for eternal life. These words will be repeated by Charicles, Brathwaite's Charles II who is featured in the second half of *Panthalia*. Rosicles's concluding "prayer" in his final letter would have called to mind for Brathwaite's readers the supplications in *Eikon Basilike* through which Charles I conditioned the possibility for a restored, divinely sanctioned monarchy.

Before the great tragedy of Charles's execution is recounted, Brathwaite offers an interset story featuring Panthalia, the insertion of tales within the main narrative being characteristic of romances, including Sidney's *Arcadia*. Brathwaite also reveals his indebtedness to Sidney in other respects: the character Panthalia begins her wayward journey as an Arcadian hero—and a not atypical Shakespearean female hero—who adopts masculine attire in order to pursue her lover, and who finds herself the object of female love. Continuing her travels, Panthalia visits a convent devoted to Diana, and is granted an opportunity to recount civil war history in an exchange with the Governess, the abyss of the convent. The inclusion of this narrative in a romantic interset story represents the interpenetration of history and Arcadian fantasy, and serves as one of the distinguishing features of the newly "emasculated" romance genre. An active commentator on governmental affairs, Panthalia provides the most extensive account of the Civil War (pp. 173–79), which has transformed Candy into a paradise lost. Spoilt by their liberty and "deep Surfet" (p. 177), the Candiots become unjustly critical of their favorable conditions and their government. Reciting the Aesopian "Fable of the *Froggs*," Panthalia explains how the Candiots, like the frogs, insisted on a new commander, which they received and before long greatly regretted (p. 175). Her diagnosis of the disease that infected the body politic from the inside is repeated in the main narrative ("*Distractions in the State of Candy in their Aristocracy; with the miseries of an innovated Government*" [p. 264]), thus further challenging Matthew Wilson Blacke's conclusion that the interset story is "indeed irrelevant" to the main theme of *Panthalia* (p. 88).

We return to the arcadian tale following the history of the civil war to find Panthalia wavering between religion and romance. She first retreats to a cloister in which the nuns imitate courtly rituals by "personat[ing] a Sister for a Compleat Courtier" (p. 186), a performance mimicking that of Ismenia and her female companions who "play the Platonick Courtiers" in Basilius's theatricalized court (p. 40). Again the historical and fictional narratives are interwoven in the text. Panthalia's return to the world of passion in the later part of the interset story is triggered by some correspondence she receives from Acolasto, which leads to her reconciliation with him. The tale nevertheless resists a romantic ending, finally recommending neither spiritual nor earthly love. Panthalia's earlier warning about admitting "one Marriage-day," which might result in "a Tragick Scene without all hope of a Comicall Conclusion" (p. 202), is realized at the end of the "*Pleasant Passages*": reduced to uxorious behavior, Acolasto becomes Panthalia's "obsequious Servant" (p. 231), an inversion of the gender hierarchy, which, as we have seen in the historical narrative, ignites civil war in the private and public spheres. Brathwaite's interset story invites comparison with the heroic plot that is presented alongside a serious plot in John Dryden's *Secret Love; or, the Maiden Queen* (1667), and which features a romantic reconciliation between the lovers Candiope and Philocles.

In his prefatory remarks to the interset story, Brathwaite characterizes the romantic tale featuring Panthalia as "varied and interwoven with much delight" and thus "quite estrang'd from the native body or Contexture of an History" (p. 146). By the end of the "*Pleasant Passages*," the connection between romance and history is underscored, and we are invited to consider: "what near dependence these incidences had to the Subject of our Discourse now in hand" (p. 224). Indeed the romantic tale does intersect with the main narrative in a variety of ways, though a tragic, somber tone pervades the historical account. The drama of seventeenth-century political history resumes with the arraignment and scaffold speech of Sophronio, Brathwaite's earl of Strafford, whom he romanticizes at least in part because Brathwaite was patronized by Strafford's family. The trial and parting words of Rosicles presented thereafter are followed by the king's memorable performance on the tragic scaffold. The supernatural occurrences, including prodigious births, that mark the great tragedy of the king's execution (pp. 248–51) are the material of romance and popular culture, though they are also reminiscent of the natural disturbances in the biblical account of Christ's Crucifixion to which the regicide was frequently compared. The final words of Rosicles to Irina that the gods might "crown" their "Cloudy day with a Clear Evening" (p. 140) recall the scene of the darkened sky at midday marking the Crucifixion. They also anticipate the opening of Charicles's (Charles II's) lament upon his first appearance in *Panthalia*: "O Heavens! When will these cloudy dayes close with a clear evening?" (p. 258), thus connecting the tragedies of Rosicles, Christ, and of Charicles who enters the narrative at this propitious moment.

Brathwaite ultimately invites us to read the concluding episodes in *Panthalia* as a tragicomedy-in-progress, featuring a king who must yet make his way onto the political stage. We encounter Charicles following the Battle of Worchester in 1651 as he is rescued "*beyond all expectancy*" by Candiope (p. 254). Candiope figures the historical Jane Lane, who disguised herself as her servant, William Jackson, in accompanying Charles II from Bentley to Abbots Leigh and Trent; or she may represent Juliana/Judith Coningsby, who accompanied the king in the journey from Trent.[35] Candiope hears a voice from the grove, perhaps suggestive of Mary Magdalene's confrontation with Christ in the garden following the Crucifixion. But Charicles only speaks of tragedy at this stage: "*O Heavens! When will these cloudy dayes close with a clear evening?... Must Theatres be erected onely for acting our tragedies? Must the fame of our family be quite razed forth of the Annals of posterity?*" (p. 258). The character Molinutus (the Cavalier general, Henry, Viscount Wilmot, the First Earl of Rochester, who attended the king in his journey to Scotland) is cast as Charicles's travel companion in *Panthalia*. As they are being received by Candiope, Charicles reminds Molinutus that the times do not permit romance: "*It was your Office, said he* [Charicles], Molinutus, *to play the Purveyer and not a suiter: Our mispent times will admit of no Mistresses*" (p. 259). Only divine intervention can convert tragedy into comedy and restore the king to the throne, Brathwaite suggests: "So as there remained no hope of a new being or breathing to the revivall of their Phænix ashes, unless some invisible hand *far above all humane expectance* should interpose it selfe, and in mercy raise it from the rubbish of division, and by degrees restore it" (p. 270; emphasis mine). Charicles, who appears "*beyond all expectancy*" (p. 254) in the narrative, is now the "new being," the instrument of the invisible hand which interposes itself "far above all humane expectance."

In a world turned right side up, shepherds and kings occupy different realms. Anarchy erupts when social distinctions are ignored or violated. At the end of *Panthalia*, Climenes—a less heroic figure than Andrew Marvell's Cromwell who moves out of "his private gardens" to overthrow the monarchy[36]—recalls his reluctant entry into politics: "I shall only tell these disaffected Ones, that I should rather have chused to keep Sheep on an hill, then born Command over such Incendiaries" (p. 283). Soon thereafter, in his "Speech to his Cabinet Councel," Climenes reasserts this position: "Yea, so dispassionately has my patience been transported with the guidance of this People, as I should have holden my condition more happy in being a Shepherd, then leading such wild Cattle" (p. 287). In a postscript added to *Panthalia* after its completion in 1658, Brathwaite describes the succession and ultimate retreat of Darchirus (Richard Cromwell), who, wearied or perhaps disillusioned by his father's unjust rule, "betak[es] himself to the innocent freedom of a Country life." With the retreat of the revolutionaries, the time had come for Charicles to leave the pastoral world behind and assume his rightful position on the throne, Brathwaite implies.

The Restoration, which Brathwaite could only glimpse at in *Panthalia*, took place the following year, thus transforming tragedy into divine comedy (or at least tragicomedy) for royalists. In "The Stationer to the Reader" of John Webster and William Rowley's play, *The Thracian Wonder. A comical History* (1661), Francis Kirkman observes that the winter of discontent has now passed, though the extraordinarily tragic nature of recent events relegates history to the realm of fiction or romance. Using the imagery deployed by royalists in the experience of defeat, Kirkman declares: "We have had the private Stage for some years clouded, and under a tyrannical command, though the publick State of *England* has produc'd many monstrous villains, some of which have deservedly made their exit. I believe future Ages will not credit the transactions of our late Times to be other than a *Play*, or a *Romance*: I am sure in most Romantick Plays there hath been more probability, then in our true (though sad) Stories."[37] Tragedies so horrific that they seem less credible than imaginary romances give way to tragicomedy in the Restoration playhouses and on the national stage.

Through the marriage between fiction and political history, royalist romances helped prepare the stage for the new king. Having made its statement, the genre receded into the background as theatrical productions took political and literary culture by storm. The king and court supplied the material for the dramas, though sometimes unwittingly: while tragicomedy celebrated the *astræa redux*, the sexual politics and antics of the court were dramatized in satirical Restoration comedies, often featuring Cavaliers as effeminate fops. Meanwhile, historical fiction lay dormant, until it would rise "phoenix-like" in the form of the historical and epistolary novels, periodicals, and in the journal literature of the coming decades. Yet as a genre, the Interregnum historical romance remained in many ways "a much more ambitious form than the preceding drama, or the Restoration novels which superseded it" (Salzman, p. 149) for its embrace of history and politics and its emasculation of the romance.

NOTES

I gratefully acknowledge the support of the Social Sciences and Humanities Research Council of Canada during the preparation of this essay.

1. D. E. Underdown, "The Taming of the Scold: The Enforcement of Patriarchal Authority in Early Modern England," *Order and Disorder in Early Modern England*, ed. Anthony Fletcher and John Stevenson (Cambridge: Cambridge University Press, 1985), p. 36.
2. John Milton, *Apology for Smectymnuus, Complete Prose Works of John Milton*, ed. Don Wolfe et al., 8 vols. (New Haven: Yale University Press, 1953–82), 1:891. All quotations from Milton's prose are from this edition and marked "*CPW*."
3. Lois Potter, *Secret Rites and Secret Writing: Royalist Literature, 1641–1660* (Cambridge: Cambridge University Press, 1989), p. 74.
4. Critics and historians who maintain that the Cavaliers retreated during the period include: Earl Miner, *The Cavalier Mode from Jonson to Cotton* (Princeton: Princeton University Press, 1971); David Underdown, *Royalist Conspiracy in England 1649–1660* (New Haven: Yale University Press, 1960),

and Paul H. Hardacre, *The Royalists During the Puritan Revolution* (The Hague: Nijhoff, 1956). Those who take an opposing position include: Robert Wilcher, *The Writing of Royalism, 1628–1660* (Cambridge: Cambridge University Press, 2001); Susan Wiseman, *Drama and Politics in the English Civil War* (Cambridge: Cambridge University Press, 1998); Dale J. B. Randall, *Winter Fruit: English Drama, 1642–1660* (Lexington: University Press of Kentucky, 1995); Potter, *Secret Rites*, Annabel Patterson, *Censorship and Interpretation: The Conditions of Writing and Reading in Early Modern England* (Madison: University of Wisconsin Press, 1984).

5. Leah Marcus, *Puzzling Shakespeare: Local Reading and Its Discontents* (Berkeley: University of California Press, 1988), p. 54.
6. By presenting women as unstable, men also had an opportunity to engage in linguistic game-playing and to create imaginative flights and mock social or political scenes. See Peter Stallybrass, "Patriarchal Territories: The Body Enclosed," *Rewriting the Renaissance: The Discourses of Sexual Difference in Early Modern Europe*, ed. Margaret J. Ferguson et al. (Chicago: Chicago University Press, 1986); and Sandra Clark, "*Hic Mulier, Haec Vir*, and the Controversy over Masculine Women," *Studies in Philology* 82 (1985): 158–59. On the effeminate tyrant and on the anxiety about threats to the integral male identity in political dramatic texts of the period, see Rebecca W. Bushnell, *Tragedies of Tyrants: Political Thought and Theater in the English Renaissance* (Ithaca: Cornell University Press, 1990), p. 20 ff.
7. The "woman controversy," associated with this period, intensified as a result of James's repressive actions. See Katherine Usher Henderson and Barbara F. McManus, *Half Humankind: Contexts and Texts of the Controversy about Women in England, 1540–1640* (Urbana: University of Illinois Press, 1985).
8. Richard Brathwaite, *Panthalia: or the Royal Romance. A Discourse Stored with infinite variety in relation to State-Government And Passages of matchless affection gracefully interveined, And presented on a Theatre of Tragical and Comical State, in a successive continuation to these Times. Faithfully and ingenuously rendred* (London, 1659).

   Benjamin Boyce examines the text as a political allegory in "History and Fiction in *Panthalia: or the Royal Romance*," *Journal of English and Germanic Philology* 57 (1958): 477–91. *Panthalia* is mentioned by Paul Salzman, *English Prose Fiction, 1558–1700: A Critical History* (Oxford: Oxford University Press: 1985); and by Matthew Wilson Black, *Richard Brathwaite: An Account of His Life and Works* (Philadelphia: University of Pennsylvania Press 1928), pp. 86–89. A somewhat lengthier discussion is found in Patterson, Censorship and Interpretation, pp. 198, 206–10.
9. Sir Philip Sidney, *The Countesse of Pembrokes Arcadia*, 9th ed. (London: Printed for J. Waterson and R. Young, 1638), p. 482. A Sixth Booke written by R. B. of Lincolnes Inne Esquire in this edition was one of many indications of the continuation of this tradition.
10. Milton, *Eikonoklastes, CPW*, 3:362; Sir Philip Sidney, *The Countess of Pembroke's Arcadia. Tenth edition. By William Du-Gard, to bee sold by George Calvert and Thomas Pierrepont, 1655.*
11. Thomas May, *The History of the Parliament of England* (Oxford: Oxford University Press, 1854), p. 91.
12. Eleanor Douglas, *To the Most Honorable The High Court of Parliament Assembled, &c* (London, 1643), sig. B3v.

13. *The Sussex Picture, or, An Answer to the Sea-Gull* (London: Printed by F. N., 1644); *The Great Eclipse of the Sun, or, Charles his Waine Over-clouded By the evill Influences of the Moon Eclipsed by the destructive perswasions of His Queen* (London: Printed by G. B. [Bishop], 1644).
14. M. A. E. Green, ed., *Letters of Queen Henrietta Maria* (London, 1857), p. 214.
15. John Milton, *Facsimile of the Manuscript of Milton's Minor Poems Preserved in the Library of Trinity College Cambridge*, ed. William Aldis Wright (Cambridge: Cambridge University Press, 1899). BM MS Facs. 133, p. 35.
16. [Henry Parker,] *The King's Cabinet Opened: or, Certain Packets of Secret Letters & Papers, written with the King's own hand, and taken in his Cabinet at Naseby-Field June 14, 1645* (London, 1645).
17. Sophie Tomlinson, "She that Plays the King: Henrietta Maria and the Threat of the Actress in Caroline Culture," *The Politics of Tragicomedy: Shakespeare and After*, ed. Gordon McMullan and Jonathan Hope (New York: Routledge, 1992), p. 202.
18. *Perfect Diurnal*, May 29, 1643, qtd. in *Letters of Queen Henrietta Maria*, ed. M. A. E. Green (London, 1857), p. 167.
19. *The Princely Pellican. Royall Resolves Extracted from His Majesties Divine Meditations* (n.p., 1649), p. 4.
20. *Eikon Basilike: The Portaiture of His Sacred Majesty in His Solitudes and Sufferings*, ed. Philip A. Knachel (Ithaca: Cornell University Press, 1966), p. 95.
21. Sir Percy Herbert, *The Princess Cloria*, 2nd ed. (London, 1661), p. 333.
22. Milton cites p. 248 of Sidney's *Arcadia*. From the fifth edition (1621) through to the thirtieth (1674), Pamela's prayer is found on this page.
23. *The None-Such Charles His Character* (London, 1651), pp. 170–71; qtd. in Ernest Sirluck, "*The Eikon Basilike*: An Unreported Item in the Contemporary Authorship Controversy," *Modern Language Notes* 70 (1955): 331–32. On Charles's performances on the page and the stage, see Elizabeth Sauer, "Milton and the "Stage-work" of Charles I's *Prose Studies: History, Theory, Criticism*, 23.1 (2000): 121–46.
24. *Mercurius Britanicus* (June 13, 1648).
25. Edmund Gayton, *Pleasant Notes on Don Quixote* (London, 1654).
26. Earl Miner, *The Restoration Mode from Milton to Dryden* (Princeton, 1974), p. 73.
27. See Salzman on the decline of chivalric romance (p. 99 ff.).
28. Sir Percy Herbert, "To the Reader" *Cloria and Narcissus. A Delightfull and New Romance, Imbellished with divers Politicall Notions, and singular Remarks of Moderne Transactions* (1653).
29. The complicated textual history of the romance includes its influence on Brathwaite (Patterson, *Censorship and Interpretation*, p. 198).
30. The Prologue to *Panthalia* states: "And if these please not Ladies, it were strange" (sig. A4v). Female readers were addressed by Lyly in *Euphues*, Sidney in the *Old Arcadia*, and often by Nashe. See Helen Hackett, *Women and Romance Fiction in the English Renaissance* (Cambridge: Cambridge University Press, 2000); and Helen Ostovich and Elizabeth Sauer, "Life-writing: Nonfiction and Fiction," *Reading Early Modern Women: An Anthology of Manuscripts and Texts in Print, 1550–1700*, ed. Helen Ostovich and Elizabeth Sauer (New York: Routledge, 2003), ch. 6.

31. See Richard Brathwaite, *The Two Lancashire Lovers: or The Excellent History of Philocles and Doriclea*, ed. Henry D. Janzen (Ottawa: Dovehouse Editions, 1998).
32. [Samuel Sheppard's] play-pamphlet, *The Famous Tragedie of King Charles I* ([London?], 1649).
33. See *A Curtain Conference, being a Discourse betwixt (the late Lord Lambert, now) J. Lambert, Esq., and his lady, as they lay abed together one night* January 1660, qtd. in William Harbutt Dawson, *Cromwell's Understudy: The Life and Times of General John Lambert and the Rise and Fall of the Protectorate* (London: William Hodge, 1938), p. 453.
34. Henry Jermyn was in reality involved not only with the queen but also others of her Platonic circle. See Quentin Bone, *Henrietta Maria: Queen of the Cavaliers* (London: Peter Owen, 1973), pp. 84–86.
35. See Samuel Pepys, *King Charles Preserved: An Account of his Escape after the Battle of Worcester dictated by the King himself to Samuel Pepys* (London: Rodale Press, 1956).
36. Andrew Marvell, "An Horatian Ode," *The Complete Poems*, ed. Elizabeth Story Donno (Harmondsworth: Penguin, 1972; rpt. 1985), 1. p. 29.
37. John Webster and William Rowley, *The Thracian Wonder. A comical History*...(London: Printed by Tho. Johnson, and...sold by Francis Kirkman...1661), sig. A2.

Chapter 11

Sidney, Gascoigne, and the "Bastard Poets"

Robert W. Maslen

In this essay I shall argue that Sidney imitated, in the *Old Arcadia*, one of the most influential and controversial English texts of the 1570s: George Gascoigne's erotic prose fiction *The Adventures of Master F. J.* (1573).[1] I shall also suggest that he may have had a number of specific reasons for wanting his own prose fiction to be linked with the work of a writer who was regarded with some ambivalence by his contemporaries. E. K., for instance—the scrupulously pedantic commentator on Spenser's *The Shepheardes Calender* (1579)—describes Gascoigne as "a wittie gentleman, and the very chefe of our late rymers, who, and if some partes of learning wanted not (albee it is well knowen he altogyther wanted not learning) no doubt would have attayned to the excellencye of those famous Poets. For the gifts of wit and naturall promptnesse appeare in hym aboundantly."[2] Sidney, it seems to me, would have been profoundly interested in a soldier-poet who showed abundant "gifts of wit and naturall promptnesse"—gifts that prompted Sidney's uncle, the earl of Leicester, to employ him as the chief deviser of his elaborate entertainments for the queen at Kenilworth in 1575. E. K.'s assessment of Gascoigne offers the perfect illustration of the current state of English imaginative writing as Sidney describes it in *An Apology for Poetry*: bursting with raw promise but stubbornly resistant to the "artificial rules" and "imitative patterns" imposed by classical precedent or pedagogic authority (133/3–4).[3] Yet in the *Apology* Sidney cites not Gascoigne but himself as an example of the resistance to "the right use both of matter and manner" among the new generation of Elizabethan poets (140/4–5). It looks as though Gascoigne and Sidney might have more in common than scholars have so far been willing to concede.

To make my case, I shall begin with an analysis of the passage from the *Apology* in which Sidney surveys the condition of English poetry at the beginning of the 1580s. It should be remembered that by "poetry" Sidney means every written form of fiction, from drama, verse, and prose romance to the fabricated anecdotes and speeches exploited by humanist philosophers and historians to spice up their allegedly factual treatises. When Sidney observes, then, that the current literary scene is dominated by "bastard poets," hack writers who sacrifice their artistic integrity for cash (132/10), he is not exempting Gascoigne's *The Adventures of Master F. J.* from his blanket condemnation of modern printed texts, any more than he exempts himself from the charge of having allowed "not only love, but lust, but vanity, but . . . scurrility" to possess the pages of his unpublished literary works (125/18–19). The *Apology* and the *Arcadia* are witty testaments to the fundamental rottenness of the Elizabethan state: and the lurking presence of Gascoigne in the latter offers a tantalizing clue to Sidney's sense of his own place in the tottering edifice of contemporary English culture.

I

Sidney did not think much of his Elizabethan contemporaries as poets. At least, this has been the assumption of commentators on *An Apology for Poetry* (ca. 1580), who have tended to take its assessments of modern English poetry at face value. The list of Elizabethan poems it selects for approval is short: the *Mirror for Magistrates, The Shepheardes Calender*, and *Gorboduc* (133/22 ff.)—and not one living English poet is mentioned by name. But we should beware of approaching a wittily combative text like the *Apology* with our critical guard lowered. In the words of the *Apology* itself, Sidney's spirited assault on poetry in England might have "another foundation, than the superficial part would promise" (121/23–34). And a glance at the section of the text in which Sidney articulates his views on English poetry—the penultimate section known as the "Digression" (131/3–141/20)—may begin to suggest where the hidden "foundation" of these opinions lay.[4]

The Digression is as much concerned with England's role in European politics as it is with the lamentable condition of Elizabethan imaginative writing. The decline of English poetry, Sidney argues, is a symptom of England's decline as a military power. The laurel, after all, is the emblem of triumphant military leaders as well as of poets (130/37 ff.), and the scarcity of laurels in England must therefore testify to a loss of martial as well as poetic prowess. Of course, he could only sustain such an argument by playing down the literary successes of the past decade, especially the achievements of writers whose work had found a favorable reception in the public arenas of the theater and the printer's shop. We need, then, to recognize that Sidney was making a *political* point in this passage rather than a literary one, and to read his judgments of his peers in the light of his acknowledgment that he himself was "sick among the rest," a victim of the "common infection" which had brought England as well as English poets into disrepute (140/1–2).

In the past, he tells us, poetry flourished in England, above all in time of war. The old song of Percy and Douglas served in its day as a trumpet-call to military action, as did the stories of "honest king Arthur" (127/7). But things have changed. An "overfaint quietness" has taken possession of "idle England" (131/32–132/1), and as a result the reputation of poetry has plummeted. "Base men with servile wits undertake it, who think it enough if they can be rewarded of the printer," while better poets refrain from printing their productions for fear of being identified with the "bastard poets" whose texts throng the bookshops (132/3–17). Poetry, in other words, is not responsible for England's political quietism—her failure to intervene in the struggle of Protestantism to protect its interests in Europe, as Sidney and the other members of Leicester's circle were continually urging her to do.[5] Indeed, the poor reputation of poets in peacetime serves (Sidney argues) as circumstantial evidence for the intimate relationship between poetry and military action, since it shows that "Poesy . . . like Venus (but to better purpose) hath rather be troubled in the net with Mars than enjoy the homely quiet of Vulcan" (131/35–37). Elizabethan England has made the poets idle, not the other way round. It is not poetry that abuses man's wit, but man's wit that abuses poetry.

The sly allusion to Venus and Mars in the middle of this passage ought to alert us to its subversion of certain contemporary views on poetry. Stephen Gosson's *The Schoole of Abuse* (1579)—which was dedicated to Sidney, and which may have goaded him into composing his defense—argued that poetry feminized its male practitioners and recipients by encouraging them to imitate women and to seek out their company.[6] This was a position (as Sidney points out) that had been frequently taken by poet-haters since Plato first took it in the *Republic*.[7] Curiously, however, it was by reference to a woman that Gosson chose to mark the difference between the "feminine" properties of latter-day Englishmen and their pursuit of "masculine" virtues in England's martial past. He tells how Bunduica, the ancient "Queene of Englande," derided her Roman enemies as "unwoorthy the name of men, or title of Souldiers, because they were smoothly appareled, soft lodged, daintely feasted, bathed in warme waters, rubbed with sweet oyntments, strewd with fine pulders, wine swillers, singers, Dauncers, and Players."[8] Poets and players were the men responsible for reducing the Romans to this state of luxuriant effeminacy, and Gosson implies that the proliferation of poets and players in modern England has reduced her people to the same degenerate condition. "God hath now blessed England with a Queene," he claims, who resembles Bunduica in her qualities as a leader, but "wee unworthy servants of so milde a Mistresse, unnatural children of so good a mother, unthankful subjects of so loving a prince, wound her royall hart with abusing her lenitie."[9] Like most Elizabethan social commentators Gosson lays the blame for the collapse of good relations between the authorities and their subjects—or the good mother and her unnatural children—squarely on the subject. And the most disastrous consequence of this social and moral collapse is that it has turned the young Englishmen of his time into a bunch of lascivious girls.

Sidney, on the other hand, maintains at the beginning of his Digression that it is England herself, the "mother of excellent minds," who has broken her bond with her poetic progeny by becoming in recent years "so hard a stepmother to poets" (131/5–7). The formerly maternal Elizabethan authorities have relinquished their traditional role as nurturers of the arts at the same time as they have abandoned the military traditions of their ancestors. Indeed, he argues, whatever writers like Gosson may claim, there has never been a period of English history when the two traditions have not gone hand in hand: "in our plainest homeliness, yet never was the Albion nation without poetry" (126/23–24). The phrase neatly demolishes Gosson's appeal to the quasi-mythical warrior-queen Bunduica—ruler of an anachronistic "Englande" where poetry was not yet practiced—by exposing its historical inaccuracy through a self-conscious use of the most ancient name for Britain, Albion. Poetry may be a female art (Sidney refers to it throughout the *Apology* as a woman), but it is not "an art . . . of effeminateness" (130/33–34)—not, that is, an art that infuses its male readers with "womanly" qualities such as passivity and sensuality, and so effectively converts them into women. On the contrary, England's abandonment of her maternal role has for the first time robbed the poets of their special relationship with male spheres of action. Poetry has not made the English womanly; instead, England (and it's hard to resist substituting "Elizabeth" for England at this point) has not been sufficiently "womanly" to encourage poetry.

Having said this, Sidney seems to concur wholeheartedly with Gosson's strictures on the current abuses of poetry. It is on the *causes* of these abuses, and on the best way of dealing with these causes, that the two writers differ fundamentally. Sidney is fully prepared to agree that contemporary poets are addicted to sensuality: "that not only love, but lust, but vanity, but (if they list) scurrility, possesseth many leaves of the poets' books" (125/18–19). He is even prepared to confess that when poetry is abused in this way, "by the reason of his sweet charming force, it can do more hurt than any other army of words" (125/36–37). And in Sidney's discussion of the current state of English poetry, as in Gosson's, the complicity of modern imaginative writing with the prevalent trend for illicit sexual acts is confirmed at every juncture. The Muses, we learn, have sold themselves into prostitution and given birth to a succession of "bastard poets" (132/10), whose insatiable hunger for financial gain recalls the dubious economic arrangements under which they were conceived. "Scurrility" dominates contemporary tragedy (136/6), and drama as a whole is so "pitifully abused" that it has come to resemble an "unmannerly daughter" who "causeth her mother poetry's honesty to be called in question" (137/21–23). In the context of the *Apology*, the first third of which is devoted to establishing the premise that the lineage and function of the poet is "princely" (104/37, 113/19, 115/33), this exposure of the sexual license exercised in Elizabethan verse, drama, and prose fiction could be taken by poet-haters as bearing out their worst suspicions of the act of forging fictions.

Throughout the Digression, Sidney associates the misdemeanors of modern poetry with a succession of imaginary women: the Muses, "mother Poesy," and Poesy's "daughter" Drama. He implies, then, that at the moment when England transformed herself from mother to stepmother, "Poesy" swapped her ancient role as the nurse of knowledge (96/12–14) for that of a flamboyant whore. This abrupt reversion to Gossonian antifeminism would seem to be fatal to Sidney's argument. In the first part of his defense, Sidney labored to demonstrate the antiquity of the male poet's pedigree and the exalted political and cultural status of his forefathers since prehistoric times. But in the Digression, the patrilinear credentials of the modern poet disappear in a morass of blots on his heraldic scutcheon. The sexual activities of the Muses mean that upstart, base-born poets are more conspicuous in Elizabethan culture than the aristocratic "right poet," while the "right poet" is reduced to exercising his art furtively, in private, for fear of being mistaken for a relation of these assertive bastards.[10] The difference between the legitimate and illegitimate offspring of the Muses seems on the verge of extinction. When Sidney speaks of the "spots of the common infection grown among the most part of writers" (140/1–2), himself included, his readers might suspect that the infection is a kind of sexually transmitted disease, which communicates itself from writer to writer irrespective of birth or social status.

What, then, is the distinction Sidney seeks to make between the "bastard poet" and the "right poet" at this stage of his argument? Their sexual practices don't seem so very different. As we have seen, "Poesy" (as practiced by "right poets") prefers acts of strenuous adultery with Mars to a life of domestic bliss with Vulcan; and the offspring of such adulterous acts would presumably be no less illegitimate than the offspring of the Muses. Later, after explaining the distinction between "laughter"—the spontaneous vocal response to sexual "scurrility," which irresponsible playwrights elicit from their audiences—and "delight," a kind of sympathetic pleasure that the responsible dramatist uses as a pedagogical tool—Sidney suggests as the ideal topic for writers of comedies a scene from classical myth that stimulates *both* responses, and which he describes in characteristically pictorial terms: "Hercules, painted with his great beard and furious countenance, in woman's attire, spinning at Omphale's commandment" (136/34–36). The "right poet," then, may not feminize his male readers as Gosson says he does, but he is fascinated and delighted by feminized masculinity. Laughter, and the scurrility that provokes it, is perfectly acceptable to him so long as it is "mixed with . . . delightful teaching" (137/2). Lyrical poetry, too, Sidney tells us, would be best employed in singing God's praises; but if a man *must* use it for secular love he should be prepared to imagine himself a woman if he wishes to produce a persuasive text: "truly many of such writings as come under the banner of unresistible love, *if I were a mistress*, would never persuade me they were in love" (137/32–34, my emphasis). What begins as a clear-cut distinction between the "bastard poet" and the "right poet"—the former favors scurrility, the latter delightful teaching, the former writes secular love-lyrics, the latter writes the "praises of the immortal beauty" (137/27–28), the former inculcates the "female" qualities of passivity and servility, the latter the "masculine" military virtues—rapidly breaks down into an acknowledgment that the topics, the interests, even the impact on a writer's and reader's sexual identity of texts by the two sorts of poets are identical. The difference between them consists in one thing alone: their "purpose."

Poesy, Sidney tells us, "like Venus (*but to better purpose*) hath rather be troubled in the net with Mars than enjoy the homely quiet of Vulcan" (131/35–38, my emphasis). What "better purpose" could possibly make the act of divine adultery—the sort of theological scandal that made Plato banish poets from his Republic—into something that "giveth great praise to Poesy" (131/34–35)? Making money is clearly not a purpose of which Sidney approves. What marks out the "base men with servile wits" as "bastard poets" is their willingness to write anything at all so long as they get "rewarded of the printer" (132/3–4). The other, related characteristic that distinguishes them from right poets is their servility. They wish only to please their paymasters (the printer, the theater audience, the reading public), and have no higher aim in writing. The right poet, by contrast, writes in order to get things done: whether it be to seduce his readers into "virtuous action" (104/35) or into bed. And in the Digression, at least, these two purposes appear to be closely linked. The delight a male reader feels when confronted by a picture of Hercules in drag is presumably the same delight he feels when he is "ravished . . . to see a fair woman" (136/20–21), and both visual impressions are in some sense instructive. But it is hardly adequate to define the "better purpose" that distinguishes the right poet as a willingness to incite readers *either* into "virtuous action" *or* into a possibly illicit sexual act. To understand the distinction between right poets and wrong ones it might be helpful to look at a moment elsewhere in Sidney's literary output in which he rewrites the work of one of the "bastard poets."

One of the most conspicuous names omitted from Sidney's list of good Elizabethan poets is that of George Gascoigne (1530–1577). Gascoigne was Sidney's immediate literary precursor: he wrote the first sonnet-sequence in English, the first essay on prosody, one of the first pieces of original prose fiction, and much of the verse for the most lavish royal spectacle of the century, the Entertainment at Kenilworth which Sidney attended in 1575.[11] Gascoigne, in other words, had more or less excelled in all the literary genres that Sidney later made his own. Like it or not, Sidney was always writing in his shadow. Yet Sidney's biographer, Katherine Duncan-Jones, implies that the dead poet's name was left out of the *Apology* because Sidney held his writing in contempt.[12] This is quite possible—although the fact that Sidney echoed one of his finest poems in *Astrophil and Stella* suggests that he may not have considered comparisons between them to be altogether odious.[13] But there is another equally plausible explanation for Gascoigne's absence from the *Apology*. His first collection of poetry, prose, and drama, *An Hundreth Sundrie Flowres* (1573), seems to have been found offensive by some of its readers, and the revised version of the collection, *The Posies of George Gascoigne Esquire* (1575), was withdrawn from circulation by the censors of the ecclesiastical High Commission.[14] So including them in a defense of poetry would hardly have strengthened Sidney's case. Regardless of one's opinion of the quality of his work, it would have been true to say of Gascoigne in 1580 that he was one of those who "no more but setting their names to it, by their own disgracefulness disgrace the most graceful Poesy" (132/7–9).

The *Apology* may even contain an indirect allusion to the fate of Gascoigne's censored poetry collection, *The Posies*. The Digression tells us that the "bastard poets, without any commission . . . do post over the banks of Helicon, till they make the readers more weary than post-horses," while the "right poets" are "better content to suppress the outflowing of their wit, than, by publishing them, to be accounted knights of the same order" (38/10–17). The censorship of *The Posies* by the High Commission might explain the phrase "without any commission"—Gascoigne's volume had been printed without the Commission's authority. And the reference to the "bastard poets" as incompetent horsemen might allude to a series of verses published in *The Posies*, "Gascoignes Memories," which Gascoigne tells us he composed with astonishing speed while traveling to and from the house of a friend on horseback.[15] One of the poems in the series, a sonnet-sequence, which might be expected to catch Sidney's eye, begins "In haste post haste,"[16] hence, perhaps, the allusion to the poets "who *post* over the banks of Helicon." Finally, Gascoigne adopts the persona of the Green Knight in several autobiographical poems in *The Posies*.[17] Thus poets who wished to dissociate themselves from his collection might well choose not to publish in order to avoid being "accounted knights of the same order" as the Green Knight, Gascoigne. If this sentence does indeed refer to Gascoigne, it would seem to confirm Duncan-Jones's view that Sidney had nothing but contempt for his unfortunate predecessor.

But whatever his faults or merits, Gascoigne was certainly one of the most influential writers to have been "rewarded of the printer" in the previous decade. Despite the censure they had incurred—or perhaps because of it—his two collections were widely imitated, finding echoes in the work of (among others) George Pettie, George Whetstone, John Grange, John Lyly, and Gabriel Harvey.[18] The text of Gascoigne's that spawned the most imitations was his scurrilous prose fiction *The Adventures of Master F. J.*, which appeared in different versions in the *Flowres* and the *Posies*. So it would hardly be surprising to find echoes of the *Adventures* in Sidney's first foray into prose fiction, the *Old Arcadia*; especially given the links modern scholars have found between the *Adventures* and the amorous escapades of Sidney's uncle, the earl of Leicester.[19] If the relationship between Gascoigne's and Sidney's prose fictions has not been noticed before, it is no doubt because Sidney has succeeded in convincing generations of scholars of his aristocratic disdain for the popular works of his English predecessors.[20] But a man who could call the tales of King Arthur "honest," when the eminent humanist

Roger Ascham and his followers (including E. K.) thought they encouraged nothing but "open mans slaughter, and bold bawdrye," need not have been averse to the *Adventures* on principle.[21] Sidney was not one of the older generation like Ascham who sought to advise the young from the vantage point of accumulated experience. On the contrary, he depicts himself in the *Apology* as a young man "sick among the rest," who is as deeply conscious of the force of sexual attraction, and the attractions of self-interest, as Gascoigne was, and who shared with his contemporaries a tendency to reject the blandishments of the authoritarian father-figures who strove to guide him. The *Arcadia* has much in common with the *Adventures.* Much, that is, except its "better purpose," and the physical form in which it was read during Sidney's lifetime. In the second part of this essay I shall consider the links between the two texts in detail, and end by considering the light these links may shed on Sidney's relationship with the "bastard poets" he affects to despise.

II

The first version of *The Adventures of Master F. J.* tells of a young man on a visit to an aristocratic household in the north of England who has an affair with his host's wife. The affair is conducted through a series of coded utterances and an exchange of secret letters and verses, and is consummated under cover of darkness, by the fitful light of the moon, on the bare boards of a gallery. Soon after this consummation the young man, F. J., begins to suspect that his mistress Elinor is having a simultaneous affair with her secretary—the man who writes her letters. His suspicions make him ill, and when Elinor comes to comfort him in his bed by night he first accuses her of infidelity, then rapes her. After this their relationship deteriorates, and the story ends with F. J. leaving Elinor's household in disgust and bestowing his indiscriminate curse on the whole of womankind.

In neither its first nor its second version does this narrative make much claim to incite readers to "virtuous action."[22] The first version claims only to demonstrate the impossibility of keeping sexual indiscretions under wraps—especially in an age of print. The narrator, who signs himself G. T., explicitly states that his text shows the willingness of his English countrymen to privilege self-promotion over edification: they seek "rather to win a passover praise by the wanton penning of a few loving lays, than to gain immortal fame" by handling themes more "profitable" to the nation.[23] G. T.'s "purpose" in writing the narrative was merely to satisfy a friend's taste for "good letters" (p. 4)—although the letters it contains, both epistles and verses, are scarcely "good" in any moral sense. And the friend for whom he wrote the story clearly had as little "good" in him as G. T.'s protagonist. Despite G. T.'s request that he keep the manuscript to himself, this friend had no sooner read it than he took a copy to the printer's shop to be published. The friend's justification for this brazen act of treachery is specious in the extreme. He describes himself as "one that thought better to please a number by common commodity than to feed the humour of any private person by needless singularity" (p. 3). And the personal "commodity" he claims to have reaped from the text is this: "to sit and smile at the fond devices of such as have enchained themselves in the golden fetters of fantasy, and having bewrayed themselves to the whole world do yet conjecture that they walk unseen in a net" (p. 3). In other words, he justifies the act of betraying secrets to the press by claiming that the secrets were already open ones. Adulterers who cultivate invisibility have already betrayed their crimes to the world, through texts and actions, and are as embarrassingly visible as Mars and Venus were once Vulcan had caught them "in a net."

This story and the tale of its illicit publication would seem to confirm all Sidney's strictures on the "base writers"—or in this case, friends of writers—who think of nothing but getting "rewarded of the printer." It even invites the kind of meditation on the state of English poetry that he composed in the Digression.[24] Yet for Sidney, if not for G. T., the best poetry is perfectly willing to be caught in sexually compromising situations—to be "troubled in the net with Mars"—so long as it is for a "better purpose." And at the center of the *Old Arcadia* lies an act of sexual exposure that corresponds very closely to the various acts of exposure and betrayal that mark the *Adventures.*

Like the *Adventures*, the *Arcadia* tells of a young man, Pyrocles—accompanied in this case by his best friend Musidorus—who infiltrates an aristocratic household and finds himself both prosecuting a clandestine love affair (but this time with his host's daughter) and erotically involved with his host's wife (but this time against his will). Like F. J., Pyrocles is forced to conduct his affair through an exchange of coded utterances, songs, poems, and narratives, whose obscurity leads to misunderstandings between himself and his lover. Again like F. J., Pyrocles soon learns that his identity as a lover is known to one of the women in the household (F. J.'s courtship is detected by Elinor's sister, Frances, while Pyrocles's is found out by Gynecia, his host's wife). Later, Pyrocles finds the development of his relationship impeded by a serious outbreak of jealousy (in the *Adventures* it is F. J. who becomes jealous; in the *Arcadia* it is first Gynecia, then Philoclea, the woman he loves). In the meantime, his friend Musidorus is courting his host's other daughter, a courtship that culminates in an elopement and an attempted rape. Pyrocles's affair achieves a more satisfactory consummation, after elaborate preparations, in the darkness and secrecy of Philoclea's bedchamber; but then, like F. J.'s, it is discovered (Frances spots F. J. returning from his liaison with Elinor; the servant Dametas catches Pyrocles and Philoclea in bed together). In the trial that follows, Pyrocles is cross-examined by the prosecution, and attempts to remove any blame from Philoclea by claiming that he had tried and failed to rape her (F. J., on the other hand, interrogates Elinor in bed, and on failing to receive a satisfactory answer, rapes her at once). At this point the two texts diverge completely: Pyrocles is condemned to death while F. J. escapes scot-free. But none of these young lovers shows any remorse. Whatever "delightful teaching" Sidney's text contains, it is by no means certain that he, any more than Gascoigne, wishes his young male readers to learn that they will live to regret their sexual misconduct—or even to acknowledge it. "We have lived," Musidorus declares before the trial, "and have lived to be good to ourselves and others"; while Pyrocles refuses to "show a repentance of the love we bear to those matchless creatures," the women they have struggled to woo.[25] If the *Arcadia* has a "better purpose" than the *Adventures*, it is not the purpose that Ascham and Gosson might have expected—to discourage clandestine courtships.

Indeed, Sidney seems almost perversely determined to ensure that his text will fall foul of Elizabethan moralists. Once contaminated by the "common infection" of love at the beginning of the book, Sidney's Pyrocles not only falls into poetry (verse, elaborately figured discourse, references to the *Metamorphoses*)—thereby confirming Gosson's theory that poetry and illicit sex are mutually dependent—but also changes into drag. He could hardly have furnished a more dramatic illustration of the feminizing effect of poetry on its male practitioners. And as a direct result of this cross-dressing, rebellion breaks out in Arcadia. The inhabitants of the Arcadian town of Phagona resolve to rebel because a "strange woman had now possessed their prince and government" (pp. 111–12). If Pyrocles had not changed his clothes, his host, Prince Basilius, would presumably not have fallen in love with him, and the Phagonians would not have thought their prince "possessed" by a foreigner. So, at least, the moralists might have reasoned. Sidney appears to be offering an irrefutable confirmation of his statement in the *Apology*, that "Poesy . . . being abused . . . can do more hurt than any other army of words."

Where Sidney differs from Gosson and other followers of Ascham, however, is in laying the blame for the abuse of poetry on the older generation rather than his own. Pyrocles adopts his female disguise in response to Basilius's withdrawal from his responsibilities as prince of Arcadia; and this withdrawal is prompted by a radical misuse of poetry in the form of the Delphic oracle. Sidney mentions the oracle in the *Apology*, both as the source of vatic pronouncements in verse, which indicate the high regard for poetry among the ancient Greeks, and as "a very vain and godless superstition" (98/35). Basilius's vanity and godlessness is such that he not only consults the oracle, against the advice of his most trusted minister, but also attempts to avoid the fate it predicts for him by concealing his daughters from the sight of men. His timidity resembles that of the "self-wise-seeming schoolmasters" of the Elizabethan age, such as Roger Ascham, author of *The Scholemaster* (1570), who argued vociferously for the protection of the young from the pernicious influence of foreign love-poetry.[26] Basilius, too, assumes that the menace to himself and his offspring hinted at by the oracle will come in the form of sexually predatory foreigners, but as we might expect, his own efforts to avert the foreign menace prove more disastrous than any threat from abroad. His protective withdrawal into secrecy forces secrecy on the foreign prince, Pyrocles. And Pyrocles's disguise seduces Basilius into a further abuse of poetry. Soon after he sees the young man in his Amazonian costume Basilius bursts into verse very far from good, either technically or morally speaking (*OA*, pp. 83–84). The situation offers a wily critique of the many wise old men who had appointed themselves the moral custodians of Elizabethan youth—and of Sidney's in particular. Through their efforts to curb other men's sexual and poetic activities, the moralists merely make a humiliating display of their own sexual obsessions—and their desire to retain possession of the bodies as well as the minds of the young.

Pyrocles's "purpose" in courting Philoclea seems a good deal "better" than Basilius's in preventing her from being courted. His desire for an alliance with Philoclea is a perfectly legitimate one; it is shared both by Philoclea and by his own father, who (we learn at a crucial point just before the closing trial) had intended to approach Basilius with a proposal that their children be married (p. 310). Only Basilius's opposition renders the match illegal. And the outcome of Pyrocles's courtship is the kind of private betrothal that, as Catherine Bates has pointed out, "was still considered legally binding in Sidney's day, and was certainly a convention of chivalric literature."[27] For all the similarities between the plots of the *Adventures* and the *Old Arcadia*, then, Sidney goes to considerable lengths to distinguish the protagonist of his narrative from Gascoigne's adulterous rapist; and in doing so he offers a radical critique of the blanket condemnation of erotic fiction by Ascham and his moralizing acolytes. A further comparison of Pyrocles's adventures with those of F. J. will serve to highlight the essential differences as well as the resemblances between them.

At the point when F. J. succumbs to jealousy—half way through G. T.'s narrative—the narrator breaks off to tell the allegorical story of Suspicion, adapted from Ariosto's *Orlando Furioso*.[28] Up to this point F. J.'s affair has been conducted in a confusing twilight, a bewilderment of torches, moonshine, and shadow that reflects his need for verbal and physical obscurity. The story of Suspicion announces his entry into total intellectual and moral darkness. Suspicion inhabits two cave-like dwellings in succession, the first of which, "so dark and obscure that scarcely either sun or air could enter into it" (p. 47), is the scene of his murder, as a mortal, by his wife. The second, a "hellish dungeon" where he lives by himself after being restored to life, is the den from which he issues "in the dead and silent nights" to plague humanity with causeless fears and sexual paranoia (pp. 49–50). From this point in the narrative F. J. can no longer penetrate the "darkness" that enshrouds Elinor's discourse or the jealous gloom that prevents him from celebrating the blaze of her beauty as he did when they first met. The *Arcadia* too, has a cave at its midpoint: a cave where in book three Pyrocles is first apprised of Gynecia's jealousy and suspicion, and to which in the same book he directs Gynecia and Basilius to consummate their desire for him. His plot to lure Gynecia to the cave arouses the jealousy of Philoclea, so that Sidney's cave, like Gascoigne's, might appropriately be dubbed the House of Suspicion. Indeed, the cave bears a close physical resemblance to the second dwelling-place of Gascoigne's Suspicion—it contains a series of chambers and has a stream running through it—despite being described in much more attractive terms (it is a "dark, but pleasant, mansion," *OA*, p. 157). It might be read as a figure for the secret places of Pyrocles/Cleophila's body to which Basilius and Gynecia desire to gain access; or for the beguiling moral blindness that drives them to seek their desire's consummation. But this cave does *not* imprison the story's young male protagonist. He uses it as a blind for others—as a means of bringing about his own secret (and, in his opinion, legitimate) liaison with Philoclea by getting her parents out of the house, and as a means of deceiving Philoclea's parents into a legitimate erotic encounter. It therefore has a function precisely the reverse of the caves in the *Adventures*, which represent the self-imposed blindness and imprisonment of F. J. and other jealous lovers. The older generation approaches Pyrocles's cave much as Sidney's censorious elders might have approached his text—with the expectation of finding something salacious at its heart. Instead, to their disappointment, they find only each other, intent on their quest for forbidden fruit. The moment of discovery is one of intense embarrassment to both parties, but especially to Basilius, who is "more ashamed to see himself so overtaken than Vulcan was when with much cunning he proved himself a cuckold" (*OA*, p. 240). The phrase exposes once again the folly of the older generation in Sidney's own time, who worked so hard to prove poetry more successful than other forms of pedagogy in seducing its readers.

Pyrocles's plot against Basilius, unlike the plot of F. J., is not adulterous: it is designed to confirm rather than to undermine the conjugal alliance between his host and his wife. Where he might seem at first to be encouraging adultery by stirring up illicit lusts in older men and women, we soon learn that the young man has a "better purpose." And his nocturnal meeting with Philoclea, too, has a different purpose from F. J.'s meetings with Elinor. The similarities between these meetings are striking. Pyrocles describes his projected visit to Philoclea as an "adventure" (*OA*, p. 201), a term that dominates G. T.'s narrative.[29] Before setting out for Philoclea's bedchamber he places "his sword under his arm" in case of unwelcome challenges along the way (*OA*, p. 200)—just as F. J. hid his "naked sword" under his nightgown on the way to his first liaison with Elinor.[30] Later, both male lovers have their swords stolen from them by an undetected witness of their sexual exploits: Frances in the *Adventures*, Dametas in the *Arcadia*. Again, on both occasions when F. J. has sex with Elinor one of the lovers is ill or feigning illness. On the first occasion Elinor goes to bed early because she finds herself "somewhat sickly disposed,"[31] while on the second it is F. J. who has taken to his bed, racked with a jealous fever. In the *Arcadia*, too, Pyrocles finds Philoclea sick in bed, tormented by the mistaken belief that he has transferred his affections to her mother. Finally—and this is the most striking parallel of all—on the second occasion when F. J. meets his mistress at night he faints dead away when she asks him the reason for his bedridden condition. Elinor revives him not by slapping his cheeks "in such sort as they do that strive to call again a dying creature" but by "pressing his breast with the whole weight of her body, and biting his lips with her friendly teeth."[32] Pyrocles, too, faints when his mistress accuses him of treason.[33] His swooning is linked by the *Arcadia's* most recent editor with the swooning of

Troilus in Chaucer's celebrated poem (*OA*, p. 206 note). But Philoclea's reaction recalls Elinor rather than Criseyde: "she laid her fair body over his breast; and throwing no other water in his face but the stream of her tears, nor giving him other blows but the kisses of her well-formed mouth, her only cries were . . . lamentations" (*OA*, p. 206).[34] Any reader familiar with the work of the most celebrated poet of the 1570s, Gascoigne, might have been expected to pick up the verbal echoes here of his popular narrative.

These echoes—the cave of suspicion, the details of the encounter between the lovers, the purloining of the hero's sword—have no equivalent in the three chief sources of the *Old Arcadia*, Sannazaro's *Arcadia*, Heliodorus's *Aethiopian History*, and *Amadis de Gaule*. Only the *Adventures* is invoked by them; and this invocation is an act of brazen impudence on Sidney's part. It marks him out as a self-conscious member of the new generation of male poets condemned by Ascham and Gosson: highly sexed and keen to take sex as the subject of their fictions; ingenious in devising plots, especially amorous ones; a generation of Icaruses, willing and eager to discard the advice of their paternalistic Daedaluses;[35] willing too to hazard the loss of their birthright and national identity for the sake of the ends they consider worth pursuing.[36] Just before entering Philoclea's bedchamber Pyrocles formally abandons his subservience to his father: "All the great estate of his father seemed unto him but a trifling pomp, whose good stands in other men's conceit, in comparison of the true comfort he found in the depth of his mind" (*OA*, pp. 200–01). More even than Gascoigne, Sidney is ready to acknowledge that he and his fellow poets are dangerous—capable of demolishing dynasties and overthrowing governments in the interests of their own "true comfort." As he approaches Philoclea, Pyrocles resembles Ovid's Tereus (he hears Philoclea singing "like a solitary nightingale" in her room, *OA*, p. 201) or Livy's sword-carrying Tarquin. Everything suggests that he is about to commit an atrocity: that he will surrender to his lust, like F. J. and Musidorus, thus fulfilling the gloomiest predictions of the poetry-hating lobby. But he does not. Instead he and Philoclea exchange prenuptial vows and sleep together as consenting adults. Later, when his phallic sword is taken from him by Dametas, Pyrocles reverts to the female role of Lucretia and seeks to kill himself with the only available weapon—the iron bar that secures their chamber window (*OA*, p. 251 ff.). And it is paradoxically at this point—when he is at his weakest and most "effeminate," in Gosson's terms—that his political dangerousness is made most manifest.

In Sidney's as in other Renaissance texts, suicide is one of the few acts of heroism available to women. Thisbe committed suicide, as did Dido and Lucretia; and all three women are associated with either Pyrocles or Philoclea in the third and fourth books of the *Arcadia*. Pyrocles tells Gynecia he will play the Thisbe to her Pyramus when he invites her to visit him in his cave (p. 195). When Pyrocles enters Philoclea's bedroom he is associated with Aeneas, "blown up and down with as many contrary passions" as the wandering Trojans who followed Virgil's hero (p. 204), which places Philoclea in the role of a potential Dido. Soon after, when Pyrocles faints, Philoclea announces her intention to die with him "with Thisbe's punishment of my rash unwariness" (p. 206)—that is, by suicide—if he should die of grief. Finally, on being discovered by Dametas, Pyrocles symbolically loses his masculinity along with his sword, and decides to end his own life as Lucretia did, in order to lend credibility to the version of events he wishes his jailers to believe: the version in which he was killed by Philoclea while attempting to rape her, or killed himself in frustration on failing to carry out the rape.

Both these versions pander to the desire of the authorities to inscribe young men as treacherous perpetrators of violent sex-crimes that are also major breaches of national security. But Pyrocles is only prepared to pander to this desire in order to defuse their equal willingness to brand young women as whores. His conscience is "clear and joyful" (*OA*, p. 256). Unlike F. J., who faints because he thinks he has betrayed Elinor's trust, Pyrocles faints because he has been *unjustly* accused of treason. That is why his decision to imitate Lucretia is so appropriate. It aims at the heart of the Elizabethan myth of women, and of the poets who celebrate them, as sexual Sirens who feminize the men whose passions they arouse. In the *Apology*, Sidney alludes to a picture of Lucretia as the supreme example of the work of the best painters, "who bestow that in colours upon you which is fittest for the eye to see," and hence of the best poets, who "range, only reined with learned discretion, into the divine consideration of what may be and should be" (102/25–37). Saint Augustine (the precursor of the Elizabethan poet-haters) had condemned Lucretia's suicide as desperate and therefore damnable;[37] but neither Sidney nor Pyrocles finds his arguments convincing. Yet it is still more appropriate that Pyrocles should have been dissuaded by a woman from his Lucretian attempt. Philoclea is fully—if somewhat anachronistically—apprised of all the Augustinian arguments against suicide, and completes the vindication of women from the antifeminism of church fathers, humanists, and poet-haters by enunciating them with unsurpassed eloquence. Love, then, may feminize the male lover by forcing him into a female role (although it is the behavior of the authorities that renders this necessary, just as it is the impasse in which he finds himself that forces Pyrocles into contemplating suicide). But in the *Old Arcadia*, as in the *Apology*, the words and actions of women are well worth imitating.

Women are also more effective than armies in bringing about revolutions. Lucretia's death offered shocking and irrefutable evidence of the misbehavior of the Roman royal family, and so sparked off the insurrection that transformed Rome into a republic. Pyrocles's adoption of a female disguise, and the events that lead to his Lucretian near-suicide, offer irrefutable evidence of the self-love that motivated Basilius's withdrawal from his princely duties. By intensifying this self-love they come close to toppling Basilius from the throne of Arcadia. They do not actually dethrone him—Basilius's desire is after all comic, where Sextus Tarquinius's is the stuff of tragedy—but they demonstrate just how easy it would be to supplant a prince who had surrendered himself (or herself, perhaps) to political seclusion.

Sidney's echo of Gascoigne, then, in the middle of the *Arcadia*, performs two functions. It both identifies him with the "bastard poets" condemned by Gosson and marks him out as distinct from them. Some of their abuses he shares: above all their sexual adventurousness and their resistance to the counsel of their elders. But he does not share their servility. His agenda in tracing the course of "love . . . lust . . . scurrility" is quite different from theirs. It is designed not to flatter the Elizabethan authorities but to aggrieve them; to expose the consequences of monarchic irresponsibility; to give "a notable example how great dissipations monarchal governments are subject unto" (*OA*, p. 277). His agenda, then, is decidedly not servile: and any Elizabethan reader could have been expected to recognize this. This, perhaps, is why Sidney left his poetry and prose in manuscript. The handwritten page, available only to "such friends who will weigh errors in the balance of goodwill" (p. 3), was subject to none of the censorial controls that governed, and to some extent determined, Gascoigne's writing career.[38] If the "bastard poets" were betrayed into servility by the medium of print, the best means of drawing attention to your difference from them, and so to your independence of the ruling authorities, was to distribute your poetic compositions personally, "in loose sheets of paper" (p. 3).

Pyrocles's female disguise marks out his heroism as of a different kind from the open military heroics of England's past. Disguised heroics are the only kind available to him. His camouflage does not, however, prevent him from being a hero. As we have seen, the *Apology* selects as the most striking "speaking picture" of virtuous action a painting of Lucretia at the moment of death, and as the most worthwhile comic subject a painting of Hercules in a dress. Pyrocles is associated with Lucretia, but he is also associated with Hercules: when he kills a rampaging beast in book one, Gynecia thinks he possesses "the very face of young Hercules killing the Nemean lion" (*OA*, p. 48). The "right poets" of Sidney's time may have been driven, like the inhabitants of England and Arcadia, into a remoteness from public affairs that might be mistaken for indolence; they may have become feminized, as Hercules was in later life; but these conditions have been imposed on them by circumstance, and neither condition is as dishonorable as it might at first seem. Hercules is Hercules, even when in love and dressed as a woman. Both conditions—being in love and being in drag—help those who embrace them to lay aside, for a time, their expected subservience to a discreditable national regime. And they also serve as the perfect cover for an analysis of what has damaged that regime and brought it to the brink of being supplanted by something else.

Sidney may also have had a more personal reason for imitating Gascoigne's *Adventures* in the third and fourth books of the *Arcadia*. Introducing his revised poetry collection, *The Posies*, Gascoigne hints that the first version of the collection had been found offensive by censorious readers because they interpreted the *Adventures* as a *roman a clef*, an insalubrious morsel of court gossip. Some "busie conjectures," he explains, "have presumed to thinke that the same was indeed written to the scandalizing of some worthie personages, whom they woulde seeme therby to know";[39] and Cyndia Clegg has demonstrated that the text might well have been associated in the minds of courtly readers with the "scandalous rumors" surrounding the love life of Robert Dudley, earl of Leicester.[40] By rewriting Gascoigne's romance in a heroic context for the exclusive perusal of members of Leicester's circle, Sidney may have seen himself as vindicating his uncle's personal reputation, as he was to do once again in his *Defense of the Earl of Leicester* (1584–85). The adventures of Pyrocles transform the knowing erotic machinations of Gascoigne's F. J. into a courageous gesture of political dissent, a bid for sexual and heroic fulfillment in a world where political leaders value personal safety and the satisfaction of their private desires above the higher national and religious interests they claim to serve. Pyrocles is not, of course, an allegorical representation of Leicester, any more than F. J. is, but the clandestine romances both men pursue offer two quite different perspectives on the Elizabethan sexual politics in which Leicester was so deeply embroiled. And the Pyroclean perspective is by far the more flattering.

One cannot help thinking that Sidney would have considered the offspring of Pyrocles's more or less illicit union with Philoclea to be of a more elevated kind than any bastards born of F. J.'s and Elinor's adulterous grapplings. But to appropriate Sidney's own phrase from the *Apology*, the "imaginative groundwork" of the *Arcadia*'s "profitable invention" was laid, in part at least, by the "bastard poet" George Gascoigne. It is time, perhaps, that we began to reassess in earnest Sidney's relationship to the literary experiments of his Elizabethan forebears.

NOTES

1. The first draft of this essay was written for discussion at a seminar, "Prose Fiction and Early Modern Sexualities," chaired by Goran Stanivukovic, at the twenty-seventh annual meeting of the Shakespeare Association of America. I am grateful to all participants at the seminar for their invaluable comments. My thanks also to Professor James Treadwell of McGill University, and to my colleagues at the University of Glasgow, Mr. Robert Cummings and Professor Willy Maley, for advice and encouragement.
2. Edmund Spenser, *Poetical Works*, ed. J. C. Smith and E. de Selincourt (Oxford and New York: Oxford University Press, 1912), p. 463.
3. References to *An Apology for Poetry* are taken from Geoffrey Shepherd's edition (London: Nelson, 1965). For an account of the "artificial rules" and "imitative patterns" recommended by classical rhetorical theorists, see Shepherd's note on this passage.
4. Geoffrey Shepherd describes the section as a "Digression" in his analysis of the rhetorical structure of the *Apology* (see pp. 13–16 of his introduction, esp. p. 15 ff.). For an account of the Digression as central to the argument of the *Apology* see Andrew Hadfield, *Literature, Politics and National Identity* (Cambridge: Cambridge University Press, 1994, ch. 5, pp. 132–39) and the Introduction to my edition of the *Apology* (Manchester: Manchester University Press, 2002).

5. For Sidney's association with the militant Protestantism of Leicester's faction, see Blair Worden, *The Sound of Virtue: Philip Sidney's Arcadia and Elizabethan Politics* (New Haven and London: Yale University Press, 1996).
6. For a full account of Gosson's argument and of its relationship to the *Apology* see Arthur F. Kinney, ed., *Markets of Bawdrie: The Dramatic Criticism of Stephen Gosson* (Salzburg: Universität Salzburg, 1970), introduction. For a discussion of the relationship between poetry and effeminacy in Elizabethan England, see Juliet Fleming, "The Ladies' Man and the Age of Elizabeth," in *Sexuality and Gender in Early Modern Europe: Institutions, Texts, Images*, ed. James Grantham Turner (Cambridge: Cambridge University Press, 1993), pp. 158–79.
7. See *Apology*, ed. Shepherd, 123/5–16, 125/2–23, 128/8 ff., etc.
8. Kinney, *Markets of Bawdrie*, p. 95.
9. Kinney, *Markets of Bawdrie*, pp. 95–96.
10. Sidney's definition of the "right poet" is as follows: "these . . . be they which most properly do imitate to teach and delight, and to imitate borrow nothing of what is, hath been, or shall be; but range, only reined with learned discretion, into the divine consideration of what may be and should be" (102/33–37). He contrasts these with the "many versifiers" of recent times "that need never answer to the name of poets" (103/19).
11. For a list of Gascoigne's achievements see *George Gascoigne: The Green Knight*, ed. Roger Pooley (Manchester: Carcanet Press, 1982), p. 7. For Sidney's attendance at the Kenilworth entertainments, see Katherine Duncan-Jones, *Sir Philip Sidney: Courtier-Poet* (London: Hamish Hamilton, 1991), pp. 91–99.
12. She suggests, e.g., that at Gascoigne's death "it is unlikely that [Sidney] felt much regret at his passing" (*Sir Philip Sidney: Courtier Poet*, p. 138). See also her account of Sidney's possible reactions to the Kenilworth entertainments in chapter 5.
13. Duncan-Jones points out the debt of *Astrophil and Stella* p. 83 to Gascoigne's *The Praise of Phillip Sparrowe* in her Oxford Authors compilation *Sir Philip Sidney* (Oxford: Oxford University Press, 1989), p. 367.
14. The best account of the publishing history of Gascoigne's two collections is that of Cyndia Susan Clegg, in *Press Censorship in Elizabethan England* (Cambridge: Cambridge University Press, 1997), ch. 5, pp. 103–22.
15. For "Gascoignes Memories," see George Gascoigne, *The Posies*, ed. John W. Cunliffe (Cambridge: Cambridge University Press, 1907), pp. 62–70. For Gascoigne's account of their composition see p. 70.
16. See *The Posies*, ed. Cunliffe, p. 66. The poem is a set of meditations on the proverb "Sat cito, si sat bene," which Gascoigne renders "No haste but good, where wisdom makes the waye." Erasmus discusses the proverb in his *Adagia*; see Margaret Mann Phillips, *Erasmus on his Times: A Shortened Version of the Adages of Erasmus* (Cambridge: Cambridge University Press, 1967), p. 17.
17. See *The Posies*, ed. Cunliffe, pp. 367–82.
18. For Gascoigne's influence on George Pettie and John Lyly, see the chapters on these authors in my *Elizabethan Fictions: Espionage, Counter-Espionage and the Duplicity of Fiction in Early Elizabethan Prose Narratives* (Oxford: Clarendon Press, 1997), esp. pp. 158–284. For his influence on Grange, see my article, "John Grange," in *Dictionary of Literary Biography, Vol. 136: Sixteenth-Century British Nondramatic Writers*, ed. David A. Richardson

(Detroit, Washington, D.C., and London: Bruccoli Clark Layman, 1994), pp. 155–58. For a more detailed discussion of the relationship between Gascoigne's work and that of Whetstone and Grange, see my doctoral dissertation, "A Study of the Works of John Lyly and his Predecessors in the Context of Changing Attitudes to Fiction in Elizabethan England" (Oxford University, 1990), pp. 208–29. Harvey imitates Gascoigne's *The Adventures of Master F. J.* in his unfinished prose fiction, "The Story of Mercy Harvey, Sister of Dr. Gabriel Harvey," printed in *The Works of Gabriel Harvey*, ed. Alexander B. Grosart, 3 vols. (London: Privately printed, 1885), vol. 3, pp. 73–97.

19. See Clegg, *Press Censorship*, pp. 117–20.
20. A. C. Hamilton, e.g., assumes that the *Arcadia* "remains largely isolated from the main tradition of English fiction," and even speaks of the "absence of native prose fiction" when Sidney was writing it. See "Sidney's *Arcadia* as Prose Fiction: Its Relation to Its Sources," in *Sidney in Retrospect*, ed. Arthur F. Kinney and the Editors of *ELR* (Amherst: University of Massachusetts Press, 1988), pp. 119–50.
21. See Roger Ascham, *English Works*, ed. W. A. Wright (Cambridge: Cambridge University Press, 1904), p. 231.
22. The *Adventures* first appeared in Gascoigne's *Flowres*, and was reprinted in *The Posies* with a number of minor alterations, the chief of which was its transference from an English to an Italian setting.
23. *An Anthology of Elizabethan Prose Fiction*, ed. Paul Salzman (Oxford: Oxford University Press, 1987), p. 5. All references to *The Adventures of Master F. J.* are taken from this edition.
24. See G. T.'s discussion of the condition of poetry in England at the beginning of the *Adventures*, pp. 4–5.
25. *The Old Arcadia*, ed. Katherine Duncan-Jones (Oxford: Oxford University Press, 1985), p. 321. All references are to this edition.
26. Sidney proposes a "self-wise-seeming schoolmaster" as an appropriate subject for comedy in the *Apology* (137/14). For an account of Ascham's attack on foreign poetry and prose fiction, see my *Elizabethan Fictions*, pp. 41–51.
27. Catherine Bates, *Language and Literature* (Cambridge: Cambridge University Press, 1992), p. 118.
28. Salzman, *Elizabethan Prose Fiction*, pp. 47–50.
29. See my *Elizabethan Fictions*, ch. 3, esp. pp. 114–15.
30. Salzman, *Elizabethan Prose Fiction*, p. 30.
31. Salzman, *Elizabethan Prose Fiction*, p. 29.
32. Salzman, *Elizabethan Prose Fiction*, p. 60.
33. In the *Old Arcadia* Pyrocles exclaims, "Let not the dangerous cunning I have used to please you be deemed a treason against you!" He then asks, if he should be proved treacherous, that "my heart empoisoned with detestable treason [may] be the seat of infernal sorrow." Philoclea replies, "you have betrayed me" (pp. 205 and 206), which leads to his collapse. In the *Adventures*, F. J. is so ashamed of the contrast between his suspicions and Elinor's kind treatment of him that he "began now to accuse himself of such and so heinous treason as that his guilty heart was constrained to yield unto a just scourge for the same" (Salzman, *Elizabethan Prose Fiction*, p. 59).

34. Troilus, by contrast, is lifted onto Criseyde's bed by Pandarus, where Criseyde and her uncle use every available means to revive him:

    Therwith his pous and paumes of his hondes
    They gan to frote, and wete his temples tweyne;
    And to deliveren hym fro bittre bondes,
    She ofte hym kiste; and shortly for to seyne,
    Hym to revoken she did al hire peyne. (Book III, lines 1114–18)

    Sidney, like Gascoigne, makes a point of saying that his heroine used *only* her "body" laid on her lover's "breast," and her mouth, in her efforts at resuscitation.
35. See *Apology*, ed. Shepherd, 132/36–133/8.
36. On this new generation of English poets, see my *Elizabethan Fictions*, introduction.
37. For Augustine's views on Lucretia, see Ian Donaldson, *The Rapes of Lucretia: A Myth and Its Transformations* (Oxford: Clarendon Press, 1982), pp. 21–39.
38. For Sidney's exploitation of so-called manuscript culture, see H. R. Woudhuysen, *Sir Philip Sidney and the Circulation of Manuscripts, 1558–1640* (Oxford: Clarendon Press, 1996), Part II: "Sir Philip Sidney." On Sidney's strategies for evading censorship, see Annabel Patterson, *Censorship and Interpretation: The Conditions of Writing and Reading in Early Modern England* (Madison, Wisconsin: University of Wisconsin Press, 1984), pp. 24–43 etc.
39. *The Posies*, ed. Cunliffe, p. 7.
40. Clegg, *Press Censorship*, p. 119.

Chapter 12

Unfolding the Shepherdess: A Revision of Pastoral

Lori Humphrey Newcomb

I started to look for shepherdesses in early modern pastoral—that is, characters *called* shepherdesses—when one made a belated appearance in Caroline reprintings of an Elizabethan romance, Robert Greene's *Pandosto*. In Greene's original text, ca. 1585, Fawnia, the lost Bohemian princess, is consistently called a *shepherd* like the Sicilian country man who adopted her.[1] So, for instance, she interpolates herself to Dorastus, the prince of Sicily: "Fawnia, thou art a shepherd, daughter to poor Porrus" (p. 182). Even after Dorastus, too, "becomes a shepherd" to woo her, she insists, "I dare not say, Dorastus, I love thee, because I am a shepherd" (pp. 185, 188). Fawnia's self-description—"shepherd" without "-ess"—marks her social status, but not, as we might expect, her gender. Then, in the tenth extant edition of the romance, dated 1632 (STC 12291), the noun is varied. The narrator reports Dorastus's "calling to mind, that *Fawnia* was a Shepheardesse" (sig. D3^{v}); then, the prince convinces himself that she is "borne to be a Shepheardesse, but worthy to be a Goddesse" (sig. D4). While the prince's emendation chimes with "goddess," the narrator's has no rhetorical motivation. Throughout this 1632 edition, Fawnia still call herself a "shepherd," as though the gendered form is not in her rustic vocabulary.[2] By the twelfth edition of 1636 (STC 12292), the change is consistent: Fawnia is now a "shepherdess" throughout the romance, even in her own rhetorical set pieces, as though no one, even the simplest of country girls, would call a woman a "shepherd." Indeed, no popular edition of this romance ever called Fawnia a "shepherd" again.[3]

Somehow, during the 1630s, *Pandosto*'s use of "shepherd" for a woman was judged to be inappropriate: the feminine-inflected "shepherdess" had become the right word. Such piecemeal emendations in reprintings of a steady seller were probably made by compositors rather than the publisher.[4] Yet they are more than mere "accidentals," outcomes of compositorial habit: a compositor does not lightly decide to cram three extra pieces of type into a line when resetting pages type-for-type (as in these editions). The compositors attended to the narrative just enough to notice and casually change the female protagonist's job title.[5] With no more deliberation than that, the change became uniform within a few editions. Thus, this gendering of pastoral labor was, as ideological changes tend to be, both compulsory and unremarked.

What did "shepherdess" say about Fawnia that "shepherd" did not? Why was that differentiation compulsory in the 1630s and not in the 1580s? A strictly modal explanation might point to the codification of pastoral in the 1630s; a social one, to shifting hierarchies of labor, gender, and sexuality over the entire fifty-year period.[6] Of course, if we accept Louis Montrose's powerful argument that "symbolic mediation of social relationships is the central function of Elizabethan pastoral forms," the modal and social explanations are inseparable.[7] For Montrose, pastoral *form* registers social change, reinventing the split between noble and common as a distinction between noble and aspirant. I propose that the pastoral *noun* "shepherdess" similarly registers changing conceptions of gender, renegotiating women's capacity for agricultural and literary production. The English Renaissance shepherd put into his pastoral simplicity the social complexity of many roles: laborer, everyman, political theorist, priest, king, courtier, desiring subject, lover of men and women.[8] In late Elizabethan usage, "shepherdess" borrowed the central tension for male shepherds, that between vital but suppressed economic production and prestigious but coded cultural production—and this alone, even with the discounting suffix, proved both ambivalent and fleeting.[9] The term was extended into seventeenth-century pastoral conventions only once its ambitions had been reduced; the shepherdess of Caroline literature and beyond is a radical simplification of what could have been a complex representation, an enameled symbol of a contestatory process that gendered agricultural, poetic, and erotic work.

Because the ideological force of conventions is cumulative, the revision that adds the word in the 1630s, when Caroline pastoralism permeated literary and print culture, requires explanation less than its absence in the 1580s, when pastoral was formulated as a prime form of English social representation.[10] Greene could have coined "shepherdess" in 1585, and yet he was far from alone in avoiding it. Early English pastoral is full of nymphs and damsels, shepherd's daughters and wives; but shepherdesses, figures familiar in Continental literature, are introduced belatedly and cautiously. And when the "shepherdess" appears, her agricultural and poetic duties are restricted far beyond the shepherd's traditional *otium*. England's resistance to women as pastoral agents, like its intolerance of women on the stage or in print, marks a specifically national discomfort with women's voices. The choice of "shepherd" or "shepherdess" was not merely semantic, but carried ideological weight: on what terms could women acquire speaking and authorial positions in pastoral? In 1585, briefly, Greene imagined a woman pastoral character could be called a "shepherd"; within five years, the inflected label would grant relative parity (not equality) to women as performers of the literary; within fifty years, "shepherdess" would be firmly established as a speaking but non-authorial pastoral subject.[11] The pattern of early uses of the term allows both the acceptance and the limitation of women's voices to be specified by genre and period, as pastoral was shaped in the poetry, fiction, and drama of the Elizabethan, Jacobean, and Caroline eras.[12] Its introduction was compelled by the imitation of Continental pastoral prose romances, for romance needed female figures who acted and spoke, unlike pastoral poetry that left them between the lines.

Literary uses of "shepherdess" over this fifty-year period prove to be powerfully double-edged: it gave social dignity to women characters and poetic opportunity to women authors, but it insistently suppressed women's economic contributions and constrained the representation of their desire. The word "shepherdess" mediates labors of animal husbandry and fictional speech, both dangerously charged with eroticism. The shepherdess both speaks and herds, and folding together those actions redoubles the fleshiness of expression and nurture. The insertion of the shepherdess into what Stephen Guy-Bray calls the "homoerotic space" of pastoral revises both European pastoral tradition and English gender codes. As he points out the Renaissance pastoral is indeed heterosexualized by the insertion of female figures; but the partial displacement of homosocial and homoerotic energies by the female presence introduces new problems.[13] As pastoral is heterosexualized, the heterosexual is also pastoralized, dragged down to earth, as female pastoral figures reintroduce the problematic animality of desire that clung to male participants in classical pastoral. In that distinctive and slippery modal space, the erotics of labor and speech are managed by gender coding, a process marked if not exhausted in the term "shepherdess."

Thus, to affiliate with the power and prestige of the "shepherd"—even diminutive form—demanded a separation of poetic making from earthier duties and pleasures. England initially resisted the *pastoral shepherdess* of Continental traditions, hoping to keep her *animal erotics* apart from women's work in *animal husbandry*, which was itself marginalized. Eventually, women were brought into Elizabethan pastoral by splitting the *speaking shepherdess* from the *sheep-like shepherdess*. In the Stuart period, the *authorial shepherdess* fleetingly gained the pastoral privilege of encoding public issues in private experience; but in the long run, only the *pasteurized shepherdess* remained, a figurine of silencing. The *Oxford English Dictionary* gives two senses for "shepherdess": "a female shepherd, a woman or girl who tends sheep. Also *fig.* in pastoral poetry" and "A representation (in painting, etc.; esp. china or earthenware) of a shepherdess." The entry slides from gendered labor to poetic convention to porcelain representation; my own history of the shepherdess tries to recover the complexity in this simple figuration, to make visible the socioeconomic, poetic, and erotic labors enameled over by convention. This essay starts to unfold the shepherdess, as she revised the pastoral tradition, and herself demanded revision.

PASTORAL SHEPHERDESS

In the Continental languages, words for "shepherd" acquired female equivalents from an early stage—"berger/bergère," "pastor/pastora"—available, as far as I can tell, in practical as well as literary contexts.[14] The English language, not requiring gender agreement, creates less pressure for inflected nouns: grammar was no obstacle to Greene's calling Fawnia a "shepherd." Nonetheless, Greene must have seen gender-inflected forms in French pastoral works, and more significantly, he used the English "shepherdess" shortly after *Pandosto*, in works of 1589 and 1590.[15] "Shepherdess" could have occurred to him earlier: a large number of feminine nouns were coined using the -ess suffix from the fourteenth century on.[16] The question is always whether such a coinage will stick, since, as Dennis Baron puts it, "the history of the English lexicon, literary and nonliterary, clearly shows a cycle of marking, unmarking, and remarking for feminine nouns" (p. 121). That the *OED*'s examples all have pastoral overtones may be traceable to the dictionary's literary bias or may mean the word was never common parlance. The first cited use is "shepheardess" in Sir Thomas Usk's elusive allegory, the *Testament of Love*, from 1387 to 1388. The next is in Greene's semiautobiographical pamphlet, *Never Too Late*, from 1590: "Consider with your selfe faire Shepheardize, that poore men feel paine as well as Princes."[17] The next entry, from Spenser's *Astrophel* (published 1595), refers to "the gentlest shepheardesse that lives this day."

The *OED*'s sampling creates the impression that the word is ubiquitous in the Golden Age of English pastoral, but in fact, Elizabethan pastoral literature before 1590 used "shepherdess" much less than its Romance-language exemplars used its equivalent. Searching through literature databases, I found that the word "shepherdess" occurred far less than criticism on pastoral would suggest: many women in pastoral, and almost all of them before 1590, were (semi-mortal) nymphs, (nonworking) damsels, or (relational) shepherd's daughters or shepherd's wives.[18] My database search found only one Elizabethan use antedating the *OED*'s reference to Greene's *Never Too Late*, and that was another work by Greene, the insistently pastoral *Menaphon* (1589).[19] The databases, confined to canonical and printed sources, identified no other occurrence of "shepherdess," in any spelling, in any genre of English fiction, drama, or poetry, that had been printed before 1589.

The apparent omission was Sidney: but that was because his works were published after 1590. Sidney could not be credited with bringing the word into print, but he had used it before 1589. "Shepherdess" occurs once in *Astrophil and Stella* (written in 1581 and published in 1591), and several times in *New Arcadia* (printed 1593, written before 1586). Why, then, had it not appeared at all in the *Old Arcadia* (written ca. 1580)? How had Greene come up with the word before the 1593 publication of *Arcadia*?[20]

And given the close confluence of interests between Sidney and Spenser, why did Spenser not use the word in *Shepheardes Calendar* or *The Faerie Queene* (Pastorella is never called a shepherdess)? Only in "Colin Clout's Come Home Again" and "Astrophel" (both written after 1591 and published 1595), did Spenser use the word; in tribute to two shepherd courtiers, Sir Walter Raleigh and Sidney, respectively. In the high seriousness of their plan to rehabilitate pastoral as political and theological allegory, Sidney and Spenser only rarely extend the title of "shepherd" to women, even with the diminutive suffix.

The explanation for the word's dramatic emergence into print in 1589–90 was not Sidney's carefully controlled uses, then; rather the impetus to gendering the pastoral protagonist—and importantly, an impetus through romance—was Angel Day's 1587 English translation of Longus's *Daphnis and Chloe.* Day was working from Jacques Amyot's translation of Longus, the first edition of the Hellenistic romance to see print in any language.[21] Translating Amyot's "berger" and "bergère" as "shepherd" and "shepherdess," Day for the first time allowed the pastoral shepherdess to speak and publish her name in English. Day's 1587 publication date, between those of *Pandosto* and *Menaphon* makes it plausible as Greene's source for the word "shepherdess."[22]

Animal Erotics

Sidney's manuscript uses and Day's print uses may precede Greene's, but they confirm that the crucial context for the English "shepherdess" is not pastoral poetry, but Longus's pastoral prose romance: relatively late, popular, and feminine by classical standards, and deeply problematic to the Renaissance in bringing a nubile woman into the world of bucolic and animal desire. Longus's *Daphnis and Chloe* represented its goatherd and shepherdess as making love, not words: their heterosexuality challenged both the homoeroticism of the Theocritan tradition and the willed ascetism of early Elizabethan pastoral poetry. As Theocritus had contrasted the hesitancies and regrets of human lovers to the instinctive drives of their animals, Longus linked the sexual awakening of his young lovers to the reproductive activities of the animals they tended. What is metaphor in Theocritus is explicitly physical in Longus: and while interspecies penetration is satirized, close and pleasurable bodily contact between human and animal is not.

In Day's translation, the "shepherdess" is constantly linked with sheep and other animals in a language of sexual or oral desire. Longus's heroine Chloe was an exposed child, found and rescued because Dryas's ewe "visited it many times with her teats, as if it had bin the proper Nurce" (p. 9). After Dryas and his wife, Nape, adopt the child, Nape and the sheep are figured as maternal rivals: Nape "feared lest the sheepe that whilome suckd the swatheled impe, should in the beastly regard it shewed be preferred before her." So that the girl "might the sooner be taken and reputed for hers"—that is, a shepherd's wife's child—"she gave it thence-from a name Pastorall, and called her Chloe," and naturally the girl becomes "a simple sheepeheardesse" (p. 11). Similarly, Daphnis, found being nursed by a she-goat, grows to be a goatherd. That Daphnis's rival is a cowherd suggests a whole scale of human rank by analogy with the rank of domestic beasts, much as Nape's fears imply rivalry between animal and human attentions. Once in love, Daphnis drops his "husband-like desire, by hardned labours, to see his cattel prosper" and dedicates himself to "heedefull attendance of blisfull Chloe, and her most daintie passages" (p. 19). Later, the gourmand Gnathon asks Daphnis to offer himself to be mounted, offering the behavior of goats as a model. Daphnis and Chloe delight in erotic pleasures that forestall only the genital: breathing into a pipe one after another, drinking from the same vessel, kissing, bathing, sleeping side by side. Their love is secret, oral, physical, animal.

Daphnis and Chloe, with its knowing innocence, its insistence on the mutuality of erotic experience, and its willingness to liken human and animal eroticism, was both troubling and compelling to English Renaissance writers. It represented the underbelly, so to speak, of pastoral, the grotesque body that threatens yet enlivens the classicizing figures of the early modern versions of pastoral.[23] The labor of the shepherdess was potentially *too* erotic, too intimately associated with the most animal elements in Longus. In English, the -ess suffix generally turns real work into an imitative and compliant gesture: poet*ess*, actr*ess*, host*ess*. In this case, this erotic force of the suffix was actually threatening, for it suggested biological *reproduction* as a shared concern of sexual desire and animal husbandry, and thus replaced the bodily desires of the homoerotic shepherd with the breeding potential of the heterosexual shepherdess. The shepherd was a maker, a poet, but he could not be involved in the sort of making that nonpoetic shepherdesses shared with sheep: the physical act of reproduction. A littering shepherdess would threaten the lettered shepherd.

The pressure of these animal associations is evident in early uses of the word, and also when it is conspicuously avoided. Spenser's Pastorella (*Fairie Queene*, Book VI, published 1596) is not called a shepherdess, but "a faire damzell" whose greene dress "her owne hands had dyde." Sir Calidore adopts "shepheards weed" and "hooke" to help guard her sheep:

> and every evening helping them to fold:
> And otherwhiles, for need, he did assay
> In his strong hand their rugged teats to hold,
> And out of them to presse the milke: love so much could. (canto 9, stanza 37)

Sir Calidore's love–service includes the physical labor of husbandry, allegorically dignified; but the mistress who needs his assistance is not called a shepherdess.

That "shepherdess" entered English usage forcibly after 1587; that Elizabethan resistance to it was erotic at base—these claims are confirmed in that central pastoral space, the cult of Elizabeth herself. Elizabeth's courtiers were much happier to call themselves "shepherds" than to call the queen "shepherdess." Peele called her "our great Shepherdesse" in his 1589 "Eclogue Gratulatorie" to the "Shepheard of Albions Arcadia: Robert Earl of Essex and Ewe."[24] Elizabeth apparently refused that dubious honorific. The queen rhetorically known as prince, supreme negotiator of gender-inflected titles, is never recorded calling herself "shepherdess." The word perhaps was tainted with excess sexuality, or perhaps excessively discounted women's labor. Montrose notes Elizabeth's poignant references to female agricultural workers: sequestered in the 1550s, she was said to envy " a certaine milkmaid singing pleasantlie"; in 1567, pondering the execution of her half-sister, she insisted the two could not coexist blithely like "two milkmaids with pails upon our arms"; in 1576 she told Parliament she was less available for marriage than "a milkmaid with a pail on my arm."[25] Elizabeth's phrase, characteristically plain and characteristically recycled, tropes the rural rather than the pastoral: milkmaids carry physical loads much lighter than queens' political burdens. But the pail, as much as the singing, euphemizes the animal parts also held in a milkmaid's arms.

This forbidden animal eroticism rears its head in courtier verse written by Spenser and Raleigh around 1591–92. Spenser had paid homage to Raleigh's cultivated pose as "shepherd of the sea" in "Colin Clout's Come Home Again" (written 1591, published 1595), praising Elizabeth as "that great shepherdess" who fed her "flocks and sheep" on the "bosom of the billows." By 1592, Raleigh was, like Peele, a rejected courtier; his bitter, fragmentary, and unpublished *Ocean, to Cynthia* claims that he suffers Elizabeth's rejection much as "the gentle lamb, though lately weaned, / Plays with the dug, though finds no comfort there."[26] Here the charge of animality damns Elizabeth as bad shepherd and bad mother.

Continental literature had proliferated shepherdess figures with little worry about animal eroticism, perhaps because Longus remained virtually unknown until Amyot appeared in 1559. In most Continental languages, shepherdesses enjoyed a name of their own, and roles in medieval and early Renaissance literature. Medieval *pastourelle* involved a "pastora" and a knight, though both used courtly language.[27] Petrarch figured his Laura as a rough mountain shepherdess in the 52nd of the *Canzone* of 1499—a sonnet the English didn't translate. The real boom came with Montemayor's 1530 *Diana*, a pastoral in verse and prose whose central subjectivities were lovelorn shepherdesses, from the titular character to a host of other. Montemayor made the shepherdess requisite in pastoral fiction—but his shepherdesses were no more working women than Laura had been. Longus may have released new animal anxieties, not least because its lovers were "real" rustics unconstrained by courtly codes. Those anxieties about hetero-sexualized pastoral faced Sidney when he took upon himself the introduction of pastoral tradition into English. Sidney worked deliberately to suppress the newly rediscovered frankness of Longus, to circumvent the complex sexualities of Theocritus, and to re-masculinize the example of Montemayor. His isolated uses of "shepherdess" follow the examples of Petrarch in *Astrophil and Stella*, and Montemayor and Amyot's Longus in *New Arcadia*, while markedly curtailing the agency of those female pastoral figures.

ANIMAL HUSBANDRY

The resistance to literary representation of women herders is only indirectly related to the material involvement of Englishwomen in animal husbandry; these erotic anxieties interfere with deeply entrenched pastoral strategies for the euphemization of labor.[28] Still, the eventual barring of the shepherdess from pastoral labor matched the sexual division of labor that increasingly barred women from outdoor farm labor.[29] Gradually, women's agricultural work was pastoralized in literature, purified of its earthier elements and perhaps of its agency. But women's work in animal husbandry had been marginal, economically and linguistically, long before pastoral vocabulary conspired with agricultural change to make women's proper place in the landscape decorative. If the contributions of women herders had been valued, the word "shepherdess" might have been commonplace earlier.

The relative invisibility of sheep-herding work makes it difficult to measure agricultural practice against poetic representation for men, much less for women. Enclosure was changing the day-to-day life of male shepherds, and may have reduced women's opportunities for herding sheep. As long as a community had a commons, a shepherd could drive the sheep there in the morning, and in the evening pen them in a cote or less permanent fold on private ground. Land enclosed into pasture or used for up-and-down agriculture (the alternation of crop growing and pasturing)—still required a shepherd to move (presumably larger) flocks across the pasturage and into portable folds at night. Enclosure made for more fulltime shepherding work, but made more shepherds "mercenary" (a usage also debuted by Greene's pastoral romances), so that fewer owned their own flocks as the pastoral tradition demanded.[30]

For women, ownership of the flock would have been exceptional at any era, and even hired herding became unlikely with larger flocks. Social historians have found few records of women herding sheep full-time. Women laborers sheared sheep in season (earning 60–80 percent of the wages of a male shearer), and young women in service might feed animals, but few spent their days at pasture.[31] Problematically, both primary and secondary sources assume a sexual division of labor falling between cows and sheep. Ann Kussmaul explains that the position of shepherd is man's work—and not always a servant in husbandry, but sometimes an adult, married laborer or husbandman—because the shepherd of a large flock bore a large financial responsibility and needed arcane knowledge gained from experience.[32] Certainly the work demanded a long-term absence from the domicile; toting heavy equipment long distances, and living in messy physical contact with animals, particularly during lambing. Paradoxically, the shepherd performed nigh-maternal duties at this time. Barnabe Googe (in a manual, not an eclogue) explained that when ewes dropped their lambs, the shepherd must be "gentle as a midwife."[33] Gervase Markham, in *Cheape and Good Husbandry*, explained that a sick lamb might need ewe's milk to be fed by hand.[34] Men manipulated folds and flocks and animals' living bodies. Meanwhile, husbandry manuals reserved women's involvement to manipulating milk, mutton, and fleece (except at sheep-shearing). Gervase Markham's *English House-wife*, for instance, begins its section on cloth production at the point when the husband brings home the fleece.[35]

On a small scale and close to home, very young women might keep sheep. Henry Best, a Yorkshire gentleman-yeoman who kept a midsized commercial flock, running to around three hundred animals in 1640–42, kept a manuscript "Farming Book." He paid his head shepherd to fold the flock on uplands in summer. But in April, when young lambs and ewes needed to be kept closer to cover, Best wrote that he usually hired a "boy or girle to tende them a dayes" close to home. In 1642, the latter job went to a boy—the eleven-year-old son of his head shepherd, paid three halfpence a day.[36] Best also commented that townspeople sent their own small flocks out with "boyes and girles to keepe them aboute the . . . Town-side and Lanes."[37] At least in Yorkshire, then, young girls helped with tending as did the ten-year-old Fawnia—but this is far from the freedom of Chloe.

Women like Best's townspeople or rural smallholders might keep a few sheep as part of their households. One implication of such small-scale husbandry by women, Alice Clark famously argued in her 1919 *Working Life of Women in the Seventeenth Century*, was that women were disproportionately harmed by the movement to enclosure.[38] But sheep were relatively rare among such household animals. Clark mentions women keeping "sheep and pigs"; an Elizabethan stepdaughter complains of being asked to feed "cattel, swyne and sheep" like a mere servant—perhaps in midwinter, when sheep were kept under cover.[39] The 1581 *Booke of Christian Prayer* ("Queen Elizabeth's Prayerbook") includes in its Dance-of-death borders a depiction of Death herding a sprightly "Shepeheardes wife." The motto: "Be thou young or olde: Thou must enter into my folde." The wife carries a sheep-tickling staff for driving her charges into their "fold"; but significantly, she is not called a shepherdess—and the verse figures her as the sheep. Moving a little later, a 1658 almanac by Sarah Jinner puts folding, breeding, selling, and feeding a few sheep among the tasks of "a country-housewifes year."[40]

In sum, early modern English women did keep sheep, but the word "shepherdess" is not a fulltime job description. The circumstances in which women kept sheep illustrate the liminality that Clark attributes to women's agricultural work, falling between domestic production and the market economy, in neither a private nor public sphere. The sheep moved from cote to pasture or common; they yielded wool, milk, and meat for the household, and perhaps wool, milk, meat, and offspring for the market. The work of sheep-keeping was conducted by women and under conditions that varied with the seasons, regions, and size of holdings; and by women of various lifecycle groups, including those too young for field work. The work might be solitary or collective, might take women to their sheepcotes, their town-lanes, to a common field, or to market. The practice slowly faded with enclosure, but the male contemporaries who ignored the practice certainly did not bemoan its loss.[41] Economically, women's sheep-keeping was invisible, falling between emergent representations of animal husbandry as men's work and housework as women's; but in everyday rural life, women with sheep could have been common sights.

Greene's *Pandosto* took female agricultural work relatively seriously. Greene's Fawnia delights in her labors but does not deny them: "our toil is in shifting the folds and looking to the lambs: easy labours" (p. 184). Her work requires cooperation: Fawnia asks a female companion to join her in going "home by the flock to see if they were well folded" (p. 179). Her work is constant and engrossing: Fawnia, "seeing that the night drew on, shifted her folds and busied herself about other work to drive away such fond fancies as began to trouble her brain" (p. 185). Greene is anxious, clearly, to establish that "folding" is the main task in the job description, even if he's vague about what it means.[42] Googe describes folds more vividly: the shepherd must carry "hardelles" (hurdles) and nets to construct folds as needed.[43] Fawnia is not herding sheep on enclosed land, it seems, since she must drive her sheep "home" at night, but she still must be prepared to move these pieces of farm equipment around: shifting folds is harder than it sounds. (Even vague references to "shifting folds" evince more awareness of substantive agricultural work than later pastoral descriptions of "tending flocks.") When Greene's Fawnia becomes Shakespeare's Perdita, she manages the proceeds of her adoptive father's flock (one thousand five hundred sheep, by the Clown's math) but never folds it. Yet at the sheep-shearing feast, where Fawnia does not do herding work or hostess work but does speak pastoral, Polixenes addressed her as "shepherdess." The embrace of animal duties and physical desires is subsumed in her desire to hold Florizel "quick and in my arms."[44]

That "shepherdess" became a fantasy vocation is confirmed by the gentle-born Dorothy Osborne, writing in 1653 from her father's estate in Bedfordshire:

> about sixe or seven a Clock, I walke out into a Common that lyes hard by the house where a great many young wenches keep Sheep and Cow's and sitt in the shade singing of Ballads; I goe to them and compare their voyces and Beauty's to some Ancient Sheperdesses that I have read of and finde a vaste difference there, but trust mee I think these are as innocent as those could be, I talk to them, and finde they want nothing to make them the happiest People in the world, but the knoledge that they are soe; most Comonly when wee are in the middest of our discourse one looks aboute her and spyes her Cow's goeing into the Corne and then away they all run.[45]

Osborne's anecdote confirms that women kept sheep intermixed with cows on community-owned property. The presence of sheep allows her to compare rural practices to the conventions of her beloved pastoral romances. Even through her patronizing romanticization of poverty, she registers the gap between reality and fiction, between "young wenches" and dignified "Shepherdesses." Their work in sheep-keeping lets them consort with their peers in a space outside the household: they are public, visible, accessible to "discourse" with a passerby. Only in that discursive sense do they attain the label of "shepherdess"—for a half-ironic moment.

Courtly Shepherdess and Sheep-Like Shepherdess

Given England's belated exposure to pastoral romance, and its inattention to women's agricultural work, it is not surprising that Elizabethan literature failed to place the shepherdess in every context where Continental literature would have cried out for her. Sidney and Spenser, the shapers of Elizabethan pastoral, innovated in rare mentions of "shepherdess" that lent authority to women, but Sidney also created shepherdess grotesques, using class lines to distance the shepherdess from the prestige of the shepherd. Sidney's uses of the word reveal that the weight of this word lay in its associations with the act of poetic making, and that its introduction was motivated by the need to account for (and perhaps discount) the presence of women in the circle of literary production. The complex associations of "shepherdess" and "fold" sketch out a subtextual debate over gendered poetic voice, through the incremental introduction of "shepherdess" through *Astrophil and Stella*, the *Old Arcadia*, and the *New Arcadia*. Following Petrarch, Sidney describes Stella as a shepherdess in the ninth song of *Astrophil and Stella*,"Go, my flocke, go get you hence." Stanza 4 praises and blames

> *Stella* fiercest shepherdesse,
> Fiercest but yet fairest ever;
> *Stella* whom O heavens do blesse,
> Tho against me shee persever,
> Tho I blisse enherit never.

As a shepherdess whose "fiercest" word has repercussions that precede her fairness, Stella comes close to being a speaking subject rather than a desired object—except that her words are not reported. The shepherdess here is not the full equal of the shepherd as *poet*, but she is certainly the poet's equal or superior in status and authority. In fact, her fierceness makes her lion to Astrophil's lamb. Astrophil claims that his love for her exceeds the maternal love of even the ewe, in a characteristic transposition of female reproductive power onto a bumbling version of Sidney himself:

> *Stella* hath refused me,
> *Stella* who more love hath proved,
> In this caitife hart to be,
> Then can in good eawes be moved
> Toward Lamkins best beloved.

He concludes the song by asking his abandoned flock to speak for him:

> But alas, if in your straying
> Heavenly *Stella* meete with you,
> Tell her in your piteous blaying,
> Her poore slave's unjust decaying.

The scenario is ridiculous, but the ridicule is transferred away from Stella, maintaining her power as, remarkably, "fierce" if unvoiced. The pattern of protecting the shepherdess heroine by deflecting the animal indignities onto another would be echoed—though none but Sidney dared to take them upon himself. It is characteristic of the latter career of the shepherdess that the 1674 edition of Sidney's works reports the song blithely as "*Stella* fairest shepherdess, / Fairest, but yet cruelest ever," flattening this first appearance of the courtly shepherdess.

The opening of the *Old Arcadia* describes Arcadia as a land where the "very shepherds themselves had their fancies opened to so high conceits," a claim quickly ironized.[46] Dametas is mocked for his expertise in "husbandry matters (as a dog sure, if he could speak, had wit enough to describe his kennel)" (p. 28), and Pamela, "whose noble heart had long disdained to find the trust of her virtue reposed in the hands of a shepherd," has only reluctantly "taken on a shepherdish apparel, which was of russet velvet, cut after their fashion" (p. 33). The costume of shepherdry is appealing only insofar as a "noble heart" can scorn it. There is no "shepherdess" in *Old Arcadia*.

The first instance of "shepherdess" in *New Arcadia* is a markedly noncommittal gesture toward Montemayor. Early in Book 1, Arcadia is described: "here a shepherd's boy piping as though he should never be old; there a shepherdess knitting and withal singing, and it seemed that her voice comforted her hands to work and her hands kept time to her voice's music."[47] The shepherdess and the shepherd's boy are analogues; both are doing work that dissolves boundaries between work and play. The shepherdess has a voice, but uses it to accompany the female duty of cloth production, while the shepherd's boy has a pipe. Is she even a shepherdess, or is she a shepherd's wife, using "ye lockes of the shepe therwith to make clothes"? (Clark, p. 49).

Split off from this innocuous and anonymous landscape figure are references that invoke the pastoral erotics of Longus without using the loaded term "shepherdess." When Musidorus adopts the shepherd disguise of Dorus, he reports Mopsa's "throwing a great number of sheep's eyes upon me" (p. 225). His song addressed to Mopsa but for Pamela lets him manipulate the erotic while avoiding its animal associations:

> My sheep are thoughts, which I both guide and serve,
> Their pasture is fair hills of fruitless love:...
> My sheep-hook is wan hope, which all upholds:
> My weeds, desire, cut out in endless folds. (p. 232)

In this context, to grant the title of shepherdess to Mopsa would rob Dorus of his claimed superiority to her; she must be something lower, a farmer's daughter who slobbers like an animal and makes sheep's eyes; a sheep and not a shepherdess. The nervousness about the Elizabethan shepherdess affects Sidney's revision of this passage: *New Arcadia* adds a lead-in, not in *Old Arcadia*, which explains his motivation: "to show what kind of shepherd I was, I took up my harp and sung these verses" (p. 232). Sidney makes it clear, indeed shows Dorus making it clear, that he's a literary, not "real," shepherd—if real shepherds and shepherdesses are as animal as Dametas and Mopsa.[48]

Both the *OED* and The English Poetry Database reported that Spenser had used the word "shepherdess" in his late elegy on Sidney, "Astrophel," published 1595. But in fact the usage tests the boundaries of authorship. It occurs in the last lines of Spenser's section of "Astrophel," and introduces the remaining section, "The Doleful Lay of Clorinda," as authored by Mary Sidney, countess of Pembroke.

> But first his sister that Clorinda hight,
> The gentlest sheapheardesse that liues this day:
> And most resembling both in shape and spright
> Her brother deare, began this dolefull lay.
> Which least I marre the sweetnesse of the vearse,
> In sort as she it sung, I will rehearse.

Although this final stanza is necessary to the numerological effect of Spenser's poem it is frequently omitted from anthologies, together with the lay itself.[49] Addressing the question of composition date, the recent editors of Mary Sidney's works link the lay to a manuscript "passion," or elegy, that Mary Sidney mentioned in a letter, ca. 1594. But the letter does not indicate anything about the history of its composition or publication.[50] The editors argue that the inclusion of Mary Sidney's lay within "Astrophel," itself combined with elegies by other authors, constitutes a form of "collaborative work," but that the graphic presentation of the transition presents her poetic work as singular: "Except that the 'Lay' is not given a separate title, it is difficult to imagine what else the printer could have done to set off 'The Doleful Lay' from 'Astrophel' while retaining them in the same volume."[51] But her name is not published, and the extent of her involvement in this publication is unknowable. The word "shepherdess" thus encodes the ambiguous status of the woman poet within the coterie figured as pastoral community. Here is a female shepherdess who shares all of her brother's pastoral work—patronage, spiritual guidance, the maintenance of an estate, the furnishing of moral example, and above all the production of skilled pastoral poetry. But she is a shepherdess whose only love is directed to her brother, a shepherdess with only sororal desires to unfold. And the lines that grant the title of "shepherdess" are not penned by her, do not necessarily reflect her will, and substitute for a more direct identification of her name.

The "Doleful Lay" concludes: "shepheards pride was he, / Shepheards hope never againe to see": within the poem, speaking collectively of their community, the shepherdess is subsumed among the shepherds.

Pasteurized Shepherdess

The shepherdess's act of "folding" emerges, along with "shepherdess" itself, as an important secondary mark of her absorption into English pastoral convention, a word that identifies the physical desire implied in both agricultural and literary work. The pun, not directly available in Romance languages, pays lip service to the materiality of labor, and brushes suggestively against the questions of physical embrace. Henceforward, then, I call attention to both words. The changes in "shepherdess" can be measured in Shakespeare's *As You Like It* and *Winter's Tale* (ca. 1599 and 1611, but not published until 1623), confirming a consolidation of the term during the Jacobean period. But difficulties remain. Lodge's *Rosalynde* (1590) repeats the splitting strategy of Sidney's ninth song: the shepherdess can be appropriated with full erotic power only if more laboring and animalistic connotations are displaced onto lower-class figures. Aliena decides to "become a shepherdess, meaning to live low." Corydon, another mercenary shepherd, suggesting she buy the farm and flock of his employer, himself a lovesick shepherd. Aliena is delighted:

> Send for thy landslord and I will buy thy farm and thy flocks, and thou shalt still, under me, be overseer of them both. Only for pleasure sake, I and my page will serve you, lead the flocks to the field, and fold them. Thus will I live quiet, unknown, and contented.[52]

The simultaneous insistence on both serving and overseeing is typical of the class confusion that will continue to haunt the shepherdess; Marie Antoinette will similarly try to have her cake and eat it too. But sedimented in this action of folding is a promise of events to unfold, of solitude to be broken, of embraces to be made once melancholic lovers unfold their arms.

Shakespeare's *As You Like It* follows Lodge closely in his pastoral usage. There are multiple references to the erotic cruelty of Phoebe—"Shepherdess, look on him better / And be not proud" (3.5.77–78). Ganymede's line to Phoebe, "What, shepherdess, so fair and so cruel? (p. 193) strikingly echoes the Petrarchan paradox of the ninth song, but now the edge of social differentiation, mockingly turned in Sidney against Astrophil, accuses the minor shepherdess of cruelty and thus lack of gentility. Even more insulting is Ganymede's references to Phoebe's ugliness, and there is another level of displacement with the sluttishness of Audrey, who is identified with her lusty goats (but never called a herdress). Aliena never calls herself a shepherdess, but Ganymede's single reference to "the shepherdess, my sister" interestingly describes the two as hanging "in the skirts of the forest, like a fringe upon a petticoat" (3.3.321). Because Ganymede is a page rather than a shepherd, "shepherdess" is not required to discursively support the friends' performance of gender difference. Instead, the word "shepherdess" is associated with the erotic power of costume. Where Shakespeare notably diverges from Lodge is in his omission of the word "fold." Aliena's plans are much less specific, much less realistic in their conventions, in Shakespeare than in Lodge: she will simply buy the "cottage, pasture, and the flock" (2.4.92).

What disappears from this play is the act of folding. It's something of a surprise, considering the importance of pairing off and secret-keeping and text-making in this play, that Shakespeare avoids the word. But when I review all of his uses of the word, I am struck by just how erotically charged it is for him, and how elite. "The fold stands empty" in *MND*, but elsewhere we have "the lord of folded arms" (*LLL*) and Hamlet's false death warrant, *Troilus*'s "unloose his amorous fold," and, most suggestively of all, the climactic lines of *The Rape of Lucrece*:

> The wolf hath seized his prey, the poor lamb cries,
> Till with her own white fleece her voice controlled
> Entombs her outcry in her lips' sweet fold. (lines 677–79).

The fold that is delicately erotic on the romance page becomes, onstage, oral, genital, violent, secretive yet shameful, courtly, private, and relentlessly heterogenital. The word Shakespeare grants to his pastoral heroines is "flock," a word that suggests indistinguishability, the pleasures of merging into a group, perhaps mindlessly homoerotic as in the Roman plays' references to mobs as the "flock," or perhaps sexlessly aesthetic as in Camillo's remark to the "shepherdess" Fawnia: "I should leave grazing were I of your flock, / And only live by gazing" (4.4.108–09).

The first literary author for whom shepherdess becomes a truly key word is not Sidney, Spenser, Greene, Lodge, or Shakespeare, but undoubtedly Lady Mary Wroth. The most striking instance is the first song of *Pamphilia to Amphilanthus* (1621). Deliberately reversing her father's (unpublished) lines "Thus sayd a shepheard, once / With weights of change opprest" (song 3, 63–64), Wroth gives the speaking voice of this pastoral song to a woman: "A shepheardess thus sayd / Who was with griefe oprest."[53] The shepherdess thus becomes a speaking subject with all the claims of pastoral authority. She is in a pastoral landscape, and wears garlands and willow, but poetry and grieving, not husbandry, are her labors. A similar strategy appears in *The Countess of Montgomeries Urania* (also 1621). Picking up on a late reference in *Arcadia* to "Urania, fairest shepherdesse" (possibly by Sidney, but that late in the posthumous volume, possibly collaborative), Wroth begins her romance with a pastoral description of Urania, clearly identified as a shepherdess—and also, like Aliena and Fawnia, immediately identified as no shepherdess by birth.[54] Such figures reappear in several of the major plots of the book, and suggest that Wroth finds a special freedom in granting the title of shepherdess to highborn female characters. In this role, they are able to write poetry and to experience desire, a word that appears often in conjunction with shepherdess figures. They are fully kitted out with "Hooke and Scrip" (p. 638), hat, garland, and elegant dress in gray or russet. They have well-behaved sheep who play nearby. They don't fold or worry about their flocks. They are contrasted, as a group, to titled queens with larger responsibilities; to "nymphs" who have foresworn love; and to "ladies" who often prove morally faulty. The shepherdess is a strong figure, pure but not sexless.

Strikingly, however, these shepherdess figures seem to come in pairs (or paired with ladies) like the *Winter's Tale*'s "twinn'd lambs," so that their expressions of desire are voiced in homoerotic pairs. Thus a lady and a shepherdess gaze at one another across the water that divides them, while "love had in their hearts a desire of meeting" (p. 639). They locate a bridge, accept the assistance of the prince in crossing it, and "then did the two (lover-like) women kisse" (p. 639), a situation complicated quickly as the two friends and their male lovers find themselves "in their crosse embracements a truelovers knot" (p. 643). Who needs animals?

The failure of Wroth's shepherdesses to "fold" is a failure to do manual work, but it is not a rejection of embodied desire. In the second book, one character reflects on the time when "pale wan lipps won kisses, where dispaire made hope, and death affection: but from these sprung my desires, which lie as deadly wrapt up now in folds of losse, no expectation of any good." The lines explicitly rewrite Sidney's: desires that once joined lips are now wrapped up in "folds of loss," an inscrutable figure for an unfilled orifice. These lips are as erotic as anything in Longus; the model for that eroticism is not Sidney, although it could be Shakespeare. An unnamed shepherd who loves the shepherdess Melantha, companion to the shepherdess Veralinda, tells the latter's lover Leonius that Melantha "takes my Songs, and sings them, happy lines that ever gaind such blisse, to kisse those sweet lippes passing into ayre, as scorning other place then her breast, when she will expose them unto eares should harbour them" (p. 426). Leonius, inspired by this, borrows a female disguise from the unnamed shepherd, and finds herself able to offer Veralinda "better than any of her fellows kisses, for this seemd more passionatly kind" (p. 435). Even before the revelation that "Leonia" is a male forestalls the same-sex possibilities, a state of confusion erupts within the sign. Leonia the nymph and Veralinda the "shepherdes" move to a fountain,

> the Nimph setting herself so, as she might both see and touch the loved Shepherdes, all the rest beholding this stranger with as much admiration, as shee did their Mistris, thinking no difference betweene them in beauty, save that the new guests fairenesse seemed more masculine... Thus they beheld each other, the Sheapherdes passionately beholding Leonia in memory of her love, and the Nimph amorously gazing on her. (p. 436)

But "Sheapherdes" is Roberts's record of a marginal correction made by Wroth in the Newberry Library copy; the word was printed "Shepheards" in

1621. Lost in the mirroring of mutual admiration and onlookers, or perhaps reluctant to admire the homoerotic, the compositor had recorded a masculine plural form denoting, perhaps, the onlookers. Wroth's correction, peculiar by modern spelling standards, insists that the person gazing on Leonia "in memory of her love, is not a plural masculine audience, but the loving shepherdess herself. It insists, in other words, that Veralinda is a desiring subject. Although Wroth has won this shepherdess's subjectivity, like her own, by suppressing the labor of pastoral's working counterparts, and the animality of their classical precedents, the intimacy and tangibility of her metaphor suggest how much eroticism can be enfolded in the name of shepherdess.

NOTES

1. The first extant edition of 1588 (STC 12285) is the base text used by Paul Salzman in his *Anthology of Elizabethan Prose Fiction* (Oxford and New York: Oxford University Press, 1987); see Salzman, p. xxvii, for evidence of a lost 1585 edition. Further references to the 1588 text cite Salzman parenthetically.
2. The 1632 edition's mixed forms seem to link the choice between "shepherd" and "shepherdess" to subject-position as well as genre. Fawnia, identifying herself as a working shepherd, tells Dorastus that being a shepherd is more than adopting apparel: as she says, it's a question of birth, and as the narrator shows, it's a question of doing work with "painful labour." For Dorastus, a royal heir, her being a shepherdess can be overcome with a change of costume, scene, and name. "Shepherd" is a line of work; "shepherdess" is a field of play. As I will show, the prince's view overestimates the ease of donning this label.
3. Chapbook adaptations of *Pandosto* appeared as *The Royal Shepherdess* in 1796 and ca. 1800–20. See Lori Humphrey Newcomb, *Reading Popular Romance in Early Modern England* (New York: Columbia University Press, 2002), pp. 173, 182, 198–200.
4. Perhaps coincidentally, the title changes in editions of 1635 and beyond, from the 1588 title *Pandosto. The Triumph of Time* to *The Pleasant Historie of Dorastus and Fawnia*, previously the running title. The new title shifts the plot emphasis from father to daughter and her lover, in effect making the romance a love story. The choice may have been made by Francis Faulk(e)ner, who published the editions of 1629, 1632, 1635, and 1636; or the compositors might have used copy without a title page.
5. The compositors would have been male. Intriguingly, the 1636 edition was the first of Faulk(e)ner's editions printed in the shop of Elizabeth Purslowe. The fact that she signed her name with an X makes it unlikely that she edited the romance, although she could have read it.
6. For the most powerful recent account of pastoral as a mode that "puts the complex into the simple," see Paul Alpers, *What is Pastoral?* (Chicago and London: University of Chicago Press, 1996).
7. Louis Montrose, " 'Of Gentlemen and Shepherds': The Politics of Elizabethan Pastoral Form," *ELH* 50 (1983): 415–59. Further references cited as Montrose, "Gentlemen."
8. See Montrose, "Gentlemen"; and, among others, Robert Lane, *"Shepheards Devises"* (Athens: University of Georgia Press, 1993); Anthony Low, *The Georgic Revolution* (Princeton: Princeton University Press, 1985);

Annabel Patterson, *Pastoral and Ideology* (Oxford: Clarendon Press, 1988); James Grantham Turner, *The Politics of Landscape* (Cambridge: Harvard University Press, 1979); and Bruce R. Smith, *Homosexual Desire in Shakespeare's England* (Chicago and London: University of Chicago Press, 1991), esp. "The Passionate Shepherd," pp. 79–115.

9. Wendy Wall points to the "shared nature of the tasks of writing and farming," each of which "bespeaks the Ur-principle of generation," in "Renaissance National Husbandry: Gervase Markham and the Publication of England," *Sixteenth Century Journal* 27.3 (1996): 779.
10. On Caroline pastoralism, see Annabel Patterson, *Censorship and Interpretation* (Madison: University of Wisconsin Press, 1984), and Lois Potter, *Secret Rites and Secret Writing: Royalist Literature 1641–60* (Cambridge: Cambridge University Press, 1989).
11. To focus the question on the word "shepherdess" is not, of course, to tell the whole story of woman in English pastoral, a story that needs to be traced in full: women can and did appear as objects, subjects, or speaking subjects whether or not so named, and the word in itself gives mixed signals about agency. But its appearance is an earmark, so to speak, of pastoral convention taking a shape in which women's presence is essential but troubling.
12. For other ideological readings of semantic change in the period, see Ilona Bell, *Elizabethan Women and the Poetry of Courtship* (Cambridge: Cambridge University Press, 1998); Catherine Bates, *The Rhetoric of Courtship in Elizabethan Language and Literature* (Cambridge: Cambridge University Press, 1992); and Andrew McRae, *God Speed the Plough* (Cambridge: Cambridge University Press, 1996).
13. Stephen Guy-Bray, *Homoerotic Space: The Poetics of Loss in Renaissance Literature* (Toronto: University of Toronto Press, 2002), p. 147.
14. In the Greek of Longus's *Daphnis and Chloe*, the first European work to feature a woman who both speaks and herds, the same word is used for both lovers, but inflected as feminine when describing Chloe.
15. All biographers of Greene agree that he could read French and relied on French translations of classical works when an English one was not available.
16. Dennis Baron, *Grammar and Gender*, p. 120.
17. The *OED* cites Grosart's *Works*, vol. 8, p. 216. The print edition of *OED* sniffs that this spelling is "*erron.*"
18. I typed "shepherdess" into the Chadwyck-Healey databases—Early English Prose Fiction, English Poetry, English Verse—and analyzed the context of each usage. The word's variant spellings confirm its novelty: *Never Too Late*'s "shepheardize"; the "shephearddesses" of the *Winter's Tale* stage directions; and Wroth's "shepherdes," a feminine singular noun.
19. "Shepherdess" in *Menaphon* is clearly honorific: "Samela," the heroine, is alternately called a "nymph" or the "new-come shepherdess" or "gentle shepherdess"; unlike ordinary "country maids," she is articulate and high born.
20. Thomas Lodge, who said "shepherdess" in his 1590 *Rosalynde*, saw *Arcadia* in manuscript; that Greene did too is less likely. See Newcomb, *Reading*, p. 63; Woudhuysen, *Sir Philip Sidney and the Circulation of Manuscripts, 1558–1640* (Oxford: Clarendon Press, 1996), pp. 302–03.
21. See Richard F. Hardin, *Love in a Green Shade: Idyllic Romances Ancient to Modern* (Lincoln and London: University of Nebraska Press, 2000), p. 26.

The first Greek edition was published in 1598, the first Greek/Latin parallel texts in 1601 and 1605 (Hardin, p. 43).

22. Day interpolates into Amyot's Longus a tilt like those in Sidney's romance; the homage could mean that Sidney, knowing Amyot, encouraged this translation, but he is not a dedicatee. See Roy Strong, *The Cult of Elizabeth* (1977; rpt., London: Pimlico, 1999), p. 151.
23. Introducing his *English Pastoral Poetry* (1952; New York: W. W. Norton & Co., 1972), Frank Kermode noted that pastoral poetry is often aware that "the natural life in fact [is] rather an *animal affair*" (p. 17, emphasis added).
24. Montrose, " 'Eliza, Queene of shepheardes,' and the Pastoral of Power." *English Literary Renaissance* 10:2 (1980): 158.
25. Montrose, " 'Eliza, Queene of shepheardes,' and the Pastoral of Power," *English Literary Renaissance* 10 (1980): 155 (quoting Holinshed), pp. 156, 157 (quoting Elizabeth).
26. Ralegh, *Selected Writings* (1984; rpt., Harmondsworth, Eng.: Penguin, 1986), p. 38. The poem more explicitly charges that he has been denied the "milk" of "Affection from the parent's breast that bare me," p. 44.
27. In some 18% of pastourelles from the North of France (though not in the originary Occitane), the shepherdess is raped. See Kathryn Gravdal, *Ravishing Maidens: Writing Rape in Medieval French Literature and Law* (Philadelphia: University of Pennsylvania Press, 1991) for this pattern and controversial claims about it.
28. On which see Montrose, "Gentlemen"; Raymond Williams, *The Country and the City* (New York: Oxford University Press, 1973).
29. The first parallel has long been noted and investigated by Turner, Low, and Patterson (not to mention the poets themselves); the latter has not. Also see *Culture and Cultivation in Early Modern England: Writing and the Land*, ed. Michael Leslie and Timothy Raylor (London: Leicester University Press, 1992).
30. Both Sidney's *New Arcadia* and John Fletcher's *The Faithful Shepherdess* (written before 1611; acted at court in 1633) insist that their pastoral shepherds own their flocks.
31. See Michael Roberts, "Sickles and scythes: women's work and men's work at harvest time," *History Workshop Journal* 7 (1979): 3–28.
32. Ann Kussmaul, *Servants in Husbandry in Early Modern England* (Cambridge: Cambridge University Press, 1981).
33. Googe, translation of Heresbach's *Foure Bookes of Husbandry* (1577, 1586).
34. [Gervase Markham], *Cheape and Good Husbandry*. London: Bernard Alsop for John Harrison, 1649, p. 117.
35. G[ervase] M[arkham], *The English House-wife*. London: B. Alsop for J. Harison, 1648, p. 167.
36. *The Farming and Memorandum Books of Henry Best of Elmswell, 1642*, ed. Donald Woodward (London: Oxford University Press, 1984), p. 86. Best mentions no adult women at sheep-shearing, but employs "two little" girls (or boys, but the rest of the passage assumes they are girls) to assist with heating the tar pot (salve) and gathering loose scraps of wool (pp. 24–25).
37. *Farming*, p. 13. During February and March, the townspeople and Best vied to graze sheep on common land to which both Elmswell manor and the Elmswell village claimed rights.

38. See the reissue of Clark's book, *Working Life of Women in the Seventeenth Century*, ed. Amy Louise Erickson (London: Routledge, Kegan & Paul, 1982). Further references cited parenthetically as Clark.
39. Clark, *Working Life of Women*, p. 57. The disgruntled young woman is mentioned in G. R. and K. R. Fussell, *The English Countrywoman* (1953; New York: Benjamin Blom, 1971); their unspecified source appears to be one of several early twentieth-century works of general social history (pp. 31, 212).
40. In Kate Aughterson, *Renaissance Woman: A Sourcebook* (New York: Routledge, 1994), pp. 219–21.
41. Women's loss is implied only in the romanticized form of later pastoral poetry and landscapes. See John Barrell, *The Dark Side of the Landscape* (Cambridge: Cambridge University Press, 1980), pp. 50–51.
42. "Shepherdess" and "fold" are similarly adjacent in John Hind's Varrona in *The Most Excellent Historie of Lysimachus and Varrona* (1604)—indeed, Hind simply plagiarized from Greene's work. Another, apparently original, speech in Hind supports readings of the fold as both poetic and phallic: "we judge you are as cunning in faining a passion, as in folding sheepe, and can as soone deceive a woman with a pen, as adde a cure to a disease." A man who pretends to be a shepherd can feign to fold sheep or unfold passion, cure the rot or seduce a woman with his pen.
43. Googe, *Foure Bookes* (1586), sig. [141v].
44. William Shakespeare, *The Winter's Tale*, ed. J. H. P Pafford (1963; London and New York: Routledge, 1993), 4.4.77, 132.
45. From *Lay By Your Needles, Ladies, Take the Pen*, ed. Suzanne Trill, Kate Chedgzoy, and Melanie Osborne (London: Arnold, 1997), pp. 187–88.
46. Sir Philip Sidney, *The Old Arcadia*, ed. Katherine Duncan-Jones (1984; Oxford: Oxford University Press, 1994), p. 2. Subsequent references are cited parenthetically.
47. *The Countess of Pembroke's Arcadia*, ed. Maurice Evans (Harmondsworth, Eng.: Penguin, 1977), pp. 69–70. Subsequent references are cited parenthetically.
48. The sheep-like shepherdess makes a revealing late appearance in the *Poems and Fancies* of Margaret Cavendish, duchess of Newcastle (1653):

    The Shepherdesses which great Flocks doe keep,
    Are dabl'd high with dew, following their Sheep,
    Milking their Ewes, their hands doe dirty make;
    For being wet, dirt from their Duggs doe take. (sig. Aa3[v])

    The general sense of ordure, not to mention the confused referent of "their Duggs," shows that Cavendish is suspicious of the pasteurized shepherdess accepted by her more conventional contemporaries. Yet oddly, "milking their ewes" echoes the lily-white Perdita (4.4.451).
49. "Astrophel" has two hundred and sixteen lines, twice the number of sonnets in Sidney's *Astrophil and Stella*; Mary Sidney's lay has one hundred and eight lines.
50. See Margaret P. Hannay, Noel J. Kinnamon, Michael G. Brennan, eds., *The Collected Works of Mary Sidney Countess of Pembroke* (Oxford: Oxford University Press, 1998), p. 287.
51. Hannay et al., *The Collected Works of Mary Sidney*, pp. 124, 126.
52. Thomas Lodge, *Rosalind*, ed. Donald Beecher (Ottawa: Dovehouse Editions, 1997), p. 134. Subsequent references are given in the text.

53. See *Poems of Lady Mary Wroth*, ed. Josephine A. Roberts (Baton Rouge: Louisiana State University Press, 1983). His song 3, lines 63–64; her song 1, lines 17–18, p. 89.
54. *The First Part of the Countess of Montgomery's Urania*, ed. Josephine A. Roberts (Binghamton, NY: Center for Medieval and Early Renaissance Studies, 1995). Further references cited parenthetically.

Afterword

Constance C. Relihan and Goran V. Stanivukonic

As we were finishing a draft of the introduction to this volume, we came upon Kate Chedgzoy's introduction to *Shakespeare's Queer Children: Sexual Politics and Contemporary Culture*. In it she writes of her own attempt to introduce her collection of revisionist adaptations and appropriations of Shakespeare's texts:

> Initially, I tried to do everything in the strictly conventional way, setting out my theoretical stall in considerable and polysyllabic detail, and decking it with my various wares.... But it didn't work... it stood in direct contradiction to everything the book itself tries to do. This is a book about diversity and multiplicity; about the subversion of the fantasied monolithic icons of a culture which believes itself to be uncontestably dominant by a polyphonic choir, in which by no means all the voices are in harmony with each other.[1]

Exactly. While we do not mean to suggest that our introduction is a failure, this project too aims to represent the "polyphonic choir" of voices that for too long have been homogenized and elided by literary history. The study of prose fiction has long been the undervalued branch of early modern studies for some time (we are tempted to call it the "weak sister" of the period's literary studies), and its scholarship has been marked, as our introduction suggests, by a philological focus on sources and influences. The traditional approaches the fiction has often evoked when it has been studied have begun to give way in the past decade to deconstructive, feminist, queer, Marxist, cultural, and other approaches that show the influence of poststructuralism, but so much more needs to be done.

The essays in this volume represent a first step toward recognizing the multiplicity of sexualities constructed by and represented in early modern prose fiction, but it is a difficult and tentative first step, often complicated by fluid definitions of desire, sexuality, and gender. This fluidity is necessarily also complicated by the subject position occupied by the critic him or herself. Our own sexuality inevitably influences our perception of textually created sexualities: it often limits and filters the kinds of desire we are able to see operating within a given text. Essays such as those in this collection are essential to help us pull ourselves out of constructions of the operation of desire based on our own experience. Just as earlier studies or race, class, and gender have limited the ability of readers to universalize their experience of texts on the basis of these categories, queer studies and analyses of sexuality, by focusing on desire rather than gender, are helping to eliminate narrow and reductive understandings of early modern texts that are blind to the ways in which these texts weave nonnormative desire into their fabric. Just as it is no longer possible to speak of a universal subject as if the experience of class status, racial politics, or socially constructed gender were negligible, essays such as those in this collection are destroying "sexuality" as an undifferentiated critical monolith as well.

The sexualities represented within early modern fiction, because they are often described in very broad or highly allusive terms, have too often evaded scholarly notice. These essays attempt to redress that imbalance—whether by highlighting the homoerotic dimension of early fiction, demonstrating the link between normative heterosexual desire, rape, and violence, or amplifying the various ways in which gender identity is altered by constructions of desire. Sexualities in fiction are always plural; these essays hope to demonstrate that.

NOTE

1. Kate Chedgzoy, *Shakespeare's Queer Children: Sexual Politics and Contemporary Culture* (Manchester and New York: Manchester University Press, 1995), p. 5.

Bibliography

Alpers, Paul. *What Is Pastoral?* Chicago and London: University of Chicago Press, 1996.

Amussen, Susan Dwyer. *An Ordered Society: Gender and Class in Early Modern England*. Oxford: Basil Blackwell, 1988.

Amussen, Susan D. and Mark A. Kishlansky, eds. *Popular Culture and Cultural Politics in Early Modern England: Essays Presented to David Underdowne*. Manchester and New York: Manchester University Press, 1995.

Archer, Ian. *The Pursuit of Stability: Social Relations in Elizabethan London*. Cambridge: Cambridge University Press, 1991.

Aristotle. *Ethica Nicomachea*. Edited by J. Bywater. Oxford: Clarendon Press, 1894.

Ascham, Roger. *English Works*. Edited by W. A Wright. Cambridge: Cambridge University Press, 1904.

Ascham, Roger. *The Scholemaster*. New York: AMS Press, 1967.

Aubrey, John. *Aubrey's Brief Lives*. Edited Oliver Lawson Dick. London: Secker and Warburg, 1950.

Aughterson, Kate. *Renaissance Woman: A Sourcebook*. New York: Routledge, 1994.

Austen, Gillian. "Gascoigne's *Master FJ* and Its Revision, or, 'You Ain't Heard Nothin' Yet!'" *Narrative Strategies in Early English Fiction*. Edited by Wolfgang Görtschacher and Holger Klein, 67–85, Lewiston, NY and Salzburg, Austria, 1995.

Aydelotte, Frank. *Elizabethan Rogues and Vagabonds*. Oxford: Oxford University Press, 1913.

Bacon, Francis. *A Selection of His Works*. Edited by Sidney Warhaft. Toronto: Macmillan of Canada, 1965.

——. "Of Friendship." *The Essayes or Covnsels, Civill and Morall*. London, 1632.

Bakhtin, Mikhail. *The Dialogic Imagination: Four Essays*. Edited by Michael Holquist. Translated by Caryl Emerson and Michael Holquist. Austin: University of Texas Press, 1981.

Barish, Jonas. "The Prose Style of John Lyly." *ELH* 23 (1956): 14–35.

Baron, Dennis E. *Grammar and Gender*. New Haven: Yale University Press, 1986.

Barrell, John. *The Dark Side of the Landscape*. Cambridge: Cambridge University Press, 1980.

Bate, Jonathan. *Shakespeare and Ovid*. Oxford: Clarendon Press, 1994.

Bates, Catherine. *The Rhetoric of Courtship in Elizabethan Language and Literature*. Cambridge: Cambridge University Press, 1992.

Baudrillard, Jean. *The Transparency of Evil: Essays on Extreme Phenomena*. Translated by James Benedict. London: Verso, 1993.

Beier, A. L. *Masterless Men: The Vagrancy Problem in England, 1560–1640*. London: Methuen, 1985.

Bell, Ilona. *Elizabethan Women and the Poetry of Courtship*. Cambridge: Cambridge University Press, 1998.

Bhabha, Homi K. *The Location of Culture*. New York: Routledge, 1994.

Billingsley, Martin. *The Pens Excellencie or the Secretaries Delight*. London: J. Sudbury & G. Humble, 1618.

Black, Matthew Wilson. *Richard Brathwaite: An Account of His Life and Works*. Philadelphia: [n.p], 1928.

Boesky, Amy. *Founding Fictions: Utopias in Early Modern England*. Athens: University of Georgia Press, 1997.

Bolsec, Hierosme. *Historie de la vie, movers, doctrine, et deportements, de Thedore de Beze*. Paris: Guillaume Chaudiere, 1582.

Bone, Quentin. *Henrietta Maria: Queen of the Cavaliers*. London: Peter Owen, 1973.

Botero, Giovanni. *The trauellers breuiat, or, An historicall description of the most famous kingdoms in the world*. London, 1601.

Bowie, E. L. "The Greek Novel." *Oxford Readings in the Greek Novel*. Edited by Simon Swain, 39–59. Oxford: Oxford University Press, 1999.

Boyce, Benjamin. "History and Fiction in *Panthalia: or the Royal Romance*." *Journal of English and Germanic Philology* 57 (1958): 477–91.

Brathwait, Richard. *The Two Lancashire Lovers: or The Excellent History of Philocles and Doriclea*. Edited by Henry D. Janzen. Ottawa: Dovehouse Editions, 1998.

——. *The English Gentleman*. London: 1630; rpt. Amsterdam: Theatrum Orbis Terrarum, 1975.

——. *Panthalia: or Royal Romance. A Discourse Stored with infinite variety in relation to State-Government And Passages of matchless affection gracefully interveined. And presented on a Theatre of Tragical and Comical State, in a successive continuation to these Times Faithfully and ingenuously rendred*. London: J. G., 1659.

Bray, Alan. "Homosexuality and the Signs of Male Friendship." *History Workshop Journal* 29 (1990): 1–19; rpt. *Queering the Renaissance*. Edited by Jonathan Goldberg, 40–61. Durham, NC: Duke University Press, 1994.

——. *Sex, Law, and Marriage in the Middle Ages*. Aldershot, Hampshire: Variorum; Brookfield, VT: Ashgate, 1993.

Brundage, James A. *Law, Sex, and Christian Society in Medieval Europe*. Chicago: University of Chicago Press, 1987.

Beecher, Donald, ed. *Critical Approaches to English Prose Fiction, 1520–1640*. Ottawa: Dovehouse Editions, 1998.

Bredbeck, Gregory. *Sodomy and Interpretation: Marlowe to Milton*. Ithaca and London: Cornell University Press, 1991.

Breton, Nicholas. *The Goode and the Badde, Or Descriptions of the Worthies, and Vnworthies of this Age*. London, 1616.

Bristol, Michael and Arthur F. Marotti. "Introduction," 1–29. *Print, Manuscript, and Performance": The Changing Relations of the Media in Early Modern England*. Columbus: Ohio State University Press, 2000.

Brown, Peter. *The Body and Society: Men, Women, and Sexual Renunciation in Early Christianity*. New York: Columbia University Press, 1988.

Bushnell, Rebecca W. *Tragedies of Tyrants: Political Thought and Theater in the English Renaissance*. Ithaca: Cornell University Press, 1990.

Butler, Judith. *Gender Trouble: Feminism and the Subversion of Identity*. New York: Routledge, 1990.

Cantar, Brenda. "Charmed Circles of Enchantment: Pre-Oedipal Fantasies in Sir Philip Sidney's *Arcadia*." *Sidney Newsletter & Journal* 12 (1992): 1–20.

C[arrier] B[enjamin]. *Pvritanisme The Mother, Sinne The Daavghter.* St. Omer: English College Press, 1633.

Carroll, William. *Fat King, Lean Beggar: Representations of Poverty in the Age of Shakespeare.* Ithaca: Cornell University Press, 1996.

Catty, Jocelyn. *Writing Rape, Writing Women in Early Modern England.* New York: St. Martin's Press, 1999.

Cavanagh, Sheila T. *Cherished Torment: The Emotional Geography of Lady Mary Wroth's "Urania".* Pittsburgh: Duquesne University Press, 2002.

Cavendish, Margaret, Duchess of Newcastle. *Poems and Fancies.* London: T. R., 1653.

Cawley, Robert Ralston. *The Voyagers of Elizabethan Drama.* Boston: D. C. Heath and Company, 1938.

Cecil, Robert. "The State and Dignities of a Secretarie of State." Bodleian Library, Oxford, Ashmole MS 826, fo. 29.

Certaine Sermons or Homilies Appointed to be Read in Churches In the Time of Queen Elizabeth I. London, 1623; rpt. Gainesville, FL: Scholars' Facsimiles and Reprints, 1968.

Charles, Casey. "Heroes as Lovers: Erotic Attraction Between Men in Sidney's *New Arcadia.*" *Criticism* 34 (1992): 467–96.

Chedgzoy, Kate. *Shakespeare's Queer Children: Sexual Politics and Contemporary Culture.* Manchester: Manchester University Press, 1995.

Cholakian, Patricia Francis. *Rape and Writing in the "Heptameron"of Marguerite de Navarre.* Carbondale: Southern Illinois University Press, 1991.

Clark, Katerina and Michael Holquist. *Mikhail Bakhtin.* Cambridge, MA: Harvard University Press, 1984.

Clark, Sandra. "*Hic Mulier, Haec Vir* and the Controversy over Masculine Women." *Studies in Philology* 82 (1985): 157–83.

Clegg, Cyndia Susan. *Press Censorship in Elizabethan England.* Cambridge: Cambridge University Press, 1997.

Colie, Rosalie. *The Resources of King: Genre-Theory in the Renaissance.* Edited by Barbara Lewalski. Berkeley: University of California Press, 1973.

Coryate, Thomas. *Coryat's Crudities.* London: W.S., 1611.

Crane, Thomas. *Italian Social Customs of the Sixteenth Century and Their Influence on the Literature of Europe.* New Haven: Yale University Press, 1920.

Cressy, David. *Birth, Marriage & Death: Ritual, Religion, and the Life-Cycle in Tudor and Stuart England.* Oxford: Oxford University Press, 1997.

——. "Gender Trouble and Cross-Dressing in Early Modern England." *Journal of British Studies* 35 (1996): 438–65.

"Cursor Mundi." Trinity College, Cambridge, MS R.3.8 (588); Early English Text Society (1875). Pt. 2. Edited by Richard Morris, lines 9247–48; rpt. London, New York, and Toronto: Oxford University Press, 1966.

Danby, John F. *Poets on Fortune's Hill: Studies in Sidney, Shakespeare, Beaumont and Fletcher.* London: Faber & Faber, 1952.

Daniel, Samuel. *Delia and Rosamund Augmented. Cleopatra.* London: Simon Waterson, 1594.

Davis, Walter. *Idea and Act in Elizabethan Fiction.* Princeton: Princeton University Press, 1969.

Dawson, Harbutt. *Cromwell's Understudy: The Life and Times of General John Lambert and the Rise and Fall of the Protectorate.* London: William Hodge, 1938.

Day, Angel. *The English Secretary, or Methode of writing of Epistles and Letters ... Now newly reuised.* London: C. Burbie, 1599.

Daybell, James. "Women's Letters and Letter Writing in England, 1540–1603: And Introduction to the Issues of Authorship and Construction." *Shakespeare Studies* 27 (1999): 161–86.

De Bèze, Théodore. *Poemata edition secunda ab eo recognita.* Geneva: Henri Estienne, 1569.

De Certeau, Michel. *The Practice of Everyday Life.* Translated by Steven Rendall. Berkeley, Los Angeles, London: University of California Press, 1988.

De Grazia, Margareta and Stanley Wells, eds. *The Cambridge Companion to Shakespeare.* Cambridge: Cambridge University Press, 2001.

De Sainctes, Claude. *Responsio ... ad Apologiam Theodori Bezae editam contra Examen Doctrinae Cluinianae.* Paris: Claude Frémy, 1567.

——. *Lantern and Candle-light.* London, 1608; rpt. Arthur Kinney, ed., 207–60. *Rogues, Vagabonds, and Sturdy Beggar.* Amherst: The University of Massachusetts Press, 1990.

——. *The Belman of London.* London, 1608; rpt. Amsterdam: Theatrum Orbis Terrarum, 1973.

Dekker, Thomas. *O per se O. Or a New Cryer of Lanthorne and Candle-light.* London, 1612.

Dekker, Thomas and John Webster. *West-ward Hoe. As it hath beene diuers times Acted by the Children of Paules.* London: Iohn Hodgets, 1607.

DiGangi, Mario. "The Homoerotics of Masculinity in Tragicomedy," 134–54. *The Homoerotics of Early Modern Drama.* Cambridge: Cambridge University Press, 1997.

Dolan, Frances E. *Whores of Babylon: Catholicism, Gender, and Seventeenth-Century Print Culture.* Ithaca, NY: Cornell University Press, 1999.

Donaldson, Ian. *The Rapes of Lucretia: A Myth and its Transformations.* Oxford: Clarendon Press, 1982.

Donovan, Josephine. *Women and the Rise of the Novel, 1405–1726.* New York: St. Martin's, 1999.

Doody, Margaret Anne. *The Ture Story of the Novel.* London: Fontana Press, 1998.

Douglas, Eleanor. *To The Most Honorable The High Court of Parliament Assembled, &c.* London: 1643.

Douglas, Robert Langton, ed. *Certain Tragical Discourses of Bandello Translated into English by Gefraie Fenton, anno 1567.* 2 vols. London: David Nutt, 1898; rpt. New York: AMS Press, 1967.

Duncan-Jones, Katherine. Review of Alan Stewart's *Philip Sidney—A Double Life. The Observer Review*, February 13, 2000: 12.

——. *Sir Philip Sidney: Courtier Poet.* New Haven: Yale University Press, 1991.

——. ed. *Sir Philip Sidney.* Oxford: Oxford University Press, 1989.

Dusinberre, Juliet. *Shakespeare and the Nature of Women.* 2nd edition. Basingstoke: Macmillan Press; New York: St. Martin's Press, 1996.

Egger, Brigitte. "Women and Marriage in the Greek Novels: The Boundaries of Romance." *The Search for the Ancient Novel.* Edited by James Tatum, 260–80. Baltimore: The Johns Hopkins University Press, 1994.

Fabricius, Gabriel. *Responsio ad Bezam Vezeliam Eceboliam.* Paris, 1567; rpt. *Correspondance de Théodore de Bèze.* Edited by Hippolyte Aubert, Alain Dufour, Claire Chimelli and Béatrice Niccolier. Vol. 10 (1596). Geneva: Droz, 1980.

Fenton, Geoffrey. *Certain Tragical Discourses of Bandello.* 2 vols. 1898; rpt. New York: AMS Press, 1967.

Fisher, Will. "Queer Money." *ELH* 66 (1999): 1–23.

Fleming, Juliet. "The Ladies' Man and the Age of Elizabeth." *Sexuality and Gender in Early Modern Europe: Institutions, Texts, Images.* Edited by James Grantham Turner, 158–79. Cambridge: Cambridge University Press, 1993.

Ford, John. *The Broken Heart.* Edited by Brian Morris. London: Ernest Benn, 1965.

Foster, Verna Ann and Stephen Foster. "Structure and History in *The Broken Heart*: Sparta, England, and the 'Truth'". *English Literary Renaissance* 22 (1988): 305–28.

Foucault, Michel. *The Use of Pleasure.* Vol. 2 of *The History of Sexuality.* Translated by Robert Hurley. New York: Pantheon, 1985.

——. *The Order of Things.* New York: Vintage, 1973.

Fraunce, Abraham. *The Countesse of Pembrokes Yuychurch. Conteining the affectionate life, and unfortunate death of Phillis and Amyntas: That in a Pastorall; This in a Funerall: both in English Hexameters.* London: [T. Orwin],1591.

Freud, Sigmund. "Femininity." *New Introductory Lectures in Psychoanalysis. The Standard Edition of the Complete Psychological Works of Sigmund Freud.* Vol. 22. Edited by James Strachey. London: Hogarth Press, 1964.

Frye, Northrop. *Anatomy of Criticism: Four Essays.* Princeton: Princeton University Press, 1957.

Fuchs, Barbara. *Mimesis and Empire: The New World, Islam, and European Identities.* Cambridge: Cambridge University Press, 2001.

Fuchs, Eric. *Sexual Desire and Love: Origin and History of the Christian Ethic of Sexuality and Marriage.* Translated by Marsha Daigle. Cambridge: James Clark, 1983.

——. *A Defense of the sincere and true Translations of the holie Scriptures into the English tong.* London: Henrie Bynneman for George Bishop, 1583.

Fulke, William. *D. Heskins, D. Sanders, and M. Rastel ... ouerthrowne, and detected of their seuerall blasphemous heresies.* London: Henrie Middleton for George Bishop, 1579.

Fussell, K. R. and G. R. *The English Countrywoman.* 1953; rpt. New York: Benjamin Bloom, 1971.

Gallagher, Catherine and Stephen Greenblatt. *Practicing New Historicism.* Chicago and London: Chicago University Press, 2000.

Garber, Marjorie. *Vested Interests: Cross-Dressing and Cultural Anxiety.* New York: Harper Collins, 1993.

Garde, Noel I. *The Homosexual in History.* New York: Vantage Press, 1964.

Gardy, Frédéric with Alain Dufour. *Bibliographie des oeuvred théologiques, littéraires, historiques et juridiques de Théodore de Bèze.* Geneva: E. Droz, 1960.

Gascoigne, George. *The Posies.* Edited by John W. Cunfliffe. Cambridge: Cambridge University Press, 1907.

——. *The Posies of George Gascoigne Esquire.* London: H. Bynneman for Richard Smith, 1575.

——. *A Hundreth sundrie flowers bounde vp in one small Poesie.* London: Richard Smith, 1573.

Gasele, Stephen and H. F. B. Brett-Smith, eds. *The Loves of Clitoophon and Leucippee. Translated from the Greek of Achilles Tatius by William Burton. Reprinted for the first time from a copy now unique by Thomas Creede in 1597.* Oxford: B. Blackwell, 1923.

Gayton, Edmund. *Pleasant Notes on Don Quixote*. London: William Hunt, 1654.

Geisendorf, Paul-F. *Théodore de Bèze*. Geneva: Labor et Fides, 1949.

Gerhart, Mary. *Genre Choices, Gender Questions*. Norman: University of Oklahoma Press, 1992.

Gesner, Carol. *Shakespeare and the Greek Romance: A Study of Origins*. Lexington: University of Kentucky Press, 1970.

Gill, Christopher, trans. *Daphnis and Chloe. Collected Ancient Greek Novels*. Edited by B. P. Reardon, 288–348. Berkeley and Los Angeles: University of California Press, 1989.

Goldberg, Jonathan. *Desiring Women Writing: English Renaissance Examples*. Stanford: Stanford University Press, 1997.

——. *Sodometries: Renaissance Texts, Modern Sexualities* (Stanford: Stanford University Press, 1992.

——. *Writing Matter: From the Hand of the English Renaissance*. Stanford: Stanford University Press, 1990.

Golding, Arthur. *The XV. Bookes of P. Ouidius Naso, Entytuled Metamorphosis*. London: Willyam Seres, 1567.

Goody, Jack. *The Development of the Family and Marriage in Europe*. Cambridge: Cambridge University Press, 1983.

Gosson, Stephen. *Plays Confuted in Five Actions*. London, 1582. *The English Stage: Attacks and Defenses, 1577–1730*. Edited by Arthur Freeman. New York: Garland, 1972.

Gravdal, Kathryn. *Ravishing Maidens: Writing Rape in Medieval French Literature and Law*. Philadelphia: University of Pennsylvania Press, 1991.

Great Eclipse. The Great Eclipse of the Sun, or, Charles his Waine Over-clouded by the Evill Influences of the Moon Eclipsed by the Destructive Perswasions of His Queen. London: G. B. [Bishop], 1644.

Green, M. A. E., ed. *Letters of Queen Henrietta Maria*. London: [n.p.], 1857.

Greenblatt, Stephen. "Sidney's *Arcadia* and the Mixed Mode." *Studies in Philology* 70 (1973): 269–78.

Greene, Robert. *A Notable Discovery of Cozenage*. London, 1591; rpt. Kinney, 155–86. *Rogues, Vagabonds*.

——. *The Second and Last Part of Cony-Catching*. London, 1592; rpt. Gamini Salgado, *Cony-Catchers and Bawdy Baskets: An Anthology of Elizabethan Low Life*. Harmondsworth: Penguin, 1972.

——. *A Disputation, Betweeene a Hee conny-catcher, and a Shee Conny-catcher*. London, 1592; rpt. Gamini Salgado, *Cony-Catchers*.

——. *The Black Book's Messenger*. London, 1592; rpt. Kinney, 187–205. *Rogues, Vagabonds*.

——. *The Third and Last Part of Cony-Catching*. London, 1592; rpt. Salgado, *Cony-Catchers*.

Guillén, Claudio. *Literature as System: Essays Toward the Theory of Literary History*. Princeton: Princeton University Press, 1971.

Guy-Bray, Stephen. *Homoerotic Space: The Poetics of Loss in Renaissance Literature*. Toronto: University of Toronto Press, 2002.

Hackett, Helen. *Women and Romance Fiction in the English Renaissance*. Cambridge: Cambridge University Press, 2000.

Hadfield, Andrew. *Literature, Politics and National Identity: Reformation to Renaissance*. Cambridge: Cambridge University Press, 1994.

Hägg, Thomas. *The Novel in Antiquity.* Berkeley and Los Angeles: University of California Press, 1983.

Hall, Kim F. *Things of Darkness: Economies of Race and Gender in Early Modern England.* Ithaca: Cornell University Press, 1995.

Halperin, David M. *One Hundred Years of Homosexuality: And Other Essay on Greek Love.* New York and London: Routledge, 1990.

Hamilton, A. C. "Sidney's *Arcadia* as Prose Fiction: Its Relation to Its Sources." *English Literary Renaissance* 2 (1972): 29–60.

Hannay, Margaret P., Noel J. Kinnamon, Michael G. Brennan, eds. *The Collected Works of Mary Sidney Countess of Pembroke.* Oxford: Oxford University Press, 1998.

Hanson, Ellis. "Sodomy and Kingcraft in *Urania* and *Antony and Cleopatra." In Homosexuality in Renaissance and Enlightenment England: Literary Representations in Historical Context.* Edited by Claude J. Summers, 135–51. Harrington Park, NY: Haworth Press, 1992.

Hardacre, Paul H. *The Royalist During the Puritan Revolution.* The Hague: Nijhoff, 1960.

Hardin, Richard F. *Love in a Green Shade: Idyllic Romances Ancient to Modern.* Lincoln and London: University of Nebraska Press, 2000.

Harman, Thomas. *A Caveat for Common Cursitors, Vulgarly Called Vagabonds.* London, 1566; rpt. Kinney, 103–53. *Rogues, Vagabonds.*

Harrison, William. *The Description of England.* London, 1587; rpt. Georges Edelen, ed., Ithaca: Published for the Folger Shakespeare Library by Cornell University Press, 1968.

Harvey, Gabriel. "The Story of Mercy Harvey, Sister of Dr. Gabriel Harvey." *The Works of Gabriel Harvey.* Edited by Alexander B. Grosart, vol. 3, 73–97. London: Privately printed, 1885.

Helgerson, Richard. *The Elizabethan Prodigals.* Berkeley: University of California Press, 1976.

Henderson, Katherine Usher and Barbara F. McManus. *Half Humankind: Contexts and Texts of the Controversy about Women in England, 1540–1640.* Urbana: University of Illinois Press, 1985.

Henderson, Judith Rice. "Euphues and his Erasmus." *English Literary Renaissance* 12 (1982): 135–61.

Henry Best of Elmswell. *The Farming and Memorandum Books of Henry Best of Elmswell, 1642.* Edited Donald Woodward. London: Oxford University Press, 1984.

Herbert, Sir Percy. *The Princess Cloria.* 2nd edition. London: 1661.

——. "To the Reader." *Cloria and Narcissus. A Delightfull and New Romance, Imbellished with divers Politicall Notions, and singular Remarks of Moderne Transactions.* London: E. C., 1653.

Herrup, Cynthia. *A House in Gross Disorder: Sex, Law, and the 2nd Earl of Castlehaven.* New York: Oxford University Press, 1999.

Heylyn, Peter. *Microcosmus, or A Little Description of the Great World.* Edited by Montague Summers. New York: Benjamin Bloom, 1928.

Hill, Christopher. "Sex, Marriage, and the Family in England." *The Economic History Review*, 2nd series, 31 (1978): 450–63.

Hind, John. *The Most Excellent Historie of Lysimachus and Varrona.* London: T. Creede, 1604.

Hinds, Stephen. "Landscape with Figures: Aesthetics of Place in the *Metamorphoses* and its tradition." *The Cambridge Companion to Ovid*. Edited by Philip Hardie, 122–49. Cambridge: Cambridge University Press, 2002.

H[odges], A[nthony]. *The Loves of Clitophon and Leucippe. A most elegant History, written in Greeke by Achilles Tatious: And now Englished*. Oxford, 1638.

Hollander, Anne. *Seeing Through Clothes*. New York: Viking, 1978.

Holzberg, Niklas. *The Ancient Novel: An Introduction*. Translated by Christine Jackson-Holzberg. London: Routledge, 1995.

Hosius, Stanislas. *Catholici cvivsdam et orthodozi ivdicivm et censvra, de iudicio & censura ministrorum Tygurinorum & Heydelbergensium, de dogmate contra adorandam Trinitatem in Polonia nuper sparso*. Cologne: apud Maternum Cholinum, 1565.

Houlbrook, Ralph A. *The English Family, 1450–1700*. London: Longman, 1984.

Howell, James. *Epistolae Ho-Elinae: Familiar Letters Domestic and Forren*. London: 1650.

Hull, Suzanne. *Chaste, Silen, and Obedient: English Books for Women, 1475–1640*. San Marino, CA: The Huntington Library, 1982.

Hutson, Lorna. *The Usurer's Daughter: Male Friendship and Fictions of Women in Sixteenth-Century England*. London and New York: Routledge, 1994.

Hyrde, Richard. Dedicatory epistle to *A devout treatise upon the Paternoster made first in latyn by the moost famous doctour mayster Erasmus Rotorodamus*; qtd. *Vives and the Renaiscence Education of Women*. Edited by Foster Watson, 166–67. London: Edward Arnold, 1912.

Ingram, Martin. *Church Courts, Sex and Marriage in England, 1570–1640*. Cambridge: Cambridge University Press, 1987.

Iser, Wolfgang. *The Implied Reader: Patters of Communication in Prose from Bunyan to Beckett*. Baltimore and London: The Johns Hopkins University Press, 1974.

Jacobs, Joseph, ed. *Daphnis and Chloe: The Elizabethan Version from Amyot's Translation. By Angel Day: Reprinted from the Unique Original*. London: David Nutt, 1890.

Jardine, Lisa and Alan Stewart. *Hostage to Fortune: The Troubled Life of Francis Bacon 1561–1626*. London: Victor Gollancz, 1998.

Jed, Stephanie H. *Chaste Thinking: The Rape; of Lucretia and the Birth of Humanism*. Bloomington and Indianapolis: Indiana University Press, 1989.

Johnson, Richard. *The Most Famovs History of the Seuen Champions of Christendome*. London: Elizabeth Burbie, 1608.

Jordan, Constance. *Renaissance Feminism: Literary Texts and Political Models*. Ithaca: Cornell University Press, 1990.

Kahn, Victoria Ann and Lorna Hutson, eds. *Rhetoric and Law in Early Modern Europe*. New Haven, CT: Yale University Press, 2001.

Kelso, Ruth. *Doctrine for the Lady of the Renaissance*. Urbana: University of Illinois Press, 1956.

Kennedy, Duncan. "Sexual Abuse, Sexy Dressing, and the Eroticization of Domination." 126–213. *Sexy Dressing Etc.: Essays on the Power and Politics of Cultural Identity*. Cambridge, MA: Harvard University Press, 1993.

Kermode, Frank. *English Pastoral Poetry*. 1952; New York: W. W. Norton & Co., 1972.

Kinney, Arthur, ed. *Sidney in Retrospect*. Amherst: University of Massachusetts Press, 1988.

——. *Humanist Poetics: Thought, Rhetoric, and Fiction in Sixteenth-Century England.* Amherst: University of Massachusetts Press, 1986.

——. ed. *Markets of Bawdrie: The Dramatic Criticism of Stephen Gosson.* Salzburg: Universität Salzburg, 1970.

Kinney, Clare. "The Masks of Love: Desire and Metamorphosis in Sidney's *New Arcadia.*" *Criticism* 33 (1991): 461–90.

Knachel, Philip A., ed. *Eikon Basilike: The Portraiture of His Sacred Majesty in His Solitudes and Sufferings.* Ithaca: Cornell University Press, 1966.

Knapp, Jeffrey. *Centuries' Ends: Narrative Means.* Stanford: Stanford University Press, 1996.

Konstan, David. *Sexual Symmetry: Love in the Ancient Novel and Related Genres.* Princeton: Princeton University Press, 1994.

Kussmaul, Ann. *Servants in Husbandry in Early Modern England.* Cambridge: Cambridge University Press, 1981.

Lamb, Mary Ellen. "Exhibiting Class and Displaying the Body in Sidney's *Countess of Pembroke's Arcadia.*" *Studies in English Literature* 37 (1997): 55–72.

——. *Gender and Authorship in the Sidney Circle.* Madison: University of Wisconsin Press, 1990.

Lane, Robert. *"Shepheards Devises."* Athens: University of Georgia Press, 1993.

Leslie, Michael and Timothy Raylor, eds. *Culture and Cultivation in Early Modern England: Writing and the Land.* London: Leicester University Press, 1992.

Levine, Laura. *Men in Women's Clothing: Anti-Theatricality and Effeminization, 1579–1642.* Cambridge: Cambridge University Press, 1994.

Lewis, C. S. *English Literature in the Sixteenth Century.* Oxford: Clarendon Press, 1954.

——. *The Allegory of Love: A Study in Medieval Tradition.* Oxford: Oxford University Press, 1936.

Lindheim, Nancy. *The Structures of Sidney's "Arcadia".* Toronto: University of Toronto Press, 1982.

Linton, Joan Pong. "The Humanist in the Market: Gendering Exchange and Authorship in Lyly's *Euphues* Romances." *Framing Elizabethan Fictions: Contemporary Approaches to Early Modern Narrative Prose.* Edited by Constance C. Relihan, 73–87. Kent, OH: The Kent State University Press, 1996.

Lisle, William. *The famous historie of Heliodorus. Amplified, Augmented, and Delivered Paraphrastically in Verse.* London, 1638.

Lodge, Thomas. *Rosalind.* Edited by Donald Beecher. Ottawa: Dovehouse Editions, 1997.

——. *Wits Miserie, and the Worlds Madnesse: Discouering the Ddeuils Incarnate of this Age.* London: A. Islip, 1596.

Louglin, Marie H. *Hymeneutics: Interpreting Virginity on the Early Modern Stage.* Lewisburg: Bucknell University Press, 1997.

Love, Harold. *Scribal Publication in Seventeenth-Century England.* Oxford: Clarendon Press, 1993.

Lovelace, William. *Eglogs, Epytaphes, and Sonettes.* London: Thomas Colwell, 1563.

Low, Anthony. *The Georgic Revolution.* Princeton: Princeton University Press, 1985.

Lucas, Caroline. *Writing for Women: The Example of Women as Reader in Elizabethan Romance.* Milton Keynes: Open University Press, 1982.

Lupton, Donald. *London and the Covntrey Carbonadoed and Quartered into Seuerall Characters.* London, 1632.

Lyly, John. *The Complete Works of John Lyly.* 3 vols. Edited by Warwick Bond. Oxford: Clarendon Press, 1996.

Machard, Alexandre. "Recherches sur la querelle des "Juvenilia." *Les Juvenilia de Théodore de Bèze.* Edited by Alexandre Machard, XVII–XVIII. Paris: Isidore Lisieux, 1879.

Manley, Lawrence. *Literature and Culture in Early Modern London.* Cambridge: Cambridge University Press, 1995.

[Markham, Gervase]. *Cheape and Good Husbandry.* London: Bernard Alsop for John Harrison, 1649.

——. *The English House-wife.* London: B. Alsop for J. Harrison, 1648.

Marcus, Leah. *Puzzling Shakespeare: Local Reading and Its Discontents.* Berkeley: University of California Press, 1988.

Marotti, Arthur F. *Manuscript, Print and the English Renaissance Lyric.* Ithaca, NY: Cornell University Press, 1995.

——. "Patronage, Poetry, and Print." *Yearbook of English Studies* 21 (1991): 1–26.

Marvell, Andrew. "An Horatian Ode." *The Complete Poems.* Edited by Elizabeth Story Donno. Harmondsworth: Penguin, 1972; rpt. 1985.

Maslen, Robert. *Elizabethan Fictions: Espionage, Counter-Espionage, and the Duplicity of Fiction in Early Elizabethan Prose Narratives.* Oxford: Clarendon Press, 1997.

——. "A Study of the Works of John Lyly and his Predecessors in the Context of Changing Attitudes to Fiction in Elizabethan England." Doctoral dissertation. Oxford University, 1990.

Masten, Jeffrey. *Textual Intercourse: Collaboration, Authorship, and Sexualities in Renaissance Drama.* Cambridge: Cambridge University Press, 1997.

Masten, Jeffrey, Peter Stallybrass and Nancy Vickers. "Introduction: Language machines." *Language Machines: Technologies of Literary and Cultural Production.* Edited by Master, Stallybrass, Vickers, 1–14. New York: Routledge, 1997.

Matar, N[abil] I. "'Turning Turk:' Conversion to Islam in English Renaissance Thought." *Durham University Journal* (January 1994): 33–41.

Maus, Katharine Eiseman. *Inwardness and the Theater in the English Renaissance.* Chicago: University of Chicago Press, 1995.

May, Thomas. *The History of the Parliament of England.* Oxford: Oxford University Press, 1854.

McCabe, Richard A. "Wit, Eloquence, and Wisdon in *Euphues: The Anatomy of Wit.*" *Studies in Philology* 81 (1984): 299–324.

McCandles, Michael. "Oracular Prediction and the Fore-conceit of Sidney's *Arcadia.*" *ELH* 50 (1983): 233–44.

McCoy, Richard C. "Gascoigne's 'Poëmata castrata': The Wages of Courtly Success." *Criticism* 27 (1985): 29–56.

Mentz, Steve. "Selling Sidney: William Ponsonby, Thomas Nashe, and the Boundaries of Elizabethan Print and Manuscript Culture." *TEXT* 13 (2000): 124–46.

Meres, Francis. *Gods Arhithmeticke.* London, 1597.

Mihil Mumchance, his Discouerie of the Art of Cheating in False Dyce Play, and Other Vnlawfull Games. Anon. London, 1597.

——. *The None-Such Charles His Character.* London: 1651, 170–71; qtd. in Ernest Sirluck, "*The Eikon Basilike*: An Unreported Item in the Contemporary Authorship Controversy." *Modern Language Notes* 70 (November 1954): 497–502.

Milton, John. *Apology for Smectymnuus.* London, 1642. *Complete Prose Works of John Milton.* Edited by Don Wolfe et al., 862–953. Vol. 1 of 8 vols. New Haven: Yale University Press, 1953–82.

Miner, Earl. *The Restoration Mode from Milton to Dryden.* Princeton: Princeton University Press, 1974.

——. *The Cavalier Mode from Johnson to Cotton.* Princeton: Princeton University Press, 1971.

Mish, Charles C., ed. *Short Fiction of the Seventeenth Century.* New York: Norton, 1963.

——. Charles. "Best Sellers in Seventeenth-Century Fiction." *Papers of the Bibliographic Society of America* 47 (1953): 356–73.

——. "Black Letter as Social Discriminant in the Seventeenth Century." *PMLA* 98 (1953): 627–30.

——. "Comparative Popularity of Early Fiction and Drama." *Notes and Queries* 197 (June 21, 1952): 269–70.

——. *Montaigne's Essays.* Translated by John Florio. London, 1603; vol. 1; rpt. Menston: Scolar Press, 1969.

Montaigne, de Michel. *The Complete Essays of Montaigne.* Translated by Donald M. Frame. Stanford: Stanford University Press, 1958.

Montrose, Louis. " 'Of Gentlemen and Shepherds:' The Politics of Elizabethan Pastoral Form." *ELH* 50 (1983): 415–59.

——. " 'Eliza, Queene of Shepheardes,' and the Pastoral of Power." *English Literary Renaissance* 10 (1980): 153–82.

More, Sir Thomas. *More's History of King Richard III.* London: 1513. Facsimile edited by J. Rawson Lumby. Cambridge: Cambridge University Press, 1883.

Moryson, Fynes. *An Itinerary Written By Bynes Moryson Gent. First in the Latine tongue, and then Translated By him into English. Containing his Ten Yeeres Travell Through the Twelve Domjnions of Germany, Bohmerland, Sweitzerland, Netherland, Denmarke, Poland, Jtaly, Turkey, France, England, Scotland, and Ireland.* London: John Beale, 1617.

Moulton, Ian. *Before Pornography: Erotic Writing in Early Modern England.* Oxford: Oxford University Press, 2000.

Mueller, Janel. *The Native Tongue and the Word: Developments in English Prose Style 1380–1580.* Chicago: University of Chicago Press, 1984.

Müller, Wolfgang G. "The Modernity of the Second Version of George Gascoigne's *Master F.J.*" *Narrative and Strategies.* Edited by Görtschacher and Klein, 87–102.

Mirror of Knighthood. The second part of the first booke of the Myrrour of Knighthood. Translated by R[obert] P[arry]. London: Thomas Este, 1585.

Navarre, Marguerite de. *The Heptameron.* Translated and edited by P. A. Chilton. New York: Viking Penguin, 1984.

Newcomb, Lori Humprhey. *Reading Popular Romance in Early Modern England.* New York: Columbia University Press, 2002.

——. "'Social Things:' The Production of Popular Culture in the Reception of Robert Greene's *Pandosto.*" *ELH* 61 (1994): 753–81.

Northbrooke, John. *A Treatise Against Dicing, Dancing, Plays, and Interludes.* London, 1577. London: Reprinted for the Shakespeare Society, 1843; rpt. New York: AMS Press, 1971.

O'Connor, John. *Amadis de Gaule and Its Influence on Elizabethan Literature.* New Brunswick, NJ: Rutgers University Press, 1970.

O'Dell, Sterg. *A Chronological List of Prose Fiction in English Printed in England and Other Countries, 1475–1640.* Cambridge, MA: Technology Press of MIT, 1954.

O'Hara, Diana. *Courtship and Constraint: Rethinking the Making of Marriage in Tudor England.* Manchester: Manchester University Press, 2000.

Orlin, Lena Cowen. "Three Ways To Be Invisible in the Renaissance: Sex, Reputation, and Stitchery." *Renaissance Culture of the Everyday.* Edited by Patricia Fumerton and Simon Hunt, 183–203. Philadelphia: University of Philadelphia Press, 1999.

Ostovich, Helen and Elizabeth Sauer, eds. *Reading Early Modern Women: An Anthology of Manuscripts and Texts in Print, 1550–1700.* New York: Routledge, 2003.

Outhwaite, R. B. *Clandestine Marriage in England, 1500–1850.* London: The Humbledon Press, 1995.

Ovidius, Publius Naso. *Ovid, Metamorphoses.* Translated by Frank Justus Miller, revised by G. P. Goold. Loeb Classical Library. Vol. I. Cambridge, MA and London: Harvard University Press, 1994.

——. *Metamorphoses Ovidii, argvmentis quidem solute oratione, enarrationibus autem & allegorijs elegiaco uersu occuratissimè expositae.* Illustrated by M. Iohan. Francoforti, 1563.

Oxford Companion to English Literature. Edited by Margaret Drabble. Oxford: Oxford University Press, 1985.

Painter, William. *The Palace of Pleasure.* 4 vols. London: Cresset Press, 1929.

Palmendos. The Famous History of Palmendos, son of the Most Renowned Palmerin D'Oliva. London: E. Alsop, 1653.

Palmerin of England. The third and last part of Palmerin of England. London: William Leake, 1602.

Parismenos. Parismenos: The Second Part of the Most Famous, Delectable, and Pleasant Historie of Parismus, the Renowned Prince of Bohemia. London: Thomas Creede, 1599.

[Parker, Henry]. *The King's Cabinet Opened; or, Certain Packets of Secret Letters & Papers, written with the King's own hand, and taken in his Cabinet at Naseby-Field June 14 1645.* London: [n.p.], 1645.

Parry, Robert. *Moderatus, The Most Delectable and Famous Historie of the Blacke Knight.* London: R. Jhones, 1595.

Patterson, Annabel. *Pastoral and Ideology.* Oxford: Clarendon Press, 1988.

——. *Censorship and Interpretation: The Conditions of Writing and Reading in Early Modern England.* Madison: University of Wisconsin Press, 1984.

Pepys, Samuel. *King Charles Preserved: An Account of his Escape after the Battle of Worcester dictated by the King himself to Samuel Pepys.* London: Rodale Press, 1954.

Pettie, George. *A Petite Palace of Pettie His Pleasure.* Edited by Herbert Hartman. London: Oxford University Press, 1938.

Phillips, Margaret Mann. *Erasmus on his Times: A Shortened Version of the Adages of Erasmus.* Cambridge: Cambridge University Press, 1967.

Pigman, G. W. "Editing revised texts: Gascoigne's *A Hundreth Sundrie Flowres* and *The Posies.*" *New ways of looking at old texts, II: Papers of the Renaissance English Text Society, 1992–1996.* Edited by W. Speed Hill. Tempe: Medieval & Renaissance Texts & Studies/Renaissance English Text Society, 1998.

——. "How to Tell a Flatterer from a Friend." Edited by Frank Cole Babbitt, 264–395. *Plutarch's Moralia.* Vol. 1. Loeb Classical Library. London: Heinemann and Cambridge, MA: Harvard University Press, 1949.

Plutarch. "On Having Many Friends." Edited by Frank Cole Babbitt, 46–69. *Plutarch's Moralia.* Vol. 2. Loeb Classical Library. London: Heinemann and Cambridge, MA: Harvard University Press, 1928.

Pooley, Roger. *George Gascoigne: The Green Knight.* Manchester: Carcanet Press, 1982.

Potter, Lois. *Secret Rites and Secret Writing: Royalist Literature, 1641–1660.* Cambridge: Cambridge University Press, 1989.

Prendergast, Maria Micaela Teresa. *Renaissance Fantasies: The Gendering of Aesthetics in Early Modern Fiction.* Kent, Ohio and London, England: The Kent State Ohio Press, 1999.

Prouty, C. T. *George Gascoigne: Elizabethan Courtier, Soldier, and Poet.* New York: Columbia University Press, 1942.

Pruvost, René. *Matteo Bandello and Elizabethan Fiction.* Paris: Librairie Ancienne Honorè Champion, 1937.

Purchas, Samuel. *Hakluytus Posthumus, or Purchas His Pilgrims.* 20 vols. Glasgow: J. Maclehose and Sons, 1905.

Quintilian. *Institutionis Oratoriae.* Edited by M. Winterbottom. 2 vols. Oxford: Clarendon Press, 1970.

Ralegh, Sir Walter. *Selected Writings.* 1984; rpt. Harmondsworth: Penguin, 1986.

Rambuss, Richard. *Spenser's Secret Career.* Cambridge: Cambridge University Press, 1993.

Randall, Dale J. B. *Winter Fruit: English Drama, 1642–1660.* Lexington: University Press of Kentucky, 1995.

Records of the Court of the Stationers' Company 1576 to 1602 from Register B. Edited by W. W. Greg and E. Boswell. London: The Bibliographical Society, 1930.

Reynolds, Bryan. *Becoming Criminal: Transversal Performance and Cultural Dissidence in Early Modern England.* Baltimore: Johns Hopkins University Press, 2002.

Relihan, Constance C. *Fashioning Authority: The Development of Elizabethan Novelistic Discourse.* Kent, OH and London, England: The Kent State University Press, 1994.

Richardson, David A, ed. *Dictionary of Literary Biography. Vol. 136: Sixteenth-Century British Nondramatic Writers.* Detroit, Washington, D.C., and London: Bruccoli Clark Layman, 1994.

Riche, Barnabe. *His Farewell to Military Profession.* Edited by Donald Beecher. Ottawa: Dovehouse Editions, 1992.

Rocke, Michael. *Forbidden Friendships: Homosexuality and Male Culture in Renaissance Florence.* New York and Oxford: Oxford University Press, 1996.

Roberts, Josephine. " 'The knott never to bee untide': The controversy regarding marriage in Mary Wroth's *Urania.*" *Reading Mary Wroth: Representing Alternatives in Early Modern England.* Eds. Naomi Miller and Gary Waller, 109–32. Knoxville: University of Tennessee Press, 1991.

Roberts, Michael. "Sickles and Scythes: Women's Work and Men's Work at Harvest Time." *History Workshop Journal* 7 (1979): 3–28.

Rose, Mark. *Heroic Love: Studies in Sidney and Spenser.* Cambridge, MA: Harvard University Press, 1968.

——. "Sidney's Womanish Man." *The Review of English Studies* n.s. 15 (1964): 353–63.

Rowlands, Samuel. *More Knaues yet? The Kanues of Spades and Diamonds.* London: Iohn Tap, n.d.

Ruggiero, Guido. "Sodom and Venice," 109–45. *The Boundaries of Eros: Sex Crime and Sexuality in Renaissance Venice*. New York and Oxford: Oxford University Press, 1985.

Rutilius. *Figuris sententiarum et elocutionis*. Edited by Edward Brooks, Jr. Leiden: E. J. Brill, 1970.

Sandbank, Shimon. "Euphuistic Symmetry and the Image." *SEL* 11 (1971): 1–13.

Sanford, J[ames]. *The Amorous and Tragicall Tales of Plutarch Whereunto is annexed the Hystorie of Cariclea & Theagenes, and the saying of the Greek Philosophers*. Ann Arbor, MI: University Microfilms, 1964.

Salgado, Gamini. *Cony-Catchers and Bawdy Baskets: An Anthology of Elizabethan Low Life*. Harmondsworth: Penguin, 1972.

Salzman, Paul. *An Anthology of Elizabethan Prose Fiction*. Oxford: Oxford University Press, 1987.

——. *English Prose Fiction, 1558–1700: A Critical History*. Oxford: Oxford University Press, 1985.

Saslow, James M. *Ganymede in the Renaissance: Homosexuality in Art and Society*. New Haven: Yale University Press, 1986.

Sauer, Elizabeth. "Milton and the 'Stage-work' of Charles I's." *Prose Studies: History, Theory, Criticism* 23 (2000): 121–46.

Saunders, J. W. "The Stigma of Print: A Note on the Social Bases of Tudor Poetry." *Essays in Criticism* 1(1951): 139–64.

Schlauch, Margaret. "English Short Fiction in the Sixteenth and Seventeenth Centuries." *Studies in Short Fiction* 3 (1966): 393–434.

Schleiner, Winfried. "Male Cross-Dressing and Transvestism in Renaissance Romances." *Sixteenth-Century Journal* 19 (1988): 605–19.

Sedgwick, Eve Kosofsky. *Between Men: English Literature and Male Homosocial Desire*. New York: Columbia University Press, 1985.

Shakespeare, William. *Hamlet. The Riverside Shakespeare*. 2nd edition. Edited by G. Blackmore Evans and J. J. M. Tobin. Boston: Houghton Mifflin, 1997.

——. *A Midsummer Night's Dream*. Edited Peter Holland. Oxford and New York: Oxford University Press, 1995.

——. *The Winter's Tale*. Edited by J. H. P. Pafford. 1963; London and New York: Routledge, 1993.

——. *The Chronicle Historie of the life and death of King Lear and his three Daughters*. London: N. Butter, 1608.

——. *Twelfe Night, Or What You Will. Comedies, Histories, & Tragedies. Published according to the Tue Originall Copies*. London: Isaac Jaggard and Ed. Blount, 1623.

Shannon, Laurie. "Nature's Bias: Renaissance Homonormativity and Elizabethan Comic Likeness." *Modern Philology* 98 (2000–01): 183–210.

Shelley, Percy Bysshe. "Peter Bell the Third." *The Complete Poetical Works of Percy Bysshe Shelley*. Edited by Thomas Hutchinson. London: Oxford University Press, 1905.

Shepard, Robert. "Sexual Rumours in English Politics: The Cases of Elizabeth I and James I." *Desire and Discipline: Sex and Sexuality in the Premodern West*. Edited by Jacqueline Murray and Konrad Eisenbichler, 101–22. Toronto: University of Toronto Press, 1996.

Sheppard, Samuel. *The Famous Tragedie of King Charles I*. [London?], 1649.

Sherman, S. P. "Stella and *The Broken Heart*." *PMLA* 24 (1909): 274–85.

Shklanka, Diane, ed. *A Critical Edition of George Whetstone's 1582: An Heptameron of Civill Discourses*. New York: Garland, 1987.

Sibley, Gertrude Marian. *The Lost Plays and Masques, 1500–1642*. Ithaca: Cornell University Press, 1933.

——. *The Old Arcadia*. Edited by Katherine Duncan-Jones. 1984; rpt. Oxford: Oxford University Press, 1994.

Sidney, Philip. *Sir Philip Sidney*. Edited by Katherine Duncan-Jones. Oxford: Oxford University Press, 1989.

——. *The Countess of Pembroke's Arcadia*. Edited by Maurice Evans. Harmondsworth: Penguin, 1977.

——. *An Apology for Poetry*. Edited by Geoffrey Shepherd. London: Nelson, 1965.

——. *The Countesse of Pembrokes Arcadia*. London: William Ponsonbie, 1598.

Skretkowicz, Victor. "Categorizing Redirection in Sidney's *New Arcadia*." *Narrative Strategies in Early English Fiction*. Edited by Wolfgang Görtschacher and Holger Klein, 133–46. Lewiston, NY and Salzburg: The Edwin Mellen Press, 1995.

Slack, Paul. *The English Poor Law 1531–1782*. Cambridge: Cambridge University Press, 1995.

Smith, Bruce. "Premodern Sexualities." *PMLA* 115 (2000): 318–29.

——. *Homosexual Desire in Shakespeare's England: A Cultural Poetics*. Chicago and London: The University of Chicago Press, 1991.

Smarr, Levarie, trans. *Italian Renaissance Tales*. Rochester, MI: Solaris Press, 1983.

Smith, Hallet. *Shakespeare's Romances: A Study of Some Ways of the Imagination*. San Marino, CA: The Huntington Library, 1972.

Spenser, Edmund. *Poetical Works*. Edited by J. C. Smith and E. de Selincourt. Oxford: Oxford University Press, 1912.

Stallybrass, Peter. "Patriarchal Territories: The Body Enclosed." *Rewriting the Renaissance: The Discourses of Sexual Difference in Early Modern Europe*. Edited by Margaret W. Ferguson, Maureen Quilligan, and Nancy J. Vickers, 123–42. Chicago: Chicago University Press, 1986.

Staub, Susan C. "The Lady Frances Did Watch: Gascoigne's Voyeristic Narrative." *Framing Elizabethan Fictions*. Edited by Constance C. Relihan, 41–54.

Stephanson, Raymond. "John Lyly's Prose Fiction: Irony, Humor, and Anti-Humanism." *English Literary Renaissance* 11 (1981): 3–21.

——. "Bribery, Buggery, and the Fall of Lord Chancellor Bacon." *Rhetoric and Law in Early Modern Europe*. Edited by Victoria Kahn and Lorna Hutson, 125–42. New Haven and London: Yale University Press, 2001.

Stewart, Alan. *Close Readers: Humanism and Sodomy in Early Modern England*. Princeton: Princeton University Press, 1997.

Stone, Lawrence. *The Family, Sex and Marriage in England, 1500–1800*. London: Weidenfeld and Nicolson, 1977.

Strong, Roy. *The Cult of Elizabeth*. 1977; rpt. London: Pimlico, 1999.

Stubbes, Philip. *The Anatomie of Abuses*. London, 1583.

Sullivan, Margaret M. "Amazons and Aristocrats: The Function of Pyrocles' Amazon Role in Sidney's Revised *Arcadia*." *Playing with Gender: A Renaissance Pursuit*. Edited by Jean R. Brink, Maryanne C. Horowitz, and Allison P. Coudert, 62–81. Urbana: University of Illinois Press, 1991.

Summit, Jennifer. *Lost Property: The Woman Writer and English Literary History 1380–1589*. Chicago: University of Chicago Press, 2000.

Sussex Picture. The Sussex Picture, or, An Answer to the Sea-Gull. London: F. N., 1644.

Sussman, Anne. "'Sweetly Ravished': Sidney's *Old Arcadia* and the Poetics of Sexual Violence." *Renaissance Papers* (1994): 55–66.

Tate, N[ahum] and "A Person of Quality." *The Aethiopian History of Heliodorus in Ten Books.* London, 1686.

Tetel, Marcel. *Marguerite de Navaree's "Heptameron": Themes, Language, and Structure.* Durham, NC: Duke University Press, 1973.

Theodori Bezae Vezelii poemata. Paris: Conrad Badius, 1548.

Tilnay, Edmonde. *A Brief and Pleasant Discourse of Duties in Marriage, called the Flower of Friendshippe.* London, 1571.

Tomlinson, Sophie. "She that Plays the King: Henrietta Maria and the Threat of the Actress in Caroline Culture." *The Politics of Tragicomedy: Shakespeare and After.* Edited by Gordon McMullan and Jonathan Hope. New York: Routledge, 1992.

Traub, Valerie. "Sex Without Issue: Sodomy, Reproduction, and Signification in Shakespeare's Sonnets." *Shakespeare's Sonnets: Critical Essays.* Edited by James Schiffer, 431–52. New York: Garland, 1999.

——. "The Perversion of 'Lesbian' Desire." *History Workshop Journal* 41 (1996): 23–49.

——. "The (In)Significance of 'Lesbian' Desire in Early Modern England." *Queering the Renaissance.* Edited by Goldberg, 62–83, 1994.

Trill, Suzanne, Kate Chedgzoy, and Melanie Osborne, eds. *Lay By Your Needles, Ladies, Take the Pen.* London: Arnold, 1997.

Tudor Royal Proclamations. Edited by James F. Larkin and Paul L. Hughes. Vol. 1. Oxford: Oxford University Press, 1973.

Turner, James Grantham. *The Politics of Landscape.* Cambridge: Harvard University Press, 1979.

Underdown, David. *Royalist Conspiracy in England 1649–1660.* New Haven: Yale University Press, 1960.

Underdown, D. E. "The Taming of the Scold: the Enforcement of Patriarchal Authority in Early Modern England." *Order and Disorder in Early Modern England.* Edited by Anthony Fletcher and John Stevenson. Cambridge: Cambridge University Press, 1985.

Underdowne, Thomas. *An Aethiopian Histories, Written in Greek by heliodorus, no less wittie then pleasant.* London, 1577.

Vives, Lodovicus. *The office and duetie of an husband, made by the excellent philosopher Lodovicus Vives, and translated into Englyshe by Thomas Paynell.* London, 1554.

Walker, Gilbert. *The Institucion of a Gentleman.* London, 1555; rpt. Amsterdam: Theatrum Orbis Terrarum, 1974.

——. *A Manifest Detection of the Most Vile and Detestable Use of Diceplay, and Other Practices Like the Same.* London, 1552; rpt. Kinney, 59–84. *Rogues, Vagabonds.*

Wall, Wendy. "Renaissance National Husbandry: Gervase Markham and the Publication of England." *Sixteenth Century Journal* 27 (1996): 767–85.

——. *The Imprint of Gender: Authorship and Publication in the English Renaissance.* Ithaca, NY: Cornell University Press, 1993.

Waller, Gary. *The Sidney Family Romance: Mary Wroth, William Herbert, and the Early Modern Construction of Gender.* Detroit: Wayne State University Press, 1993.

Waterman, William, trans. *The Fardle of facions conteining the aunciente maners, customes, and Lawes, of the peoples enhabiting the two partes of the earth, called Affrike and Asie.* London: Jhon Kingstone and Henry Datton, 1555.

Webster, John and William Rowley. *The Thracian Wonder: A Comical History.* London: Tho. Johnson, 1661.

Weisner-Hanks, Merry E. *Christianity and Sexuality in the Early Modern World: Regulating Desire, Reforming Practice.* London and New York: Routledge, 2000.

Whately, William. *A Bride-Bush, Or a Wedding Sermon: Compendiously describing the duties of Married Persons.* London, 1617.

Wilson, Richard. "Voyage to Tunis: New History and the Old World of *The Tempest.*" *ELH* 64 (1997): 333–57.

Winkler, John J. "The Invention of Romance." *The Search for the Ancient Novel.* Edited by James Tatum, 23–38. Baltimore: The Johns Hopkins University Press, 1994.

——. Trans. *Leucippe and Clitophon. Collected Ancient Greek Novels.* Edited by B. P. Reardon, 175–284. Berkeley and Los Angeles: University of California Press, 1989.

Webster, John. *The Tragedy of the Dutchesse of Malfy.* London: J. Waterson, 1623.

Weiss, Adrian. "Shared Printing, Printer's Copy, and the Text(s) of Gascoigne's *A Hundred Sundrie Flowres.*" *Studies in Bibliography* 45 (1992): 71–104.

Wilcher, Robert. *The Writing of Royalism, 1628–1660.* Cambridge: Cambridge University Press, 2001.

Wilson, Katharine. " 'An ensample to all women of lightnesse': Lyly's Lucilla and Her Influence." *Imaginaires* 2 (1997): 31–46.

Williams, Raymond. *The Country and the City.* New York: Oxford University Press, 1973.

Wiseman, Suan. *Drama and Politics in the English Civil War.* Cambridge: Cambridge University Press, 1998.

Wolff, Samuel Lee. *The Greek Romances in Elizabethan Prose Fiction.* New York: Columbia University Press, 1912.

Worden, Blair. *The Sound of Virtue: Philip Sidney's Arcadia and Elizabethan Politics.* New Haven and London: Yale University Press, 1996.

Woudhuysen, H. R. *Sir Philip Sidney and the Circulation of Manuscripts, 1558–1640.* Oxford: Clarendon Press, 1996.

Wright, F. A., ed. *Heliodorus: An Aethiopian Romance.* London: Routledge, n.d.

Wright, William Aldis. *Facsimile of the Manuscript of Milton's Minor Poems Preserved in the Library of Trinity College Cambridge.* Cambridge: Cambridge University Press, 1899.

Wrightson, Keith. *English Society, 1580–1680.* London: Routledge, 1982.

Wroth, Mary. *The First Part of the Countess Montgomery's "Urania".* Edited by Josephine A. Roberts; completed by Suzanne Gossett and Janel Mueller. Medieval and Renaissance Texts and Studies. Vol. 140. Binghampton, NY: Center for Medieval and Early Renaissance Studies State University of New York at Binghampton, 1995.

——. *The Second Part of the Countess of Montgomery's "Urania".* Edited by Josephine A. Roberts; completed by Suzanne Gossett and Janel Mueller. Medieval and Renaissance Texts & Studies. Vol. 211, Tempe, Arizona: Arizona Center for Medieval and Renaissance Studies, 1999.

——. *Poems of Lady Mary Wroth.* Edited by Josephine A. Roberts. Baton Rouge: Louisiana State University Press, 1983.

Index

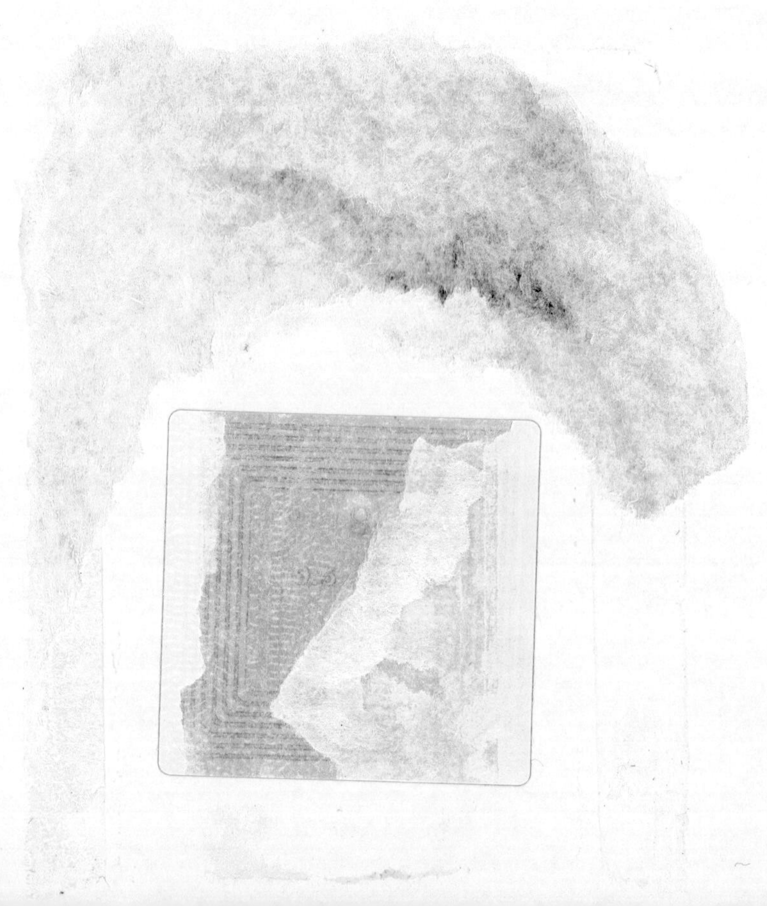